Small Group Communication in Organizations

Second Edition

Small Group Communication in Organizations

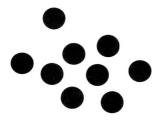

H. Lloyd Goodall, Jr.
University of Utah

 WCB **Wm. C. Brown Publishers**

Book Team

Editor *Stan Stoga*
Production Coordinator *Carla D. Arnold*

WCB **Wm. C. Brown Publishers**

President *G. Franklin Lewis*
Vice President, Publisher *George Wm. Bergquist*
Vice President, Publisher *Thomas E. Doran*
Vice President, Operations and Production *Beverly Kolz*
National Sales Manager *Virginia S. Moffat*
Advertising Manager *Ann M. Knepper*
Marketing Manager *Kathleen Nietzke*
Production Editorial Manager *Colleen A. Yonda*
Production Editorial Manager *Julie A. Kennedy*
Publishing Services Manager *Karen J. Slaght*
Manager of Visuals and Design *Faye M. Schilling*

Cover design by Benoit and Associates

Library of Congress Catalog Card Number: 89–60877

ISBN 0–697–04891–8

Printed in the United States of America by Wm. C. Brown Publishers,
2460 Kerper Boulevard, Dubuque, IA 52001

10 9 8 7 6 5 4 3 2

Contents

Preface

Small Group Communication in Organizations is written for persons planning to pursue successful and productive careers in American organizations and agencies. It is a book written during a time of rapid change in the way American free enterprise is managed, when the values and goals of American citizens are beginning to stabilize. In what were once characterized as "top-down, inside-out" American organizations, we have witnessed a radical, but gradual, shift over the past twenty years, as the patterns of American business and industry evolved into group-centered, community-conscious, communication-valuing systems. Within this newer framework, built by the work of individuals in small groups responsible for carrying out tasks, making decisions, and resolving dilemmas, we observe that the values attributable to effective and efficient communication between and among group members emerge as those skills most likely to determine an individual's worth, character, and promise.

This book was written because group communication skills can be learned. Purposeful speaking, active listening, creative participation in group work, effective leadership of group activities, the tools of reasoning, data-collecting, and analysis are processes that can be taught. While there are always some individuals who work well in small groups without any special preparation or training, the great majority of people who work in groups must be trained and educated to do so. *The premise of this text is that students can become skilled in and knowledgeable about the work of small groups and develop responsible communication to carry out the work while still in school. Moreover, those students who demonstrate competency in college or university courses devoted to small group communication will be better prepared to demonstrate these skills on the job.*

The research for this project capitalized on three interrelated and important sources of information. First, the traditions of scholarship related to communication, and particularly communicating in group settings, provided a rich basis for understanding what skills are important and how group processes are used in American business and industry. Second, the testimonies of individuals who work in American organizations provided a pragmatic basis for determining how group work is actually accomplished, how individuals who do the work view the problems, paradoxes, and promises of group activity. And third, the experiences of the author as an organizational consultant and trainer provided the ways and means of translating the theories and practices of small group communication into a workable plan for instruction. Throughout this text you will find these three sources of information used to convey ideas, procedures, and ways of resolving difficulties commonly encountered in a variety of group settings and tasks.

The book is divided into eleven chapters. The first five chapters are devoted to explanations of the skills and knowledge necessary for productive communication in small groups. Within these chapters you will find guidelines for effective entry into the group, participation and leadership skills, and the roles of communication used to carry out organizational tasks. Chapters 6 and 7 investigate decision-making and the implementation of decisions made by small groups. Chapters 8 through 10 propose ways and means of improving communication in groups, indicating how knowledge of group communication may be used to obtain and maintain jobs in American businesses and industries. Chapter 11 details the processes and tools of observing and evaluating the work of small groups, and reveals how communication is central to any appraisal of the quality and quantity of work done by group members. In each chapter you will also find exercises designed to sharpen your communication skills, as well as references you may want to consult to deepen your understanding of the concepts and skills related to small group communication.

The Second Edition

The second edition of *Small Group Communication in Organizations* capitalizes on several subtle, but important, changes that have occurred since the introduction of the original edition in 1985. Chief among these changes are the updating of research sources and the inclusion of recent findings in the areas of leadership, participation, and agenda-management in groups. This second edition also profits from the advice of users of the text who have contributed their ideas about resources and pedagogy, and who, collectively, have convinced me to move the chapter on observation and evaluation of groups toward the end of the book to more closely align with syllabi.

The place of small groups in organizations—both as a practical aspect of organizational life and as a prominent feature of the research literature—has expanded significantly since the publication of the first edition. Fresh insights provided by organizational theorists, such as Gareth Morgan, Linda Smircich, and Linda Putnam, combined with a better understanding of the role played by small groups in the development, maintenance, and change of organizational cultures as found in the work of Michael Pacanowsky, Nick Trujillo, Anne Swidler, and others have also found their way into this second edition. Finally, my own research into the meaning of small groups in high technology firms has evolved sufficiently to be occasionally included in this volume.

Hence, this second edition should offer colleagues more and better material. I have not, however, fiddled very much with what users found useful in their classes. I continue to be enthusiastic about the support this book has received and look forward to continuing the dialogue with those interested in seeing it evolve with the discipline.

No book is ever written alone. I wish to express my sincere appreciation to the many individuals and organizations who cooperated with me while I completed this project. I am especially grateful to the persons whose words are reprinted within these pages, whose experiences and insights greatly contributed to what is presented here. While their names have been changed to guard their identities, I wish to take this opportunity to convey my gratitude to them and their parent organizations: United Technologies, Division of United Space Boosters, Inc.; Pittsburgh Paint & Glass, Division of Aircraft Windshields; Huntsville Utilities; the United States Army, Divisions of the Missile Command and the Army Corps of Engineers; Rockwell International; Computer Sciences Corporation; Sperry Systems, Inc.; IBM; Intergraph; and Chrysler Corporation. I would also like to acknowledge the reviewers of the original manuscript: Jack L. Whitehead, University of Texas at Austin; Gerald L. Wilson, University of South Alabama; Olaf E. Rankes, University of Miami; Lawrence W. Hugenberg, Youngstown State University; and Sue De Wine, Ohio University. I also want to thank the reviewers for the second edition: Judith Hoover, Western Kentucky University; Alan Shiller, Lindenwood College; and Julie Zink, Spring Hill College. I am also indebted to my research assistant from The University of Alabama in Huntsville, Beth Gonsewski, whose contributions to this volume are numerous, and without whose help this project would not have been completed on time.

To the Instructor

Using Small Groups in the Course

Small Group Communication in Organizations is designed to be a flexible text, adaptable to your individual needs and pedagogical methods. The chapters are intended to be complete instructional units; and every chapter ends with an exercise, or series of exercises, developed and tested for classroom use. I wish to explain some alternatives for using small group exercises to facilitate classroom instruction.

Traditionally, small group communication courses use a lecture/discussion format. The text is used to aid students' comprehension of the lecture material, and to provide interesting points for classroom discussion or debate. In-class exercises from the text, or prepared by the instructor, are used to "test out" ideas from the lectures and to provide each student with the opportunity to develop group communication skills. Should you prefer this traditional method of instruction, *Small Group Communication in Organizations* provides detailed in-class exercises you may want to use. I have found, however, the use of this lecture/discussion/exercise format is enhanced by:

1. *Organizing small groups for the whole term or semester:*   Because small groups mature with age, and since one of the basic communication skills for group members is the ability to adapt to other group members over a period of time, I recommend making *permanent* group assignments at the beginning of the term. Students should be told these assignments will not change (you may want to have a "bail out" mechanism for serious disturbances). Use of permanent in-class groups facilitates appreciation of the human relationships, social and task goals, and adaptive skills. It also provides the groups with a sense of shared identity.
2. *Selecting group members based on an equitable distribution of basic skills:*   As every small group communication instructor knows, there is no "ideal" method for assigning individuals to groups. However, I have found that students respond favorably if the instructor makes the assignments based on skills they can claim. For example, on the second or third class meeting I ask students to select one of the

following skills: (a) speaking in public, (b) experience leading a small group, (c) researching a subject in the library, (d) conducting surveys or informational interviews, (e) typing, and (f) writing clear technical reports. I explain that claiming a skill does *not* mean the student will be responsible for *performing* the skill for the group! It is only a way to apportion useful resources equitably among the in-class groups.

3. *Rotating the leadership and recorder functions among group members on a weekly/bi-weekly basis:* To gain communicative competencies in small groups requires the opportunity to practice them. After the groups are assembled, ask them to decide on a leader/recorder rotation for the *first half* of the term/semester. Leaders will be responsible for preparing agendas, calling the meetings to order, and directing the group's work on a task or through the prescribed exercises. Recorders will be responsible for taking minutes of the meeting and keeping a formal record of what the group has accomplished (it is advisable to ask the group to use *one* common group notebook for the term/semester). After the first half of the term the groups should be free to decide how they want to handle the leadership role for the remainder of the course. Some groups may prefer keeping the original rotation, others may vest the leadership role in one person who demonstrates competency while the recorder role may continue to rotate among the other members, and still other groups may prefer to share the leadership role among themselves without designating a formal leader.

4. *Assigning a regular meeting time for all in-class groups:* Groups tend to work best when they establish a routine. Instructors can help groups establish a routine by allotting group meeting time at the end (or beginning) of each class, or every other class meeting. This schedule will help leaders prepare agendas for the allotted time, and will simulate real organizational meetings.

5. *Asking the groups to formally evaluate their own performance at the end of the term/semester:* Using the material in Chapter 10, ask each group to design and implement an evaluative procedure capable of assessing (a) the individual contributions of the group members, and (b) the overall performance of the group.

The above guidelines should prove useful to instructors who plan to use the exercises at the ends of the chapters, combined with a lecture/discussion format.

A second method for organizing small group work in courses is to develop an organizational simulation.[1] The goal of this format is to promote an organizational environment within the classroom capable of inducing students to treat each other as working professionals while learning small group communication

---

1. See H. Lloyd Goodall, Jr., "Organizational Communication Competence: The Development of an Industrial Simulation to Teach Adaptive Skills," *COMMUNICATION QUARTERLY* 30 (Fall 1982), 282–295, for a comprehensive account of how to design a simulation course.

skills. *Small Group Communication in Organizations* is amenable to the simulation format because the chapters are organized for systematic skill development, using Standard Agenda, Delphi Technique, and a combination of the two methods to make group decisions. Your syllabus can be designed according to the following guidelines:

1. *Make permanent group assignments, rotate leader/recorder roles, and base group member selections on an equitable apportioning of basic skills:* As in the traditional format, the simulation-based course should require students to develop working group histories, productive relationships with other group members, and learn to synthesize task and social goals. Use the guidelines for the traditional format (see previous page) to organize the in-class small groups.

2. *Use Standard Agenda to organize the first half of the term/semester:* Students can solve organizational problems/case studies using Standard Agenda. Standard Agenda is also a fundamental way to organize group work systematically within a classroom. Allow one group meeting per phase of Standard Agenda, two or three meetings for fact-finding. This schedule will help group leaders learn the requirements of agendas, and will demonstrate the importance of the effective communication principles found in the first five chapters of the text. At the end of the first half of the term/semester, ask the groups to prepare a final report (oral or written) and present it to the class for critique.

   The second half of the term/semester provides creative alternatives for organizing the student groups. For example, new group assignments can be made, new decision-making techniques can be used (e.g. Delphi Technique, or a combination of Standard Agenda and Delphi Technique), and new ways to organize leadership/recorder roles can be developed. Or, you may prefer to keep the original groups and Standard Agenda, but allow the groups to determine how leader/ recorder roles should be enacted. Regardless of the method you prefer, the goal of the second half of the term should be to ask each group to accomplish *one major project.* In complex simulations these projects overlap, hence requiring student groups to integrate their work and share information among the groups. For example, you may want to use the following broad topics to design specific organizational problems for group decision-making assignments: (a) a financial planning problem, (b) a strategic forecasting problem, (c) a marketing/advertising problem, (d) a public relations problem, (e) a personnel policies problem, (f) a hiring/firing/grievance problem, and (g) an evaluation problem. (Note: The evaluation group should be responsible for designing the organization's group communication evaluation instrument.) For each group problem, the group members *must be made responsible* for all work leading to the final group report. The instructor(s) should serve only in liaison/consulting capacities.

3. *Lecture a little, encourage productive time in groups:* The role of the instructor in a simulation-based course is analogous to the CEO in an organization. You provide the overall objectives, monitor the work of the groups, and encourage useful expenditures of time and effort. When I use the simulation format I limit my lectures to 15–20 minutes per class session, and use the rest of the time to observe and monitor the groups.

4. *Make the demonstration of communication competencies a major basis for grading decisions:* The simulation format is not a traditional classroom. Unlike the familiar setting, the simulation format values systematic acquisition of the performance skills necessary for communication competence. Therefore, I advise you to rely less heavily on traditional methods of measuring individual progress (e.g. exams, term papers), and to place more emphasis on the acquisition of communication skills. How will you evaluate the individuals and the groups? I suggest making the group assessment instrument count for at least 50% of the final grade—the group members know who has contributed to their effort, who has learned the skills, and who has demonstrated them. The other 50% or so you can use to include an exam or two, a term paper, or perhaps your own assessment of student's progress. But a major objective for the course should be to encourage students to see the relationship between their *communication competencies* and *evaluations made of and about them* by other group/organization members.

5. *Make the simulation setting as "real" as possible:* One major purpose of any organizational simulation using small groups to organize the in-class work is actually to *simulate* real organizational conditions. Of course this goal must be tempered with an appreciation of the need to establish a learning environment in which mistakes can be made and deficiencies may be overcome. But the tone of the classroom should be kept professional. To accomplish this objective I recommend using formal memos to group leaders as the basis to distribute necessary information. I also encourage group members to go to the group leaders for advice rather than to me, the instructor, (unless they have a personal problem or a genuine grievance). Furthermore, I collect all group records at the end of the term and pass them on to the next class—the simulated organization actually develops a real history!

For large classes (simulations tend to work best when relative anonymity is guaranteed) I use students who have received an "A" in the course previously as mid-level managers and supervisors. This addition to the class encourages a sense of hierarchy, and allows the student/managers to help the groups. These student/managers serve a vital function in the simulation because they convey information between the groups and the instructor, and serve as mediators of information and disputes. I also use the student/manager evaluations of individual and group performances in my final assessment of term grades.

The above guidelines can help you design an organizational simulation using small groups and this text. Should you choose to use a simulation-based format, I hope you find it as creative and rewarding as I have. Whatever format you choose, I hope the second edition of *Small Group Communication in Organizations* proves to be useful and adaptable. If you have any questions about using this text or the formats I have just outlined, please call or write me and I will be happy to help you.

H. Lloyd Goodall, Jr.
Salt Lake City, Utah
July, 1989

An Orientation to Small Groups in American Organizations 1

Introduction

An organization is defined as a human group whose activities are designed to seek specific goals. The goals vary with the nature of the organizational activity. There are groups whose primary goal is manufacturing (such as General Motors, IBM, and Sony). There are other groups whose primary goal is research and development (such as United Technologies, TRW, and NASA). We have groups whose primary goal is public service (such as the United States Government, the American Red Cross, and local police departments and hospitals). We even encounter groups that are designed to help other groups function more smoothly, more profitably, or more efficiently (such as Communications Consulting and Training Corporation, E. F. Hutton, and the Consumer Protection Agency). Many modern organizations may carry out two or more of the above activities, and have more than one specific goal. The question becomes, then, how is the work accomplished?

Organizations are composed of human beings in small groups interacting with a variety of technologies and other human beings. The larger the organization, and the more complex the technology, the greater is the need for dividing the labor into smaller, more manageable units. Three or four people can command billions of bits of information stored in a single computer. Five or six individuals are required to assemble automobile radios on a production line. Nine or ten junior and senior accountants, their secretaries, and one or two tax specialists may comprise an accounting department. Although most people say they are employed by large organizations, their daily work in the service of the organization is usually carried out as members of small groups.

This chapter addresses the small group processes affecting the modern organization. First, we will explore the uses of small groups in organizations, focusing on the meaning of interactions between and among formal and informal groups involved in organizational processes. Second, we will examine what organizations expect from small group members, and conversely, what small group members expect from organizations. Finally, we will help you to understand what benefits you can derive from reading this book and participating in this class.

The Uses of Small Groups in Organizations

Types of Goals   Organizations must meet their goals if they are to survive. To meet goals, organizations must *direct* the activities of employees, *coordinate* all of the activities of groups of employees, and *account* for the quality and productivity of the employees and the groups striving to meet organizational goals. When organizations are small, and the employees come to know each other and each other's tasks, there is less need for specialization and more opportunity for flexibility in daily activities. Consider the following statement made by an employee of a small company.

> **Michael H., 29**   In my company there are about twenty employees. We manufacture small tools, and our specialty is the chisel. Sure, we all have our titles and our assignments, but almost everybody can cover for someone else if we have to. A guy gets sick and I do his job for a day or two, someone else helps me out with my work, and there are no hard feelings. The old man understands and doesn't interfere. He owns the company, but I have seen him working at the bench during rush periods when we had deadlines to meet.

Larger organizations seldom encourage the kind of behavior exemplified by Michael's company. For example, TRW employs about 100,000 individuals in the United States. TRW's recruiters and personnel officials hire people because of their specialties, and then provide intensive training in the organization's activities relating to a specific task. An accountant in a TRW office in Huntsville, Alabama, probably has very little knowledge about the organization's activities in California or Ohio. TRW is a progressive organization in its treatment of employees, but the potential chaos that could occur if the employees behaved like employees in Michael's company would soon undermine TRW's organizational objectives. The company is simply too large and too complex to operate effectively at the level of informality allowed, and often encouraged, in smaller organizations.

The need for smaller groups to direct, coordinate, and account for quality and productivity in larger organizations is a major factor in the survival of the organization. For this reason, organizations are divided into departments or divisions with specific goals to guide their operation. One way to discover how formal groups are constructed and used in organizations is to examine an organizational chart. (See Figure 1.1.)

Interdependence   When we examine an organizational chart we can note the divisions of labor re-
of Small Groups   quired to carry out the objectives of the company. We also see the *interdependence* of the smaller units; if the accounting department does not receive accurate information from the marketing and sales division, both groups suffer and the overall objectives of the organization may not be met. If there is a delay in one of the manufacturing divisions, all of the other manufacturing operations may be curtailed.

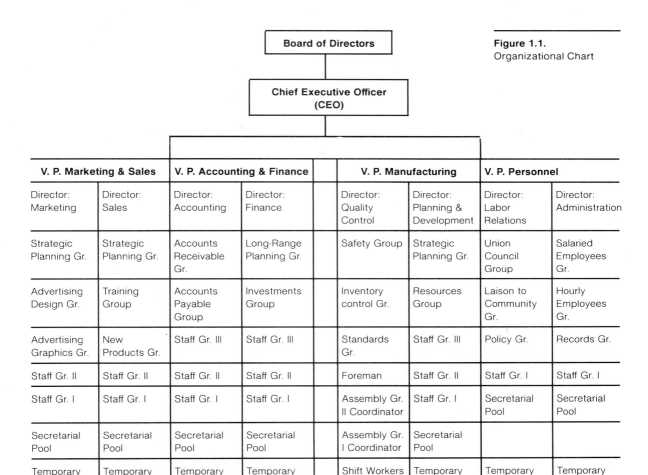

Figure 1.1.
Organizational Chart

	Board of Directors			

Chief Executive Officer (CEO)

V. P. Marketing & Sales		V. P. Accounting & Finance		V. P. Manufacturing		V. P. Personnel	
Director: Marketing	Director: Sales	Director: Accounting	Director: Finance	Director: Quality Control	Director: Planning & Development	Director: Labor Relations	Director: Administration
Strategic Planning Gr.	Strategic Planning Gr.	Accounts Receivable Gr.	Long-Range Planning Gr.	Safety Group	Strategic Planning Gr.	Union Council Group	Salaried Employees Gr.
Advertising Design Gr.	Training Group	Accounts Payable Group	Investments Group	Inventory control Gr.	Resources Group	Laison to Community Gr.	Hourly Employees Gr.
Advertising Graphics Gr.	New Products Gr.	Staff Gr. III	Staff Gr. III	Standards Gr.	Staff Gr. III	Policy Gr.	Records Gr.
Staff Gr. II	Staff Gr. II	Staff Gr. II	Staff Gr. II	Foreman	Staff Gr. II	Staff Gr. I	Staff Gr. I
Staff Gr. I	Staff Gr. I	Staff Gr. I	Staff Gr. I	Assembly Gr. II Coordinator	Staff Gr. I	Secretarial Pool	Secretarial Pool
Secretarial Pool	Secretarial Pool	Secretarial Pool	Secretarial Pool	Assembly Gr. I Coordinator	Secretarial Pool		
Temporary Staff	Temporary Staff	Temporary Staff	Temporary Staff	Shift Workers	Temporary Staff	Temporary Staff	Temporary Staff

Because of the interdependent nature of modern organizations, the need for people trained in effective group communication, in addition to a specific trade or skill, cannot be overlooked. The following statement is from a major corporate recruiter:

> **Lynn L., 24** As the company recruiter I am often asked what impresses me most about candidates for managerial positions during the interview. What I say is this: after reviewing the resumé and checking the references, I look for a person who demonstrates communications skills and a strong desire to succeed. More and more I find myself asking candidates about their background and training in small groups. I call these questions my "eliminators." Very often I see otherwise qualified applicants who tell me they do not enjoy working in group settings, or who have no idea what it means to run a meeting. Because working with others in groups and participating in

group meetings is what most of our managers do, I eliminate candidates who do not possess group skills. And when I find a candidate who can talk to me about organizing a group, and managing a meeting, I know I've found a "winner."

Sandra O'Connell, one of America's leading organizational consultants, reports that the higher a person rises in the company, the more time will be spent in meetings (1979, p. 28). William Ouchi, a management theorist, believes effective group operation is the key to modifying American business practices to meet the challenge of the Japanese (1981). There can be no doubt if you plan a career working in an organization, the need for training in group communication skills is as necessary as training in finance, marketing, accounting, management, computer science, economics, or any other business specialty.

To begin your study of effective group communication, and the skills you will need to be a competent group member, you need to examine two important human groups affecting an organization's operation: formal and informal small groups.

Formal Small Groups

Formal small groups are usually established to accomplish specific tasks within divisions of an organization. If you look at an organization chart, you will see managerial operations divided according to specialities: accounting and finance division, marketing and sales division, manufacturing division, personnel division. Each one of these divisions has objectives that must be met by the people who are members of the various small groups.

When an employee says "I work for the personnel department," she or he is making a statement about group membership. The personnel department is a *formal* group because it has a specific objective to guide the activities of each group member. The *work* done by the individual group members to accomplish the group's objective, *rather than personal objectives,* makes the personnel department a formal group setting. When personal goals override group objectives, then the formal nature of the group is threatened. This does not mean people don't have personal goals when they work in formal groups; what it does mean is that people have a responsibility to do the group's work, that is, an obligation that is more important to the group than are any one member's personal goals.

Most of the literature on the uses of small groups in organizations focuses on formal group settings (see Hampton, Summer, and Webber, 1978, for an overview). As a result of this emphasis, we have been able to see the operation of formal groups the way managers see them. Formal groups exist to help the organization accomplish its objectives. There are five precise uses of formal groups in most organizations:

1. *Production Teams:* Are formal groups of people whose activities are coordinated to produce a marketable product or service. The line workers who assemble automobiles, televisions, or clothing are members of production teams. Because of the prescribed nature of the

production team's task, and the level of specialization required to accomplish it, this formal group is characterized by the least amount of group communication pertaining to the task.

2. *Committees:*   Are formal groups of people who investigate problems, evaluate the progress of other groups and individuals, or plan activities for the members of the organization. There are many different kinds of committees, some requiring more specialization than others. As a result, this formal group is characterized by varying amounts of group communication. For example, the Rand Corporation assigns individuals to committees which seldom, if ever, meet. These committees accomplish their tasks by circulating written memos and reports to other group members for advice and consent. Other organizations may use committees which meet and interact regularly. Still other organizations use committees who meet only once or twice and then disband.

3. *Decision-Making Groups:*   Are formal groups of people who collect and evaluate information used to make a decision affecting the organization's operation. Decision-making groups are characterized by a high level of goal-oriented communication, and the use of formal procedures, policies, and guidelines to ensure the quality of the decision-making process.

4. *Problem-Solving Groups:*   Are formal groups of people whose activities are designed to overcome any obstacles or deficiencies in the organization's operation. Problem-solving groups, like decision-making groups, are characterized by a high level of goal-oriented interaction, and the use of formal procedures, policies, and guidelines to ensure the quality of the problem-solving process.

5. *Quality Circles:*   Are formal groups of people whose activities vary depending on how the organization chooses to use them. In some cases, quality circles are used for decision-making and problem-solving activities. In other cases, quality circles are used to monitor all activities within an organization, including planning and carrying out directives. The concept of a "quality circle" is relatively new in American business and industry, although it has been used with success in Japan. For a comprehensive treatment of the subject, see Stohl and Jennings (1988), Baird (1982), or Dewar and Beardsley (1977).

Formal groups are used by organizations to accomplish every phase of the company's operation. From planning and financing the organization, through the manufacturing of the final product or service, formal groups are used to direct, coordinate, and account for the quality and productivity of employees responsible for attaining the organization's objectives.

Because formal groups permeate the organizational structure and are ultimately responsible for the success or failure of the organization, much emphasis is placed on an individual's ability to work in small formal groups. Since formal groups have specific tasks to accomplish, and certain procedures must be implemented and followed by group members in order to accomplish them, much emphasis is placed on an individual's ability to visualize the completion of a task as the primary goal of formal groups. Unfortunately the organization's view of formal groups often does not take into account the *human* factors involved in getting people to work closely and effectively with each other. There is more to the success of a group than merely accomplishing a task; in fact, there is much more to the success or failure of a formal group than formality and the organizational chart can reveal:

> **Drew A., 22** When I got this job, I was assigned to work in three separate groups. I .was given no information about who was in the groups, no idea of what had happened in those groups prior to my assignment. So I was shocked when I found out just how much some of the people actually *hated* each other. You talk about a mess—I wasn't on the job two days until I saw one of our senior execs cuss out an engineer in a group meeting. It was embarrassing. Then I met with the second group and saw people falling asleep. The third group was okay. The woman in charge knew what she was doing, and she didn't try to dominate our discussions. You can bet when appraisal time rolls around I'm going to ask to be reassigned out of two of my groups—to protect my sanity!

Well, we are only human after all.

Drew's experience with groups is unfortunately fairly typical. Despite what an organization chart indicates *should* happen when groups are assembled, what really *does* happen depends on the ability of group members to do more than simply accomplish the task. When people work with other people, there should be some way of promoting friendly, instrumental interaction between and among group members. Organizations are primarily concerned with groups accomplishing tasks. However, people in those formal groups are equally concerned with liking the people they must work with while they accomplish those tasks.

The two interdependent goals of effective formal small groups are (1) accomplishing tasks and (2) promoting productive interpersonal relations between and among group members. We can talk about accomplishing tasks, and we can talk about promoting productive interpersonal relations among group members, but the reality of group situations prevents us from separating these two important goals. They must both be accomplished if the formal group is to be successful.

Informal Small Groups

Organizational charts do *not* account for informal small groups, but no organization denies their existence or importance. Informal groups are, in many ways, very much like extended families, consisting of people working in an organization with whom you enjoy nontask related interaction, or on whom you rely to help you research personal and social goals. Unlike families, there are no common bonds of blood or intimacy; but like families, informal groups serve as people and places you can go to for comfort, kindness, fun, and aid:

Paula B., 25   If it weren't for people I know but do not have to work with there would be very few good reasons for keeping this job. I mean, I do enjoy my work, but you have to have friends between nine and five too. Mostly my friends are not the people in my division because I learned early on what can happen if you make an enemy there. So I got to know people from different parts of our plant. We meet regularly for lunch and play bridge until it is time to go back to work. If I need some information, I know who I can call to get it without having to hassle with the "proper" channels, if you know what I mean. It helps to have friends who support you. Working would be pretty awful without them.

Paula's luncheon-bridge group is an example of an informal group within an organization. Unlike formal groups, these people meet because they want to see each other for personal or social reasons. Usually they do not see their group as a "group," nor do they talk about having a specific objective. Yet they are a group, and clearly they have objectives.

One difference between formal and informal groups is the method by which an individual becomes a member. In formal groups, membership is usually assigned because of a skill or specialty the individuals possess. In informal groups, membership is voluntary. It is very difficult to cease being a member of a formal group; it is relatively easy to cease being a member of an informal group.

A second difference between formal and informal groups is the nature of their activities. Formal groups must generally meet during company time, abide by company policies, and implement agendas and procedures to conduct their meetings. Informal groups are not directly affected by company time or policies (except as time relates to when they can meet and policy relates to what their activities should or should not include), and they seldom use formal agendas or procedures.

Now you have considered the nature of informal groups. Let's examine four varieties of informal groups commonly found in modern organizations:

1. *Information Networking Groups:*   Are collections of individuals who are acquainted with each other on a personal or social basis, but who use their personal and social ties to improve their organizational effectiveness (see McPhee, 1986; Eisenberg, Monge, and Miller, 1983; Albrecht and Ropp, 1982; Schwartz and Jacobson, 1977; and Wickesberg, 1968). For example, Paula mentioned knowing people she could call on to avoid the hassles of using organizational channels. Very often informal networks are established to serve informational needs and to cut through bureaucratic tape (see Tichy, Tushman, and Fombrun, 1979). Recently, the concept of networking has evolved to a more formal way of imparting information about the organization to new members. Women's support groups have been particularly effective in establishing informal networks to acquaint new female employees with the do's and don'ts of the particular organizations.

2. *Political Alliances:* Are collections of individuals who are also acquainted on a personal or social basis, and who use these ties to advance themselves in the organization (see Baker, 1981). Politics is a major part of organizational life (see Van Maanen and Barley, 1984) and of particular interest to people who plan to rise through the ranks, or exert influence over who does and does not receive promotions. Political alliances are also formed to keep abreast of company policy changes and major decisions affecting the work of these individuals. Like networking groups, political alliances are characterized by gaining access to information through non-traditional channels.

3. *Social Alliances:* Are collections of individuals who attempt to blend social and professional interests on a regular basis (see Roberts and O'Reilly, 1977). Paula mentioned the luncheon-bridge association as being important to her concept of rewards in the organization. Social alliances are often characterized by members meeting outside of the workplace as well as inside of it. Friendships are made during working hours, and alliances are formed that carry over into weekend and evening activities.

4. *Recreational Teams:* Are groups of individuals who enjoy getting together to participate in recreational activities. Many organizations sponsor softball, volleyball, tennis, or bowling leagues, and encourage interested parties to become involved in these team-sport activities. Teams are more structured than other informal groups, and they generally have a more carefully defined purpose than do social or political alliances, or informational networks (see Goodall, 1989).

Informal groups affect the operation of the organization both directly and indirectly. Although not recognized officially by any organizational chart, informal groups influence a variety of activities, both during working hours and beyond them. Some informal groups exert powerful influences over the direction and policies of an organization, including the ability to change or subvert decisions made by formal groups.

We know very little about the effects of the interdependence between formal and informal groups on an organization's activities. We know that most people working for modern organizations hold memberships in both kinds of groups, and we believe that as the workplace becomes more democratic and decision-making more decentralized, the interplay and cooperation between formal and informal groups will become a major focus of organizational research and theory-building (see Goldman, Stockbauer, and McAuliffe, 1977).

The central concern in this text is necessarily on communication in formal groups. Where appropriate we will examine the influences that informal groups exert on the work of formal groups. In all cases the emphasis will be consistently placed on the development of *effective communication skills* adaptable to both informal and formal groups.

Sanda R., 24 I think it all comes down to knowing what you can say and do with people. Sure, we all have technical expertise—or else we wouldn't have been hired in the first place. Sure, we all work using agendas and schedules and we try to meet deadlines and everyone feels the pressure. But working in an organization means working with people, and knowing how to work with people means learning communication skills.

What Organizations Expect from Group Members

Most organizations establish policies and guidelines for all employees. Policies may include procedures for completing tasks and filing grievances, how sick leave will be handled, and when, where, and how promotions and raises are determined. Policies govern the operation of the organization in formal, legal, and binding ways. Guidelines are generally more flexible than policies, and are adapted to the specific needs of divisions within the organization. Guidelines describe procedures for group operations, the formal chain-of-command, where to go and who to ask for help with a specific problem or question, etc.; they are generally drawn up by company employees for the benefit of company employees.

Policies and guidelines provide basic *rules* for the organization. From an administrative point of view, these rules provide general descriptions of the kinds of behavior expected from employees. If all else fails, a rule is always applicable to the given situation.

But we all know that organizations also use unwritten codes of conduct to evaluate individual and group behavior. Records of past achievement, personal views of employees' motivation, competence, and skills, of the character of an individual, of the personality of a group, and of the management's expectations for performance in a given appraisal period all figure into an account of what ought to happen during work. Often the unwritten codes of conduct carry as much or more weight in the organization, precisely because they are based more on human experiences than on formalized policies.

When we discuss what organizations expect from small group members, we are referring to both the rules and the unwritten codes of conduct of the organization. Every new employee should read and remember the formal policies and procedures governing life in the organization; knowing these policies is often a source of power and influence when working with others who don't know what the policies are. Every new employee should also try to discover the unwritten codes of conduct within the organization. Through informal discussions with other group members as well as conferences with the supervisor, a great deal of important information can be acquired if the right questions are asked. Unless questions are raised, there is no need for anyone to provide the information.

Here are four basic types of questions new employees need to ask to discover what an organization expects from them:

1. *Attendance:* All organizations expect group members to arrive on time, work the day's schedule, break when breaks are usually taken, and be available when needed. Attendance is the first law of any

group operation; unless the group members are present no work can be accomplished, no real consensus can be reached. Essential information can be gained by asking questions about the attendance policy of the organization and of the particular division and group employing you. Find out how you can make up work missed due to illness or leave; ask who is to be called upon to provide direction about making up assignments or the group's decision-making during your absence. Your goal should be to attend all group meetings; your concern upon entering the group is to find out whom you can contact if you are absent.

2. *Participation:* All organizations expect group members to participate actively in the interactions governing their operation. Participation means communicating (Phillips, Pedersen, and Wood, 1985); asking questions, making statements, responding to arguments, providing summaries, making and accepting individual assignments are how you participate in small groups. Hunt (1980) characterizes participation in organizations as (a) engaging in interpersonal communication, (b) contributing to small groups, (c) developing leadership skills, (d) demonstrating presentational skills, and (e) disseminating information internally and externally using oral and written communication skills. Using Hunt's listing of participatory acts, we can see how everything that is accomplished in the organization is done through the use of one or more communication skills. In the organization, nothing exists or happens until it is communicated. Learning to ask questions about how to improve your participation in small groups is vital. What skills are you competently demonstrating, and what skills should you attempt to develop more fully? How are other group members responding to your communication?

3. *Performance:* All organizations expect employees to perform according to some standard. Most organizations rely on quarterly or annual reviews or appraisals of performance to determine promotions, raises, and new assignments. Most of the *Fortune* magazine's 500 companies use the concept of MBO (Management By Objectives) to organize work in the departments and divisions, and to establish goals for individual employees (Hampton, Summer, and Webber, 1978). The established objective or goal becomes the standard by which performance is measured. When goals are achieved, employees can expect to be rewarded. When goals are not met, they can expect some hard negotiating about why they were not achieved and what can be done to improve performance next time. It is absolutely essential for new employees to discover what standards are being used to evaluate their performance. Learn to ask questions about the standards, the evaluation periods, who does the evaluating, and how the evaluations or appraisals are used by the organization.

4. *Loyalty:* All organizations attempt to inspire loyalty from their employees. Loyalty is defined as a sense of commitment to the goals and objectives of the organization and a corresponding feeling of pride and satisfaction derived from the work experience. Ouchi (1981) suggests American corporations have difficulty instilling a sense of loyalty because of high rates of worker turnover and the sense of freedom and independence in the American worker. He contrasts the American worker with the Japanese, who, because of the strong cultural, social, and professional pressures to remain with one company for life, experiences disgrace upon leaving a job or company. The new employee needs to find out how loyalty is determined by the organization and what rewards and incentives are offered for it. Perhaps even more important for group situations is the need to assess the loyalty of other group members. Find out who is committed to the organization and why they are committed. You should also find out who is not committed to the work of the group. Answers to these questions can provide useful information which should influence your decisions about whom to associate with and whom to avoid knowing in the company.

These four sources of questions for the new employee can provide important information about the expectations held by the organization and group for individual members. Unless these questions are raised, you might find yourself feeling as Tom does:

Tom A., 26 I wish I had known then what I know now. When I started to work for the company I had no idea what they expected from me. The people who told me what was what I later found out were the malcontents, and I was branded as a "problem employee" simply because I hung around with them. During my first appraisal, I was given an unsatisfactory rating and given three months to "shape up or ship out." Then I got scared and began asking questions. I found out that being quiet during meetings was perceived as being hostile or worse—that I was not doing anything productive. I thought I was being polite. I thought I was showing deference to the older, more experienced employees. Boy was I wrong. It took a long time to gain respect in my group, and I missed at least two opportunities for promotion because of it. Things are better now, but some people still remember me as the "rebel" and I'm not sure I will ever shed that image.

Tom, like most new employees, wanted to do a good job. Unfortunately, since he had no idea what a "good" job meant, he suffered the consequences. Learning what the organization and your group members expect from you is one of the best ways to establish a favorable reputation.

One of the major themes of this text is that you can influence the ways others respond to you and your work by learning to make productive choices about your own behavior in small groups. Your choices must be based on the information you acquire about the goals and objectives as well as the policies and unwritten codes of conduct in the organization employing you. If you do not gain the information you need, your ability to make informed choices will be seriously diminished, and the results may be costly. Learn to ask questions to find out what others expect from you. You may not always be able to meet those expectations, but at least you will understand how evaluations of your behavior and performance will be made.

What Small Group Members Expect (and Fear) about Small Groups

Grouphate

Sorensen (1981) offers the intriguing idea that most individuals do not like or enjoy working in groups. She developed a scale for measuring what she terms "Grouphate" and found a direct correlation between absence of training in communication skills associated with effective group operation and high levels of hostility toward working in groups. Sorensen's finding should not surprise you. Like any skill, learning how to communicate in group settings requires time, effort, and training.

Because modern organizations are composed of small groups responsible for carrying out activities designed to meet objectives, the individual who possesses skill and training in small group communication has a decided advantage over other potential employees. Unfortunately, most people do not receive such training, and consequently they do not develop the necessary skills enabling them to contribute to the group. In this section we want to examine some of the common expectations and fears associated with group work.

Assumptions Made about Groups

Let's begin by trying to determine what individuals may think a "group" is. The first problem concerns the assumptions we make about the meaning of a "group." Philosophically, if we consider a "group" as a collection of individuals, all working together to accomplish some task, we are encouraged to view *free will* and *motivation* as primary influences on the effectiveness of the group's operation. We could call this view of a "group" the "sum of its parts" perspective. The effectiveness of the group will depend on the level of skills and knowledge contributed by each individual member of the group. Thus, the group is only as effective as the sum of its parts. The individuals in the group are viewed as *instruments* used to function collectively for the group's purpose. Phillips and Wood (1980) describe this philosophical attitude toward the group by using the metaphor of the machine. The group can be made better, more productive, by replacing the "parts" which don't function efficiently, or by adding more parts to compensate for the weaker elements. Most people do not like to be thought of as simply cogs in a wheel, or parts in a machine. Viewing the group as a collection of individual parts diminishes the importance of learning how to be effective in the group; it separates the concept of a communication process from the idea of what it means to be a participant in a group. For these reasons, viewing a group as a collection of individuals is unsatisfactory.

Melanie N., 23   I hate working in groups. I have always hated working in groups, and I have very good reasons for it. Back in high school we were often put into small groups to "discuss" something. Those "discussion" sessions ended up being about everything except what we were supposed to "discuss." They were boring, and in the end I had to make up the wasted time on my own. The same thing happened in college, only worse. There we had to use groups to develop term projects, and usually this meant that I had to do most of the work because most groups just don't know how to work well together. After a while people in the group gave up. If you wanted to do well in the class, get a good grade, accomplish something, you ended up doing all the work for the rest of the group. It wasn't fair.

Another way of viewing what a "group" means is to consider it as an entity *greater* than the sum of its parts. Organizations normally assume this to be the case; there is no good reason to assign a decision-making or problem-solving task to a group when it could be accomplished by an individual. Groups are used in business and industry because we assume that when a number of people are gathered in a room something more than their individual personalities and skills emerges. Through the process of communication the group assumes a character above and beyond the individual characters of the group members; the cluster of people now functions as a group, rather than as a collection of individuals. The persons in the group assume *roles* which are capable of modification and change based on their ability to make choices about their own behavior, and to influence the responses they receive from others. The group uses a method for directing communication, such as an agenda or procedure; and the use of a system encourages the group to work together to accomplish the task, rather than to work independently to satisfy individual goals. Individuals make choices affecting the action of the group, but the group also affects how individuals make those choices and produce results. Viewed in this way, a group is not a machine with interchangeable parts. Replacing group members changes the dynamics of the interaction and may not be productive.

Considered thus, the group consists of *actors* (Phillips and Wood, 1980) who contribute to the meaning which the group has for its members as well as for the organization. Process is important to this view, because over a period of time and through interactions, group members learn how to behave with each other and how to make more accurate predictions about their own behavior and that of others. The group also develops a history of its communication, a record capable of influencing present and future actions. For these reasons, it is more satisfactory to view the group as more than the sum of its parts, and to consider the individuals in the group as actors capable of creating and shaping the meaning of the group's interaction through choices made about behavior. This view allows us to look at human beings as human beings rather than as machines or parts of a machine; it encourages us to focus on the choices which people make as actors interpreting the drama of the group interaction.

A second problem associated with expectations and fears of working in small groups is the question of *leadership*. Again, it makes a difference whether we view leadership as a power vested in a single individual or as a "thing" to be shared among all group members. In Chapter 5 we will explore fully the question of leadership, but for the present we need to look at leadership as a potential problem for any group. Consider the following statement made by a person who experienced a lack of leadership in a small group:

> **Grace V., 19** I work for a radio station in a medium-sized market. Every Monday we have a group meeting to decide what needs to be done during the coming week. The meetings are a pain in the a--. Nobody knows what to say or do. We smoke cigarettes, drink coffee, hash over old problems, talk about our friends, talk about our competitors, and nothing gets accomplished. I think the problem is a lack of leadership, although I know that sounds like a cliché. Our thing has been to treat each other as equals, from station manager to secretary, and generally that is good. But in meetings, someone needs to be in charge! Somebody's got to call the meeting to order, tells us what we are supposed to talk about, give deadlines, make decisions, and so forth. Equality is killing us, and our ratings are showing it.

Grace makes a good case for having a strong leader. But the issue is not as simple as she makes it sound. Consider the following testimony of Anthony, who has a different perspective on leadership in groups:

> **Anthony C., 21** When they interviewed me for this job they said I would have a lot to say about public relations for the university. Bull. I haven't had diddly to say because of the way our meetings are run. Once every two weeks the directors of university activities meet in the Vice-President for Student Affairs' office. It's like being committed to Hades for two hours. We all sit around a table while she leads. She pontificates on subjects of her own choosing, and because she is the VP no one tries to shut her up. She makes all the decisions, which makes us wonder why we are supposed to meet with her at all. She says she wants our "input," but when we give it to her it had better correspond to what she thinks or else we are given the cold shoulder. I've applied for another job. I can't take this group crap anymore.

Anthony was in a group with a strong leader, but apparently there was no group interaction. There was a leader who delivered public speeches, instead of a group who worked together to make decisions. Unfortunately, Anthony's response to the ineffectiveness of the group situation is fairly typical of many frustrated group participants—he was ready to quit. He seems to hold to the view of the group as a machine with interchangeable parts, which in this case was essentially true, unless the group acts to correct the leader's behavior.

Somewhere between having no leader and having a domineering one is a happy medium. Effective groups are characterized by a variety of leadership styles; no one style of leadership is right for every group. But the extremes given here are usually to be avoided. What is needed is to see *leadership as a set of communication skills that may be vested in one person or shared among group members*. If the style of leadership is not conducive to effective interaction among group members, then the group members are responsible for altering it.

A third problem too often associated with expectations and fears about group meetings is a feeling of personal *ineffectiveness*. Human beings interact most effectively and efficiently when they feel that they have contributions to make, and that their contributions are rewarded. Ineffectiveness in a group setting is like inertia: there are strong forces operating *against* each other, rather than using the group's resources to promote effective participation. Consider the following statement made by a member of an ineffective group:

> **Wilhelmina H., 27**   We have R and D meetings on Thursday afternoons. We are supposed to plan for new research projects and make recommendations about the company's priorities. What we do instead is listen to Frank and Jesse argue with each other about who gets what in terms of research money and computer time. I usually draw pictures to pass the time. Some group members quit attending, and our leader tells jokes. I used to care, but it doesn't matter as much to me anymore.

Wilhelmina's problem is a common one. When groups become ineffective it is difficult to rebuild a sense of contribution among group members. Ineffectiveness has many causes, ranging from not adhering to an agenda to not having effective methods for countering conflict between and among group members, or not encouraging participation.

Ineffectiveness is a major cause of two other problems associated with expectations about small groups. When nothing seems to happen in group meetings, members are *bored*. When members become bored with the group's operations, people learn to see the group's activities as a *waste of time*. No wonder Sorensen was able to establish the "Grouphate" concept as pervasively affecting people's feelings about working with each other!

The human need to establish order prevents us from accepting chaos and confusion in our dealings with others. Without specifying a goal, finding a method to work toward it, and gaining a sense of accomplishment from participation in groups, we have no good reason to want to work with others. Because organizations are making increasing demands on individuals to participate in small groups, and since we know that the ultimate success or failure of modern organizations depends on our ability to train people as effective group participants, this text and this course should be taken seriously.

What You Get Out of Reading This Book

No one can make you an effective group participant by telling you to read a book. No one can make you an effective group participant by simply placing you in a small group and telling you to "work things out." Learning group interaction skills requires a combination of two forms of education—accumulation of intellectual understanding and applied experiential training. This text can help you acquire the knowledge you need to perform well in groups. Your class can help you to apply these understandings by allowing you to experience working in small groups.

Learning small group interaction skills is not a passive procedure. Like learning how to play a musical instrument or riding a bicycle, you must consciously apply to your small group experiences the principles contained in this book. You will make mistakes, but hopefully not repeat the same mistakes. You will find yourself frustrated, but you will learn ways to overcome this feeling by working in groups. You will experience conflicts with other group members, but you should be able to manage these by applying the information you read to the diagnoses of the causes and symptoms of the conflict. And you will also find yourself progressively more comfortable with group interaction as a method for making decisions and solving problems.

Organization of the Text *Small Group Communication in Organizations* is designed to promote systematic learning on your part. This chapter is an introduction to the uses, problems, expectations, and fears of groups in modern organizations. Chapter 2 is an introduction to how small groups develop over a period of time, and how they accomplish group work. Chapter 3 explains what you should know about communication skills in the small group. Chapter 4 discusses the nature of participation in the small group, and provides an extensive listing of types of statements to make and questions to ask while working with others. Chapter 5 develops the idea of leadership in small groups as a set of communication skills that can be learned by almost everybody. Also in Chapter 5 we discuss how problems associated with too much or too little leadership can be overcome. These first five chapters provide you with a synopsis of intellectual understandings to guide your performance in small groups. Each chapter also includes exercises designed to be used in your class to demonstrate the principles you need to know.

Chapter 6 addresses how decisions are made in small groups. Two systematic procedures for implementing the decision-making process, together with a summary of the duties of participants and leaders, show you how to encourage group decision-making.

Chapter 7 addresses problem-solving in small groups. We take the approach that in most modern organizations problem-solving usually follows decision-making. Consequently, we present two procedures for implementing problem-solving processes based on decisions previously made. One special case study is provided at the end of Chapter 7, enabling you to make productive use of the skills and understandings presented in this chapter.

Chapters 8 and 9 are concerned with improving your effectiveness in small group settings. Chapter 8 explores the "mixed-motive" interactions that often disrupt group work, then investigates a variety of strategies used by group members which can result in this problem. Chapter 9 is primarily concerned with how you can help improve the performances of *others* in small groups. In this chapter the emphasis is on the analysis of particular communication problems commonly encountered by groups and methods of solving them by means of strategic intervention. In both chapters the emphasis is on developing *adaptive* approaches to group effectiveness.

Chapter 10 explains how to observe and evaluate small group interaction. If you plan a career in management or any of its allied disciplines, you should be able to apply what you learn from reading this chapter to the behavior of the groups you lead or in which you participate. This chapter shows you how to discover what individual behavior means in terms of the *process* of group interaction. Chapter 10 is an "interlude" in the text, following the theoretical foundations of group communication and preceding the practical examinations of specific group settings. You will learn to refer to Chapter 10 as you continue to progress through the course.

Chapter 11 is the last chapter in the text, but it may serve as the foundation for your future small group communication activities in organizations. This chapter explains how to implement the information presented here when you enter small groups in business or industry. Practical advice is given about how to talk about your group communication skills in job interviews, how to approach a superior about the use of a small group, and how to fit into existing groups with a minimum of disturbances. Finally, the chapter offers some advice about the profession of communication consulting as it relates to small group interaction, and speculates on the future of small group activity in the American free enterprise system.

If you read each chapter of this text carefully, and make a conscientious attempt to apply these principles to your decisions about behavior in small group settings, you should be able to improve your ability to get work done in small groups. As soon as you can make these principles an integral part of your thinking about interactions with others, they will cease to be intrusive guides, and become a part of your repertoire of communication skills. The purpose of this book is to enable you to develop competencies which you can then refine as required.

Remember this: when you enter a small group, you assume a responsibility perhaps more demanding than any other responsibility in organizational life. This is associated with your commitment to working with others to the best of your ability. Whenever you avoid an assignment, show up late for a meeting, fail to follow the appropriate agenda, or do not try to communicate an idea accurately, *you are adversely affecting the lives of all other group members.* The success of a small group depends on a high level of commitment to the goals of the group on the part of each group member. Nothing less can be tolerated.

Think about the advantages to be gained from learning how to work with others in group settings. Now ask yourself: are you ready and willing to make the necessary commitment? If your answer is "no," then return this text to the shelf and plan to come back to it some time in the future. If your answer is "yes," then you are ready to begin a journey through the uses and abuses of small group communication in organizations. Welcome!

Summary

This chapter introduced you to small group processes in the modern organization. An organization is defined as "a human group whose activities are designed to attain specific goals." There are three basic kinds of modern organizations, manufacturing, research and development, and public service; many firms use two or more of these activities to reach their goals.

Organizations are composed of small groups of people working with technologies and other people. Because of the size and complexity of many modern organizations, tasks are broken down by divisions (e.g., accounting and finance, marketing and sales, manufacturing, and personnel), and these divisions in turn further subdivide the work by assigning specific tasks to smaller groups. An organization is responsible for directing, coordinating, and accounting for the quality and productivity of its employees. All organizational activities are interdependent.

There are two basic kinds of small groups in organizations. Formal groups are responsible for carrying out tasks assigned to them; membership in formal groups is determined by an organizational chart. Informal groups are aggregates of individuals who interact regularly to attain personal, social, or political goals within the organization. Membership in such informal groups is voluntary, and does not correspond to official titles and task responsibilities contained in the organizational chart. Modern organizations are characterized by an interdependence of formal and informal groups. There are basically five uses of formal groups in organizations: production teams, committees, decision-making, problem-solving, and quality circles. There are basically four varieties of informal groups in organizations: information-networking, political alliances, social alliances, and recreational teams. The emphasis in this text is on the development of communication skills for formal group settings, although these same skills can be used in informal group settings.

Most organizations establish policies and procedures guiding the work of formal groups. These policies and procedures comprise the rules of the organization. However, there are always unwritten codes of conduct affecting human behavior in groups; these codes may be more important to individual success. When you enter an organization there are four sources of important questions you need to ask to discover how your work will be appraised or evaluated: attendance, participation, performance, and loyalty.

To improve your understanding of and performance in small groups, you need to determine what the group expects from you. Many people do not like working in groups because they are not trained to interact effectively in them. You need to understand what a "group" is from the perspective of your organization. Is it a kind of machine composed of interchangeable human parts, or is it an entity greater than the sum of its parts, which relies on individual decision-making about behavior and goals? You also need to understand the function of leadership and participation in the group to guard against ineffectiveness, boredom, and a sense of wasting time in group settings. Remember that the need to establish order in human groups depends on setting up and defining a goal for the group's operation, finding methods capable of reaching those goals, and contributing to the relative satisfaction of all the members engaged in group interaction.

You must learn how to be an effective participant in small groups. Reading this text and applying what you have read to individual group activities is the best way to train group members in effectiveness. To become effective, you need to recognize and respond to the idea of commitment to the group, and to accept responsibility for the outcomes of group interaction.

References

Albrecht, T. L., and V. A. Ropp. "The Study of Network Structuring in Organizations Through the Use of Method Triangulation." *Western Journal of Speech Communication* 46 (1982): 162–78.

Baker, P. M. "Social Coalitions." *American Behavioral Scientist* 24 (1981): 633–48.

Baird, Jr., J. E. *Quality Circles.* Prospect Heights, Ill: Waveland Press, 1982.

Dewar, D., and J. F. Beardsley. *Quality Circles.* Midwest City, Okla.: International Association of Quality Circles, 1977.

Eisenberg, E., P. R. Monge, and K. I. Miller. "Involvement in Communication Networks as a Predictor of Organizational Commitment." *Human Communication Research* 10 (1983): 179–201.

Goldman, M., J. W. Stockbauer, and T. G. McAuliffe. "Intergroup and Intragroup Competition and Cooperation." *Journal of Experimental Social Psychology* 13 (1977): 81–88.

Goodall, Jr., H. L. "A Theatre of Motives: A Longitudinal Interpretive Study of One Organization's 'Meaningful Orders of Persons and Things' with Implications for the Ethnography of Organizational Cultures." *Communication Yearbook 13.* Edited by J. Anderson. Beverly Hills, Calif.: Sage, 1989.

Hampton, D., C. Summer, and R. Webber. *Organizational Behavior and the Practice of Management,* 3d. ed. Glenview, Ill: Scott, Foresman, and Company, 1978.

Hunt, G. T. *Communication Skills in the Organization.* Englewood Cliffs, N.J.: Prentice-Hall, 1980.

McPhee, R. D. "A Model of Serial Network Development in Organizations." *Central States Speech Journal* 37 (1986): 8–18.

O'Connell, S. E. *The Manager as Communicator.* New York: Harper & Row, 1979.

Ouchi, W. *Theory Z: How American Business Can Meet the Japanese Challenge.* Reading, Mass.: Addison-Wesley, 1981.

Phillips, G. M., D. J. Pedersen, and J. T. Wood. *Group Discussion: A Practical Guide to Participation and Leadership,* 2d ed. New York: Harper & Row, 1985.

Phillips, G. M., and J. T. Wood. "Metaphysical Metaphors and Pedagogical Practice." *Communication Education* 29 (1980).

Roberts, K. H., and C. A. O'Reilly, III. "Organizations as Communication Structures: An Empirical Approach." *Human Communication Research* 3 (1977).

Schwartz, D., and E. Jacobson. "Organizational Communication Network Analysis: The Liaison Communication Roll." *Organizational Behavior and Human Performance* 18 (1977): 158–74.

Sorensen, S. "Grouphate." Paper presented to the International Communication Association annual convention, Minneapolis, May, 1981.

Stohl, C., and K. Jennings. "Volunteerism and Voice in Quality Circles." *Western Journal of Speech Communication* 52 (1988): 238–51.

Tichy, N. M., M. L. Tushman, and C. Fombrun. "Social Network Analysis for Organizations." *Academy of Management Review* 4 (1979): 507–20.

Van Maanen, J., and S. R. Barley. "Occupational Communities: Culture and Control in Organizations." *Research in Organizational Behavior* 6 (1984): 287–365.

Wickesberg, A. "Communications Networks in the Business Organization Structure." *Academy of Management Journal* 11 (1968): 253–62.

Exercises

The following exercises are designed to be used in class. Please follow your instructor's guidelines for organizing your group and making decisions within the group. After each group completes the three exercises, ask a representative from each group to write the results on the board. Compare the results from the different groups. Which items achieved consensus among all the groups? Which items did not? Why?

The following 10 items direct you to achieve consensus within your group. Use "A" for agree; "D" for disagree; and "U" for undecided. After all items have been marked "A," "D," or "U," go back over the ones marked "U" and change the arrangement of the item in a way capable of producing an "A" consensus among group members. REMEMBER; THIS IS A GROUP *COMMUNICATION* EXERCISE. Avoid asking each group member to simply mark her/his own answers; discuss the issues among all group members.

_____ 1. The group is like a machine—it is only as good as the sum of its parts.

_____ 2. The group is like a drama—it is more than the sum of its parts.

_____ 3. A group should have a strong, directive leader to guide discussions.

_____ 4. A group should not have a designated leader. All persons in the group should help accomplish leadership functions.

_____ 5. Persons should be encouraged to say whatever they feel like saying in a decision-making group.

_____ 6. The primary objective of a small group should be to accomplish the task given to it.

_____ 7. It is just as important to have group members like each other as it is to accomplish the assigned task.

_____ 8. You need a lot of experience in groups before you can work well in these clusters.

_____ 9. Working in small groups is a boring waste of time.

_____ 10. I want to learn how to work efficiently in small groups.

The second exercise asks your group to rank the following items (1 = most important; 5 = least important) based on how each item contributes to friendly, productive group work.

_____ 1. A group experience should improve a person's self-esteem.

_____ 2. A group should obey the rules of conduct established by the organization.

_____ 3. A group should focus its activity on accomplishing its task.

_____ 4. A group should follow a procedure or agenda for all discussions.

_____ 5. A group should get rid of unproductive group members.

The third exercise asks your group to rank the following items in terms of their importance to the overall effectivenss of the group (1 = most important; 5 = least important).

_____ 1. Establishing an agenda for orderly discussion.

_____ 2. Encouraging group members to make statements or express opinions.

_____ 3. Encouraging group members to ask questions.

_____ 4. Encouraging group members to follow the directions of the designated leader.

_____ 5. Keeping the group on schedule to meet all prescribed deadlines.

After you have recorded your answers and discussed them in class, you should have a good idea about the initial norms and personal standards used by the individuals in your group. While there are no "right" answers to any of the above items, it is useful to know how the individuals in your group view group communication. You will notice some members seem to be more concerned with task accomplishment than social goals; others may feel more inclined to "follow the leader" rather than assume a leadership role themselves. Knowing how your group feels about these issues can help you make more accurate predictions about each other's behavior. Remember, you have just provided information about yourselves to the group. This information should be used to guide decisions about how to communicate more effectively by adapting to the needs and expectations of the individual group members. Note also that this information will *change* as you gain more information about each other and about effective group communication.

2 What You Should Know about Small Group Processes and Functions

Introduction

It is a relatively simple task to describe what is meant by the term "small group." A small group ideally consists of five to seven members (Bales and Borgatta, 1955), who interact regularly in a specific context (Thompsen and McEwen, 1958), using an agenda or procedure to guide communication (Phillips, Pedersen, and Wood, 1979), to accomplish a purpose. This generalized description of an ideal small group may bear very little resemblance, however, to small groups operating in American business and industry. For example, although the size of an ideal small group is between five and seven members, the actual size of small groups within organizations varies with the nature of the task and history of the division. Quality circles, for instance, may include as few as four or as many as fifteen group participants. We can use this ideal description to discuss a small group, but we cannot use it to generalize about what happens within particular small groups in American organizations.

For example, our ideal description of a small group presents a static view of the unit, and fails to account for the group *process*. Etzioni (1964) suggests most human groups within organizations are characterized by movements toward or away from their goals, and may seldom actually accomplish their given objectives. While our ideal description may imply that groups accomplish their objectives, evidence suggests that less than ideal groups (which account for most small groups in American organizations) are characterized by communication that reveals a process of movement toward and away from objectives. For example, a long-term goal for a particular marketing and sales group might be complete market saturation. Because of the high degree of difficulty associated with attaining this objective, the marketing and sales group may never actually reach their goal. However, while they make and fail to make progress toward their objective, they will be characterized by communication processes and evaluations of individual and group effectiveness.

Another characteristic absent from our ideal description of a small group is an assessment of the functions served by the group within the organization and for specific group members. By "function" I mean that the presence of the group and its activities contributes to the meaning of the organization and the meaning which the organization holds for individual group members. Our ideal description deprives group communication of its humaneness, its heroes, its sense of humor, and transforms an active and changing process into one that is sterile and static. As excerpts from the comments of actual group members consistently demonstrate, people interpret their participation in small groups very personally. They ascribe meanings to their work and to each other on the bases of the stories they tell, the memories they recall, and the lessons they learned. Small groups, and the individuals within them, are active components of any organizational culture; to fully appreciate how a small group functions within an organization requires an understanding of how the culture is served and shaped by communication.

This chapter discusses what you should know about small group processes and functions within American organizations. First, we will examine the organization as the product of a culture, and of various small group subcultures within it. Second, we will investigate the nature of group membership, its meanings within an organization, and then consider how joining a new group influences that group's history and procedures. Third, we will examine individual and group goals, observing how they shape small group processes and reveal small group functions. Fourth, we will note in detail some agendas and procedures used by small groups in American organizations, and describe how these agendas and procedures can be used effectively to operate group processes and to organize group functions. Following the chapter summary you will find exercises and references designed to deepen and broaden your understanding and awareness of small group processes and functions.

Organizational Culture and History in the Small Group

If you conceptualize an organization to be like a *culture,* complete with shared meanings for symbols, rituals, rules, and codes of conduct (Beyer and Trice, 1987; Morgan, 1986; Pacanowsky and O'Donnell-Trujillo, 1983; Hawes, 1980), then you can make productive use of small group communication as representing or reflecting what happens in *subcultures* comprising the culture. Every culture and every subculture develops its own unique history. Moreover, the process of making history contributes to the vital relationship between the subculture and the culture in which it exists. In this section we will examine the effects of cultural and historical evolution on small group processes and functions.

Culture is a difficult term to define. It can be used globally, as when we speak of an "American culture," or more narrowly, as when we speak of "being cultured." Essentially a culture is an abstraction, a term we use to express the sum total of *shared meanings* that have evolved over a period of time. Anthropologists such as Clifford Geertz (1972) despair about our ability to interpret a culture unless we are part of it; communication research tells us that "culture" is a term we usually apply to someone else, working in some other organization, to explain differences between them and us (see Chaney, 1983; Pacanowsky and O'Donnell-Trujillo, 1982).

Evolution of Organizational Cultures

Sociologists often speak of culture as the defining structure of a society. Thus, we can talk about the "American culture" as a system of interrelated processes and functions served by government, industry, communities, and institutions. Because these processes and functions must change and yet remain stable for the United States to survive, we say the structure of American culture is both evolving and established.

Cultures do not just happen. Cultures develop over periods of time, using the historical processes that affect the evolution of shared meanings to shape and define such cultures. We often hear arguments about Europeans having a richer cultural history than we have; the argument generally used to support this claim is that Europe has been a center of civilization for a longer period of time. Because European history was, at least until the later Renaissance, *the* history of Western Civilization, weighty influences of European history and tradition are found in every country once discovered or ruled by a European nation.

When we use the term *culture* to describe an organization, we are pointing out how shared meanings evolve (Goodall, 1989; Pacanowsky and O'Donnell-Trujillo, 1982). Hawes (1974) indicates that the outcome of these shared meanings, as revealed in communication, *is* the organization. Over a period of time these shared meanings tend to stabilize. The organization develops a structure and processes, and functions for groups are specified. An organization, as a culture, consists of a structure, processes, and a set of functions that remain stable and yet change. International Business Machines' (IBM's) organizational chart has not changed very much during its year of operation, despite its obvious expansion and diversification of interests. As a culture develops a history, that history influences what people know and believe about the culture. As IBM developed a history, new employees were given instruction in the shared beliefs about IBM's mission and ways of accomplishing the mission. New employees of IBM inherit a cultural tradition which influences their perceptions of the organization, of their tasks, and of themselves. The same is true of any organization with a history.

We will consider organizations as cultures, because when we view them this way we can better understand the influence of history and shared meanings on the ways in which individuals and small groups interact. For example, in our culture we have a strong belief in establishing a precedent to govern how interpretations should be made. Organizations also establish precedents based on their own history of decision-making policies, problem-solving procedures, productivity, and their ideas of leadership and participation. The actions of employees are often *evaluated* according to these standards. Perhaps the best early treatment of how organizational standards affect individual behavior can be found in William H. Whyte, Jr.'s *The Organization Man* (1956). Referring to the fear of loss of autonomy resulting from pressures to conform to organizational standards, Whyte's book details overt and subtle influences which companies exert upon the behavior, attitudes, values, and beliefs of their people. The longer the organization has been operating, the more likely rigid standards will be established and adherence to them compulsory for the individual. For example, for many years IBM workers could be readily identified by their "uniform": white shirt, dark tie, conservative suit, polished shoes. Everyone in the organization, from type-writer repair personnel to senior executives wore the uniform, thus contributing to the shared meaning of the company's values while continuing a historical precedent.

More recent critiques of America's organizational cultures and the enormous influence they have over individual choice-making among employees, appear in a variety of literature (see Shorris, 1983; Dandridge, Mitroff, and Joyce, 1980; Benson, 1977; Silverman, 1971). Unfortunately, some authors have taken a disturbingly negative view of the influence generated by organizations, inducing us to see employees as faceless, nameless, almost mindless entities, instead of active choice-makers capable of exerting an influence on the organization's operation (see Scott and Hart, 1979).

Five major areas of organizational behavior are influenced by the development of an organizational culture:

Characteristics of Organizational Culture

1. *The Evolution of Rituals:*   Organizations develop and encourage ritualized forms of interaction among employees. The ability or inability of people to address one another by surnames, the habitual ways in which people in superior and inferior positions speak to each other, company sponsored retreats and picnics, as well as organizational development programs, or styles of dress, are all manifestations of influence generated by the history of an organization.
2. *The Establishment of Authority and Uses of Power:*   Organizations develop a history of leadership ideals and failures, using past experiences with leadership functions as guides to decisions about how authority should be vested and how power can be most productively used. Formal chains-of-command and ideas about uses and abuses of power are inherent in any organization.
3. *The Use of Formal Groups:*   Organization charts reveal how the structure and functions of the company are arranged. As we have seen, these charts provide us with a way of visualizing how formal groups are integral to the organization's accomplishment of objectives. The history of an organization, its rituals, and its uses of power influence how these formal groups are used; they also provide insight into how membership in formal groups is assigned.
4. *The Use of Standard Operating Procedures:*   Organizations develop regular and routinized methods of making decisions, solving problems, and directing the activities of individual employees. History influences how standard operating procedures are developed and used, illustrating how SOPs become the company's methodological imperative.

5. *The Appraisal/Review Process:* Organizations periodically review the achievements and failures of divisions, while these, in turn, review the productivity of formal groups and individuals. Most organizations use standardized evaluation forms developed empirically (historically) as appropriate devices for assessing the behavior of employees. Because behavior is evaluated according to historically derived forms and formats, we can observe the influence of an organizational culture on the behavior choices made by individuals and groups.

These five influences reveal how an organization's cultural understandings and values permeate every aspect of the operation. Although there are many similarities among organizations, there are also intriguing differences in how history has determined these cultural understandings. In the next section we will see how these differences can arise in an organizational setting, but first let's examine the following statement made by an employee of two companies who saw how some of the cultural influences were manifested:

Robert T., 26 I worked for ( ) for two years before coming to ( ). When I worked for the first network, we all had to wear a suit and tie, arrive at work a half-an-hour before the sales manager, and have tightly planned schedules for sales calls. Everything was planned, and there was very little room for individuality. When I came to this network I had to make a real attitude adjustment. Nobody wears a suit, and seldom do you see anyone wearing a tie. You are given incentives to make sales, and your time is truly your own. If I don't feel like coming to the office, I don't. So long as the sales manager knows where to get in touch with me, everything is cool. I remember trying to turn in a sales plan after my first week on the job—Jerry (the sales manager) just stared at me and then shook his head back and forth. "You guys from ( )," he said, "are all alike. Look, I don't care what your plan is so long as you meet or exceed your sales quota. You gotta learn how to act around here if you plan to stay around here."

Evolution of Small Groups as Subcultures

In view of the many influences generated by the organizational culture, people have many opportunities to create their own unique set of shared meanings, especially in small groups. If we can conceptualize an organization as a culture, we can see how that culture is made up of various smaller subcultures or small groups (Carbaugh, 1988; Martin and Siehl, 1983).

A good analogy can be drawn from the city of Pittsburgh. As an American city, Pittsburgh draws on the culture and shared meanings of the United States, as established by historical precedents and use of a common language, English. But when we look more closely at the city of Pittsburgh, we distinguish a complex of smaller subcultures, many of which are built on ethnic ties and specialized uses of old world languages. Traveling through the city of Pittsburgh, we can hear people speaking Polish, Italian, Yiddish, German, and other languages in communities made up of people who share those cultural heritages. We can see subcultural influences in the rich variety of shops and restaurants, in the ways homes are painted and decorated, in the style of dress exhibited by Pittsburgh's citizens. While they all share in the American cultural experience, these subcultures have created unique ways of maintaining independent identities based on their own histories and experiences.

Similarly, an organization is made up of divisions, each one a composite of its individual members. While the organization has organizational objectives, each division has its own objectives guiding the activities of individuals and groups. If we think of the division as a subculture, we can appreciate how special understandings and interpretations characteristic of the subculture facilitate effective interaction. Although everyone may use the English language, there are technical terms and phrases peculiar to each part of the organization's operation. While each division is ultimately responsible to the organization, it usually has its own historically derived ways of reaching divisional goals.

Most of the work accomplished by divisions is carried out by small groups. The latter develop a history of their own, complete with records of past accomplishments and failures, myths about their operation, codes of conduct for group members, and legends about individual and group performance. To understand what you need to do to be effective in a small group, you should learn about the group's history. Historical precedents and commonly shared understandings form the core of any group's collective comprehension of goals and procedures. Consider Barry's case:

Barry V., 29   When I was transferred to the research-end of the organization, I made the mistake of believing what happened here was like what happened in the production-end of the organization. Back there we were more or less equals, like one big happy family. Our supervisor was a company man who played by the rules, but as long as we did the work on time he never complained. Over here I work with a team of experts. We make reports to each other, and leadership depends on who has the expertise on a particular subject. When I came on board Liz was the group leader because she was directing a research project in her area. I thought she was *the* leader, and treated her as such. You know what happened? People began thinking I was trying to put the moves on her! I can see why they thought that way now, but then I was terrified. I mean, I'm a married man with kids—the last thing in the world I need is that kind of trouble. I alienated Liz by my actions. She still doesn't trust me, but I'm learning. In a way I can see how the whole thing was my fault, but I wish someone would have explained how this research group worked before I joined them.

As Barry discovered, very often community understandings are so well comprehended by members of the community that transgressions by outsiders or new group members easily occur.

When you enter a small group, you should try to remain an observer until you can find out some of the community's shared understandings. Ask questions about the history of the group, and try to discover how the group uses its history.

Let people know why you are asking the questions, and ask them for help when you become confused. As the old saying goes, "Fools rush in where angels fear to tread." You need to gather information before you can make informed choices about your behavior in small groups. Pacanowsky and O'Donnell-Trujillo (1982) list seven possible sources of information about the organization's culture which you may wish to investigate:

Possible Sources of Cultural Information

1. *Relevant Constructs:* Try to discover the group's general and specific goals and what their shared meanings are. These notions will become important to you as you gain experience in the group and can rely on them for important information.

2. *Facts:* From the relevant constructs you should be able to gain an appreciation for what counts as information for the group and for each individual member. You will discover, for example, which problems, authorities, vested interests, and preferred actions the group uses as bases for decisions.

3. *Practices:* Try to find out how this particular group knows when it has completed the task, and how communication practices are viewed in relation to accomplishing the task: for example, how does the group keep records, process new information, punish violators of the group's code for behavior? (Pacanowsky, 1987)

4. *Vocabulary:* Try to learn the particular argot, jargon, or technical language used by the group and its members. The more you learn to use the group's language, the more likely they are to accept you into the culture.

5. *Metaphors:* Listen to how the group members talk about themselves and the organization. What are the typical metaphors they use to describe their organizational experiences? This can reveal valuable information about how they see themselves within the group or organization. Are they "playing the game," or "changing the system?" (Morgan, 1986)

6. *Stories:* Listen to the stories individual group members tell about themselves and others. There will be ritualized "screw-ups" when the boss was away, or perhaps an important event that happened when the computer broke down. In stories we reveal significant information about the group and the organization (Dandridge, Mitroff, and Joyce, 1980; Mitroff and Kilmann, 1975).

7. *Rites and Rituals:* Every subculture has it own ceremonies and important dates or observances. Examples are the semi-annual reviews of performance, weekly staff meetings, and daily coffee breaks. Knowing these rites and rituals provides valuable insight into the inner workings of the group, as well as a sense of what the operating rules are (Roy, 1960).

In this section we have examined how history influences the development of organizational cultures and small group subcultures. I have consistently tried to demonstrate how history affects perceptions about the meaning of behavior, and how performance will be judged according to historically derived standards. We are now ready to investigate the nature of group membership in organizational subcultures.

The Nature of Group Membership

Ideally, people seek membership in small groups that reflect their individual attitudes, values, and beliefs (Phillips and Erickson, 1970). With this principle in mind we can examine the membership of formal and informal groups within organizations, and trace the networks of commonly held meanings and interests (Deetz, 1982). Because of the voluntary nature of informal group membership, we can gather data about the types of informal groups members of an organization belong to and generalize about those shared meanings and interests.

Formal groups are usually composed of people who have been specifically *assigned* membership in the group. Assignments to small groups in organizations are often made on the basis of skills or special experiences which may improve the group's performance. Within academic decision-making groups, representatives are drawn from the upper ranks of the faculty. Deans, directors of programs, chairpersons, and vice-presidents are selected for membership because each should be able to express the viewpoints of the respective academic areas and cost centers. Major corporations establish small groups responsible for long-range strategic planning, assigning individuals who have expertise in the areas relevant to the decisions being made. Because of the involuntary nature of formal group membership, we have a more difficult task trying to locate generalizable attitudes, values, and beliefs. As a result, the shared meanings and preferences of a formal small group are likely to evolve more slowly than they do in informal small groups. Consider Fred's experiences and the impact of time on his understanding:

> **Fred H., 32**   I guess it took me about three years before I felt like I knew the other group members. We met once a month, maybe twice a month, and we worked under pressure most of the time. There wasn't much push to get to know each other as people; we were there to accomplish our tasks. I remember thinking that Al was a jerk for the longest time because he used to sit in meetings and just stroke his beard and make humming noises. Then I saw him in the cafeteria one afternoon, and, well, it would have been awkward if I'd have not sat down with him. We were the only two people there. So I did and we talked, and I found out what a really interesting fellow Al is. I tend not to pay much attention to his beard-stroking and humming these days.

Virginia is a different story. I liked her from the start. She seemed warm and friendly and yet businesslike. You know, the "I'm a liberated woman asserting myself on the way up" style you see a lot of these days. I respected her for being that way, for knowing what she wanted. Then I found out how she screwed over a friend of mine, a technical writer. She knew what she wanted all right: his job. Played up to him like he was a saint, then, when she got the information she wanted, she made it seem like *he* was the one spreading rumors. For awhile it was very tense around Virginia in meetings. We all knew. We just wanted to let her know her game was up.

As Fred's experiences point out, membership in formal small groups is fraught with hazards, particularly if you have information about other group members which is unfavorable. Formal small groups do the work of the organization despite these hazardous conditions; the chances are good that if you are assigned membership in a small group within an organization, there will be people with whom you would rather not associate, there will be tasks to accomplish that seem to demand more expertise or skill than the group can collectively muster. But despite all these problems, you and other members of your small group will meet the challenge.

Why?

The formation of a small group, even when members are assigned, constrains people to act in ways that promote the group's ability to master the assigned task. Membership is critical because assignments should be made on the basis of expertise, experience, and skills which accent the group's goal-orientation rather than their ability to get along with each other. In most American organizations, there is an attitude of ambivalence about individual group members *liking* each other: the objective is not to enjoy each other's company, but to accomplish the goal in a given period of time.

Unfortunately, this ambivalence runs counter to human nature. People generally do care whether or not they get along with each other. More and more, the quality of our interpersonal relationships at work contributes to our sense of belonging, and to our motivations for work (Yankelovich, 1981).

Managers making assignments of group members should strive to form groups in which each individual can contribute to the positive outcomes of affiliation and task accomplishment among group members. Consider the following example of how this goal was met in one group setting:

Cheryl C., 30   Our project leader was present during the first meeting of our group. He explained the group's charge, and then told us why each one of us was important to the group. In a sense, he established our reasons for being group members, and I think this helped us treat each other fairly. We all knew what our areas of expertise were to be, and so we all had a good idea of our territory. It was easily the best group I have ever been part of. We learned to respect each other's talents, and to direct questions to the appropriate group member.

Group selection should be a primary concern of any group leader. It is essential to find individuals who have the required expertise, experience, or skills, and to explain why they were assigned to the group. Intuitively we know we work better with people we like, and we generally feel more comfortable in group settings when we understand our role in relation to the group's task and objective.

The Nature of Group and Individual Goals for Small Groups

All human groups have purposes or goals. The family protects, nurtures, and guides the behavior of its younger members while advancing the welfare of all. The American Public Health Association lobbies for legislation designed to protect the health of communities and individuals. *Alpha Psi Omega* promotes undergraduate and graduate theatre activities on campuses across the United States. These are generalized objectives. Although they serve to establish general goals or statements of purpose of these groups, they do not tell us very much about the more specific objectives of the smaller groups that compose these organizations. If all we had were generalized goals, the actions and interactions of small groups would be seriously impaired. Each individual would be free to interpret the goals and invent ways of reaching them without reference to a common plan of action to guide the group's activities.

While there may be instances when having no precise goal would be advantageous (such as the meetings of a streetcorner gang or a casual literary discussion group), organizations must operate in a more formal, more structured, more goal-oriented fashion. Organizations hold individuals and groups accountable for their actions, using performance-based evaluations to make critical decisions about company policies, long- and short-range planning, the use of incentives, pay raises and promotions. Without specific goals for each of the organization's small groups, the objectives of the organization probably could not be met. In other words, the organization would be irresponsible.

What is a goal? It is what you want to have happen, an outcome, an end product. A goal is a way of guiding meaningful discussion toward optimal conclusion or solution. As I pointed out earlier in this chapter, not all organizational or small group goals are met. However, unless a precise outcome, a desired end product, can be specified for the group, the chances of getting there are materially reduced. For a moment consider the operation of a large organization responsible for manufacturing automobiles and trucks. At any given minute, there are many different goals for the organization, depending on whom you ask. The stockholders may see the goal as returning a fair dividend on earnings. The board of directors may see the goal as producing a quality car or truck, using the most advanced technologies to reduce overhead while ensuring consistent productivity. The general managers of each car or truck division may be interested in increasing the sales and reputation of their division, which in turn may create a favorable impression about their managerial skills with the board of directors.

Mid-level managers and engineers may be responsible for ensuring that a specific product (e.g., a one-ton light duty, four-wheel drive truck) meets the blueprint specifications, while also being accountable for the performances of individuals in their respective divisions. Regional managers may be responsible for collecting data about consumer behavior, bidding for new labor contracts, handling customer complaints, hiring and firing employees. Individual dealers must interpret the decisions of higher level managers, direct the activities of employees, establish sales quotas, maintain the neat appearance of the property, and attempt to make a reasonable profit. The sales managers' goals usually deal with the efficient direction of other sales personnel while making a comfortable income and keeping up with new developments and ideas in the automobile trade. The sales personnel try to improve their sales records, often with the hope of moving up to sales manager. The secretaries and office workers must keep accurate records, do the bidding of the bosses, and win the respect of the members of the organization. The maintenance staff must keep the property neat and clean, make sure the products are presentable, and be available for routine situations. The mechanics and service personnel must repair the products, perform routine checkups, keep the parts department informed about tool and parts needs, etc. From the top to the bottom of the organization, there are different goals which must be met if the organization is to succeed.

Organizations, then, have several *interdependent* objectives. Unless most of the more specific goals are met at the different levels, the entire organization suffers. Seldom, if ever, are all of the goals met all the time, so that most people learn to live with a constant sense of ambiguity and minor frustration in their work.

> **Sally L., 28** I used to get nervous around budget time. In college, everyone taught us to believe that organizations were so efficient, so orderly, so precise in their routines. It took me about two years of worry and being nervous to realize that organizations want you to believe that, but they tolerate more inefficiency than they admit. For instance, our budget was due on the first of October, but the final draft of the document, with all the revisions, didn't come out until the fifteenth. I thought I would be fired. Instead, the project director complimented me on doing such a fine job. When I apologized for not having the budget ready on time, he said, "that's okay, hell we haven't met a budget deadline in twelve years!" You learn to live by the standards of the organization. You try to improve your own performance, but sometimes you just can't.

Sally knew what her objective was, but her group was unable to meet it on time. Although this practice is never a good one, it is sometimes a necesary evil. The efficient image an organization tries to present to the public does not always reflect the real, day-to-day operations of human beings who strive to meet deadlines and attain goals.

Organizations have objectives to guide the work of people in groups. The groups themselves have goals to guide the behavior and performance of individual members. And individual group members have personal ends they try to satisfy through communication while working in groups. The purpose of an organizational objective is to organize the activities of its employees; the goals of the individual employees should be to monitor their communication in the service of the group, and of the organization.

As an old Chinese proverb has it, "If you don't know where you are going, any road will get you there." A group goal should provide the individual group members with an idea of where the group should go, and how to get there through effective interaction. Now that we have examined the nature of goals for small groups, we need to take a closer look at how to set goals in small groups.

Consider the following two examples of goal statements. Which one do you think is the better statement?

The Skill of
Establishing Goals

> I want the other group members to like me.
>
> I want the other group members to look at me when I speak, to answer my questions, to act on my recommendations, and to rely on me to provide useful information for discussion.

You should have selected the second statement. It supplies the needed behavioral data to support the goal of "being liked" by other group members. The first statement is deficient because how would you know "liking" if you saw it? The second statement specifies *exactly* how you would know.

The more precise the statement of a goal, the better your chances are of attaining it. While consulting with a group of engineers for an aircraft windshield manufacturer, I discovered that they had no precise goals for their group work, although their goals for design specifications were very precise. Consequently, their designs often lost contracts because the groups responsible for packaging and presenting them were not well organized. They did not need help with their designs; they needed precise group goals. Many groups fail to define a purpose, they meet regularly but accomplish nothing. The need for human groups to make precise statements of goals to guide their discussions is the critical first step in promoting effective interaction.

Groups need to establish goals to make the group more *cohesive* (Davis, 1969). Cohesiveness may be defined as the ability of the group members to work together productively while enjoying their interactions. Cohesiveness is a primary component of effective groups; it is in and of itself a goal for groups whose members must necessarily be together for any long period of time. We know most people do not enjoy group work if they have no purpose (Sherif and Sherif, 1956).

Consider the following example:

Philip C., 30   I used to like the people in my group as individuals until we had to work as a group. Now I admit I am a pragmatic person, but just sitting around a table for an hour or so twice a week exchanging gossip would get to anybody. For the first few meetings we were okay. We made big plans and talked about the future of our sales team. We wanted to be "the best"— whatever that means. But after that things just got progressively worse. The discussions deteriorated into minor arguments, pet peeves, and talk about what we had accomplished years ago. People stopped attending the meetings, and soon a few of the guys found other jobs. I used to have two close friends in that company, but we hardly ever speak to each other anymore. I blame the whole thing on the ineffectiveness of that one small group. In that room, on Wednesday afternoons, we really learned how weak and fragile we were. None of us needed that.

Philip's experience is typical of small groups who operate without a goal. Unless there is some purpose for the meeting, some objective to be reached, people will find other matters to discuss, usually having nothing to do with why the group is together, and in Philip's case, causing more problems than any group should.

Goal setting is a skill. There is very little magic involved in figuring out what you want to have happen and working systematically toward accomplishing it. Here are three common forms goal setting can take in groups:

Forms of Goal Setting

1. *Goal established outside of the group and presented to the group as a "charge"* (assignment).   Many organizations are composed of standing committees or formal small groups. Often these groups have very little to say about the nature of their activities. Someone higher up in the organization determines what needs to be done and directs the group to accomplish it. When the charge is given to the group, group members need to ask questions about the (a) precise goal guiding the work of the group; (b) deadlines and timetables affecting the group's progress; (c) resources available to the group—financial, material, human, technological; and (d) limitations affecting the accomplishment of the goal.

2. *Goal established within the group as a response to a particular need or urgency.*   Organizations expect their various divisions to keep up with developments inside and outside of the organization. At any time a small group within a particular division may decide something needs to be done and then direct the work of group members toward accomplishing the task. When the charge is formulated in the small group, the members need to (a) ask the appropriate official in the organization for permission to work on the task; (b) formally articulate the group's charge, making sure all group members understand it in the same way; (c) establish a discussion procedure to follow during group meetings; and (d) determine what the final outcome will be: a written report, an oral presentation, a brief, a recommendation, or some combination of the above.

3. *Goal established outside of the group, presented to the group as a "charge," but modified by the group as new information becomes available.*   Organizations are usually dynamic structures capable of responding to change. Many times organizations will perceive a need and assign to a particular group the responsibility for investigating it. The group charged with this task may find that no real reason exists for continuing the investigation after certain facts are collected. It is then their responsibility to inform the organizational official of their

findings. A second possibility may be that the group finds there is a problem, but not the problem originally described by the person presenting the charge. In this case it is the group's responsibility to present the information collected and argue for a modified charge to be given. A third possibility may be that the group finds there is a need for their activity, but not in the way specified in the original charge. The group should then explain their perception of the task to the official, and argue for their revision of the plan of action.

As you can see by the above examples, goal setting is a skill that requires an understanding of the *situation* the group faces, the *alternatives* available to the group, the *audience* for whom the group is responsible, and the *resources* allocated to the group to conduct its activities. Without this vital information, the group is in danger of establishing a goal they cannot reach, should not reach, or may reach incorrectly.

Mager (1972) makes a useful distinction between "doable" and "desirable" goals. A "desirable" goal is one a group wants to reach, but may not be able to attain with the resources they have available. A "doable" goal is one a group can reasonably be expected to accomplish with the resources they have available. For example, a desirable group goal may be to put their competition out of business in the next six months. A "doable" version of this goal may be to gain a 51 percent share of the market during the next year. Desirable goals make intriguing informal conversation; "doable" goals make productive group discussions.

Goals must be expressed in non-abstract language (Hayakawa, 1978). The more abstract the language, the less precise the goal, and the less precise the goal, the slimmer the chances for the group to accomplish it. Consider the following examples of how goals can be expressed in abstract and non-abstract language:

Reducing Abstraction in Goal Setting

Abstract Goal	*Non-Abstract Goal*
I want this meeting to be successful.	I want this meeting to allow us to reach a decision by five o'clock.
Let's talk about the advertising department.	Let's talk about the role the advertising department will play in the introduction of our new product next April.
I think we have some problems.	I think we have three problems: first, we are not getting timely information from the accounting division; second, the information they do give us is biased in favor of equipment purchases; and third, because no one is presently in charge in accounting, we have to figure out whom to make our recommendations to.

The use of abstract language in goal setting creates problems for small groups. First, it encourages open-ended discussions that may or may not have any direct bearing on the problem at hand or the desired outcome of the meeting. Second, abstract language usage may confuse group members about the meanings of the words; "talking about the advertising department" may mean a variety of things to the group members, including how to introduce the new product, the personalities of the advertising department staff, or anecdotes about the history of the advertising program. Third, abstraction tends to reproduce itself in the talk of group members. When the leader begins by saying "I think we have some problems," the group members may feel free to discuss those problems (whatever they are) in equally ambiguous language. To set a positive example, the members of small groups must limit their own use of abstractions, and strive to be more precise and direct.

Transcript of group meeting (excerpted):

Maurice W.:	"I guess we all know what the problem is. . . ."
Mary C.:	"Yeah, I know I do."
Pat R.:	"Me too. Something's got to be done."
Maurice W.:	"What do you suggest?"
Pat R.:	"I dunno. Maybe we ought to talk about it first."
Mary C.:	"Yeah, I agree. Let's talk about it."
Maurice W.:	"Okay, I'm game. Where should we begin?"
Mary C.:	"I guess we all know the story. The problem is definitely in not knowing what we're supposed to do here."
Pat R.:	"I know what to do, in fact, I think we all know what to do, we just don't do it."
Maurice W.:	"We don't know *how* to do it. That's the problem."
Pat R.:	"Doesn't that mean we don't know *what* we're supposed to do, I mean, if we don't know *how* we must not know *what,* either."
Mary C.:	"I dunno. Maybe we do know what and how, but other things seem more important at the time."
Maurice W.:	"Could you be more specific?"
Mary C.:	"Hey Maurice, don't pull that on me. You know exactly what I mean!"

This meeting went on for another forty minutes before someone established a goal. Notice how the use of abstraction encouraged abstract responses. Observe how meanings were misconstrued because no precise definitions for words were given. Also note how the group suffered because of their inability to specify a goal, and making the mistake of *assuming* everyone in the group knew what the goal was and how to proceed.

Goal setting is a skill at the heart of effective group communication. Every statement made, every question asked, every decision rendered, depends on the ability of the group to establish a "doable" goal and achieve consensus on what the goal means. Establishing a goal is perhaps the most important task confronting group members at the beginning of a meeting. The goal is a major influence on the interaction following it. Now that we have discussed the idea of goal setting, we are ready to look at how goals may be translated into agendas and procedures to guide small group communication.

The Idea of Agendas and Procedures

Groups need an orderly procedure to follow to prevent personal biases, misinformation, or Groupthink (Janis, 1972) from exerting undue influence over the quality of the group's decision-making or problem-solving. By *orderly procedure* I mean a method for controlling the verbal and written communication used by a group to achieve concensus. Such orderly procedure allows consideration of topics to flow in a directed sequence, indicating where and how to introduce new topics, specifying outcomes, identifying responsibilities of participants and leader. When people know what they can reasonably expect to occur during a group discussion, they can better prepare to communicate effectively.

In this section you will examine three basic types of agendas. First, you will look at *Standard Agenda,* one of the most commonly used methods for directing interaction in organizational groups. Second, you will explore the *Delphi Procedure,* an alternative method for incorporating written consensus-seeking forms into group interaction. Finally, you will examine *hidden agendas,* or the effects of personal plans of action or expectation of reward on the group decision-making or problem-solving process.

The orderly procedure known as Standard Agenda is derived from John Dewey's classic work *How We Think* (1910). Dewey set forth what he believed to be the five steps in problem-solving or scientific reasoning:

Standard Agenda

1. An individual responds to some difficulty or problem, recognizing it as a problem.
2. The individual defines the problem, carefully putting into words the fundamental difficulty.
3. The individual gathers information about the problem, and establishes some standards capable of testing a proposed solution.
4. The individual generates several proposed solutions and selects one.
5. The individual applies the solution to the problem and sees whether or not it overcomes the problem.

McBurney and Hance (1950) adapted Dewey's five steps for use in group discussion, and soon other writers and teachers experimented with the basic idea, making necessary modifications. Perhaps the most detailed and pragmatic discussion of Standard Agenda as adapted for problem-solving small groups can be found in Gerald M. Phillips, Douglas Pedersen, and Julia Wood's *Group Discussion: A Practical Guide to Participation and Leadership* (1979).

Standard Agenda is useful because it is easily amenable to both decision-making and problem-solving groups. It can be successfully used to guide committee work, as well as to serve as a logical basis for discussions of virtually anything. There are a few key elements in the use of Standard Agenda that must be followed if the procedure is to allow a group to arrive at an optimal conclusion:

1. *Group members must understand the use of Standard Agenda.* It is not a good idea to put people in a small group and fail to explain what procedure will be used to guide their interaction. Standard Agenda consists of seven steps that can be learned by almost anyone. Leaders using this procedure should take time to explain to group members how it works, what constraints are placed on communication because of it, and how to prepare for productive group discussions.

2. *Group members must be prepared to interact.* As useful as Standard Agenda may be, the ultimate quality of the interaction will be determined by the ability of the participants to prepare for each group meeting. As group members learn to understand the procedure, they should be given instruction in the kinds of preparation necessary for successful completion of each step of the Standard Agenda.

3. *Group members must be willing to undergo a process of mutual influence.* The most productive uses of Standard Agenda are made by individuals who accept role-taking as a natural part of group discussion, and who are willing to undergo the strain of adapting talk and action to the needs of situation and others. In essence, Standard Agenda relies on the ability of group members to *exchange persuasions* toward reaching consensus. As a rhetorical process, Standard Agenda works best when the group members are flexible in their choice of behavior.

4. *The group leader must be willing to lead and capable of exhibiting leadership behavior and skills.* Successful use of Standard Agenda requires the presence of an effective leader. As we will see, leadership skills can be learned by virtually anyone. An effective leader realizes the need to carefully monitor one's own behavior and that of others in the discussion situation. Someone is needed to call the meeting to order, to explain the items on the agenda, to set forth the freedoms and constraints on talk, and to specify an outcome for the meeting. The leader is also responsible for encouraging interaction, making summaries, asking for decisions leading to consensus, and preventing the interaction from becoming purposeless or chaotic.

These four principles underlie the use of Standard Agenda by small groups in organizations. Though many authors believe Standard Agenda is one of the best techniques of group communication, it can be disadvantageous to implement the procedure with individuals who do not understand why and how it should operate. For this reason you must be careful to explain the operation of Standard Agenda, and its basic assumptions, *prior* to using it. This task is normally carried out by the group leader, or by the person responsible for forming the group.

Now that we have examined the basis for using Standard Agenda, let us consider each step in the procedure. In later chapters we will provide a more extensive examination of the issues and outcomes of each step in the process, but at this point we are interested only in *previewing* the components of Standard Agenda.

1. *Understanding the charge:*   Before a group can discuss anything, it must know (a) what the goal of the interaction is, (b) who formed the group and why, (c) what resources are available for the group to use during the process, including financial, material, and human support, and (d) when the group must make its final report, in what form, and to whom. These four issues should be resolved before any further exploration of the problem ensues.

Phases of Standard Agenda

2. *Phrasing the question:*   Before a group can discuss the problem, they must achieve consensus on what the problem is. For this reason, the second step in Standard Agenda asks the group to phrase the question to guide future discussions. The phrasing of the question should (a) allow maximum utilization of the resources available to the group, (b) be directly related to the kind of outcome specified in the charge, and (c) prepare the group to enter the next step of the process with a clear idea about what should be accomplished. These three issues must be resolved before the group can progress to the third step in the process.

3. *Fact-finding:*   The goal of this step is to collect as much factual information as possible about the nature of the problem, and to inform each group member about these available facts. Interactions will focus on (a) presentations of the facts, (b) critical examination of the quality and utility of the facts, (c) effects of the facts gathered on the original question expressed by the group, or the ability to carry out the original task given to them, and (d) whether or not enough quality information has been gathered to warrant moving to the next step of the process. These four issues should be discussed *in order* before moving to the fourth step.

4. *Establishing Criteria:*   This step is absolutely essential for the ultimate completion of the task! The goal of this step is to produce a set of carefully worded statements to guide the group in the selection of the final solution. These are called "statements of criteria" and are designed to keep the group from using non-objective measures to arrive at a solution. Interactions should focus on (a) the nature of an ideal solution, (b) the elements in the ideal solution which could allow the group to find a reasonable, but less-than-ideal solution, (c) the standards to be used for constructing a final solution, and (d) any limitations on the group, including financial, material, legal, moral, logistical, suasory, or human, which may prevent a solution from being implemented. These four issues should be discussed *in order,* and resolved, before moving on to the fifth step of the process.

5. *Generating alternative solutions:*   The goal of this step of Standard Agenda is to present to the group for their examination as many alternative solutions to the original problem as possible. To accomplish this task, the interaction should (a) use the "brainstorming" technique to discover real and imagined alternatives, and (b) record the alternatives for later use. This step of the process is often believed to be the most creative because the interaction is only limited by the imaginations of the participants. Care must be taken, however, to agree that the "brainstorming" session is over before moving on to the sixth step.

6. *Testing the alternative solutions against the criteria:*   The goal of this step is to find, if possible, the best solution to the original problem. If this goal cannot be reached, the group must be able to discover, workable elements, using two or more of the proposed, but unacceptable solutions to guide the construction of a feasible final solution. To accomplish the task, the group's interaction must (a) identify and separate each of the alternatives proposed, (b) consider the merits and limitations of each alternative by comparing it to the criteria, (c) rate each alternative based on its ability to meet the criteria, and (d) recommend how the final solution should be constructed. These four issues should be resolved *in order* before moving on to the seventh step of the process.

7. *Constructing the final solution and preparing the final report:*   The goal of the final step of the Standard Agenda is to make a case for a final solution to be presented to the proper authority. To accomplish this, the interaction should (a) review all of the steps in the process of decision-making, (b) scrutinize the group's determination of a final solution *or* carefully construct a final solution still capable of overcoming the problem and meeting the criteria, (c) make assignments about the preparation of the final report, and (d) assemble the final report and rehearse the final presentation. These four issues should be discussed *in order*.

Advantages of Using Standard Agenda

One major advantage of using Standard Agenda is that with proper instruction every group member knows exactly what will happen in every group meeting, and hence can prepare for interaction. Because people working in groups often complain that nothing is accomplished because no one knows what to do, Standard Agenda provides an excellent method for overcoming "Grouphate" as well as "Groupthink."

A second advantage of using Standard Agenda is that group members can know what they are supposed to accomplish, what means are available to achieve their purpose, and how they will know when they have completed their task. Because group members often experience anxiety over the goal of interactions and knowing when they have completed the task, Standard Agenda provides a resolution of these dilemmas, thus reducing anxiety and increasing productivity.

A third advantage of using Standard Agenda is that it is perhaps the most systematic procedure capable of ensuring *quality* decisions and solutions to problems. There are goals and outcomes for each step of the process. Moreover, as we shall see later, there are specific duties and responsibilities for group members and leaders at each of the steps. Because organizations encourage systematic operation, Standard Agenda is amenable to the logic of organizational behavior.

Standard Agenda is not perfect. Some critics, such as Brilhart (1978), believe that such systematic procedures for group interactions may stifle creativity, and limit the kinds of discussion that can naturally occur in group settings. I respond to such criticism by arguing that creativity has never been carefully defined, that too often groups use the concept of creativity to account for non-productive outcomes. Second, talk always occurs naturally. All talk is purposeful, either in the intent of the speaker to gain a desired response or in the interpretation which the listener ascribes to a speaker's message (Goodall, 1983). To the extent that we can encourage group members to behave purposefully, we can limit some of the problems that befall small group interactions.

Criticisms of Standard Agenda

Other critics have argued that the use of *any* systematic procedure can be shown to produce better outcomes than using no procedure (Hirokawa, 1988), but that Standard Agenda is only one systematic procedure (Hirokawa, 1980). I agree in principle with this argument: orderly procedures are necessary if the group is to achieve its purpose. I believe Standard Agenda can be used by most groups to achieve their purpose. I believe Standard Agenda can be used by most groups because it consists of a learnable, teachable, systematic set of procedures proven effective over a period of time. There may be better procedures, but as yet none has proved more effective than Standard Agenda.

Now we have examined how Standard Agenda works. Let us consider a second formal procedure which makes use of written communication among group members *prior* to any verbal interaction.

The Delphi Technique

First introduced by some researchers for the Rand Corporation to generate opinions about technological forecasts, this method of group interaction can be considered as the thinking person's response to unproductive group meetings. Researchers have long recognized that valuable time is often wasted in small groups by either (1) not having time to think about the issues being discussed, or (2) being diverted by arguments which appear to uncover fundamental disagreements among group members when in fact group members do not disagree (Thomas, 1979).

The Delphi Technique permits group members to formally consider the merits and limitations of an idea proposed for group discussion *privately*. Simply put, Delphi requires a group leader to suggest, *in writing,* an idea or problem, and to circulate the written document among group members for commentary. In the privacy of a group member's own office or study, the idea or problem can be thought out, and a written response can be made to it. The original document, with each group member's suggestions or criticisms, is passed on from person to person until most of the difficulties are resolved. In this way the group achieves *consensus* on issues related to the idea or problem *before* a formal meeting is scheduled for discussion of it.

> **Wade H., 43** We use the Delphi Technique in our research and development operation. Let's say I get an idea for a research project. I write down what I hope will be accomplished by working on the project, and the resources both needed and available to us. I will then send the report to one of my project members, who has three or four days to consider it. He or she then writes down any objections to the idea, or any ideas about problems we may encounter. Then that person sends the document to the next person, who adds his or her own material to it. And so on. We usually circulate the document three or four times among the members of the project, and by the time I schedule a meeting to discuss it, we know where everyone stands. Beyond that advantage, we also don't have to waste time in the meeting figuring out what we want to accomplish. And let me say this, by getting people to write down what they think, we force them to really think it through.

Delphi is *not* a group discussion technique. The members of the group do not meet and exchange ideas until the Delphi process is completed. For this reason I believe the most productive use of Delphi can be made as a logical adjunct to Standard Agenda. Group members can circulate the written document to establish primary consensus areas, then implement Standard Agenda to govern the operation of the meeting when open discussions are held.

Advantages of Delphi Technique

Delphi has advantages. First, in organizations characterized by time constraint for group meetings, this procedure can be useful because it limits the actual time people have to meet as a group. Second, because most organizations require the gathering of a mass of information before any decisions can be made, Delphi encourages the individual group members to collect data on their own and analyze it, while thinking through the proposal. This advantage may save the organization both time and money. Third, Delphi allows the group members to discuss only those issues they have not reached consensus on during the private, written stages. This limits the nature of group interactions, and may help groups make decisions or solve problems more expeditiously.

Disadvantages of Delphi Technique

Disadvantages of using Delphi include:

1. The emphasis on individual, rather than group, effort.
2. The assumption that all group members possess the necessary writing skills to facilitate the effective use of the technique.
3. The potential for the most persuasive writer to dominate the group's decision-making.

4. The potential for reaching a false consensus because of the failure of the group members to adequately assess how other members have thought through the idea or problem.

Later chapters will show you how Delphi can be used effectively in conjunction with Standard Agenda. I believe group interaction is necessary to the decision-making and problem-solving processes associated with formal group work; while Delphi can be useful it may not by itself be a good method for conducting group activities.

Now that we have considered two methods of working in groups, we need to look at what is often referred to as the "hidden agenda."

Hidden agenda is defined as "an objective of an individual member (or a subgroup of members) which is different from the avowed group purpose" (Brilhart, 1978, p. 23). One way to see how a hidden agenda operates is to consider the following statement made by a group member who experienced it:

The Hidden Agenda

Laura L., 23   At first everyone liked Bill. He seemed to always be prepared for group meetings, and he was a very articulate person. We all thought he would be a good contribution to our group. Well. Very soon we got to know what he was really after: a promotion. He was sly, and I must admit we were all taken in by his glib ways. He was very careful about always making sure he was assigned the task of recording what went on during our meetings. When you read his reports, it seemed like *he* was the only person in the group who was accomplishing anything. He knew the record would be passed on to our divisional head, and he hoped it would put him in a favorable light. It did. He was promoted, but I can tell you that we all made a concerted effort to warn his new group members about his ways. No one likes to have to put up with someone who is only working in the group for personal gain. I mean, that's not what a group is for, right?

Hidden agendas have nothing to do with procedures used to accomplish the group task. Instead, as Laura's testimony points out, a hidden agenda is what a single group member (or subgroup of members, as in a clique) wants to have happen for him or her. There are six basic reasons behind a hidden agenda.

1. *Personal advancement:*   Some individuals use a group to further their own cause on the job. Being an active participant draws attention to the quality of one's own work, instead of the quality of the group effort.
2. *A need for affection:*   Some people use group experiences to make friends or to explore the possibilities for relationships. By constantly asking for affiliation responses, by directing attention toward oneself and away from the group's task, a personal need for affection can seriously undermine a group's operation.

Reasons for Hidden Agendas

3. *A desire to limit the effectiveness or productivity of the group.* As I have noted earlier, some people detest working in groups. This hatred of group work can lead some individuals to find devious ways of undermining the group's operation. By actively promoting disruptive conflict, by withholding needed information from other group members, and by seeking to gain support for the ineffectiveness of the group, some people can attempt to dissolve a group.

4. *A desire to use the group setting for personal, social or professional therapy:* Nearly everyone experiences problems in organizations which can be brought to the attention of others. Unfortunately, some people tend to use a group decision-making or problem-solving session as the place to explore personal *angst,* social injustice, or professional limitations. It may be difficult for groups to resist an attempt by an individual member to obtain help or advice, but unless the group can overcome this difficulty, their productivity may be seriously diminished.

5. *A need to demonstrate competence:* There are people who become group members to show everyone in the group how astonishingly competent they really are. Unfortunately, their displays of competence can result in wasted time for the group, or can lead to discord among group members who feel equally competent.

6. *A need to exercise power:* Power is usually defined as the ability of an individual to direct the actions of other individuals while resisting the attempts of other individuals to make similar requests. Power is a necessary part of any group, and every group member should have some basis for exerting influence over the group's actions. However, excessive demands for power by an individual or subgroup can harm the group and cause feelings of helplessness among other group members. The productive group harnesses its power and directs it to the accomplishment of its task. The unproductive group abuses power, and the group meeting suffers.

The above list is not exhaustive. There are as many reasons for hidden agendas as there are individual goals which regard the group as a means to an end. I am not saying you should avoid having personal goals in the group setting; I am advocating that your goals be associated with the successful completion of the group task.

How would you know a hidden agenda if you saw one? In the following chapters we will explore the processes of communication, participation, and leadership in small groups. Through analyses of behavior, an assessment of motive or cause for the behavior, group members can discover hidden agendas and learn to deal with them in productive ways.

Group Conflict and Negotiation

Conflict is a natural part of small group work. If not properly managed, conflict may lead to negative outcomes and poor group performance. If properly managed, conflict may lead to enhanced group communication, deeper exploration of issues and agendas, and improved overall performance. Therefore, understanding conflict and learning to manage it within the group are essential skills.

What is a "conflict?" Perhaps the following testimony on the subject can provide some insight:

> **Carolyn A., 32**   When we walked into the conference room there was tension. Eddie and Jeff weren't getting along, in part due to Eddie's macho displays and verbal agility and in part due to Jeff's feelings of failure because of his problems getting continuing support for his project. Then there was Angela, who viewed every question raised as a threat to her company loyalty or personal initiative. And myself, of course—because I was part of the problem—I thought Jeff's project was badly managed and I thought Angela was a pain. So there we were, a small group of people who the company asked to work together on a project and who couldn't do our best because we were in conflict with each other.

As you can see from Carolyn's description, there are many sources of group conflict: personality differences, differences in points of view, sources of conflict external to the group that find their way into group discussions, feelings of past injustices or inequities, fear of what the future might bring (or not bring). Whatever the source of the conflict may be, its presence in a group discussion is something that is *felt,* thus adding an emotional dimension to group work that often interferes with orderly procedures, planned agendas, and rational decision-making.

Throughout this book I discuss the presence of conflict and suggest certain remedies for conflict situations. It is important to realize from the outset, however, that conflict is a normal part of any small group and that not all sources of conflict can—or even should—be resolved. Some authorities believe that many important sources of conflict can be reduced or managed, but seldom actually "resolved." In other words, conflict must be dealt with but can rarely be erased. In this introductory section, then, I will concentrate not on the various types of conflict or suggested management strategies. Instead, I will discuss what researchers can tell us about the idea of negotiation and bargaining in conflict situations.

The Idea of Negotiation and Bargaining

To reduce the negative effects of conflict requires a style of communication known as negotiation and bargaining (Gouran, 1982). The aim of this style of communicating is to (1) acknowledge differences of opinion, (2) shape a definition of the situation that focuses on mutual goals rather than individual desires or demands, and (3) work toward the accomplishment of those goals by presenting arguments and narratives that reveal reasons for, and potential solutions to, the conflict situation.

According to Putnam and Geist, "in negotiation the two parties have opposite goals (1985, p. 230)." This fact must be acknowledged when the conflict arises, and care must be put into choosing appropriate words to define those opposite goals and the reasons for them. Consider the following statement, taken from a participant in a group experiencing conflict:

> **Tim B., 25**   We were discussing what should be done to ensure funding for the group. Ellen suggested reworking the proposal, but Dave disagreed. We were at a standstill, because in our group there had been very little open disagreement. No one knew what to do. So Ellen finally sighed and just asked for clarification. Dave thought about it for a minute and then said he thought that if we changed the proposal now it would look like we were groveling. Ellen said that we were, in fact, groveling. In retrospect it was a poor word choice. "Groveling" is not something anyone wants to do, ever. Had Dave said anything else we might have gotten through that period. But he didn't, and the result was that we fought about it, changed the proposal at the last minute, and lost the contract. Did that one word make that much difference? I think so, I really do.

What happened in the above scenario is, unfortunately, fairly typical in American organizations. It is not simply that inappropriate language causes poor group performance, for everyone probably knows of situations in which all that could have gone wrong went wrong and the group still performed well enough to accomplish its purpose. Instead the problem is that when confronted with disagreement, Tim's group *did not alter its style of communicating.* When disagreement is present, it is important for the group to acknowledge it and enter into negotiations aimed at mutual understanding and bargaining aimed at mutual gain. To do this requires an appreciation of the functions of argument and narrative in bargaining and negotiation.

Argument   Argumentation is a "communication process aimed at presenting statements and providing reasons why the audience should believe them" (Crable, 1983, p. 161). In negotiation and bargaining within a group, argumentation creates an understanding of the opposing points of view. Each participant is responsible for articulating what she or he wants the group to believe and then give reasons why they should believe it.

> **John W., 27**   I told the group that we should support the new "quality first" program because it was clear that the company had already endorsed it. Gary disagreed, and said he thought we ought to use this opportunity to send a message to corporate about how silly an idea this was to begin with. He said that by adopting this program it would seem to our customers that we had

neglected quality before we put this program into effect. And he resented this deeply. "Gimmicks," he said, "are no substitute for product." I told him I thought he was right, but that this was not the forum for that particular debate. I asked him what harm could be done by adopting this program now and requesting another meeting with corporate about the whole idea later. Oddly enough, when I said that outloud it occurred to me how silly *my* idea was, how I actually agreed with him. About then we all laughed, and that was the end of it.

In this example, you can see how the articulation of reasons for a position had a dramatic effect. Put simply, most people do not know why they feel the way they do until they have to put what they are feeling into words. This is why it is vital for groups to acknowledge conflict, define the situation, and then work out—through bargaining and negotiation—some resolution or at least reduction of it.

Humans are not only defined by our ability to reason and to argue, but also by our incredible ability to make and to tell stories about our experiences. Since the time of the ancient philosophers such as Plato and Aristotle, it has been understood that any audience can be moved both by appeals to reason and by examples, illustrations, analogies, or stories. Therefore in your study of small group communication, an important ingredient will be your understanding of, and skill in, developing narratives.

Narrative

A narrative is any account of an experience—real, imagined, or hypothetical—in which events and outcomes are vividly rendered. In other words, a narrative is a story, and to use a narrative in a group is to engage in storytelling with a purpose. Consider Marie's experience:

> **Marie Y., 28** Clearly there was some major resistance to the idea that we change our advertising campaign. In this business continuity is important, and your audience expects reinforcement. But Judith was adamant, so we listened to her. What she did then is something I will never forget. She told us a story about how her father convinced her to save money. It was a simple story, but it had definite and immediately recognizable resonances with our group's situation. That story won all of us over to her side. You know, if she would have done the usual thing with an overhead projector, charts, graphs, or numbers, I don't think we would have changed the campaign. But her story did it.

Stories are effective communicative tools in groups because they are emblems of human experiences that can be shared, and because they are (when most effective) entertaining as well as informative. They provide another way of conceptualizing a situation, another mode of understanding. And, as everyone knows, we tend to listen to people who tell good stories, according them attention and respect.

As you acquire the skills of leading and participating in a group, pay attention to the functions of narrative and argument in bargaining and negotiation patterns within your work group(s). Chances are good that you will come to see narrative and argument as two choices, two methods, of accomplishing communicative goals within the style of talk appropriate to reducing or resolving conflict.

Summary

This chapter examined the processes and functions of small groups in American organizations. I described an ideal small group as represented in research literature and then demonstrated how this description fails to account for important processes and functions performed by small groups within organizations.

First, I explored organizational culture and history in small groups, defining organizational culture as the sum total of shared meanings which have evolved within particular organizations. I listed five primary areas of organizational behavior affected by the development of an organizational culture: (1) the evolution of rituals, (2) the establishment of authority and uses of power, (3) the use of small groups, (4) the use of standard operating procedures within small groups, and (5) the appraisal/review process. We concluded this section with a description of how you can gain productive information about an organization's culture.

Second, I explored the nature of group membership. I explained that assignments are generally made to formal small groups, whereas membership is voluntary in informal groups. I discussed the necessity of appropriate choices for group selection, recommending that these choices be predicated on (1) assessments of the experience, expertise, and authority represented by the group, and (2) assessment of the probability that group members will communicate effectively among one another.

Third, I discussed the nature of individual and group goals, explaining the interdependence of goals between an individual and her or his small group, together with the interdependence of goals among group members. I identified three possible ways in which goals are established for small groups: (1) goals established outside the group and presented to the group as a "charge"; (2) goals established within the group as a response to a particular need or urgency; and (3) goals established outside the group and presented as a "charge," but later modified by the group as new information becomes available. I recommended that goals be established in clear and precise language, and that groups be trained to distinguish between "doable" and "desirable" goals.

Fourth, I discussed the idea of agendas and procedures within small groups. I explained the steps in Standard Agenda, also describing how Delphi Technique can be incorporated into Standard Agenda. I detailed the advantages and disadvantages of each method, and proposed a procedure for combining the strengths of each in a formal group plan. I then explored the notion of "hidden agendas," or personal, social, and professional objectives which may threaten the accomplishment of the group's goal. I listed six possible reasons for hidden agendas, and recommended analysis of motives for behavior to deal productively with hidden agendas when they occur in small groups.

Finally, I discussed the idea of group conflict and negotiation. I dealt with the presence of conflict as a natural aspect of group work, and explained how argument and narrative function as ways to improve understanding and enhance group outcomes.

References

Bales, R. F., and E. F. Borgatta. "Size of a Group as a Factor in the Interaction Profile." In *Small Groups: Studies in Social Interaction,* edited by A. P. Hare, E. F. Borgatta, and R. F. Bales, 396–413. New York: Knopf, 1955.

Benson, J. K. "Innovation and Crisis in Organizational Analysis." *The Sociological Quarterly* 18 (1977): 3–16.

Beyer, J. M., and H. M. Trice. "How an Organizations's Rites Reveal Its Culture." *Organizational Dynamics* (1987): 4–25.

Brilhart, J. K. *Effective Group Discussion,* 3d ed. Dubuque, Ia.: William C. Brown Company Publishers, 1978.

Carbaugh, D. "Cultural Terms and Tensions in the Speech at a Television Station." *Western Journal of Speech Communication* 52 (1988): 216–337.

Chaney, G. "On the Various and Changing Meanings of Organizational Membership." *Communication Monographs* 50 (1983): 342–62.

Crable, R. E., "Evidence, Warrants, and Reservations in Public Speaking." *Principles of Human Communication,* 2d ed., edited by Barry Brummett and Linda L. Putnam. Dubuque, Ia.: Kendall/Hunt, 1983.

Dandridge, T., I. Mitroff, and W. Joyce. "Organizational Symbolism: A Topic to Expand Organizational Analysis." *Academy of Management Review* 5 (1980).

Davis, J. H. *Group Performance.* Reading: Addison-Wesley, 1969.

Deetz, S. A. "Critical Interpretive Research in Organization Communication." *Western Journal of Speech Communication* 46 (1982): 131–49.

Dewey, J. *How We Think.* Boston: Heath, 1910.

Etzioni, A. *Modern Organizations.* Englewood Cliffs: Prentice-Hall, 1964.

Geertz, C. "Deep Play: Notes on the Balanese Cockfight." *Daedalus* 101 (1972).

Goodall, Jr., H. L. *Human Communication: Creating Reality.* Dubuque, Ia.: William C. Brown Company Publishers, 1983.

Goodall, Jr., H. L. *Casing a Promised Land.* Carbondale, Ill: Southern Illinois University Press, 1989.

Gouran, D. S. *Decision-Making in Groups.* Glenview, Ill.: Scott, Foresman, and Company, 1982.

Hawes, L. C. "Social Collectives as Communication: Perspectives on Organizational Behavior." *Quarterly Journal of Speech* 60 (1974): 497–502.

Hawes, L. C. "Viewing Organizations as Cultures." Paper presented to the Purdue University Lecture Series, 1980.

Hayakawa, S. I. *Language in Thought and Action,* 4th ed. New York: Harcourt, Brace, Jovanovich, 1978.

Hirokawa, R. "A Comparative Analysis of Communication Patterns Within Effective and Ineffective Decision-Making Groups." *Communication Monographs* 47 (1980): 312–21.

Hirokawa, R. "Group Communication and Decision Performance." *Human Communication Research* 14 (1988): 487–515.

Janis, I. *Victims of Groupthink.* Boston: Houghton Mifflin Co., 1972.

Mager, R. F. *Goal Analysis.* San Francisco: Fearon Publishers, 1972.

McBurney, J. H., and K. G. Hance. *Discussion in Human Affairs*. New York: Harper Brothers, 1950.

Martin, J., and C. Siehl. "Organizational Culture and Counterculture: An Uneasy Symbiosis." *Organizational Dynamics* (1983).

Mitroff, I. I., and R. H. Kilmann. "Stories Managers Tell: A New Tool for Organizational Problem Solving." *Management Review* 64 (1975): 19–20.

Morgan, G. *Images of Organization*. Beverly Hills, Ca: Sage, 1986.

Pacanowsky, M. E., and N. O'Donnell-Trujillo. "Organizational Communication as Cultural Performance." *Communication Monographs* 50 (1983): 126–47.

Pacanowsky, M. E., and N. O'Donnell-Trujillo. "Communication and Organizational Cultures." *Western Journal of Speech Communication* 46 (1982): 115–30.

Pacanowsky, M. E. "Communication in the Empowering Organization." In *Communication Yearbook* 11, edited by J. Anderson. Beverly Hills, Ca: Sage, 1987.

Phillips, G. M., and E. Erickson. *Interpersonal Dynamics in the Small Group*. New York: Random House, 1970.

Phillips, G. M., D. J. Pedersen, and J. T. Wood. *Group Discussion: A Practical Guide to Participation and Leadership*. Boston: Houghton Mifflin, 1979.

Putnam, L. L., and P. Geist. "Argument in Bargaining: An Analysis of the Reasoning Process." *Southern Speech Communication Journal*, 50 (Spring 1985): 225–245.

Roy, D. F. "Banana Time: Job Satisfaction and Informal Interaction." *Human Organization* 18 (1960): 158–68.

Scott, W. G., and D. K. Hart. *Organizational America*. Boston: Houghton Mifflin Co., 1979.

Sherif, M., and C. Sherif. *An Outline of Social Psychology*. New York: Harper and Row, 1956.

Shorris, E., *Scenes from Corporate Life*. Baltimore, Md: Penguin, 1983.

Silverman, D. *The Theory of Organizations*. New York: Basic Books, 1971.

Thomas, L. "On Committees." In *The Medusa and the Snail*, New York: Viking, 1979, 115–20.

Thompsen, J., and W. J. McEwen. "Organizational Goals and Environment: Goal Setting as an Interaction Process." *American Sociological Review* 23 (1958): 23–31.

Whyte, W. H. *The Organization Man*. New York: Simon and Schuster, 1956.

Yankelovich, D. *The New Rules: Searching for Self-Fulfillment in a World Turned Upside Down*. New York: Random House, 1981.

Exercises

The following exercises are intended to help you understand the importance of the material covered in this chapter. The first two exercises require your group to *define* itself, and to establish common *goals* for itself. Please do these two exercises *in order*.

1. Assemble your group. You have twenty minutes (20) to decide on a *definition of your small group*. Your group must achieve consensus as to the definition, and be willing to use it as a common group referent for the remainder of the term.

2. Assemble your group. Use the class period to determine what are the *goals* of your small group. Be precise. You may want to divide the list into two parts: task goals and interpersonal goals. You may want to

combine the two under the heading "task interaction goals." Have no fewer than three (3) and no more than ten (10) goals when you finish. Compare your group's goals to the goals of other small groups in your class. What do these goals tell you about the nature of your small group?

The third exercise instructs your group to develop a plan for achieving the goals you specified in exercise #2. The following questions should provide starting points for your discussion.

3. **Group Planning Exercise.**
   —What are your goals?
   —Must some goals necessarily be reached before other goals can be attained?
   —Can you describe your goals in the behaviors used to recognize them?
   —What is a rough timetable for reaching these goals?
   —What additional information do you need from your instructor, or from your class, before you can complete this assignment?

This exercise should take at least one full class period (50–75 minutes) for preliminary discussions and at least one additional class period to report on additional information collected and to make a final decision. Use the results of this exercise to guide your group's performance evaluation for the remainder of the term. You may revise your goals and methods of attaining them as you progress through the term, but only as a last resort, and never because you believe you don't know how to reach them. Consult your instructor.

The fourth exercise asks your group to exchange biographical information. In most organizational settings this task is accomplished informally through conversation, but because you are a student in a college class, we have to formalize it a bit.

4. **Group History Exercise.**
   Assemble your group. Ask each group member to present a brief (2–3 minute) biographical sketch to the other group members. Each group member should take notes. When every member has spoken, ask each member to present a brief (2–3 minute) talk about past group experiences, using the following outline:
   —Name of the group or organization
   —Membership assigned or voluntary
   —Role(s) played and for what reason
   —Leadership experience and degree of ease experienced as a leader
   —Best remembrances of the group experiences
   —Worst remembrances of the group experiences
   —Expectations for this group experience
   All group members should also take notes about this information.
   Now make a journal entry using the data obtained from this exercise. List each group member's name, and write a brief entry summarizing their experiences in groups and what *you* expect from them this term.

The fifth exercise is designed to demonstrate how you make decisions about persons whom you might have to work with. You will find it a challenging test of your group's ability to achieve consensus on an issue based on subjective interpretations rather than hard data. In many organizations this kind of decision-making is considered one of the most difficult because personalities are involved, and often "hidden agendas" take precedence over practicality.

5. **Group Selection Exercise.**

Assemble your group. Ask each group member to read over the following list of fictional individuals who have made an application for membership in your small group. Use what you have learned about Standard Agenda to arrive at a decision based on the following charge: "Whom should we choose to become a member of our small group for the remainder of the term?"

Applicants:

Russell B., 18. Freshman in college, no declared major, but interested in the general area of business administration. Active in high school leadership club, debate team, and member of the band. Works part-time at the Baptist Student Union, and is a regular church-goer. Height: 5'10"; Weight: 155 lbs. When asked to make a personal statement about career goals, he responded: "I am dedicated to a life in Christ. After I receive my college degree, I want to become more active in the Church, possibly going into ministry."

Angela M., 19. Sophomore in college, majoring in biochemistry, minoring in statistics. Active in campus Young Republicans, and a sorority. Works part-time in the biochemistry lab. No church affiliations. Height: 5'5"; Weight: 125 lbs. When asked to make a personal statement about career goals, she responded: "I want to become a scientist, perhaps with the space program. I spend a lot of time in the lab, even when I'm not working. I have a 3.8 (on a 4.0 scale) average, and intend to keep it. After college, I want to receive a doctorate in biochemistry. I have no plans for marriage, although I have been dating the same guy since high school."

Keith K., 21. Senior in college, majoring in management, minoring in physical education. Member of the football and tennis teams. Active in Future Business Leaders of America. Height: 6'6"; Weight: 245 lbs. When asked to make a personal statement about career goals, he responded: "I am a jock at heart. I spend my spare time in the gym working out. I haven't done real well in college, but I will receive my degree. I am hoping for a try-out with the Jets. If that doesn't come through, I will probably go into sales because my father made a lot of money selling. Basically I like having a good time—drink a few beers, be around good-looking women, don't think about things too much."

Roxanne D., 20.   Junior in college, majoring in broadcast journalism, minoring in speech communication. New editor, campus newspaper, part-time disc jockey at the campus FM station. No other campus affiliations. Attends Presbyterian Church occasionally. Height: 5'4"; Weight: 115 lbs. When asked to make a personal statement about career goals, she responded: "I know exactly what I want. I am going to be a superstar television journalist and make a ton of money. I know I'm beautiful, talented, and smart—a pretty unbeatable combination, don't you agree?"

Thomas B., 20.   Sophomore in college majoring in secondary education. President, Black Student Union. Active in the Campus Crusade for Christ. Member, campus fraternity. Married, no children. Height: 6'0"; Weight: 185 lbs. When asked to make a personal statement about career goals, he responded: "I am a very responsible individual. I plan each day what I want to accomplish, and then I accomplish it. My family and my relationship with my friends is very important to me. I would like to become a high school history teacher, and educate people about the importance of Blacks in American society."

Serena R., 29.   Freshman in college, no declared major. Reports being interested in accounting, but also has strong desire to pursue a lifelong interest in art. Recently divorced, two children living with her at home. Active in the University Women's Club for many years because her ex-husband was a faculty member. Member of the Methodist Church. Height: 5'7"; Weight: 160 lbs. When asked to make a personal statement about her career goals, she responded: "Oh gosh, I don't know. I'm back in school to help me straighten out my life. I have always felt a little out of place because I didn't go to college. My children take up a lot of my time, as you can imagine. I like every course I've taken so far, because there is so much to learn these days. I know I need a skill to get a good job, but I really would like to be a sculptor. I met a person in the Art Department on campus who I think can help me straighten things out. Overall I guess I just want to be happy for a change."

Remember: the person you choose will affect how your group operates. You need to consider their goals in light of your own. After completing this assignment, discuss why you made the choice you did and what your interactions revealed about personal biases and perceptions of other people.

3

What You Should Know
about Communication
in the Small Group

Introduction

Communication may be defined as any response to a message (Johnstone, 1966). The key word in our definition is *response*. Communication does not "just happen," it is not "spontaneous." Communication occurs in situations marked by an urgency or a need to modify some element of the situation with talk (Bitzer, 1968). Communication is how we deal with situations, rather than simply allowing situations to act on us. Because of the responsive nature of communication, both the messages emitted from our mouths and the messages conveyed by our bodies are forms of communication. Literally *any* response—from a yawn to a direct statement, from a raising of the eyebrow to a pointing of the finger—is communicative.

Communication is learned. Like any skill the ability to communicate effectively is based on systematic application of principles and careful evaluation of outcomes. No one is born with speaking, reading, writing, listening, or figuring skills. These aptitudes are developed over a period of time, as we learn how to shape responses to our situations and others. A child makes squeaks, shouts, moans, and cries, and thus learns to associate them with attentive responses given by parents. As the child grows older and has more experience with the different kinds of responses to its communication, it learns to choose among them to receive just the right or desired response (Fry, 1977). To the extent that a child receives the desired responses, and learns how to adapt communication to situations and others to receive those responses, it grows to adulthood learning how to become an effective communicator.

You can acquire skill in becoming a more effective participant in small groups by learning how to make better choices about your communication. What I am asking you to do is to make *conscious* choices about verbal and nonverbal messages. For most people communication may be a response to a situation, but it is usually an unconscious response. We do not think about communication very much, except when it goes wrong. We seldom pause to consider whether a particular statement or question is the best one, or the right one, to meet the needs of others, or to reach the goals we have in this situation. To learn *how* to improve communication we must strive to make conscious these unconscious thought processes, emphasizing our delivery of words and actions in given cases. Think systematically about communication, make active choices about *what* you want to say, how to *arrange* and *support* your thoughts, and how to *evaluate* the effectiveness of what you said in reaching your goal. Since the time of Aristotle, such choices and their results have been the focus of training effective communicators.

Communication in small groups is complicated by the presence of other individuals, each with unique goals for words, each with characteristic ways of articulating and evaluating communication. Very often verbal or other expressions in a small group include many different messages, designed to attain various goals, and are sent and received simultaneously. If any one group member attempts to keep track of all forms of communication, *information overload* may result. We know when human beings receive too much information to process effectively they tend to stop processing any information at all. This is one reason for advocating restraint and controlled communication. Rather than saying whatever pops into your mind while in a small group, it is wiser and more considerate to choose what you will say and when you will say it, while being mindful of the response you are seeking.

This chapter addresses communication in the small group. First, we will examine communication as participation in small groups. Second, we will discuss communication and information used to operate an organization. Third, we will provide instruction in effective listening: what we spend most of our time doing while working in small groups. Fourth, we will explore the question of how to formulate responses to others and to certain situations. We will be concerned with the differences between asking questions or making statements, and how to know which form to choose. Fifth, we will discuss problems associated with communication in the small group and suggest some possible solutions. Sixth, we will examine the relationships between communication and evaluations of participation in small groups. Following the summary and references you will find some exercises to apply what you will learn in this chapter.

Communication and Information

One consistent problem facing people who work in organizations is the presence or absence of information needed to accomplish tasks. If the information is available, it may not be readily accessible; if it is not available, then the task is delayed until the necessary information can be found. Organizational researchers intuitively believed that there was an important relationship among information adequacy, communication, and job satisfaction (Goldhaber, *et al,* 1978; Muchinsky, 1977), but it was not until recently that they understood how important information is to satisfaction with relationships in small groups.

Consider the testimony of Al:

Al A., 29 Sure information is important to our group. We can't do anything productive without it. When we can't get what we want we argue needlessly about not having it and who's responsible. When we do have it, we work better as a group. You see, without information there is very little point to communicating, and there is every opportunity to talk about how dissatisfied you are with the company because they never give you the information you need. So unless you have good information, your communication will suffer, and you will become less satisfied with your job.

Al's statement is also confirmed by research literature. For example, in a study of eighteen organizations, Spiker and Daniels (1981) discovered that the ability of employees to gain access to information they needed to complete tasks was positively correlated to their expressed satisfaction with the quality of their working relations with others. In other words, if there is adequate access to information, group members will probably be more satisfied working with each other on the task.

The access we have to information necessary to complete our work is also related to how well we participate in groups, and what our level of participation means to us. In the same study, Spiker and Daniels confirmed Weick's (1979) hypothesis which suggested that information adequacy was more important to organizational workers than participation. This does *not* mean participation is less important to the group than information is; it means that a group needs to use information effectively to encourage participation among members.

Information may exist somewhere in the organization, but it performs no useful function until someone communicates it. One possible extension of the conclusion is that the person who has access to information and can effectively articulate it to the group is highly valued. Consider Tonya's case:

> **Tonya E., 24** I learned very quickly how to become useful and valuable to my group. I did my homework and found out where all the information relating to our task was housed in the computer and how to gain access to it. Because I was always able to get a quick printout when we needed it, the other people in the group came to rely on me for information.

Tonya was able to communicate information to her group. This not only increased her level of participation, but also provided her group with information which made their collective task easier. We can only conclude that Tonya's ability to gain access to information needed by her group contributed to positive working relations among her group members. It is very difficult not to appreciate someone who furnishes information which makes your job easier because of it.

Information provides the evidence necessary for a group to make decisions and solve problems. Access to information is an important element in any formal group, but communicating the information is how the data is literally brought into existence for the group. While it is true that without information, participation becomes less valuable even useless in achieving results, it is equally true that unless the information is properly and precisely communicated to the group, there cannot be productive participation. Now let's examine how such participation occurs in small groups.

Communication and Participation in Small Groups

Communicating—listening, making statements, asking questions, providing summaries, leading discussions—is how you participate in small groups (Phillips, Pedersen, and Wood, 1979). Unfortunately, despite the truth of this statement, many people mistakenly believe the *more* you communicate the *better* your record of participation in the small group. Because the group is a cooperative endeavor, communication must be shared among group members. Each group member should have equable access to participation, and one or two individuals should not coerce or dominate a discussion.

Communication is often said to be synonymous with *exchange*. In a small group setting, the members exchange information, persuasions, and responsibilities for the outcomes of decision-making or problem-solving. Thus, the principle of exchange is fundamentally involved in the evaluation of participation in groups. George Caspar Homans (1958) identified three common sources of exchange between and among members of groups: *goods, services,* and *sentiments.* Phillips and Metzger (1976) applied the principle of exchange to human communicative relationships, adding a fourth element, *time.* It is necessary to understand the nature of your exchanges with others in groups because what is exchanged often defines the nature of the relationship.

Communication as Exchange

> **Quentin S., 24**   You have taught me to think about the exchanges I make with other people. Frankly, at the beginning of this course, I thought this would be another one of those useless theories you know, remember it for the test, forget it for the rest of your life. But I was wrong. I discovered that I really do have clearly defined relationships based on what I exchange with others. For example, I exchange services with Vick: I help him tune his car and in return he looks over the books for my store. That is a very important part of our friendship, and if either one of us stopped providing the service, who knows what would happen to our friendship. With John and Walter I exchange sentiments. We have known each other since high school basketball, and we get together on weekends to play a little ball and remember. Honest, I think we ought to be on those Michelob beer commercials because that is pretty much how we act. I have a good relationship with my specialty delivery man: he gives me the goods and I write him a check that won't bounce. That is the mainspring of our time together. If my check bounced, or he didn't come across with the goods on time, our feelings about each other would change. It is strange to think in the exchange model, but damn it, it does make sense!

The principle of exchange is built on the "give a little—get a little" foundation of human relationships. *Giving* contributes to our sense of self-esteem and participation in the activities around us. *Getting* is our reward for making those contributions.

We can see how the principle of exchange applies to organizational communication. At each separate level in the organizational hierarchy, information and persuasion are generated between and among people who are responsible for carrying out tasks and maintaining solid working relations with others. The good, service, sentiment produced at one level is ultimately consumed at another level as the organization directs the flow of messages and activities over a period of time. The marketing and sales division uses the information supplied by the research and development division, which, in return, receives the information supplied by sales and marketing to project future needs and market demands. These exchanges reveal the degree of interdependence between and among organizational divisions, and the small groups of people who comprise them.

Communication is the articulation of exchanges. Through statements and questions received and sent, by activities performed and acted on, communicative behaviors reveal that exchanges are being made. The goals of one person or small group usually require the cooperation of other people or groups to be attained. The "give-and-receive" of exchanges between and among people have given rise to a theory of participation in human relationships based on the ideas of fairness, justice, or the maintenance of *equity* in the ways people respond to each other.

Exchange and Equity: A Theory for Participation in Small Groups

We communicate with others to reach goals. Yet, we know if we reach goals at the *expense* of others, we should feel guilty. We realize that this is true, because if others reach goals at *our* expense we feel resentment toward them and expect them to feel guilty. The delicate balance of human relations requires us, in most cases, to establish a system for dealing justly with others. We need to know when and how to punish wrongdoers and reward the actions of people who treat us fairly. The result of this thinking is summed up in the four propositions of Equity Theory (Walster, Walster, and Bersheid, 1978).

Four Propositions of Equity Theory

1. Individuals will try to maximize their outcomes (where outcomes equal rewards minus costs).
2. (a) Groups can maximize collective reward by evolving accepted systems for equably apportioning resources among members. Thus, groups will evolve such systems of equity, and will induce members to accept and adhere to these systems. (b) Groups will generally reward members who treat others equably, and will generally punish (increase the costs for) members who treat others inequably.
3. When individuals find themselves participating in inequitable relationships, they will become distressed. The more inequitable the relationship, the more distress individuals will feel.
4. Individuals who discover they are in an inequitable relationship will attempt to eliminate their distress by restoring equity. The greater the inequity that exists, the more distress they will feel, and the harder they will try to restore equity.

The exchanges made by individuals in small groups constitute adherence to or deviation from their evolved system of equity. In the last chapter we explored the influence of history on the group. We discussed how procedures for operating are historically derived, and noted the communal evolution of rules, codes of conduct, and ways of participating in groups. What we now have are four propositions that can be used to explain (and correct) the participation of individuals in small groups. Equity Theory also points out the vital need for people entering new groups to assess the influence which historical developments have had on the established system of equity.

Participation in small groups is not (should not be) a chaotic, confused activity. People participate in groups to attain goals *and* to maintain or modify equable ways of apportioning resources among members. If you think of the equity of your small group as a common constitution, then you can understand how justice is maintained. You can also see, as in the following example, how amendments are made:

Andrea B., 33   For a few weeks I observed how the people in my group did business. Everyone was given an equal opportunity to express opinions, but more often than not the person who knew parliamentary procedure won out. I thought this was unfair. There seemed to me to be a better way of running a group meeting. Finally, after about the fifth week, I proposed that we agree not to use *Robert's Rules of Order* to conduct our meetings. Instead I suggested more could be accomplished by implementing Standard Agenda. I explained how Standard Agenda worked, and promised to provide a brief written document to each group member, showing how the steps were to be used. They were amenable to the change, as it turned out. I later discovered that most of the folks were glad to drop parliamentary procedure in favor of something simpler. They too felt somewhat cheated when the few parliamentarians in the group displayed their skill at the expense of a good idea. What did I do about the parliamentarians? I suggested they be made leaders of the group. In exchange for their cooperation in using Standard Agenda, I offered them what they really wanted anyway. It worked.

As Andrea demonstrated in the above example, it is wise to figure out what rewards are *valued* by the members of the small group. In her case it was leadership, and she was more than willing to exchange it for the use of Standard Agenda. By finding the appropriate source of exchange, persuasion can occur equitably.

The use of Equity Theory to develop a way of understanding participation in small groups requires each group member to answer the following questions:

1. What does your investigation of the history of this group tell you about their evolved system of equity?   *Questions to Assess Group Equity*
2. What are the goals (personal, social, professional) of each group member, and how does participating in this group either contribute to or detract from his or her ability to reach them?
3. What is regularly exchanged between and among group members? How do these regular exchanges contribute to your sense of what is valued by each group member?

4. How are rewards and punishments meted out in your group? How can someone "increase the costs" of someone else's participation?
5. If inequity exists in your group, what is currently being done to restore equity? Are the individuals making *real* restitution or *psychological* restitution? How does the inequity affect the group's operation?

This is not an exhaustive list. However, these five basic questions should provide you with a way to assess the system of equity in your group setting and the exchanges used to maintain or modify it. Remember: the key to understanding equity in any group setting is to focus on the *communication* between and among group members. A good way to chart the communication of exchanges in a small group is to keep a record of *who says what to whom with what effect.*

Exchange and Persuasion: Sequence and Hierarchy in Group Communication

By keeping a record of who says what to whom with what effect you gain access to two valuable sources of information about communication in small groups: sequence of talk and hierarchy of influence (Haley, 1976; Bochner, 1978). By asking who says what to whom, and by charting the flow of talk in a group, you discover the *sequence* a message passes through from person to person. By finding a routine or a pattern of these sequences, you can begin asking questions about the *hierarchy* of influence prevalent in the group.

A useful way to understand the concept of sequence in group interaction is to think of exchanges as occurring in some order. Johanna introduces a topic, Rob comments on it, and Johanna then comments on his response; Paul takes Rob's side in the issue, and Johanna remains silent as Eileen agrees with what Paul has said. This is a way of tracing the sequence of the exchanges of messages among and between group members. If the sequence just described is typical of exchanges among these group members, we have a way of understanding the persuasions operating in the group, as well as the hierarchy of influence maintained by the group members.

Let's broaden our previous example to illustrate the point:

Johanna: "I think we ought to look at the language used by physicians as a potential source of conflict with their patients."

Rob: "Language isn't the only source of conflict . . ."

Johanna: "That's exactly what I'd expect you to say, Rob."

Paul: "Wait a minute, Jo, Rob's got a good point. Besides language, we can also look at educational level, expertise, credibility, etc."

Eileen: "He's right, Johanna. Maybe we ought to brainstorm for a while about possible ways of approaching our subject."

Aside from the apparent hostility Johanna and Rob feel toward each other, this little sequence of interaction can provide us with useful information about how the group operates.

First, assuming the above exchange is *typical* of sequences of talk between these people, we make tentative predictions about future interactions within this group. If Johanna introduces a similar topic, Rob may respond negatively to it, at which time Johanna may comment on Rob's negativism. Paul may join Rob's side in the cause, and after momentary hesitation, Eileen may agree with Paul. If this sequence, or any proximate variation of it, occurs regularly in the group, we can say we have isolated the sequence of interaction. But simply isolating the sequence does not tell us much.

Second, we use the isolated sequence to generate ideas about status differences created by the social hierarchy in the small group. If we think of status as being a "position" on a ladder, and the ladder itself as representing the hierarchy of group members, we can conceptualize status differences in a group. If, using sequential analysis as a critical technique (Hewes, 1979), we are able to come to a basic understanding of who says what to whom with what effect, we can begin to attach status labels to the group members:

Paul (Group leader)

Eileen (Paul's "yes" person, recorder of
the group's activities)

Rob (Point man for the group's attack on Johanna)

Johanna (Bears the brunt of criticism in the group)

Third, we can use the sequences to make tentative generalizations about who says what to whom with what effect in the group. For example, Scheidel and Crowell (1966) provide the critical label "double interact" to describe the routine sequence between Johanna and Rob. If we can regularly find Johanna introducing a topic, Rob commenting on it, and Johanna responding to his comments, we have a way of predicting the appearance of a double interact any time she presents an idea to the group. We can also describe Eileen's behavior. If she usually waits until Paul makes a statement before saying anything, and if she then usually agrees with him, we can predict that when Paul makes a statement following a conflict between Johanna and Rob, Eileen will agree with him. We must *always be careful about our tentative generalizations;* people can change their communicative styles and thus dramatically affect the sequence and hierarchy within a particular group. However, if we can understand the routines of interaction, we can better comprehend how persuasion is manifested.

Fourth, from knowledge gained about the sequence of interaction, we can begin to understand *influences* within the group. For example, in a small group *coalitions* between or among members may develop (Fisher, 1974). In our example, Paul and Eileen may become united as a coalition which might also include Rob (if his behavior toward Johanna remains constant, and if Paul and Eileen consistently take his side in arguments against her). We might also be surprised if Eileen began *dis*agreeing with Paul, or if she took Johanna's side in an argument with Rob. If Eileen and Johanna formed a coalition, the persuasive setting would be altered.

Sequence indicates how communication is connected and channeled through a group interaction. Hierarchy refers to our understanding of the relative status positions of group members based on their sequences of interacting. Thus far our analysis of communication as participation in the small group has focused on talk. We are now ready to consider the equally important communicative function of listening.

Listening as Participating in Group Interaction

Because of the interactive nature of group discussion, individuals spend most of their time in small groups listening. Some authors distinguish between active and passive listening. *Passive listening* refers to hearing the message without engaging in the mental processes necessary for understanding it. Passive listening is what happens when you allow your mind to wander during a discussion, or you focus attention on any extraneous matters instead of what is being said. *Active listening* refers to conscious attempts to understand the meaning of a message given by another. Active listening should be the goal for people engaged in small group interactions because attention is focused on communication.

Friedman (1978) makes an intriguing distinction between *soft* and *hard* listening. As a result of years of observing discussions, Friedman was able to identify occasions or situations when people were formulating responses to the messages of others while listening to them (hard listening), because the listening is directed toward attainment of a specific goal. When listening to another group member describe problems encountered while gathering facts about a specific problem, you may find yourself jumping to a conclusion or formulating a solution to the problem in your own mind. Unfortunately, this "hard" form of listening often interferes with your understanding of the speaker's message because of internal noise. While you are thinking about a response to make, you are missing information.

Soft listening refers to an attempt to "tune into" the message while avoiding the temptation to formulate a response or to ascribe a motive for the message. Rather than attending to *your* reactions to the message, you focus instead on the meaning of the other's statement or question. Consider the following example of "soft" listening:

> **Carla T., 25**   During group meetings I try to listen very carefully to what others are saying. I have found that by allowing my mind to gain impressions without trying to evaluate them, I come to a better understanding of what any one group member really means. I think the other group members sense my doing this because they often ask *me* if they are responding appropriately to someone else's ideas. I guess I help clarify the communication of group members. They trust me, although it has taken a long time for them to realize that my silence did not mean I wasn't listening, or even that I was shy. In a way I have established a good role for myself simply by being able to listen carefully and well. They call me their "philosopher," and I go along with the label even though I know there is nothing philosophical about it. I just am happier when I behave this way.

Carla is actively participating in her group by listening. While she finds the "soft" style of listening more comfortable, there are times when "hard" listening is appropriate. For example, a group leader must listen to what is being said by group members, but should the leader see the discussion wandering from the purpose of the meeting, she or he must be able to redirect the communication. Sometimes it is helpful to evaluate the purpose of statements to direct the group's discussion more productively.

We have examined some of the conceptual bases for effective listening. These bases should create an awareness of the attitude you should adopt toward effective listening in groups, and how your attitudes may influence your ability to listen. Charles Kelly (1979) provides six ways to improve listening habits in small group settings:

1. *Remember the characteristics of a poor listener:* Research indicates that the poor listener is likely to be less intelligent and less emotionally mature than the good listener (Kelly, 1963; 1967). If you want other group members to respond to you as an intelligent and emotionally mature person, then you need to cultivate the skills of empathetic listening (listening in support of the speaker, to determine what you can derive from what she or he is saying).

Improving Listening Habits in Groups

2. *Make a firm initial commitment to listen:* You must be mentally prepared to listen. Tell yourself that listening is important and that you need to listen to improve the quality of your participation in the small group. Remind yourself of past errors caused by not listening, and focus on improving your listening skills.
3. *Be physically and mentally ready to listen:* Before the discussion begins, remind yourself to sit up straight in your seat, to rid your mind of distractions, fears, worries, or other thoughts. Lean forward in your chair and concentrate on what each person is saying.
4. *Concentrate on the other person as a communicator:* Try to think of each person in the group as an individual with unique and significant contributions to make. Avoid categorizing group members because you only reinforce a rigid posture toward them, i.e., thinking of Roberta as a "sexy broad" will tend to devalue her contributions; regarding Stanley as a "typical Republican bureaucrat" will make it more difficult to focus on the potential value of what Stanley has to say.
5. *Give the other person a full hearing:* Remember the rules of communicative etiquette. Do not interrupt a speaker, do not engage in extraneous conversation while a person is making a point, do not become impatient with someone who is providing information, and try to avoid premature consensus for the sake of convenience. All of these distractions tend to divert your attention from the speaker. Here the golden rule of listening applies: Listen to others as you would have them listen to you.

6. *Use analytical skills as supplements to, not replacements for, listening:* Our own note-taking or mental review of the evidence provided to support a claim often distracts us from listening. Sometimes we become so concerned with our need to counter a point that we do not listen to what we want to argue against. Analytical skills are valuable for the group, but they must be used properly. Listen first, then analyze what you have heard. Do not attempt to do both at the same time.

There are many good sources on developing better listening skills. Some you may want to consult are included in the chapter references (see Malandro and Barker, 1983; Egan, 1973; Weaver, 1972; Johnson, 1956).

Skill in listening is critical to effective group interaction. Unless each member of the group is willing to listen, there can be no real discussion. Instead, there will be several group members simultaneously giving brief public speeches to unappreciative audiences. Effective communication requires both listening and speaking skills: the ability to receive and interpret information as well as transmit it to others.

Formulating Responses to the Communication of Others

We have defined communication as *responses* made to situations and to others. We have talked about the importance of being able to make productive *choices* of the most appropriate responses to make in group communication situations. In this section we want to examine closely the possible responses which can be made to the communication of others and how to choose the most appropriate responses.

Choices about the Form of Responses to Communication We make three responses to the communication of others: statements, questions, and silence. These three categories represent choices to be used responding to situations and others. Let's consider each category separately.

1. *Making statements:* We make statements when we want to gain the acceptance of a fact, idea, person, or opinion. We also make statements in response to someone else's statement of a fact, idea, or opinion, to let the other person know how we have responded to it. Four categories of statements are available to us, each with a corresponding burden of proof (Toulmin, 1958; Ehninger, 1974):
   —*Statements of fact,* or declarative claims: When we state a fact we either assume the audience already knows the statement to be a fact (as when we say the earth is more or less round), or else we must be able empirically to verify the fact as a fact (as when we show a photograph of the earth taken by an orbiting satellite).

—*Statements categorizing facts,* or classificatory claims: When we state that something should be defined or categorized in a particular way, we assume the responsibility for furnishing a reliable source of the definition or classification. For example, we began this chapter by defining communication and attributing the definition to a credible source.

—*Statements evaluating facts or classifications of facts,* known as evaluative claims: When we pass judgment (good/bad; right/wrong; appropriate/inappropriate) we assume responsibility for (a) establishing criteria or standards used to make the judgment, and (b) demonstrating the applicability of the criteria to the object being evaluated. For example, if I make the statement "This is a good group discussion," I incur the responsibility to establish criteria for the evaluation (e.g., by "good" I mean the group attains its goals by equitably apportioning resources among members, and reasoning through problems using Standard Agenda), and then apply the criteria to the group discussion being evaluated (e.g., this group meets the criteria because . . .).

—*Statements recommending a future course of action,* or activating claims: When we propose that something be done, we incur the communicative responsibility for demonstrating *why* it should be done. For example, if we suggest the group use Standard Agenda to guide future discussions, we must explain why Standard Agenda will be productive. Usually when we propose a new course of action, we also must show why the course of action we recommend is *better* than other alternative courses of action (e.g., Why we should use Standard Agenda instead of Delphi Technique or Parliamentary procedure, etc.).

Making statements usually involves more *self-risk* than asking questions or remaining silent. Any time we make a statement, we assume the burden of proving the worth or validity of the statement. For this reason, to improve the effectiveness of the choices we make about participating in groups, we need to understand our responsibilities when we make statements.

2. *Asking questions:* We ask questions when we want to gain information about an issue, idea, person, or agenda. We can also ask questions when we want to respond to someone else's statement, question, or silence, thereby gaining access to information which we otherwise would not have. Because there are many different ways of categorizing questions, we will limit our discussion of them to questions raised in group interactions:

—*Questions about the charge, the objectives, or the goal of the interaction:* When we ask questions about the purpose or end of the group interaction we provide leadership and direction by either initiating or refocusing the talk.

—*Questions about the procedure or agenda used to guide the interaction:* When we ask questions about the operational method used to arrive at a decision or solve a problem, we elicit formal definition or description of the means used to reach the specified end.

—*Questions about the content or meaning of a statement made by another group member:* When we ask questions about the content or meaning of someone's statement, we are trying to gain clarification or amplification of his or her argument.

—*Questions about the reliability of the source of information presented to the group for discussion:* When we ask questions about the reliability of testimony or evidence, we are seeking to establish a standard by which to measure the validity and appropriate nature of the information.

—*Questions about previous decisions or solutions reached by the group or by a similar group:* When we ask questions about the past, we are seeking to establish a common referent for work already accomplished, to discover whether or not past decisions or solutions are applicable to present or future needs, and to gain information that may be helpful in attaining the group's objective.

Asking questions usually involves less self-risk than making statements, because you are seldom required to provide reasons for the questions you ask. Whenever you ask a question, however, you should be mindful of the goal you have for it. Repeatedly asking needless questions will make you appear foolish to other group members, and impede their ability to work.

3. *Remaining silent:* There are three major uses of silence during group communication: (a) silence as communication of *acceptance;* (b) silence as communication of *ambivalence;* and (c) silence as communication of *mystery, uncertainty, passivity,* or *relinquishment.* Silence is a form of nonverbal communication that requires a knowledge of the history of a person's communicative style prior to accurately assessing it. While there are many ways of regarding silence, we will focus on the uses of silence during small group communication.

—*Silence as communication of acceptance:* When we do not make statements or ask questions and appear to be in agreement with what other group members are accomplishing, we may use silence as a vehicle for communicating our acceptance of the group process and the interaction of the group members.

—*Silence as communication of ambivalence:* When we do not make statements or ask questions, and we do *not* appear to be either in agreement or disagreement with the other group members, we may be using silence to reveal our ambivalence about the group process and the interaction of group members. Ambivalence refers to our capacity simultaneously to possess two conflicting emotions about an event, object, process, or person. Ambivalence as communication in small groups may result from dissatisfaction with the group's operation or leadership, or it may simply indicate a disinterested attitude toward the topic being pursued.

—*Silence as communication of mystery, uncertainty, passivity, or relinquishment:* Brummett (1980) used these categories to discuss political strategies of silence. He defined political silence as the absence of talk when talk is *expected.* By withholding comments or questions, a group member may be communicating dissension or signalling to others that something is wrong but cannot be discussed openly. The problem of silence, as Brummet notes, is that as a strategy it too often allows *others* to shape the meaning. Receivers of silence in a small group may misinterpret its message, either by attributing acceptance or ambivalence to it; or they may commenting on why the person is silent, thus defining for him or her the meaning of the act. Silence may also be used to gain control or power in the group, by focusing group attention in the absence of verbal expression from someone whose talk is valued.

Silence is a *choice* available to any member of a small group. As relations with group members develop over a period of time, there will be greater understanding of how silence communicates and how it should be interpreted.

The term *openness* when used in connection with communication, refers to our choice of communication style and degree of self-disclosure in the presence of others (Montgomery, 1980). For example, when we are participating in a small group with other people we like and with whom we have a successful history of past task accomplishments, we may tend to behave in a more relaxed, flexible, and responsive style than if we were participating in a group with people who make us feel uncomfortable. Our "openness" toward them would be revealed in our choices of words and actions (Montgomery, 1982), which in turn would affect how other group members responded toward us (Miller, 1980; Infante and Gorden, 1979).

Choices about Openness and Communication Style

There does not appear to be one "right" choice of openness for all occasions (Eisenberg and Witten, 1987). We must be mindful of the status and power of our audience (Infante and Gorden, 1982; Jablin, 1979). Thus, to be extremely "open" with our boss in stressful circumstances could be damaging. Consider Ellen's case:

Ellen D., 22   I knew Larry—that's my boss—liked me from the start. And I knew that sooner or later he would probably try to seduce me. But I figured I'm a big girl now and besides I don't have to do anything I don't want to. So we were in that important meeting on the budget, and Larry was admiring my legs, and I just politely smiled and maintained eye contact with him. I didn't really mean anything, but he certainly thought I did. He quickly ended the meeting and asked me to remain. The rest of the story is private, but you can read about it in any one of a dozen magazines. Only this time let me give you some advice I hope you pass along to your readers: don't play along unless you plan to come across with the goods. I didn't and I lost my job because of it. And you wouldn't believe the stories I hear about me now. . . .

It is also usually true that superiors in any organizational setting will expect to be treated deferentially. To become too open with them may be read as a sign of disrespect. To know how to make productive choices about the degree of openness, you need to understand the nature of your audience and the expectations of the situation. You also need some more information about behaviors associated with "openness" and communication style.

Barbara Montgomery (1982) defines open communication as "the process of transmitting information about the self." She then describes five categories of open style in communication:

Categories of Open
Communication

1. *Negative openness:* Specifically deals with "showing disagreement," or negative affect toward a person's attitudes, values, beliefs, or opinions.
2. *Nonverbal openness:* Refers to the communicator's facial expressions, vocal tone, and body movement which signal openness. The "approving smile" that Ellen gave her boss signalled a degree of openness she was unwilling to substantiate.
3. *Emotional openness:* Reflects whether one's emotional state is "easy to read," which includes letting others know your mood, not hiding or changing your feelings.
4. *Receptive openness:* Refers to those behaviors which indicate that a person is willing to receive others' openness; typically these behaviors include attentiveness, interest expressed in the other, and demonstrated receptivity to others' ideas and opinions.
5. *General style openness:* Focuses on the overall evaluation you make of a person's openness to communicate.

To make productive choices about your own degrees of openness with other small group members, you need to assess your goals for communicating with them, and their goals for communicating with you. While openness in communication style is generally a positive approach to others, you must understand that it may be considered an invitation to friendship or intimacy. We know from studies of self-disclosure that when one person reveals her or his "true feelings," or "opinions" about self, or the stage is set for the person to reciprocate. If you tell others about yourself, they probably will also tell you about themselves. Depending on your relationship with the other person or people, the goals that you establish the relationship, self-disclosure and openness in communication style may violate social and professional rules for conduct, and create discord among the group.

However, communicator style is often correlated with degree of satisfaction in organizational settings. Infante and Gorden (1982) studied communicator style of interaction between subordinates and superiors in thirty-five organizations, and reported that:

1. Subordinates' satisfaction was related to being *similar* to superiors in the ways jokes, anecdotes, and stories are told, and in the degree of animation used to express themselves (gestures, facial expressions, body movements).
2. Subordinates' satisfaction was related to being *dissimilar* to superiors' degree of openness in communicating, including how relaxed they felt around them and how attentive they were to them.

Although it is difficult to generalize from these findings, it would seem that you are safer expressing openness with your peers than you are with your superiors. Perhaps, when applied to small group settings, these findings would encourage the members to be less open toward their group leaders and superiors and to observe carefully their behavior for clues as to what will be considered appropriate openness within the group.

Your communication style should be flexible. Remember, you always have choices to make about behaviors, about what you say and do while in the presence of other group members. To be open to everyone would probably be a mistake. To use openness to develop relationships with others in the group whom you like and would respond favorably to is an option you can use at your own discretion. The critical consideration here is to realize that what you communicate in words and actions defines your communication style. You should choose the degree of openness and expression you think will attain the ends for which you and your group strive. Perhaps Cindy's statement is a good way to end this section:

> **Cindy G., 25**   I used to think you could act the same way around anybody and if they didn't like it, it was their problem. But that just isn't true. You need to treat others as individuals, and part of that treatment means adapting your style of communication to them. For instance, let me tell you about Frank. Frank is a nice old man who has worked here for thirty years and is almost ready to retire. He wears a tie and jacket every day. He is always clean-shaven and he is a good Christian. Now I have a tendency to curse when things go wrong. But to curse in front of dear old Frank is entirely inappropriate. He just doesn't believe a woman should do things like that, and I appreciate him enough to try to please him. Then there's Jim. Jim is a macho kind of guy who looks very much like Tom Selleck and wants people to like him. With him, even though he is my superior, I can relax. He is nearer my age, my attitudes, my experiences than other people are. We can be more open and honest with each other, but it evolved slowly. At first I thought he was just a body without a head or a heart, the kind of guy to use one woman after another, but he really isn't like that at all. He is happily married and has two children and his family means everything to him. I can joke with him, but I do not come on to him. There is a difference and we both know it. That's what I mean about adapting to others. You need to be flexible, to keep your options open, and to watch very carefully how others are treating you.

Choices about Appropriateness of Responses: A Developmental View How do you know whether to make a statement, ask a question, or remain silent when participating in a small group interaction? How do you make choices about openness and style of communication? To answer these questions, you will need to investigate three interrelated sources of information about appropriateness.

First, you need to develop a feeling for the *needs and expectations* of the group members and the discussion situation. It is important to observe each individual's style of communicating, including considerations of the *roles* assumed during discussions, *choices* about making statements, asking questions, and remaining silent, openness, and style.

Many taxonomies have been used to describe the roles played by individuals in small groups. Some categories are based on functions performed, such as initiator, gatekeeper, and tension-reliever (Benne and Sheats, 1948); others are based on motivational characteristics inspiring talk, such as wanting to get ahead in the organization or wanting to make a friend (Phillips, 1982). To understand the needs and expectations of individuals in your group, it is necessary to determine how their group roles relate to their motivational characteristics. What do they say and do in the group, and why do they choose to say and do it? Answering this question should provide a tentative understanding of the reasons for a person's communicative openness and style.

Understanding the needs and expectations of the individuals in your small group should induce you to investigate the relationships between what *you* contribute and the satisfaction/dissatisfaction of their needs and expectations. Unless you ask these questions, you might make Marc's mistake:

Marc M., 23 I always thought of myself as a bright person who said what was on my mind. I know now you shouldn't always do that. At work, I am part of a team responsible for instituting Quality Circles in an effort to involve employees in decisions. I was not the group leader, although I secretly wanted to be. So, I acted as if I *was* the leader. I opened the meetings, directed the talk, provided summaries, and the rest. The real group leader seemed amused, but the other group members were confused. They didn't know who was really in control of the meetings, and since this participatory management idea is very new to them, they thought my acting as leader even though I wasn't the leader was part of it. As you might imagine, the group failed. The real leader, of course, actually wanted the whole concept to break down because he felt threatened by involving lower-level employees in decision-making. That's why he let me make a fool out of myself. I should have known better, but I didn't. The unfortunate part of this story is that participatory management is a good idea, and the other guys in the group really wanted to make it work. If I hadn't been such a schmuck it might have. I have only myself to blame.

Marc should have paid more attention to the responses he received from the group's appointed leader. He should have assessed those responses by scrutinizing them for motivational characteristics. By ignoring this significant base for behavior, he failed to see the relationship between the needs and expectations of the group leader and the responses he was receiving to his choices about participation.

Second, you need to *compare your goals with the group's objectives.* The choices you make should communicate concern for helping the group reach its objectives. Strive to gain a sense of credibility and esteem from the group's reputation as well as from your help in creating that reputation. You will also have goals, personal goals, you want to attain in the group setting. When these objectives become hidden agendas they can hamper the group's ability to reach its objectives. However, when you understand what your goals are, you can better *monitor* your choices about behavior. In our previous example, Marc didn't know what his goal was until *after* he contributed to the collapse of the group. Then, in retrospect, he saw his actions as attempts to achieve status in the group, a leadership role which actually undermined its purpose. Hindsight is usually clearsighted. But we need to develop skills to think through to our goals and the group's objectives *before* we engage in group communication.

If you know what your goals are, you have a way of measuring your ability to reach them in the group. You can gauge the responses you receive from other group members in order to analyze your participation in the group. Also, by knowing what you want to have happen, you are in a bargaining position. If others are willing to help you reach your goals, you should be willing to help them reach their's. When you understand what makes you behave the way you do in small groups, you discover the mediums of exchange capable of motivating your own and other's work efforts.

Third, you need to take a *developmental view* of group communication. Communication is a process that creates relationships between and among individuals in small groups. Spending time, sharing space, and exchanging information provide people with better understanding of how to achieve their goals. As the group develops a history of interaction, its members begin to rely on each other to perform certain tasks or functions (Krayer and Fiechtner, 1984). All these influences should induce you to take a developmental view of the choices you make about participation in the group. Until you come to know the other group members, until you establish your ability to make accurate predictions about the outcomes of communication with them, you are limited in your selection of appropriate strategies. Your ability to make appropriate choices of behavior should develop as you spend more time with your small group:

Melinda A., 21 It took about ten weeks of meeting three times a week before I felt really comfortable in my committee assignment. My opinions of the group members changed, and my way of dealing with them changed. In the beginning I was quiet. I took careful notes and watched how the people responded to each other. I played a game with myself. I tried to think of each person in the group as a country, you know, like in the game *Diplomacy*. Then I tried to see who wanted to invade whom, and what coalitions were being formed. It helped me analyze the group, as you say. I figured out that Tom and Nancy were old lovers who tolerated each other, and that Sammy wasn't nearly as tough as he wanted people to think. It was fun. After awhile I started talking. I began by asking questions because I wanted people to know I was alert. Later I began presenting my views, and making active choices about my behavior, as you say. But it did take time before the group seemed like a group to me. Before that happened, it was just me versus them. Now it is "us."

Melinda learned how to make effective choices as a participant in her small group. She began cautiously, and proceeded cautiously, because she had been trained in small group interaction. She knew the value of gathering information about the group before plunging into discussions.

We cannot always be as cautious as Melinda was. We are often put into a group and expected immediately to begin participating actively. But as a general rule, what Melinda did is a good example to follow. She took a developmental view of the group and her role in it. She gathered information about the other group members and used it to guide her choices about communication.

The critical point here is that you do have *choices* about communicative behavior. The more conscious your choice-making becomes, the more goal-oriented your talk will be, and consequently, the better you will become in evaluating the effectiveness of your participation. Now that we have discussed the formulation of responses in small groups, let's examine some of the problems of communication experienced by people working in group settings.

Problems Associated with Communication in the Small Group

No matter how carefully you monitor communication in the group, problems will arise. No matter how skillfully you make choices about participating in the small group, your decisions will inevitably conflict with those made by other group members. In this section we will examine five common sources of communication problems experienced by people in small groups:

Sources of Communication Problems in Groups

1. Interruptions while someone else is speaking.
2. Conflicts because of statements made.
3. Conflicts because of questions asked.
4. Conflicts because of remaining silent.
5. Conflicts because of talking too much or not enough.

Before we begin to examine these problems systematically, let's consider the following humorous (and sad) report made by an individual who suffered most of these difficulties while working in a group:

Ted M., 22   . . . So I didn't say anything. Then Roberta accused me of holding out. I said, "Roberta, I am just doing what you told me to do." She said I was trying to make her look like a fool in front of the others. So then I asked her, "What do you want me to do?" She said I had no business asking that question; I was old enough to make my own decisions. So I said, "Okay," and began presenting my idea about how we could best solve the problem. Then Lenny interrupted me, which, incidentally, he always does, and told me not to make a speech. I told him to wait until I was finished before asking me any questions. I was angry by then and he knew it.

So I ask you, what is a person supposed to do? Is there any way to improve the group's productivity when we spend most of our time bickering? Well, is there?

The answer is *maybe*.

The term *communication problems* has become a cliche. Many books are available promising easy ways for overcoming such problems. Depending on how you define your communication difficulty, the answer may be any one or two of a dozen or more marketable solutions, ranging from asserting yourself to taming your need to be assertive. Of course, if you define the problem incorrectly, you may select a solution that will only aggravate the situation. There are no easy solutions to communication problems. However, there are better ways of defining what the communication problem really is. If your difficulty is a *communication* problem, it will be recognizable in speech or verbalization, rather than in personality attributes or psychological causes. We can make changes in communication behavior to overcome communication problems.

One of the most common communication problems is interrupting someone else while he or she is speaking. Not only is this behavior rude, it also may lead to retaliation by the individual who was interrupted. Remember the exchange principle: what you are willing to give you must also expect to receive. When a person interrupts another, we can identify at least three additional communication problems contributing to the difficulty:

Interrupting

1. *Failure to listen:* If you interrupt someone, you are not concentrating on the meaning of his or her message. To interrupt is to make a statement or ask a question, both of which require thought. If you are thinking about a response you want to make to them, you are not actively listening to what he or she is saying.
2. *Failure to monitor your own communication:* If you interrupt someone, you are not controlling your talk. You are failing to concede to others what you demand others allow you: the opportunity to make an uninterrupted statement. Since effective participation requires the opportunity to monitor talk, you violate this principle of effectiveness when you interrupt someone.
3. *Failure to provide the possibility for mutual influence:* When you interrupt someone, you are in effect saying, "Look here, what I talk about is more important than what you are talking about, so give me the floor." You are revealing a reluctance to be persuaded, no matter what the content of the argument might be. If you are unwilling to *be* persuaded, you may encounter resistance the next time you try to persuade. The group member who suffers the violation may increase the costs for your participating.

Interrupting a speaker is insensitive. Little is to be gained, and much is to be lost, by this action. People esteem the views of those who respect the right of everyone to express a view. Saying "I'm sorry" may not restore the loss of equity (Walster, Walster, and Bersheid, 1978).

Conflict over Statements The second source of communication problems is conflict over statements made. Whenever someone in a group makes a statement, that person probably believes the statement is both true and rational (Coombs and Snygg, 1959). To deny this is to challenge an individual's sanity, intelligence, good sense, honesty, or all of these. For this reason, you must learn to take seriously the statements other group members make, and your responses to them. Simply blurting out "that's silly," is likely to be perceived not only as an attack on the statement, but also as an evaluation of the speaker's character. I am *not* advocating avoidance of conflict over statements. *Conflict* is a neutral term when its source of conflict is managed appropriately by the participants. There are ways to introduce objections to statements which reduce the likelihood of offending the proponent. Here are some guidelines:

1. *Do not interrupt the speaker to register an objection.* We have already discussed the problem of interruptions. To interrupt someone to object to a statement is to increase the injury. Wait until the person completes the argument, then express the objection.
2. *Introduce the objection as one of fact rather than belief.* Arguments about the content of a message are productive. Arguments over facts or classifications of facts can be resolved by verification. Arguments over evaluations can be resolved by establishing the standard used to make the evaluation or appraisal, and then determining the reasonableness and appropriateness of applying them. The focus must remain on the content of the argument. Do not introduce an objection with the words "I believe"; it is more difficult to argue against someone else's beliefs than against her or his facts. Do not say you "know" something is true unless you are able and willing to supply the necessary evidence.
3. *Do not escalate the conflict.* If agreement or consensus cannot be reached over the issue, agree to delay the argument until new information can be found. Do not become a victim of your own ego by escalating the conflict into one over personalities or beliefs; restrict the argument to the basis of its claims and evidence, not its source.
4. *Do not withdraw from the conflict.* Conflicts are productive when they are mutually resolved, not when one person withdraws or is bullied into false submission. Unless both parties to an argument find appropriate resolution, the conflict will remain despite the fact that one or both parties withdraw. When this happens, restoration of equity is made more difficult because the perception of injury outweighs the real cost of the injury.

Statements should spark controversy in small groups. One major reason for using groups to make decisions or solve problems is to increase the diversity of opinions and information available to the group. Care must be taken, however, to object to statements in ways which move toward the goals of the group without injuring the individual members.

A third communication problem affecting a group's operation is conflict over questions asked. This is very similar to the problem of conflict over statements made. Again, the question will be perceived by the questioner as being important, rational, and necessary at the time when the question is posed. Any attempt to dismiss the rationality or minimize the importance of the question will most likely aggravate the conflict. We must learn to accept the statements people make and the questions they ask seriously when working in small groups. Consider the following tale of woe:

Conflict over Questions

> **Peter P., 29** I knew I was right to ask about the limits of our responsibility on the problem. But no, Sal refused to consider it. The other group members probably agreed with me, but no one said anything because we all know how Sal is. So we made a mess out of the job, and the VP gave Sal and the rest of us hell over it. Frankly, I enjoyed the criticism. I knew it was all Sal's fault. Had he listened to me in the first place and answered my questions like any reasonable person should, we wouldn't have screwed up like we did. Everybody's complaining now because we all have to do overtime to make up for the error. You can bet Sal will never hear the end of this, not as long as I have anything to do with it. I figure he owes me about a grand in overtime. I won't get the money, but there are other ways of getting even.

Hostility over perceptions of unfair treatment may be the root of most, if not all, inequity in small groups. When a person asks a question, however trivial, he or she and the question deserve the group's attention and cooperation.

A fourth communication problem is conflict concerning silence during small group discussions. As we have noted, silence may express many different meanings. Because of the inevitable *ambiguity* of silence, there is often conflict over what the silence means. Sometimes groups resent the silent member because she or he may not be contributing much to the group. If the silence is caused by shyness or anxiety associated with speaking, the shy person may unwittingly be increasing the costs of participating in the group (McKinney, 1982):

Conflict over Silence

1. Because reticent group members participate less in group interactions, they are perceived as less effective in interactions.
2. Reticent group members are perceived as less competent and less attractive than non-reticent group members.
3. Reticent group members are less likely to emerge as group leaders than non-reticent group members. This characteristic is related to:
   —Seating choice (reticent persons tend to seat themselves in less dominant discussion positions).
   —Lack of communicative skills to structure the group's work.

If the silence is caused by ambivalence, the group may decide to reciprocate. At some future time when the previously silent member speaks, the other group members may inexplicably fall silent, paying him or her back for the ambivalence with ambivalence. If the silence is strategic, if it is designed to evoke a particular response, the silent person must be careful to monitor the responses actually received to ensure accuracy of meaning. Effective uses of silence can be coordinated with meaningful eye contact, facial expressions, body posture, or gestures to amplify the intent. Silence is a choice for communication in the small group, but as yet it has very little to recommend it. Verbal messages have the advantage of being negotiated openly; they also aid in reducing the ambiguities of communication, while silence contributes to such uncertainty.

Too Much or Too Little Communication

A fifth source of problems associated with communication in small groups is *too much or too little talk*. This problem arises when expectations are violated. For example, if a single group member dominates the discussion, there will be too much talk on his or her behalf and not enough talk on behalf of the other group members. The speaker is violating the rule of equably apportioning resources (including the right to speak) among group members. Unless what the speaker is saying is very important, chances are the group members will feel the inequity and respond by increasing the costs of participation for the member next time.

The converse problem is too little talk. Silence may be perceived as strategic communication; but too little input is usually considered a failure to participate in the group's activities (McKinney, 1982). Often too little communication is associated with negative outcomes. Because none of the above associations are positive ones, too little talk should be avoided. If you have nothing to say, make that statement in the group. Let other people know you are interested in what is being discussed even if you have no particular view on the subject.

What can be done to overcome the problems of too much or too little talk? In either case, the leader should exert influence to change the behavior. The leader can address the group member who speaks too long, reminding him or her that other group members have statements to make as well. The leader can encourage the reticent group member to express his or her point of view. If the leader does not control these problems, then responsibility falls to the other group members. Here is one way to deal with the problem:

> **Cheryl S., 24** I got sick and tired of listening to Ron spout off. Cal, who was our leader, did not make any effort to shut him up. I knew the other group members were as put off by his behavior as I was, so I was the one who told him that he was taking too much time. I recommended that he prepare better for the meetings and learn to limit his remarks. Cal was embarrassed, but he didn't say anything. Ron was offended, but I didn't care. We adjourned shortly after that. You could say I wasn't diplomatic enough, and that I ruined one group meeting. But the next time we met, Ron actually brought notes to the meeting and when he spoke he did limit his remarks. He winked at me when he was through and I applauded. To both of our surprises, the rest of the group applauded too!

Cheryl's style was more blunt than I usually recommend. She not only attacked Ron's communication, she also attacked him (and indirectly the group leader). Cheryl was lucky. Her outburst could have alienated Ron, making him defensive and spiteful. Fortunately, Ron followed her advice, won her approval (as well as the group's), and the faulty behavior was corrected.

We are now ready to consider the relationship between participation and evaluation of communication in small groups.

Evaluating Communication in Small Groups

If communication represents how we participate in small groups, then it is also the source of evaluations about participation in such groups. Even when the mode of communication is silence, the effects of silence on the group are assessed as a form of participation. In this section we will examine the basis for evaluating communication in small groups; in Chapter 10 we will provide a detailed account of exactly how to observe and classify behavior in group settings.

Any evaluation depends on the observer's prior assessment of the *appropriateness* of communication. For example, as a member of a small group you have preconceived ideas about what *should* happen in your group, and how communication *should* function to obtain those goals. These desired results form the basis of your evaluative schema. During the group interactions you are consistently making judgments of the appropriateness/inappropriateness of talk, based on the evaluative schema you bring to the group. If the group, or its individual members, act within your framework for assessing their behavior, you evaluate their communication positively; if they do not meet your criteria, you evaluate their communication negatively.

For years professionals have attempted to discover or create a universal classification schema capable of producing systematic evaluations of communicative behavior in groups (Bales, 1951; Brilhart, 1967; Bodaken, Lashbrook, and Champagne, 1971; McCroskey and Wright, 1971; Leathers, 1971; Bales and Cohen, 1979). These methods have provided intriguing uses of human observation, statistical procedures, computer programs, as well as a myriad of "instruments" designed to measure behavior. For individuals trained to "see" (observe) communication in small groups using any one or more of these techniques, assessments can be systematic. However, the vast majority of individuals who work in groups, especially those in organizations, do not have the benefit of such training. Their judgments may be equally valid or truthful, but they rely on their goals, instincts, and sense of equity as criteria to determine the strengths and weaknesses of the group's communication efforts.

Any observation of communication with the intention of evaluating it relies heavily on past experiences. The impressions or conclusions of past experiences influence judgments made about communication in the small group in three interrelated ways:

1. *Past experience with the group:* What you understand about the historically derived meanings shared by group members, and past patterns of reciprocal interaction and influence among group members, will shape the way in which you make evaluations of present communicative behavior.

Past Experiences

2. *Past experience with individual group members:* What you know or believe to be true about any member of the group will influence how you respond to his or her communication. If your responses are influenced by past experiences, so also are your evaluations.
3. *Past experience with other groups and individuals:* Because the act of evaluation relies on *comparisons* between this group and previous groups or other groups, any experiences you have had in groups shape your ability to perceive and respond to the communication present in this group. You may also be influenced by past communicative acts involving other individuals outside the group who have contributed to what you believe should happen when you communicate with others.

Because of the pervasive influence of past experiences in communicating on evaluations of present group activities, you must always be careful to *identify the bases for comparison.* Try to find out to what and to whom you are comparing this small group. We cannot separate our past from our need to evaluate present actions, but if we can account for influences on our judgmental abilities, we can prevent some serious errors being made. Consider the following testimony:

Jason J., 35   I'll never forget my first day of working with the group. There were two people who physically resembled old friends of mine from college; one was an ex-lover. You can imagine my surprise! I found myself wanting to relate to them as if they were the old friends, not the new people I was dealing professionally with. Fortunately, I understood what was happening: what Freud called "transference" was occurring in me. I tried to block it but it was difficult. As I got to know the group members better, I also found myself comparing their work to the work of my last small group. Talk about learning from past mistakes; in my last group I was usually uneasy about what we were doing. I mean we had a charismatic leader whom everyone followed. It was scary. I was glad to be transferred into this group, where no one personality dominates. You can bet I try not to let my previous negative experiences affect how I act with these people.

Jason is especially sensitive to his own reactions to other people and situations. Most group members we work with are not as capable of understanding the reasons behind their own actions. The best we can try to accomplish is to discover what influences our past communicative experiences, especially our group experiences, have on what we are responding to now.

Process and Content Evaluations   A second source of judgments about communication in the group emerges from a necessary distinction between *process and content* evaluations (Brilhart, 1967). We have seen how in the course of time groups develop, how individual group members learn to adapt to the needs and expectations of others. We can speak about the "process" of communicating as an on-going, continuous activity, constantly changing because of the changes of people in the group. Conversely, we can talk about specific group interactions, dialogues or confrontations which occur in a precise setting, and are thought of as a single "event." We tend to recall the "events" of group interaction and negate the importance of "process" when we make our evaluations. *Events* encourage us to remember *content* of discussions; *process* encourages us to think developmentally of the *relationships* between and among the participants.

We must understand what it is we are evaluating. Process and content are interwoven and interdependent; unfortunately, we tend to separate them to evaluate communication among group members. We need to understand the process in order to shed light on what the content of any one or more interactions meant. Here is how one expert describes it:

> **Gerry M., 57**   One of the hardest tasks to accomplish when observing small groups or operating within them is to see how *process* works. We easily remember the times when we were actively involved in a dispute, or when we served as leader, or how we got the best of someone else. But we tend to forget how we developed relationships with the group members, and we tend to not think about how those relationships affect our perception of what really went on. For instance, I work in an academic setting, and serve on several different committees. One committee is a search committee. We are charged with the task of hiring three new faculty members this year. There are six people on that committee, two of whom I have known well for over twenty years, two others whom I hardly know at all. When one of the folks I know speaks, I listen carefully and tend to agree with them. I know them well enough to understand, in a very short period of time, what they are really saying. And I trust them. On the other hand, I don't know the new guys well enough yet. When they speak I ask questions, and probably they think I'm giving them a hard time. I'm not, but I understand how they might feel about it. The point is, when I review the work of the committee, I seldom think of our *process;* instead, I think of the individual encounters we've had. I have to force myself to see the process, and when I do, I often find good reasons for re-evaluating the participation of the new guys.

A third source of judgments about communication in the small group stems from the ability of the group to accomplish its *task or purpose.* We know groups who accomplish their objectives feel better about themselves than do groups who fail to attain their goals. Our goal orientation in small groups affects how we perceive the nature of our interactions, how we evaluate the participation of group members, and how we focus on relationships between and among the participants.

Purpose of the Group

In organizations, the accomplishment of a task is the group's primary obligation. All evaluations stem from the ability of the group members to produce the desired result. Externally, the division managers or supervisors look at the quality of the group's effort *when they have produced the end product.* Seldom do managers intervene to see how the group is doing. Consequently, most judgments about participation in the group are formed *after* the group completes its task. Internally, group members often see the task as something to be accomplished *as a result of* the success or failure of interpersonal relations in the small group. In other words, if we like each other and get along with each other, we will meet our objectives. If we don't, we won't. This either/or dichotomizing of internal evaluations is *not* recommended; however, it does occur. Because most organizations use performance appraisals to evaluate employees for raises and promotions, and since "performance" is usually defined by them as accomplishment of the task, the best way to do well in your performance appraisal is to help your group accomplish its objective.

Research into appraisal processes provides useful guidance for group members. Asherman and Vance (1981) regard documentation as the primary source of data about performance in organizations. For any group, "documentation" refers to the written record of group activities kept by the secretary or group recorder. This record should be reviewed by group members periodically to determine the accuracy of entries, and the thoroughness of coverage of the group's interactions. In some organizations the group's written record may be used to establish quantifiable standards for performance (Dertien, 1981). These organizations assume that certain quantifiable characteristics of jobs can be used to determine a formula for appraisal uses. For example, a leader could be characterized as being responsible for carrying out the following duties: beginning the meeting on time, announcing the agenda, reviewing old business, introducing new business, monitoring interactions between and among group members, providing summaries, and calling for consensus. If the group record reveals compliance with these postulated characteristics, the group leader may *quantifiably* be shown to be accomplishing his or her objectives. The *quality* of leadership, however, may or may not be related to these quantifiable characteristics.

Thus far we have examined three primary sources of influence on evaluations made about communication in the small group: past experiences, process and content factors, and accomplishment of the objectives. These factors shape our judgment of individual communicative acts. However, they are *not* very useful standards when attempting to understand the communication or interaction between and among group members. Here we need to identify specific communicative behaviors. In the following chapters we will focus on the responsibilities of participants and leaders of small groups, and provide specific standards to use when evaluating their performances. In Chapter 10, we will demonstrate how to observe and evaluate group behavior based on these understandings and competencies.

At this point it is useful to answer the following question: *How would you go about establishing a method for evaluating communicative behavior in groups?* What would be your standards? How would you know a specific behavior if you saw it? How much emphasis would be placed on quantifiable characteristics? How would you make judgments of quality?

You may make these evaluations without thinking very much about *how* you make them. If you are to improve your skills in small group interaction, you need to begin assessing your own ability to evaluate the behavior of your small group.

This chapter addressed what you should know about communication in the small group. Communication was defined as "any response to a message." Communication was shown to occur in specific situations; and the purpose of communication is to modify or change some element of the situation using talk. Communication is learned behavior, and you can learn to be a more effective communicator by learning how to make more informed choices about what you say and do.

Group communication is more complicated than individual communication because more individuals are involved, thus increasing the chances for distortion of meaning, ambiguity, and variance of goals. Despite these constraints, you can learn how to improve your communication in small groups by concentrating on the goals you seek to attain in relation to the group's objectives, and by coordinating your choices about communication with the group's norms or standards. Your ability to do well in small groups often depends on your skill in adapting to the needs and expectations of other group members and the situation.

Communication is how you participate in small groups. I discussed the importance of exchange of communication between and among group members, showing how the principle of exchange led to the development of a theory of participation in groups, Equity Theory. The Equity Theory allows us to see how groups develop standards for behavior, and how they enforce these standards. The key to understanding Equity Theory lies in the communication between and among group members. One good way to assess communication in a group is to ask, "*Who says what to whom with what effect?*" Asking this question can lead to explanations of the sequence of talk and the hierarchy of status in the small group. Understanding these bases is useful in discovering how persuasions are expressed in groups.

Individuals spend most of their time in small groups listening. I discussed the distinctions between active and passive listening as well as "soft" and "hard" listening. Listening is a critical skill for learning how to improve communication in the small group, because through listening to what others say you learn what is important to them, and you can then make more informed choices about how to adapt to and persuade them.

Because we defined communication as a *response* given to a message, we need to study how responses are formulated. I discussed the choices you can make about the *form* of communication (making statements, asking questions, remaining silent), and about the *appropriateness* of given responses. Under the latter heading we examined the importance of adapting to the needs and expectations of group members and situations, learning how to make choices about openness and communication style, and how to develop choices about roles taken in interactions. I also pointed out the skill of understanding the functions carried out by individual group members within the group so as to discover motivational characteristics. I demonstrated the need for establishing a developmental view of group interaction.

No group exists without problems. I defined five common problems of communication related to small groups: interruptions while someone else is speaking; conflicts because of statements made, questions asked, or silence; and talking too much or not enough. I discussed causes of each of these specific communication problems, and recommended ways of dealing with them.

Finally, we explored the criteria for evaluating communication in small groups. I isolated three factors influencing generalized judgments about group participation: past experiences, process and content factors, and accomplishment of the task. We examined some of the influences generated by these factors, explaining that in subsequent chapters we will develop standards for evaluating the competency of individual communicators in the group.

References

Asherman, I. G., and S. L. Vance. "Documentation: A Tool for Effective Management." *Personnel Journal* (1981): 641–43.

Bales, R. F. *Interaction Process Analysis.* Cambridge: Addison-Wesley, 1951.

Bales, R. F. "In Conference." *Harvard Business Review* 32 (1954): 44–50.

Bales, R. F., and S. P. Cohen. *SYMLOG.* New York: Free Press, 1979.

Benne, K. D., and P. Sheats. "Functional Roles of Group Members." *Journal of Social Issues* 4 (1948): 41–49.

Bitzer, L. F. "The Rhetorical Situation." *Philosophy and Rhetoric* 1 (1968): 1–14.

Bochner, A. P. "On Taking Ourselves Seriously: An Analysis of Some Persistent Problems and Promising Directions in Interpersonal Research." *Human Communication Research* 1 (1978): 178–91.

Bodaken, E. M., W. B. Lashbrook, and M. Champagne. "*PROANA 5:* A Computerized Technique for the Analysis of Small Group Interaction." *Western Journal of Speech Communication* 35 (1971): 112–15.

Brilhart, J. *Effective Group Discussion.* Dubuque, Ia.: William C. Brown Company Publishers, 1967.

Brummett, B. "Towards a Theory of Silence as a Political Strategy." *Quarterly Journal of Speech* 66 (1980): 289–303.

Coombs, A., and D. Snygg. *Individual Behavior.* New York: Harper & Row, 1959.

Dertien, M. G. "The Accuracy of Job Evaluation Plans." *Personnel Journal* (1981): 566–70.

Egan, G. "Empathetic Listening." In *Bridges, Not Walls,* edited by J. Stewart. Reading, Mass.: Addison-Wesley, 1973.

Ehninger, D. *Influence, Belief, and Argument.* Glenview, Ill.: Scott, Foresman, and Company, 1974.

Eisenberg, E., and M. G. Witten. "Reconsidering Openness in Organizational Communications." *Academy of Management Review* 12 (July 1987): 418–26.

Fisher, B. A. *Small Group Decision-Making.* New York: McGraw-Hill, 1974.

Friedman, P. G. *Interpersonal Communication: Innovations in Instruction.* Washington, D.C.: National Education Association, 1978.

Fry, D. *Homo Loquens.* Cambridge: Cambridge University Press, 1977.

Goldhaber, G. M., M. P. Yates, D. T. Porter, and R. Lesniak. "Organizational Communication: 1978." *Human Communication Research* 5 (1978): 79–96.

Goldhaber, G. M. *Organizational Communication,* 2d ed. Dubuque: William C. Brown Company Publishers, 1981.

Haley, J. *Problem-Solving Therapy.* New York: Harper & Row, 1976.

Hewes, D. E. "The Sequential Analysis of Social Interaction." *Quarterly Journal of Speech* 65 (1979): 56–73.

Homans, G. C. "Social Behavior as Exchange." *American Journal of Sociology* 63 (1958): 597–606.

Homans, G. C. *Social Behavior: Its Elementary Forms,* 2d rev. ed. New York: Harcourt, Brace, Jovanovich, 1974.

Infante, D. A., and W. I. Gorden. "Subordinate and Superior Perceptions of Self and One Another: Relations, Accuracy, and Reciprocity of Liking." *Western Journal of Speech Communication* 43 (1979): 212–23.

Infante, D. A., and W. I. Gorden. "Similarities and Differences in the Communicator Styles of Superiors and Subordinates: Relations to Subordinate Satisfaction." *Communication Quarterly* 30 (Winter 1982): 67–71.

Jablin, F. M. "Superior-Subordinate Communication: The State of the Art." *Psychological Bulletin* 86 (1979): 1201–222.

Johnson, W. *Your Most Enchanted Listener.* San Francisco: International Society for General Semantics, 1956.

Johnstone, H. W. "The Relevance of Rhetoric to Philosophy and of Philosophy to Rhetoric." *Quarterly Journal of Speech* 52 (1966): 41–46.

Kelly, C. M. "Mental Ability and Personality Factors in Listening." *Quarterly Journal of Speech* 49 (1963): 152–56.

Kelly, C. M. "Listening: A Complex of Activities—and a Unitary Skill?" *Speech Monographs* 34 (1967): 455–66.

Kelly, C. M. "Empathetic Listening." In *Small Group Communication: Theory and Practice,* 3d ed, edited by R. Cathcart and L. Samovar, 350–57. Dubuque: William C. Brown Company Publishers, 1979.

Krayer, K. J. and S. B. Fiechtner. "Measuring Group Maturity: The Development of a Process-Oriented Variable for Small Group Research." *Southern Speech Communication Journal* 50 (Fall 1984): 78–92.

Leathers, D. "The Feedback Rating Instrument: A New Means of Evaluating Discussion." *Central States Speech Journal* 22 (1971): 32–42.

McCroskey, J., and D. Wright. "The Development of an Instrument for Measuring Interaction Behavior in Small Groups." *Speech Monographs* 38 (1971): 335–40.

Malandro, L., and L. Barker. *Nonverbal Communication.* Reading, Mass.: Addison-Wesley, 1983.

McKinney, B. C. "The Effects of Reticence on Group Interaction." *Communication Quarterly* 30 (1982): 124–28.

Miller, L. D. "Correspondence Between Self and Other Perceptions of Communication Dominance." *Western Journal of Speech Communication* 44 (1980): 120–31.

Montgomery, B. M. "Verbal Immediacy as a Behavioral Indicator of Open Communication." *Communication Quarterly* 30 (1982): 28–34.

Montgomery, B. M. "Trait, Interactional, and Behavioral Assessment of Open Communication." *Communication Research* 7 (1980): 479–94.

Muchinsky, P. M. "Organizational Communication: Relationship to Organizational Climate and Job Satisfaction." *Academy of Management Journal* 20 (1977): 592–607.

Phillips, G. M., D. J. Pedersen, and J. T. Wood. *Group Discussion: A Practical Guide to Participation and Leadership.* Boston: Houghton Mifflin Co., 1979.

Phillips, G. M., and H. L. Goodall, Jr. *Loving and Living.* Englewood Cliffs, N.J.: Prentice-Hall/Spectrum Books, 1983.

Phillips, G. M., and N. J. Metzger. *Intimate Communication.* Boston: Allyn & Bacon, 1976.

Phillips, G. M. *Communicating in Organizations.* New York: Macmillan Co., 1982.

Scheidel, T. M., and L. Crowell. "Feedback in Small Group Communication."
    Quarterly Journal of Speech 52 (1966): 273–78.

Spiker, B. K., and T. D. Daniels. "Information Adequacy and Communication
    Relationships: An Empirical Examination of 18 Organizations." *Western Journal
    of Speech Communication* 45 (1981): 342–54.

Toulmin, S. *The Uses of Argument.* Cambridge: Oxford University Press, 1958.

Walster, E., G. W. Walster, and E. Bersheid. *Equity Theory and Research.* Boston:
    Allyn & Bacon, 1978.

Weaver, C. H. *Human Listening: Processes and Behavior.* Indianapolis: Bobbs-Merrill,
    1972.

Weick, K. E. *The Social Psychology of Organizing.* Reading: Addison-Wesley, 1979.

Exercises

The following exercises are designed to help you demonstrate the skills covered in this chapter. The first two exercises show you how well (or poorly) you *listen*. The third exercise is designed to help you understand how asking questions and making statements differ in their affect on group discussions. The fourth exercise should help you determine how to deal with talkative and reticent group members. Follow the directions provided for each exercise.

1. Assemble your group. Arrange to have a tape recorder. Record a discussion on the topic "What should be done to improve the services offered to students and faculty members by the library." The discussion should last no longer than thirty (30) minutes. Immediately following the discussion, ask each group member to list, in the order they occurred, the major topics raised by the group. Then ask the group members to list the name(s) of the person responsible for initiating the topic. When these tasks have been completed, play back the recorded tape and check your answers for accuracy. Try to answer the following questions:

   —How many topics did you omit?
   —How many topics did you add?
   —How many topics did you attribute to the wrong source?
   —How many topics did you attribute to no source?
   —How many topics did you list inaccurately (e.g., used the wrong words to describe, or confused with another topic)?

   Compare your answers with others in your group. Discuss possible reasons for the interferences with your listening. Ask the person with the best record to explain why he or she did so well. Ask the people with the worst records to account for their difficulties. Try to formulate a resolution concerning your group's future listening habits.

2. Make a journal entry about the communication problems *you* experienced during the listening exercise. Refer to the text for definitions of the problems and ways of identifying them. Why do you believe these problems occurred? What will you do to overcome them next time your group meets? List at least three behavioral objectives concerning communication problems you intend to attain during the term. Keep track of these objectives and your progress.

3. Assemble your group. Count off, using the "odd-even" method. All odd members must restrict themselves to *making statements,* and all even members must limit their talk to *asking questions,* during the next group discussion. Your topic is: "What students really want to learn from a course in small group communication." If possible, tape record your session. If a tape recorder is used, play back the tape and keep a record of the rule-breakers. If you do not use a tape recorder, assign someone in the group to keep a record of infractions. After the exercise, discuss why the infractions occurred, and how each member felt about not being able to make choices about communicative behavior.

4. Assemble your group, and prepare to discuss the issue of talking too much or too little. You have thirty (30) minutes to make a recommendation to the instructor about how to evaluate the behavior of people who dominate or fail to contribute to the group interaction. Do not concentrate only on ways of rewarding or punishing these people; the best comments should include suggestions about how to correct unsatisfactory behavior. After all the recommendations have been submitted, the instructor should read them aloud to the class. Use the remainder of the class period to discuss the merits of each recommendation. You may want to formulate a formal class policy as a result of this exercise.

4

Participating in the Small Group

Introduction

From the perspective of organizational management, participation at work should come naturally. People are employed on the strength of resumés and interviews which are supposed to provide the recruiter with indices of promise and desire to succeed (Posner, 1981). The person selected for a position with an organization should be inspired initially, ready to enter the group, capable of adapting to others and to situations, able to immediately apply the knowledge and skills necessary for competent and efficient completion of any task. After all, many managers ask, isn't this what the selection process is designed to do?

Most organizations assume that the candidate will participate. The idea of training people to work with others in small groups is either ignored or delegated to the OD (organizational development) program office. The organization is more a *proving* ground than a training ground. Training is acquired at your own expense in college, on weekends, or after work in the evenings. From the perspective of most modern organizations, you arrive on the job ready to do what you have been trained to do. As you work you will naturally develop maturity and expertise because of your ability to learn from experience and your need to overcome any deficiencies. The modern organizational employee is a symbol of the most educated, most motivated, most capable and cared for worker in the history of free enterprise (Scott and Hart, 1980).

These are the organization's expectations. The question is: Can you live up to them? Not, do you *want* to, but *can* you? We assume most people want to do well in their occupations. We take for granted that they want to attain a level of competence and reward derived from participating in work activities (Yankelovich, 1981). We also assume people will meet goals, if they understand what these are, and if they know what they need to do to reach them. Given these assumptions, there should be no conflict between organizational expectations and the ability of individuals and groups to meet them. Unfortunately, this is not the case. Despite good intentions and formal training in the skills enumerated in task descriptions (e.g., accounting, management, finance, marketing, computer science, statistics, etc.), many people experience a deep sense of *anxiety* when they arrive on the job. They have been trained to accomplish tasks alone; they have learned to be self-reliant; they have been trained to work on their own initiative, and to ignore others or work around those who do not perform as well. But they enter an organization equipped with the understanding that they must now work with others, a fact which may cause anxiety.

Here we confront some common problems. Most people *think* they know how to work with others, even when they do not. Most persons *believe* their ways of accomplishing tasks are the right ways, even when they conflict with proven organizational techniques, or their ways are demonstrably inferior. Most individuals *assume* that others will understand them, even though we know that differences of interpretation are as numerous as similarities. Last, but certainly not least, most people *want* others to be as concerned about their welfare as they are, even though they are not willing to reciprocate with equal concern. Consider the following dialogue taken from one of Oscar Wilde's fairy tales:

> "Pray, what are you laughing at?" inquired the Rocket. "I am not laughing."
> "I am laughing because I am happy," replied the Cracker.
> "That is a very selfish reason," said the Rocket angrily. "What right have you to be happy? You should be thinking about others. In fact, you should be thinking about me. I am always thinking about myself, and I expect everybody else to do the same. That is what is called sympathy."

Participating in small groups is not the same thing as "being natural." When we act naturally we are concerned with ourselves, much in the style of Oscar Wilde's Rocket. Participating in groups requires us to adapt to situations and others, to demonstrate a concern for others that we hope will be reciprocated. Through effective participation we can accomplish the tasks we are given, and thus have a better chance of meeting the expectations that organizations have set for us.

This chapter examines the idea of and necessary skills associated with participating in small groups. First, you will explore the special problem of entering a group for the first time, then draw upon this typical experience to explore the nature of participation in groups. Second, you will investigate two essential aspects of the group affecting our participation in them: the rules governing participation in the group, and the roles played or taken by other group members. Third, you will learn the skills of participating. I will provide a step-by-step analysis of participation in groups, from attending the initial meeting to planning a strategy for a future meeting. Fourth, you will examine in detail some of the problems associated with participating in small groups, and methods available for solving them. Following the chapter summary and references there will be some exercises to enable you to apply what you have learned in this and previous chapters.

Entry into the Group: Understanding the Nature of Participation

It is twenty-five minutes after eight. Your meeting is at eight-thirty, sharp. You don't want to arrive too early because there would mean a few minutes of embarrassing silence after the initial "hellos." You check your appearance one last time in the hall mirror. The clock says eight twenty-eight. One deep breath, and you're ready. You open the door to room 31-A.

"Glad to see you could make it on time," says a voice from the end of the table. "Why don't you just take this seat here next to me."

On your way to the assigned seat, you nod a greeting to the other group members. Some nod back, others seem preoccupied with the papers spread before them on the table.

The meeting begins. You are briefly introduced to the other group members, and fail to hear any of their names. The group leader apologizes for not having the time to "do a proper introduction," but says time is "a real problem today." For some reason, the group laughs when he makes this statement.

You hope you don't look as confused and uncomfortable as you feel. You stare at the papers in the space in front of you. The group leader says he hopes everyone has already had an opportunity to read the proposal, and asks for any initial reactions.

There is a moment of long silence before the woman seated next to you says "I think the idea is basically sound, but I can't understand what procedure we are supposed to use."

"Marge, if you look on pages nine through twelve I think that's all explained," replies the group leader.

"I've read those pages, Bob. I don't want to make the same mistake twice, if you know what I mean," Marge snaps back.

"I agree with Marge," pipes in a voice from the other side of the table.

A discussion over the issue of a procedure ensues. You are reading pages nine through twelve, but as yet cannot follow the arguments. Just as you complete the reading the group leader calls for consensus, gets it, and announces the next item on the agenda.

The meeting lasts nearly an hour. Time passes very quickly, and you forget to take notes. When the meeting adjourns, and you are collecting the papers given to you, you notice everyone seems to be in a hurry to get somewhere else. You had hoped that someone would stay behind to let you know what was going on. A little anger builds as you move toward the door. You hear Bob, the group leader, ask someone else what he thinks about you.

"Dunno. Didn't say anything, didn't take notes, didn't ask any questions. Looked bewildered. Hey, I wouldn't be surprised if this one doesn't last a week."

Bob laughs.

"Yeah, you may be right. I wonder what they teach these kids in college. I mean, what do they think a meeting is *for?*"

During this initial group experience our new group member suffered in a way many organizational employees can readily recognize. We know first impressions are important, but too often we prepare for our first day on the job in the wrong ways. We pay too much attention to what we are wearing, and too little attention to what we should be saying.

Our new group member made several significant mistakes. I will refer to these mistakes in examining what you should and should not do when entering a group.

Perhaps the first major mistake made by our new group member occurred long before he or she entered room 31-A. This mistake or problem confronts anyone who enters an organization and is assigned to work in a small group. We are taught to be protective of ourselves, to be concerned primarily with our own personal welfare, to "look out for number one."

Self-Centeredness versus Group-Awareness

Unfortunately, this self-centeredness is the very reverse of what must be learned if effective group communication is part of your professional responsibility. You need to learn to be aware of the group, to see it as a holistic entity, alive and changing as the inputs and and outcomes of communication are directed toward accomplishment of task and interpersonal goals. I am *not* advocating a lack of self-concern; instead I am stressing the need for balance between awareness of the group and awareness of our individual selves.

The reason you must learn to be aware of the group is analogous to why you need to learn the letters of the alphabet. In both cases these are your primary sources of information. Without knowing the letters of the alphabet you do not have access to any written document. Without acquiring an awareness of the group, you do not have access to what the group *means*. If you are to learn to understand and adapt to the needs and expectations of others in the group and to the group situation, you must acquire an awareness of the group.

How may this goal be accomplished? What should the new group member have done prior to coming to the group meeting? What should he or she have done once the meeting began?

1. *Research the organization:* You should understand the formal organizational chart, the objectives of the organization, and have some idea about how you fit into the operation. If possible, call the personnel office and ask for the names of the people working in your group or division. Explain to the personnel manager that you have just been hired and wish to become familiar with the names of your co-workers and their duties before "coming on board." Do not ask for personal information about them. It is essential to know their names and their job descriptions; do not prejudice yourself against or for them on the basis of secondary information.

Acquiring Awareness of the Group

2. *Study what you find out about the group:* Prior to attending your first group meeting, you should have a good working knowledge of its members and tasks. You should prepare a list of possible questions to ask concerning tasks and limits of responsibility. Think about the group you will be working with, and spend less time worrying about yourself. After all, you already have the job; now you must prove you can do it.

3. *Arrive a few minutes early and introduce yourself:*   Most people feel uneasy about making introductions. Do not make the mistake of believing that your group leader feels any better about introductions than you do. Arrive five to ten minutes before the meeting, and use a rehearsed introduction when you greet the other group members (e.g., "Hello, my name is _____ . I have been assigned to work with you on this project.). If you do not hear the person say his or her name after you introduce yourself, *ask what the name is.* The sooner you can associate names with faces, the better off you will be.

4. *Before you arrive know what you are supposed to do:*   Our new group member had no idea that a proposal would be the subject of discussion. Consequently, he or she looked unprepared. If necessary, call your group leader to find out what business will be conducted during your first group meeting. Arrange to obtain a copy of any printed or packaged material prior to the meeting in order to familiarize yourself with its contents. If possible, ask for a copy of the meeting's agenda. Use these sources of information to plan any statements you wish to make or questions you want to raise during the meeting.

5. *During the meeting keep a record of the interaction:*   Prepare for the meeting by developing a flow chart to fill in who-says-what-to-whom-with-what-effect. As you take notes on what is being said, also take notes on the patterns of interaction between and among group members. Our new group member failed to do this, and will probably waste considerable time trying to remember what happened during the meeting. Do not trust your memory! Write down what you can. The other group members will notice your activity and respect your integrity. Even if you say nothing during the initial meeting, your record of the activities will serve as an indication of your participation.

6. *Do not fear asking questions:*   Our new group member was confused and did not say so. He or she probably was afraid to look uninformed, and instead was thought incompetent. Which is worse? Most people respect those who ask questions, especially when the group knows that the new member probably does not have the information necessary to make a reasonable decision.

7. *Arrange to be debriefed by the group leader after the meeting:*   Our new group member expected someone to stay behind and explain what was going on in the meeting. This may occur, but do not plan on it. Ask the group leader for a brief conference following the group meeting. If you do not initiate the interaction, the group leader probably will not suggest it. People who work for a living are willing to help you out *only* when you ask for help. Avoid people who want to help you out when you don't feel you need help; these may be people more interested in spreading gossip or biasing your opinion of others than in providing you with useful information.

Each one of the above seven paragraphs directs your attention away from yourself and toward the group. People in groups want to know how you can help them, what you are able to contribute, what kind of professional image you intend to establish. These strategies can improve your awareness of the group, indicating to them your involvement with *their* tasks. Do not make the mistake made by our new group member, or by Roger:

Roger R., 21   When I graduated from college I went to work for a hospital as a staff assistant in Medical Records. I had completed a major in Health Administration with a minor in management. You've heard about the meaning of the term "sophomore"—a wise fool? Well, let me tell you there is no wiser fool than a recent college graduate. I mean I thought I was a hot number. I went to these meetings and told them what was wrong with their system. I complained about the lack of control to the division leader, and about the replication of paperwork to the secretaries. I don't think I could have made any more stupid mistakes. I was so sure I was right, and they were wrong, and I built an antagonistic relationship with everyone. Somehow, in my confused mind, I thought that by displaying my brilliance I would make them like me. The whole problem was me. I only thought about me, my needs, and my advancement. I never once gave a thought to their concerns. I was fired at the end of the summer, without references.

Our new group member wanted to make a good first impression. Because the newcomer focused on the event (e.g., the group meeting) rather than on the process of interaction represented by the event, several problems occurred:

Thinking about the "Process" versus Thinking about the "Event"

1. *A win/lose attitude was developed:*   When we are concerned about the result of an event, we tend to think in dichotomous, either/or terms. In this case, either we make a good impression or we make a bad impression on the group. Not only is this a symptom of self-concern instead of group awareness, it is also a false goal. Most judgments are both good and bad, a few minor blessings mingled with a few minor concerns for improvement. Because of the attitude of our new group member, the probable interpretation of the remarks overheard as he or she was leaving the room would be damaging instead of encouraging.
2. *A lack of attention to the interaction tended to isolate the individual from the group:*   Our new group member read the proposal instead of focusing attention on the exchanges between group members; he/she did not ask questions but chose to remain silent; the newcomer apparently did not look at the group members as they spoke. Each of these problems separated the individual from the group. Again, the problem is an inappropriate focus on the event instead of on the process of interaction.
3. *Anxiety increased instead of decreased, as a result of the meeting:* We tend to feel better about ourselves and our jobs when we make contributions to the group's activity. We may feel worse about

ourselves and our jobs when we expect to make a contribution but fail to do so. Our new group member was anxious upon entering the room, and left the room even more anxious after the experience. Instead of thinking about what could be learned from the meeting, our newcomer was concerned about how the group members responded to him or her as a person. This inappropriate attention to the event reduced the ability to derive useful information from the process of interaction.

Communication creates relationships between and among people. When you fail to consider the notion of process, you fail to see the connection of the individual events and thus lessen your ability to adapt to them.

Entry into the group can be an anxiety-producing situation. You can overcome feelings of anxiety by (1) developing group awareness, and (2) thinking about the process of communication. In this section I have reviewed procedures for assuring your successful entry into a small group. I do not claim to be able to rid you of anxiety; I do believe you can make better use of anxiety if you are prepared for communication. If I have made entry into the group seem like a terrifying experience, then listen to the report made by Sara, a young woman who followed my advice:

> **Sara McQ., 23**   I know you'll appreciate this, after all the guff I gave you in our groups' class last summer. I took your advice about how to prepare for entering the group. I knew I was hired in part because I'm female, and I'm an engineer, and they needed me for the wrong reasons. But I wanted to prove myself. I prepared for the meeting just like you said I should, and when I went into the meeting room for the first time, I established myself as a thoroughly prepared member of the team. I know I surprised these guys, and I loved every minute of it. But I didn't carry it too far. I realized the need to think about the process of creating relationships and took my time. You know what? Last month I was promoted—and I've got to admit that studying how groups operate has made a real difference in my professional life.

Participating in small groups requires preparation and communication. Preparation includes *thinking* about the nature of the group, its membership, its goals, its methods of reaching goals, and its history. Preparation means *determining* what you can say and do in the particular situation in order to gain the responses you want. Preparation means *adapting* to the needs of the group and the situation by thinking through the group process, then determining whether or not your personal goals can be met in the group. Preparation is the key to effective entry into the group and to each subsequent group meeting. By thinking about the group, determining what you can say and do, adapting to the needs of the group and situation, you prepare yourself for communicating in the group.

Communication includes *what you say and do* to gain responses from other group members, the *responses* (both verbal and nonverbal) you receive from them, and the *exchange of talk* between and among group members who are solving problems, making decisions, or carrying out tasks. Communication is the life-blood of any group, because through exchanges of information and persuasion group members accomplish their goals (or fail to accomplish them). Communication depends on the ability of the group members to prepare adequately for the discussion situation, and to adapt their words to the needs of the situation and of others.

Preparation and communication are interdependent activities. You prepare for a meeting to communicate more effectively; you communicate more effectively better to prepare for future group interactions. In this section I have defined participation in the small group as the result of *choices* made about the outcomes desired from working in the group. Two additional influences affect how these choices are made by group members: the rules governing participation in the group, and the roles taken or played by group members.

Rules and Roles in the Small Group

All groups operate with rules. Societies develop laws for the protection of their citizens. Nations ratify constitutions governing internal affairs and foreign policies governing foreign affairs. Towns and cities allocate taxes to improve schools or build new highways. Corporations develop guidelines for employee relations, and regulations which determine how the company will operate. Even when we come together informally we are aware of rules of etiquette and social politeness. When we play games we want to know what the rules are; when we invent games we draw up new rules to govern the action.

A rule is a "norm" or standard for the group. I have already discussed how rules are created by individuals in groups or organizations. You have studied the effects of formal regulations and informal codes of conduct. You have seen how the four propositions of the Equity Theory explain the development of rules in groups as well as their enforcement. Important as all of these preliminary considerations are, you still may only be able to offer very generalized descriptions of how rules operate, how they may affect a given group. In this section you will look more closely at rules and groups, with the object of establishing ways and means to recognize the existence of group rules, and procedures for altering them.

You are also familiar with the term *roles*. I have discussed the concept of roles as identifiable characteristics of individuals which enable us to relate to them in specific and predictable ways. We know people can "play" roles in small groups; we also know that individuals can choose roles, making them up as they go along. In this section you will examine more closely the concept of roles in small groups, with the object of identifying some common roles acted out by group members. Using these roles as a standard, you will then investigate how individuals create new roles for themselves in group settings. I will propose an *active* view of the role-making and playing process, based on the predicted outcomes projected by the group member making the choice among roles. Let's begin this section with an examination of the rules affecting small group operations.

We probably know rules when we violate them. Watzlawick, Beavin, and Jackson (1967) point out rule-violators are thought to be either "mad or bad." Shimanoff (1980) argues for a way of conceptualizing rules and rule-violations from behavior: the existence of rules can be inferred from the behavior of individuals as they communicate. If she is right (and most researchers agree she is), then you should be able to identify the rules affecting a group's operation and adapt to them *before* you unknowingly violate them and are judged "mad or bad." The important question is "how?"

Before you can know how to recognize rules in groups, you need to understand more precisely what a rule is. Shimanoff (1980, pp. 37–136) defines three common characteristics of a rule:

*Characteristics of
Communication Rules*

1. *A rule can be obeyed:* If the existence of a rule is known, then individuals have the ability to choose to follow (or not to follow) it. Ganz (1971) uses the followable principle of rules to distinguish them from laws. You cannot choose to obey the laws of motion or gravity or the speed of light. To be obeyed, a rule must be such that one is *physically* capable of obeying it.

2. *A rule is prescriptive:* If the existence of a rule is known, then violating the rule can result in punishment. Rules do not exist for themselves; they are created by people who have *uses* for them. Rules are used to guide an operation, to provide a way of recognizing good or bad, right or wrong, appropriate or inappropriate actions, to reward adherence and punish deviations. To be prescriptive, a rule must specify a preference for certain behavior, which may be used by group members to evaluate all other behaviors.

3. *A rule is contextual:* Rules may be familiar for a number of group situations; or they may also change according to the specific needs of a group in a particular situation. For example, it is generally unacceptable to eat food with your hands. However, at picnics and other informal situations, we may eat chicken with our hands and not be judged mad or bad. Though we all know or admit the existence of a general rule regarding eating, we are also conscious of circumstantial modifications of the general rule.

Using Shimanoff's three characteristics of a rule, you can understand how rules are created by groups, and how they use rules to guide their activities. Knowing what a rule is, you can now recognize how rules affect behavior.

Think about what would happen if there were no rules to govern a group's activities. Anyone could say and do anything, regardless of whether what was done helped or hindered the group's ability to reach a goal. Essentially, given your constitutional right of free speech, you are at liberty to say or do anything. However, you also have corresponding responsibilities not to infringe on the freedoms of others while exercising your own. There are laws which protect us from chaotic behavior.

But laws are not enough; we also need rules. We need to be aware of generally accepted systems of treating each other equitably while pursuing our own goals. Because people differ in the goals they pursue, we need *flexible* rules. In Shimanoff's terminology, we need rules that can be modified because of situational or circumstantial differences. These rules govern our communication. They inform us how we ought to speak in the presence of others, although we always have the choice of *not* following them or of formulating new rules when the old rules seem inapplicable. But how do rules govern communication? Shimanoff provides three identifying characteristics of rule-generated communication:

1. *Rule-generated communication is controllable.*   People are accountable to other people for their words and actions; and rules are often the source of this accountability. When you wish to exercise *control* over someone else, you usually make use of a precept rule to direct the other person's actions. This individual still can choose not to follow your advice, but if he or she does not follow it, that person is accountable to you.

Characteristics of Rule-Generated Communication

2. *Rule-generated communication is amenable to criticism.*   Behavior is the primary source of information about people. When you criticize someone, you are judging behavior by a rule which you think allows you to evaluate it. All behavior is thus open to criticism; however, the critic is responsible for identifying the rule or standard used to make the evaluation.

3. *Rule-generated communication is contextual.*   Again, there are different rules for different situations and groups. Some scholars argue that in order to be ascribed to a rule, behavior must occur at least 95% of the time if we are to attribute the communication to the rule (in Shimanoff, 1980, p. 103). The use of 95% as a guide is based on statistical reliability, however, and may not be the best determinant of whether or not a rule actually exists; what if the behavior only occurs 90% of the time? In my view it should still count as a rule, despite the fact it lacks statistical reliability.

These three characteristics of rule-generated communication provide fertile ground for observing the operation of rules in small groups. Whenever a group member criticizes another group member or attempts to use a norm to control behavior, you *may* be seeing the operation of a rule. (You may also be seeing the operation of a personal preference not indicative of the group's shared feeling.) If the behavior is consistently controlled by more than one group member, a group rule may apply. If no other group member objects to the criterion or control, then you may assume the existence of a group rule.

Now let's take a closer look at some rules operating in small groups. When we look at *participation* in groups, we must first specify the type of group so as to understand how rules governing participation may be inferred. Julia Wood (1979) found three types of small groups, each with its preference in leadership behavior.

Rules in Groups

You can use Wood's typology of groups and their leaders as a starting point to discuss how rules are created by different kinds of groups (from Wood, 1979, p. 269).

1. *Task-oriented groups:* The ideal leader of a task-oriented group is expected to possess very high intellectual and organizational competencies and to display a moderately high degree of team spirit. He or she need not be particularly attractive personally.
2. *Socially oriented groups:* The ideal leader of a socially oriented group is expected to be extremely attractive personally and to display a moderately high degree of team spirit. He or she is not necessarily expected to possess keen organizational or intellectual abilities.
3. *Dually oriented groups* (Integration of task and social goals): The ideal leader of a dually oriented group is expected to possess very high intellectual and organizational competencies, to display moderately strong team spirit, and to be moderately highly attractive personally.

The expectations group members have for the leader reveal some starting points for rules. Because task-oriented groups look for leaders to possess intellectual and organizational competencies, you can expect that rules about how group work is conducted will be a major concern of group members. Because task-oriented groups assume that leaders will reflect team spirit, you can expect rules about cohesiveness to emerge from the group. From the general characteristics of what group members require of a leader, you may infer the presence of certain rules and the absence of others. If you are not sensitive to these rule-governed features of the group, you may learn as Susan had to:

Susan A., 20 When I was in high school I was very active in groups. I was a cheerleader and the president of a sorority. So when we were asked to choose a leader for our groups in class, I was not surprised to be chosen. I know how to get along with others, I always have. Unfortunately, I did not know how different this group would be. We were assigned tasks, given time limits, and our grades depended on the quality of our oral reports. All the skills I learned in social groups did not make me an effective leader of this task group. After the third miserable week I resigned and turned the leadership role over to Vince. Vince is kind of dull, but he gets the work done. Nobody likes him very much, but that doesn't seem to matter here.

Susan's problem was inability to adapt to the specific needs of her group. She was a very effective leader in social groups, which, as you have seen, required different attributes for leadership. But when she was placed in charge of a task-oriented group, she lacked the organizational skills necessary to accomplish the work and win the loyalty of group members. The rules had changed, but Susan didn't know it.

Organizations make use of the three kinds of groups. The majority of organizations believe task-oriented groups to be the focus of most organizational work. Problem-solving and decision-making groups must accomplish their tasks if the organization is to survive. Production teams, committees, and other groups within the organization rely on the ability of smaller groups to accomplish tasks. Organizations also include social groups, some more official than others. In an earlier chapter I discussed the role of informal groups in the organization, pointing out the voluntary nature of their membership. Since informal or social groups operate with organizational information but without organizational sanction, these groups greatly influence the work of task-oriented groups. Perhaps the most powerful group in an organization is dually oriented. Within such groups, tasks are accomplished with a high premium being placed on good relations and team spirit among group members.

These three kinds of groups indicate where you should look for rules. They do *not* tell you what the rules are. Remember, changes in circumstances or situations often mean changes in rules affecting group members. A task-oriented group of mechanical engineers may not place much value on interpersonal attractiveness; however, a task-oriented group of fashion models may place a great deal of value on such traits. Now that you have examined some of the bases for rules in groups, you should observe how specific rules emerge in specific group contexts. Read through the following examples:

Diego VeJ., 23 At work it is the youngest guy who gets coffee at break for everyone. I don't know how it got started, I just know it is, man.

Candy P., 29 When a new woman joins our firm, I always make sure one of us takes her to lunch during the first week. We provide the basic information about the company she won't find in the policies manual, and we find out what kind of human being she is. She won't know she's being interviewed, but essentially that is exactly what we do. If we decide the company has made a mistake, we put the information through the right channels and usually get our way. We will not sacrifice our end of the office for anyone.

Jack W., 18 We begin with a prayer and then get down to business. No business is ever discussed before the prayer. We are serious about asking God's blessing on our work.

Phyllis S., 25 At lunch we all get together and play cards. For the last two months we haven't had anything to do; I've read six novels at work during that time. So I asked Ben why we just don't continue to play all afternoon. You wouldn't have believed the response he gave me! It was like I had just committed murder. "That's going too far," he said. He didn't speak to me for the rest of the week, but I think everything is back to normal now.

Wendy N., 31 Working for the government you learn the importance of being stupid. Don't ask too many questions, just fill in the blanks. If you don't know something, never ask anyone about it, just pretend you do know. Maybe I sound a little harsh, but I work in procurement and I see how the money is spent. It irks me to see just how important knowing the GS-15 is. Whatever Mr. J _____ says is the law around here, even when he's too hungover to hand it down himself.

As a participant in a small group you need to discover what rules govern the operation of your group. Here are some rules for finding the rules of your small group:

1. *What does your group do regularly?*   First, define the nature of your small group: task-oriented, social, or dually oriented activities. Second, observe the process of interaction. Who calls the meeting to order? Who says what to whom with what effect? Who has power and why? Third, observe whether there is punishment for infractions of rules. What behaviors are regularly corrected? What behaviors are sanctioned?

2. *What do the rules induce the group to accomplish?*   Rules are used to help guide a group toward its goal. *Why* are certain behaviors sanctioned and others forbidden? What purposes do the rules serve? Who benefits from enforcement of the rules? Who suffers from enforcement of the rules? Do the rules change with the addition of a new group member? If so, why?

3. *Do the rules carry over into other organizational contexts?*   Some rules are more compelling than others. Certain precepts operate only within a specific small group context, while others operate across organizational lines. For example, the manager or supervisor is usually accorded the respect of his or her position regardless of the place. Rules governing communication in the presence of a manager usually do not change during working hours, or even beyond the workplace.

Rules existed prior to your entry into the group. These are the precepts you *confront;* they are already being used to govern the behavior of group members. Rules can also be *created* (see Donohue, et. al., 1980, for a review of the rules' perspectives). When rules are drawn up, they are formulated by virtue of agreements by group members to act in a prescribed way. For example, the decision to implement Standard Agenda or Delphi Technique to organize the group's work, instead of any existing procedure would constitute a major change of rules.

For group members seeking to improve participation, a necessary task is to determine what rules are currently in force. Because of the existence of a system of equity within any group, rule-violators are generally punished rather than rewarded. Before any new rules can be formulated, the wise group member acquires a thorough understanding of the precepts now in force.

The Roles: Creating and Confronting Identities and Scripts

What is a role?

When you think of roles you generally associate the term with actors and actresses on stage, the roles they play. In this sense a role is a dramatization of a character or person. You understand that actors play many different roles, often contradictory in nature. For example, you may have seen the actor Richard

Chamberlain play both Dr. Kildare and Hamlet, or the actress Meryl Streep play a variety of characters, from Woody Allen's ex-wife in *Manhattan,* Robert DeNiro's companion in *The Deer Hunter,* or the fateful temptress in *The French Lieutenant's Woman.*

Just as actors and actresses play different roles in films and on stage, so also people play various roles in diverse group settings. Think of the variety of roles you play: student, child, sibling, worker, lover, companion, enemy, perhaps parent or teacher. In each one of these roles you choose behavioral patterns to fit the mental image you have of what you are supposed to be and to do. Your word choices vary from the simple to the complex, your manner may change from the easy-going to the frantic, your sense of humor may alter from the polite to the profane. You alter behavior in different roles to elicit the desired responses from others who try to coordinate their roles with yours. This is the one way in which we "coordinate the management of meaning" (Cronen and Pierce, 1978).

Think of a rule this way: Unless you have someone to act as a parent, you cannot play a child; unless you have someone to listen and take notes while you lecture, you cannot be a teacher. Roles are adapted to the needs of other people and of situations. The role you play out in one situation with a particular small group usually changes when you have to adapt to the needs of other people in a different small group.

Researchers examining the roles played by small group members usually use verbal statements as bases for determining what roles are available, and what roles are chosen (see Goldhaber, 1979, pp. 238–40 for an overview). Based on the early work of Benne and Sheats (1948), researchers generally discuss three types of roles in groups: task-oriented roles, maintenance-oriented roles, and self-oriented roles.

Task-oriented roles contribute to the ability of the group to accomplish its objectives. With this goal in mind, behaviors generally associated with organizing and evaluating work accomplished by the group can be identified. The behaviors include:

1. *Initiating interaction:* Stating the task or charge, defining the problem, establishing the procedure or agenda, contributing new ideas or opinions, asking questions.

   Task-Oriented Roles

2. *Giving information/seeking opinions:* Making statements relative to the task, asking questions about statements made by others, presenting data, and asking for evaluations.
3. *Giving opinions/seeking group's evaluation of the opinion:* Making statements based on guesses, hunches, inferences, etc., and then asking group members for responses to the statements made.
4. *Elaborating or clarifying ideas:* Making statements about the meaning or intention of a statement made or a question asked by another group member, providing additional information about the idea or opinion.
5. *Orienting and summarizing:* Provides reviews of past decisions or actions made by the group pertaining to this problem, and also furnishes reviews of ideas presented during the meeting.

6. *Consensus testing:* Asking whether or not the group is ready to make a decision or reach tentative agreement about a statement, idea, or suggestion.

These are the *communicative* behaviors associated with accomplishing the task. If one group member consistently provides a particular communication behavior (e.g., elaborates or clarifies an idea), then the group will probably rely on that person to perform that role. When the communication in the group becomes routinized or standard, you then say the group members have *established roles.*

Maintenance Roles *Maintenance-oriented roles* contribute to the ability of the group to create and maintain efficient, effective, and pleasant interpersonal relations between and among group members. With this goal in mind, it is possible to identify communicative behaviors generally associated with organizing and evaluating how group members relate to each other. These behaviors include:

1. *Harmonizing:* Reducing tension, usually with the introduction of humor.
2. *Compromising:* Offering a consensus-producing accommodation involving two or more alternative positions being argued by group members.
3. *Supporting and encouraging:* Giving praise or agreement with statements or questions contributed by other group members.
4. *Gatekeeping:* Opening the discussion to reticent or unincluded group members; channeling the flow of interaction between and among group members.
5. *Establishing criteria and assessing group feelings:* Defining standards by which to measure the effectiveness of a solution or decision, or asking for group member's feelings about an issue.

These are *communication* behaviors associated with facilitating pleasant and effective small group relationships. If one individual in the group consistently exhibits a particular kind of behavior (e.g., offers a compromise position), the group will probably rely on him or her to continue to act in that way. When the group begins to expect behavior of a particular kind from a particular individual, then that individual is said to be performing a *role* in the group.

Self-Oriented Roles *Self-oriented roles* do not contribute to the well-being of the group or to the group's ability to accomplish the task. As you learned earlier in this chapter, focusing attention on one's self is not a productive way of entering a group. Communication behaviors associated with self-oriented roles include:

1. *Blocking:* Refusing to accept the ideas or opinions of others in the group, preventing the group from achieving consensus.
2. *Withdrawing:* Refusing to contribute to the group's interaction, avoiding the topic, remaining indifferent to the discussion.

3. *Dominating:* Interrupting other group members, refusing to accept the conclusions of others as more reasonable than one's own, trying to procure a leadership position by intimidating others.
4. *Being aggressive:* Boasting, criticizing, threatening other group members.

All these are *communication* behaviors associated with self-oriented roles. If a particular group member regularly acts in one or several of these ways, the group will expect that person to continue to do so (unfortunately). When this occurs, the group establishes a *role* for the individual.

When the characteristics of each behavioral category are combined in a description of an individual group member's behavior, you have a composite picture of his or her *role*. For example, simply focusing on the maintenance behaviors, without also including task and perhaps self-oriented behaviors, produces a weak or one-sided view of how an individual communicates in the group.

If people always behaved consistently, then roles would be easily defined. However, people change their roles by adapting their choices of behavior to the goals they have for the given case. Consider the following example:

Mary C., 35   Sure I made an effort to change. In the beginning, I was always doing the "woman's" work for the group: keeping a record of the meeting, typing, filing, you know, the secretarial skills. I had a master's degree in biochemistry and I was still being treated like a high school graduate. But I came to realize it was at least partially my own damn fault. I *acted* like a secretary. I volunteered to keep the records, and when I saw a coffee cup empty, I filled it. No wonder my group treated me as they did. I asked to be treated that way. But I didn't like it, so I changed. It took awhile; you can't change the way people act toward you overnight, but now things are very different. I made substantive contributions where I used to just agree with what somebody else said. I question more, I do more homework. I'm too busy to get coffee now.

As you can see by Mary's testimony, the idea of a role is very closely connected to the concept of identity. To change her identity, Mary had to make a concerted effort to change her role. But to change her role, she had to alter specific communication behaviors.

Communication Roles and Identity

Before you investigate communicative behaviors associated with effective participation in small groups, you need to consider the connection between role and identity. Phillips and Metzger (1976) argue that *confirmation of identity is the prime human goal.* In our minds we create an image of who and what we are, then we use communication with others to determine how successful we are in confirming our mental image. For example, I can declare myself to be a great American writer, but unless others treat me as a great American writer I cannot reasonably confirm the identity I seek.

People enter groups with pre-established identities. However, they also enter groups seeking to confirm or alter their identities, and this may cause problems for the group. For example, if an individual who has a history of leading small groups is suddenly placed in a group setting where he or she is not the leader, the old mental image and the present situation may come into conflict. The individual can choose to sublimate the desire to lead to enable the group to accomplish its objectives, or that person can try to show for why he or she should be the leader. In the latter choice, the likely outcome is conflict in the group.

Identity is so vital to us that we are willing to do almost anything to confirm it. In a positive vein, this is why we have goals and work systematically to reach them. In a negative sense, this explains why we suffer the human impulses or envy, lust, jealousy, greed, and other maladies of interpersonal relations (Farber, 1978). Some researchers (Pierce, 1976) explain the relationship between role and identity by examining what they refer to as *lifescripts*.

A *lifescript* is how you see yourself in relation to others and to goals. For example, most students create their lifescripts based on the majors they choose and on the images of success beyond college which they associate with these interests. Marketing majors may see themselves as corporate vice-presidents in the near future (despite the fact that very few individuals achieve this goal). They envision their path to the vice-presidency, and imagine what their lives will be like *en route*. Very often these goals influence how individuals conduct themselves while still in school. Instead of wearing tennis shoes, dirty t-shirts, and faded jeans to class, they choose three-piece suits. They may enter into relationships with older people, especially their instructors or people working in the business community. The thrust of this example is not to evaluate the behavior as good or bad, but rather to point out the connection between one's lifescript and its influence on day-to-day activities (especially the choices they make about how they look and act.)

When you work in groups, you must understand you are working with people, who, like yourself, have visions of the future which inform the choices they make in the present. You do not simply respond to behaviors; you also respond to what you perceive to be *images, personalities,* and *lifescripts.* The role a person chooses to play in a small group may or may not accurately represent the actual image, personality, or lifescript. If a person seems consistently dissatisfied, or habitually performs self-oriented behaviors, that individual may be making a statement about *identity* rather than about the group or its task.

One small group researcher, Ernest Bormann (1972), elaborates the idea of identity of individuals as a key factor of participation, roles chosen, and patterns of interaction, to discuss the group's identity. In a fascinating critique, Bormann develops the idea of *fantasy themes* based on the group's image of itself and its work. A fantasy theme is analogous to a lifescript. It is an image of the identity of the group based on shared perceptions, communication, and feelings about future destinies. We tend to think of influences as being generated by individuals; Bormann provides an alternative view of influence as being shaped by the group's vision of itself.

You have observed how rules influence choices made about communication in small groups. You have also perceived how roles are created by group members in relation to their goals for communication and their sense of personal and group identity. Now you need to consider how rules and roles coalesce in small groups to influence choices concerning participation.

Integrating Rules and Roles

I have repeatedly stated that you have choices to make about your own behavior in small groups. You can choose to live by the rules or violate them, to play a particular part or to select some other role. You can elect to make a statement, ask a question, or remain silent. Your ability to *choose among available behaviors* based on your own assessment of goals, outcomes, needs of situation, and needs of others points to the *active* view of participating in small groups. You are *not* a passive receiver of the group's influences; you are active in shaping its activities.

The questions then arise: How can I make the best choices about my behavior in my group? How can I best participate? How can I make the most of my knowledge of rules and roles to adapt my behavior to the particular challenge in a rewarding way? Since no two groups or situations are exactly alike, there is no one way to make your decisions about participation. However, there are some useful guidelines. In virtually every group situation, you will find (Phillips & Metzger, 1976; Phillips, Pedersen, and Wood, 1979):

1. *Goals* being sought by each participant.
2. *Approved rules, procedures, and constraints* exerting influence upon the choices made by the participants about behavior.
3. *Strategies in the form of roles* directed by individuals at individuals and the group.
4. *Monitoring of behavior* and selection of responses.

Guidelines for Participating in Groups

All these sources of influence should be considered in preparing for group interaction. To integrate best what you know about rules and roles, you should prepare for interactions by (Phillips & Metzger, 1976; Phillips, Pedersen, and Wood, 1979):

1. Setting goals and showing awareness of other's goals.
2. Understanding what is legitimate (acceptable) and what is illegitimate (unacceptable) as talk and behavior in the group.
3. Analyzing the recipients of communication to discover what appeals would be most effective (think about *their* goals).
4. Selecting appeals to be used and fitting them within the role you have established in the group.
5. Maintaining, modifying, discontinuing the role depending on whether it can further the attainment of your own good and that of the group, as well as confirm your desired identity within the group.
6. Estimating the cost of your behavior against the rewards received in the group, and making decisions about whether the role will elicit the desired responses and develop the desired relationships with others in the group.

The above procedure should be used in making decisions about participating in groups. This procedure does not guarantee success in the group; it merely provides a way of determining what you want to have happen as a result of participating and how you best attain the desired outcomes through statements made, questions asked, and silence in the small group.

We have reviewed the general standards for choices about participation in small groups. Now you are ready to investigate specific communication behaviors associated with participation.

The Skills of Participating in Small Groups

Before you read this section, consider what Tommy found out about participating in small groups:

> **Tommy W., 24**   I went to work for _____ and they put me in a group. I was told to attend group meetings, prepare to discuss what was on the agenda, and add items to the agenda at least twenty-four hours in advance of any meeting. That was it. No other instructions were given. I consider myself a reasonably bright fellow; when someone tells me what to do, I am usually able to deliver. So I followed the instructions I was given. I attended the meetings, prepared myself for discussions, added items to the agenda, and found myself on probation four months later. Why? Because I did not understand what participation meant. I interrupted people, I added items to the agenda the group had already discussed, I spent most of my time trying to get the group members to like me, and I did not monitor what I said or did in the meetings. In retrospect, I acted like a fool. Why didn't somebody tell me there was more to a group meeting than that? I thought participating was telling a good joke. Unfortunately, the joke ended up being on me.

Tommy thought he knew what participation meant.

I began this chapter by pointing out that most organizations assume competence in group communication skills. Based on this assumption, organizations establish standards to measure individual and group performances on the job. If you do not measure up to those standards, you may find yourself like Tommy, on probationary status or worse. No matter what you think "ought" to be the case, you should know organizations expect people to arrive for work already possessing the skills of participation which will allow them to contribute effectively to the group's work.

In this section you will proceed through a step-by-step analysis of the skills of participating in a small group.

1. Attending the Meeting   You cannot participate unless you attend. You should arrange your schedule to arrive on time, prepared to discuss the items on the agenda. Remember there is an important difference between *active* and *passive* participation. To be an active participant in the group, you need to prepare for discussion. Do not assume you will "know what to say" or "when to say it." Always prepare for group interactions.

Prepare for the items on the agenda. Most group leaders will circulate an agenda prior to a group meeting. Read through these items and write down any initial responses you have to any of them. If you need to add an item to the agenda, inform the group leader and arrange to modify the agenda at the beginning of the group meeting.

Prepare for specific discussions. Based on your past experiences with the group, you should be able to predict what items will spark controversy or consensus. Use this information to determine how you can best contribute to the group's operation during the meeting. For example, should you play "devil's advocate" on an issue on which the group will achieve unanimous consensus? Do you have special information to furnish to the group? Have you thought of an important question to raise? When and how you will contribute to the group should be part of your preparation for the interaction.

Prepare a list of personal goals for the meeting. It is essential for each group member to know what he or she wants to have happen as a result of participating in a group interaction. Think about the *task;* what goals do you have concerning it? Think about the *interpersonal relations* in the group; what goals do you have concerning relations with other group members? Think about *yourself;* what personal goals do you have for the meeting? How do these goals fit into the group's objectives? If they conflict, what can you do about it?

I have emphasized the goals and objectives of group meetings, since I believe it is easier to attain objectives and goals if you know what they are before you talk. Consequently, I advise you to read over the agenda with the objectives of the group in mind.

2. Understanding the Charge and the Objectives of the Group

Know the group's charge. If you are entering a group, ask the leader what the charge is. If you are already in the group, make sure you understand what the task or assignment is, who is responsible for it, and to whom the group must finally report after the work is carried out. Keep the charge in mind as you prepare items for the agenda, and think about how you want to contribute to the group's operation at the meeting.

Establish group objectives for the meeting. Beyond your own personal goals for the meeting, you should think about what the group ought to accomplish at this session. If you were the leader, what would be your objectives for this meeting? How would you attempt to reach them?

Listening is a critical communication skill. Paying attention to others provides information about them and their perceptions of the group's task. No one likes to feel as if he or she is not being listened to. In most group settings, special listening courtesy should be accorded to the group leader.

3. Listening to the Leader

Prepare to listen to the leader. You need to be mentally and physically ready to listen. Try exclude distracting or extraneous ideas and concerns from your mind prior to attending the meeting. When you arrive, your only concern should be what will be covered by the participants during the session. Any other subject must be excluded. The leader will open the meeting; pay close attention to what she or he says and does. Items may be added to the agenda, and you will need to note them. The leader may introduce new information or procedures during the first few minutes. Look at the leader, listen to what is being said, and respond as an *informed* participant.

Provide verbal and nonverbal responses. As you listen, make nonverbal responses to the message: nodding your head, frowning, or smiling. After the leader has spoken, formulate your verbal response to the message. Remember: it is not always necessary to provide verbal responses. Ask yourself whether or not what you intend to say has bearing on the discussion. You should think about the outcomes of your responses before deciding to speak.

4. Listening to Other Group Members

Although the leader usually provides direction for the discussion, the other group members contribute to it. People who listen only to the leader develop poor reputations with the rest of the group. Courtesy requires that if you want the other group members to listen carefully to what you say then you must reciprocate by listening carefully to what they say.

Prepare to listen to the group. Before each group meeting prepare yourself for how you believe each group member will respond to the subjects on the agenda. What possible conflicts may arise? What will each group member contribute? Who could make a valuable contribution, but will need you to involve him or her in the discussion? Prepare a mental map for the communication territory of the small group meeting.

Prepare to respond to others. Providing verbal and nonverbal responses is indispensable to effective group interaction. Let other group members know how you are responding to their messages. Do not wait until you have the opportunity to speak; prepare the other group members for your comments.

5. Preparing for the Discussion

You are responsible for being prepared at each group meeting. Preparation means more than simply knowing what items are to be discussed, or simply attending the meeting and being a polite listener. Preparation means that you spend time and effort to analyze the *issues* before the group and the *group members*.

Prepare to contribute ideas and arguments to the discussion. The issues confronting the group affect you. You should have some ideas on which to base your communication or statement. You should therefore be able to prepare cogent arguments in support of your case. Remember, "groupthink" occurs when consensus is reached for any reason other than acceptance of the best argument. Help prevent "groupthink" by preparing the best arguments to support your position. If you believe "groupthink" may be operating, you may need to play the "devil's advocate" role in order to present alternative positions.

Prepare to exhibit flexible behavior with the group members. You realize that group interaction consists of exchanges of messages designed to persuade others to reach consensus. People are encouraged to disagree, conflict is brought out and must be managed. You know that effective group members prepare for discussions by analyzing the situation, the agenda, the issues, and the other group members, so as better to predict and to control the outcomes. One important aspect of your preparation for discussion is to become flexible in choosing appropriate behaviors. The person capable of flexible behavior realizes that any message can be expressed in a variety of ways and accepts responsibility for selecting a form of expression adapted to the situation and the needs of others. There is no good reason to hurt the feelings of those in your group. In preparing to communicate, think about how your messages could exhibit most consideration for the rights of others in your group. Remember: A group rewards those members who treat others *equitably*.

One of the best ways to prepare for discussion is to think about the questions you can raise concerning items on the agenda. You have already learned that questions are a safer form of speech than are statements. Questions elicit responses from group members, often initiating interaction on an important issue, or redirecting the talk to the issue at hand.

6. Asking Relevant Questions

Prepare questions about facts. Learn to be responsive to the group's need for accurate information. Think about the information available to the group and ask whether or not there is more or better information elsewhere. How can you obtain the information? How long will it take to receive the information? How do we know the information we have is the best available information? Should be rely on these sources? What other sources are available? Is this reliable information? Is the source of the information dependable?

Prepare questions about values. Learn to be sensitive to the underlying values expressed by other group members. Be able to ask whether or not the values being represented are the most appropriate for the issue being discussed. Be concerned about the ethical implications of the group's decision-making and problem-solving processes. What are the marks of a "good" decision? What does a "reasonable" solution include? Who is likely to profit from your outcomes? Who would probably be hurt? What is your responsibility to whomever uses the information or policy you furnish? Would I be willing to have the solution based on my proposal?

Prepare questions about policies. Groups often are used to generate ideas leading to statements of policy or procedure in an organization. The policy may be the solution to a company problem, or it may be based on the group's decision about some issue. Groups responsible for providing input to develop policy decisions should know what questions to raise so as best to shape a policy decision.

Who is being harmed? What is the weakness in the present system?
How can we document this weakness or harm?
What is likely to happen if we do nothing?
What criteria should we use to judge the worth of a proposed solution?
What are the financial limitations?
What are the logistical limitations?

What are the limitations for persuasion? (Who must we persuade?)

What are some alternative proposals?

How do these proposals meet the criteria and limitations specified?

Is the proposal practical?

Is the proposal feasible? (Can it be implemented?)

Is the proposal advantageous? (Will it cause new weaknesses or harms?)

In later chapters you will study each of these questions in greater detail. At this point, you should be aware of the need to ask these questions when policy issues are brought before the group.

7. Offering Suggestions and Giving Advice

Everyone has opinions, and if pressed, nearly everyone is willing to give advice about almost anything. Offering suggestions and giving advice are valuable tasks and interpersonal skills in small groups, but care must be taken to use these skills sparingly.

Do not give advice or offer suggestions about matters outside the purview of the group. Your concern should be with what happens *during* group meetings, not what goes on elsewhere. Do not use the group meeting as an encounter session or a truth-telling session about the deficiencies or misdemeanors of the organization.

Ask yourself whether or not the advice you are about to give is really necessary. Always try to be aware of the purpose to be served by statements you make or questions you ask. Avoid self-serving motives and concentrate on other-centered outcomes when offering suggestions or giving advice. Think about how the suggestion or advice will affect the group.

8. Providing Useful Information

The duty of each small group member is to provide useful information reflecting her or his expertise and past experience with the issue being considered. Most people are chosen to be members of small groups in organizations because they possess a special talent or knowledge relevant to that group's activities.

Know what you are expected to contribute to the group. Find out why you were assigned to the group and ascertain the limits of your informational responsibilities. When you receive an agenda, examine it for items specifically pertaining to your area of expertise and prepare to speak on it.

Present your ideas in an organized manner. Effective group participants are organized speakers. Aristotle pointed out the best form for statements over two thousand years ago: state your claim and then provide support for it. In the last chapter we developed the bases of argument according to this basic form. Learn them and use them to present your ideas to the group in an organized manner.

Invite responses to your statements. If you are uncertain about how your information is being received by other group members, ask them. Do not be afraid of inviting responses; it is better to share meaning than to make guesses about it. Also, by asking for criticism from other group members, you encourage a reciprocal arrangement whereby you may be asked for your responses to their messages. Such reciprocity should aid the group in accomplishing its tasks.

During the group meeting your attention should focus on the exchange of messages between and among group members. Listening and responding in the immediate situation is different from considered evaluations formed after you have had time to reflect on the content of exchanges during the meeting. When you have some leisure time, think back over the meeting, consulting your notes. How did what actually happened during the meeting fit your expectations? What new information did you acquire about (1) the task, (2) the interpersonal relationships between and among group members, and (3) your standing with the group?

9. Evaluating the Responses Made by Others

To think of the *process* of group communication reflects an appreciation of the connectedness of group activities. Avoid considering each meeting as an "event," a single happening during which messages are exchanged. Train yourself to be responsive to the process of the interaction, the flow of ideas in and out of all group meetings, the relationships between and among group members developed over a period of time. Learn to accept the tentativeness of group communication, the complexity of human relationships.

10. Preparing for the Next Group Meeting

When you learn to perceive group communication as a process of creating relationships and actions, you need to develop a systematic and disciplined approach to participating in your group. Effective group participation is a skill that must be cultivated over a period of time; the more practice and experience you gain, the better able you should be to interact effectively. You should try to set aside at least thirty minutes to debrief yourself about the content of the group meeting. Compare your expectations with the actual outcomes. Compare the agenda with what really transpired. Assess the progress made by the group toward attaining its objectives. Assess the relationships between and among group members. Evaluate your own standing and participation in the group. What can you do to improve?

When you have been given an assignment, complete it thoroughly as soon as possible. Do not procrastinate! If you are to do the job in a manner that will gain the respect and praise of other group members, you will need as much time as you can find. You may need to research the assignment in the library, through interviews with experts, through informal talks with people who can provide assistance. You will then need to condense the available information into a brief coherent statement to make to the group. You may need to outline what you have found and have a copy made for each group member. Or you may want to make your information available to the group prior to the next meeting. You never have time to waste.

If you can help someone in the group complete an assignment, volunteer to do so. Cooperation should be the spirit of the small group. You may know someone you can talk to, or a special source in your department unknown to the group member charged with the responsibility for completing the task. Offer to assist a group member if, and only if, you can make a positive contribution without interfering with the completion of the task. Do not just tag along for the sake of companionship; when an assignment is made, there is work to be done.

Make arrangements to remove any uncertainties you have about your role or responsibilities in the group. If you are unsure about how to proceed on an assignment, ask the group leader for a conference to clarify procedure. If you need the help of others in the group, ask for it. Make sure you understand *both* the freedoms and constraints affecting your assignment.

These ten skills should help you improve your ability to participate effectively in the small group. You are now ready to consider some problems associated with effective participation.

Problems of Participating in the Small Group

Whenever groups of people gather for any purpose there may be difficulties. Participating in small groups, however well-planned and executed, may draw people together in dispute as well as cooperation. In this section you will examine five problems affecting participation in a small group: the hierarchical imperative, territorial conflicts, interpersonal conflicts, "groupthink," and the battered bureaucrat syndrome (or burnout). You will examine each problem independently although they often overlap.

The Hierarchical
Imperative

The concept of "hierarchy" is natural to human beings working in groups (Wilson, 1978). Sociobiologists believe we may be genetically predisposed to look for and establish hierarchies to assure the survival of the strongest members of any human group. When people form groups they also establish a hierarchy of status. In modern organizations status is often determined by seniority, job title, or appointment to the group as leader or expert. Even when status is articulated in this way, individual group members will attempt to establish their own sources of power, authority, and influence within the group.

Hierarchies, despite their natural foundation in human nature, often cause difficulties in small groups. There are at least three types of hierarchical influences operating within any group at almost any time.

1. *A hierarchy of needs:* Maslow (1954) described individual human needs using the concept of hierarchy. He posited the existence of a hierarchy of needs, identifying the sources of individual motivation for work and play.

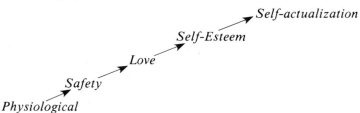

Maslow believed people do not work for the satisfaction of higher-level needs until lower-order needs are satisfied. Many management theorists borrowed Maslow's concept of a needs hierarchy to determine how motivations can be found to improve employee performance.

The usefulness of Maslow's theory can be seen in small groups. Based on which needs are being satisfied at any given moment, each group member strives for satisfaction of a higher-level need. If there are problems at home and the need for love (e.g., affiliation or acceptance) is not being met, the group member may need kind words from other group members more than greater self-esteem. Since Maslow's theory is highly generalized and different people define their needs in different ways, it is precipitous to blindly attribute motivations to others in the group. At best you can acknowledge that everyone in the group is striving for needs' satisfaction, and perhaps speculate about how you may contribute to their well-being.

2. *A hierarchy of values:*   Organizations assume that individuals are prepared to participate fully in groups. Ideally, even the individual group members believe that other group members are ready and willing to participate. Unfortunately, this is not always the case. The *value* of participating in the group may fluctuate as the individuals involved gain or lose interest in the subject, or suffer problems at home or elsewhere in the organization. Too often we take for granted that people place a premium on discussion and interaction. But participation can lag when group members reduce participation because of extraneous concerns.

3. *A hierarchy of status:*   Group members tend to arrange the roles they play according to the status attributed to them. Status may be described as an outcome of communication processes which determine an individual's relative standing within the group. Status may be ascribed on the basis of expertise or experience, the level of vigilance in group discussions, the degree and quality of participation, and the vested authority or office. Status often implies power and the ability of one or more group members to influence the outcomes of any interaction. Hollander (1958) found that high-status group members are able to deviate from group norms more than do low-status members. Inasmuch as individuals value their own sense of self-esteem, status may lead to interpersonal or territorial conflicts within the group. It is desirable for groups to provide some basis for influence so that each group member may overcome potential status difficulties.

These three sources of hierarchy may contribute to or interfere with the group's operation. When status is at stake, it is expedient to identify the sources of status for each member of the group. When values or needs are an issue, it is wise to acknowledge the difficulty and then try to get on with the work. Listen to Kim's case:

Kim K., 26 I was part of a group where everybody was very much "into" making the group a rewarding personal experience. We took time to discuss each other's personal problems, we tried to empathize, to harmonize, to find solutions to our individual *angsts*. I thought, "Wow, what a wonderful group of human beings I work with." Little did I know that Murray, one of the guys in the group, was quietly collecting all this personal information to use against us, to manipulate us. Not only was he the one who refused to reveal his problems to the group, he was the first to use our problems against us. I remember one time when he listened to Patricia's reasons for making a design decision, and then said, "We all know what you've been going through, Patricia. Unfortunately, I think this time it has affected your judgment." What could she do? No matter how hard she tried to say it wasn't so, she made it look more and more like it was. Now I say, let's get down to work in the group and stop all this moaning about our personal lives. It doesn't do anybody any good. If you need help, see a doctor.

Territorial Conflicts

We all know animals stake out territories. Place a domestic house cat in a new surrounding and it will slink around sniffing for evidence of another animal while leaving a trail of its own. We also know that groups like countries, nations, or organizations, similarly stake out territories and defend their borders. Anyone who has lived in a suburb knows how much value a family attaches to its own backyard. A sense of ownership and control is implicit in any territory we call our own, and often we are prepared to defend this territory with our lives.

Small groups operate within *physical* and *mental territories*. The physical territory is literally where the group meets regularly, where the business is conducted. Group members typically think of "our room," and even "my chair in our room," and you hear talk reflecting these territorial boundaries. If you enter the room one day and find someone you dislike sitting in *your* chair, you bristle. You see the occupation of your chair as an invasion of your space. You resent it, and furthermore, because you dislike the individual, you perceive in the act an intent to harm. If the person occupying your chair is a friend you may dismiss the invasion; but you wonder why it happened, and you certainly notice it.

Organizations are replete with tales of space invasions. I have seen managers who believe they are performing heroic acts when they attempt to gain additional office space for their groups. Employees become entangled in conflict when they perceive their territories to be invaded by other employees. "What do you mean you were just looking for a record of our last group meeting!! You know that's my job, Alice! What are you trying to do, get rid of me?" We may laugh at these intrusions, but they are an important source of difficulty for group members.

Mental territories present unique problems for small groups. You are usually assigned to a group because of your expertise or experience with a particular aspect of the group's task. This constitutes your mental territory; you protect it as you would a physical space you called your own. For example, consider the following dialogue:

Transcript of a Group Meeting

Vanessa: I think we ought to be more concerned with the cost of the proposal.

Jim: Hey, I'm the cost specialist here. I've looked over the plan and it seems reasonable to me. . . .

Carl: Yeah, but I think Vanessa's right. When you consider—

Jim: Hey Carl, I resent you butting in on my area. I don't come nosing around the auditing division, do I?

Vanessa: Calm down Jim. Nobody's questioning your ability. We just raised the issue of cost. We just need more information. . . .

Jim: Bull. I know backstabbing when I see it! I say I gave careful consideration to the cost of the plan, which is *my job here,* and it looks okay. Is that perfectly clear?

No doubt it was perfectly clear. Jim perceived the other group members to be invading his mental territory, and he was ready to defend himself against real or implied charges. Although Jim's example is dramatic, there are many other instances of equally hostile territorial disputes played out at more subtle levels.

Territorial disputes affect group participation because they impair or impede communication. When territories are staked out and defended, they are difficult to question. If a group cannot investigate issues freely, then effective participation suffers and the group is likely to fall victim to "groupthink." To avoid territorial disputes, group members need to establish a climate conducive to open discussion of issues. Unless good reasons are advanced, there should be no arbitrary termination of relevant discussions. As we shall see, territorial disputes are often related to interpersonal disputes; and it is the group's responsibilities to *separate issues from personalities* when disagreements arise. Unless a group can make this distinction, escalation of the conflict is inevitable.

We are born alone and we die alone. We tend to be suspicious of others until they prove themselves friendly. As I pointed out in an earlier chapter, most individuals resist group work. Indeed, most of us would rather work alone. For this reason, participating in small groups is a learned skill that involves adapting messages to others. While we learn this precious skill, we very often make mistakes that lead to interpersonal conflicts.

Interpersonal Conflicts

There are many sources of interpersonal conflict. The following are based on my own observations of small groups in American business and industry. While obviously not exhaustive, this list should provide you with a basic understanding of some of the causes of interpersonal conflict in small groups:

Causes of Interpersonal Conflict

1. Conflict emerging from *differences of opinion;*
2. Conflicts arising from *differences in values* affecting the group's outcome, task, or approach to the outcome or task;
3. Conflicts attributable to *disagreements about the quality of evidence* used to make decisions or solve problems;
4. Conflicts ascribable to *personal loyalties or friendships* which may affect or be affected by a decision made by the group;
5. Conflicts originating in *simple to complex misunderstandings* about the intentions, purposes, or goals of talk exchanged by group members;
6. Conflicts rooted in a *lack of perceived reward for participating* in the small group;
7. Conflicts arising from *personal prejudices, biases, or other matters* unrelated to the group's task, but revealed in discussions about it;
8. Conflicts originating in *ambition, motivation, or drive* by one or more group members, and perceived by other group members as potentially threatening;
9. Conflicts based on *physical appearance or attractiveness,* and favors dispensed by other group members because of it;
10. Conflicts attributable to *personal style* (including lifestyle, style of communicating, style of responding, style of leading, and general style of being).

As you can see, there are *many sources* of interpersonal conflict. The question most often posed by novice small group participants is: "How can I become sensitive to interpersonal conflicts in groups and contribute to managing or reducing them?" To answer this question would require another textbook, together with much more evidence than is currently available. But understanding the evolutionary paths of conflict can at least create an awareness of it. By "evolutionary path" I mean the common developments in interpersonal conflict that tend to create cooperation or division among group members caught up in it. Consider the model in Figure 4.1.

You will notice four distinct evolutionary paths based on the same initial feelings of wrongheadedness, inequity, injustice, or exasperation. If the disputants voice the disagreement, first monitor how they talk to each other about it. Then try to identify goals of their conflict within the group setting, to determine whether there are reasonable ways of resolving the conflict. If the disputants do not monitor how they talk to each other or reach mutual agreement about dis-

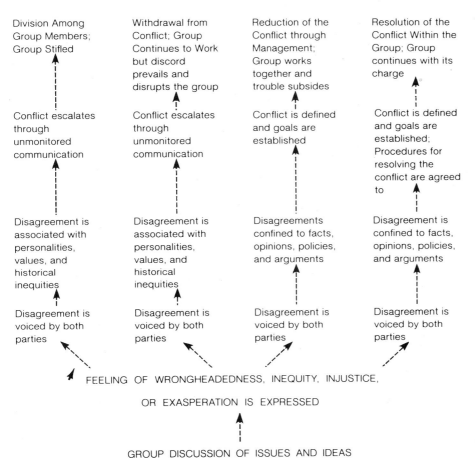

Division Among
Group Members;
Group Stifled

Conflict escalates
through
unmonitored
communication

Disagreement is
associated with
personalities,
values, and
historical
inequities

Disagreement is
voiced by both
parties

Withdrawal from
Conflict; Group
Continues to Work
but discord
prevails and
disrupts the group

Conflict escalates
through
unmonitored
communication

Disagreement is
associated with
personalities,
values, and
historical
inequities

Disagreement is
voiced by both
parties

Reduction of the
Conflict through
Management;
Group works
together and
trouble subsides

Conflict is defined
and goals are
established

Disagreements
confined to facts,
opinions, policies,
and arguments

Disagreement is
voiced by both
parties

Resolution of the
Conflict Within the
Group; Group
continues with its
charge

Conflict is defined
and goals are
established;
Procedures for
resolving the
conflict are agreed
to

Disagreement is
confined to facts,
opinions, policies,
and arguments

Disagreement is
voiced by both
parties

FEELING OF WRONGHEADEDNESS, INEQUITY, INJUSTICE,
OR EXASPERATION IS EXPRESSED

GROUP DISCUSSION OF ISSUES AND IDEAS

Figure 4.1. Evolutionary
Paths in Conflict

puted goals within the group, then the conflict probably will continue to escalate
and impede the group's work. The purpose of this model is to demonstrate how
important it is to *monitor communication* to peacefully resolve interpersonal difficulties. To eliminate or settle interpersonal disputes requires sensitivity to the
nature of the dispute and its development, ability to monitor communication during
the exchange. This also demands knowledge and skill enabling the group to create
a spirit of cooperation based on an understanding of the value and worth of *conflict management*. When people clash over ideas or issues, the group should encourage open discussion of the *reasons* for the disagreement. There must be a
concerted effort to avoid escalating the conflict to involve personalities or egos.
Interaction should deal with issues and arguments, not the people presenting them.

Groupthink   When group members consciously avoid conflicts of ideas, "groupthink" may be operating. Groupthink is a problem that affects groups striving for consensus at the cost of considering alternatives and information that contradict the wisdom of the group (Janis, 1972). "Groupthink" is a special problem impairing participation in the group when people equate participation with consensus. Listen to Ralph:

> **Ralph S., 21**   I guess part of the problem is what our parents teach us about avoiding conflict. We grow up thinking we should be kind to people, even if we disagree with them. We do not learn *how* to disagree with people's ideas without at the same time revealing our dislike of them. So when we work in groups the natural tendency is to agree with each other, even when we have doubts. We are so concerned with being liked by other group members we forget the importance of saying what we believe. We give up being ourselves to be a part of the group.

Ralph may be right. We learn to avoid conflicts and often have difficulty knowing *how* to disagree. We believe that "united we stand, and divided we fall." Unfortunately, we do not learn that we can be united by a spirit of cooperation that *includes* encouraging productive disagreements. Too often we equate disagreement with division.

The Battered Bureaucrat Syndrome ("Burnout")   Organizations assume that employees remain at a constant level of energy and enthusiasm for their job. But anyone who has ever worked in any organization knows that people vary in their energy and ability to perform tasks. One health communication expert, Stewart Auyash (1976), described the problem as "the battered bureaucrat syndrome." More recently, the term *burnout* has been used to describe what happens when *the will to participate* in groups diminishes.

There are various causes suggested for burnout. Auyash believes a chief source is information overload: having too much information available makes group decision-making a dull and laborious task. Another cause may be the feeling that no matter what the group accomplishes, small reward is bestowed on the members. The group will continue to meet, and to work, but no matter how "effective" it becomes, they will derive little satisfaction from participation. Without a value being ascribed or credited to individual effort, group members may develop the feeling that "if I don't do the work, somebody else will, so who cares?"

There are apparently several stages of burnout. Initially, group members are excited by their task and responsibilities and expend a great deal of time and effort working together. The second stage occurs when the work is being done, and group members may become complacent about their ability to do the job. The third stage is characterized by a reported feeling of "being tired" when the group assembles. The individuals in the group lack motivation to complete the task and avoid productive conflicts because they don't want to expend the energy to disagree. The final stage of burnout seems to be withdrawal from the group. Members may cease attending group meetings, report in sick, and become more and more isolated from other group members.

What can be done to prevent burnout? The easy answer is to keep group energies high and to establish a reward system which can motivate the group members. Unfortunately, this ideal solution may be very difficult to implement. If the problem is information overload, the group should find ways to reduce the amount of information any one group member must deal with. If the difficulty is boredom, institute productive conflict by appointing a "devil's advocate." There must be *value* attributed to participating in the group. In the end, the value of participating may be more important to group members than the decisions they make or the problems they solve.

In this section you have reviewed some of the problems associated with participating in small groups. Awareness of the existence of these potential problem areas must be developed, and sensitivity to their symptoms and causes should be encouraged. As necessary as awareness and sensitivity are in recognizing problems of participating in small groups, effective communication is the only way to overcome these difficulties. Communication is *how* we participate in groups, and nothing can happen without it.

Summary

You have received a large amount of information in this chapter. Participation is defined as what people say and do in small groups. You discovered that organizations assume participation will occur when people work together, but they seldom provide training in effective group participation. As a result, many people are anxious about group work and enter the group with self-centered rather than group-centered concerns.

First, you examined entry into the group. Using a fictional scenario you observed how problems occur for the uninformed group member. I discussed the need to develop an "other-centered" awareness when entering the group, with a "process" rather than "event" orientation toward group activities. I concluded this section by discussing the need for preparation and communication as logical components of effective participation in groups.

Second, you examined the concepts of rules and roles in groups. I defined a rule as a standard used to evaluate individual and group behavior. I discussed the principles of defining rules in groups by examining consistent behavior, explaining how rules allow us to determine what modes of participation are most appropriate for the kind of group we are in. I differentiated between rules existing prior to our entry into the group and those created by the group to meet situational or contextual needs. Then you explored roles played by group members. I explained the difference between roles associated with completing the task while maintaining effective interpersonal relations and the self-oriented roles that often interfere with productive participation. I discussed the relationship between roles and identities of group members, suggesting a method of describing how life-scripts can be determined by examining the communication behavior of individuals. I then extended the idea of individual identity and role to encompass a group's identity. Finally, I discussed how information about rules and roles can be integrated. Among various communicative behaviors, an individual can learn to choose those most likely to elicit the desired response within the particular group setting.

Third, you examined the skills needed for participating in small groups. I listed and defined behaviors associated with ten skills necessary for effective group interaction. Each skill was discussed in relation to how an individual group member can best prepare for communication and adaptation to the needs as well as the expectations of the other group members and the situation.

Finally, you explored the problems associated with participating in small groups. I discussed the hierarchical imperative, territorial conflicts, interpersonal conflicts, groupthink, and burnout. Under each heading I reviewed the symptoms or causes of the problem and provided suggestions about ways of overcoming the difficulty in small groups.

> **Stew A., 34**   They tell you that stress is a killer. In my case it killed my job and left me with high blood pressure and sleepless nights. I was working in this group, and we were under a lot of deadline pressures to deliver a project for the space shuttle. Then, somehow, we were falling behind and getting on each other's nerves. Arguments broke out in the group. People gossiped about each other, and I got sick of the whole thing. My work suffered, and then one day I said, "To hell with it, I'm not living like this anymore," and I quit. I thought that would make my life easier, but instead it became worse. You ever heard of "Delayed Stress Syndrome?" I hadn't either. Apparently, it is like what some guys coming back from the war experienced, but in my case my war was in my small group. That was three years ago, and I still wake up with the shaking sweats at night. Don't let them tell you burnout isn't real. It is, it happened to me.

References

Auyash, S. "The Battered Bureaucrat Syndrome." In *Proceedings of the National Conference on Child Abuse and Neglect,* 1976.

Benne, K. D., and P. Sheats. "Functional Roles of Group Members," *Journal of Social Issues* 1, 4 (1948): 41–49.

Bormann, E. "Fantasy and Rhetorical Vision: The Rhetorical Criticism of Social Reality." *Quarterly Journal of Speech* 58 (1972): 396–407.

Cronin, V. E., and W. B. Pierce. "The Logic of the Coordinated Management of Meaning: An Open-systems Model of Interpersonal Communication." International Communication Association, Chicago, May 1978.

Donohue, W. A., D. P. Cushman, and R. E. Nofsinger. "Creating and Confronting Social Order: A Comparison of Rules Perspectives." *Western Journal of Speech Communication* 1, 44 (Winter 1980): 5–19.

Farber, L. H. *Lying, Despair, Jealousy, Envy, Sex, Suicide, Drugs, and the Good Life* New York: Harper & Row, 1978.

Ganz, J. S. *Rules: A Systematic Study.* Paris: Mouton, 1971.

Goldhaber, G. *Organizational Communication,* 2d ed. Dubuque, Iowa: William C. Brown Company Publishers, 1979.

Hollander, E. "Conformity, Status, and Idiosyncratic Credit." *Psychological Review* 65 (1958): 117–27.

Janis, I. *Victims of Groupthink.* Boston: Houghton Mifflin, 1972.

Maslow, A. H. *Motivation and Personality.* New York: Harper & Row, 1954.

Phillips, G. M., and N. J. Metzger. *Intimate Communication* Boston: Allyn & Bacon, 1976.

Phillips, G. M., D. J. Pedersen, and J. T. Wood. *GROUP DISCUSSION: A Practical Guide to Participation and Leadership.* Boston: Houghton Mifflin Co., 1979.

Pierce, W. B. "The Coordinated Management of Meaning: A Rules-based Theory of Interpersonal Communication." In *Explorations in Interpersonal Communication,* edited by Gerald R. Miller, 17–36. Beverly Hills: Russell Sage, 1976.

Posner, B. Z. "Comparing Recruiter, Student, and Faculty Perceptions of Important Applicant and Job Characteristics." *Personnel Psychology,* 34 (1981): 329–39.

Scott, W. G., and D. K. Hart. *Organizational America.* Boston: Houghton Mifflin Co., 1980.

Shimanoff, S. B. *Communication Rules Theory and Research.* Beverly Hills: Sage, 1980.

Watzlawick, P., J. Beavin, and D. Jackson. *Pragmatics of Human Communication.* New York: W. W. Norton, 1967.

Wilson, E. O. *On Human Nature.* Cambridge: Harvard University Press, 1978.

Wood, J. T. "Alternative Portraits of Leaders: A Contingency Approach to Perceptions and Leadership." *Western Journal of Speech Communication,* 4, 43. (Fall 1979): 260–70.

Yankelovich, D. *The New Rules.* New York: Random House, 1981.

Exercises

The exercises presented below are designed to help you attain the participative competencies described in this chapter. The first exercise is a detailed one, asking you to use the Standard Agenda format to guide decision-making about a common problem on your campus. Depending on how much time you can allot to it, this exercise can become a valuable basis for your understanding of how participation affects group performance and policy-oriented decision-making.

1. Assemble your small group. Begin a discussion of commonly experienced problems affecting students at your school. Narrow down the discussion to one good topic about which all members of the group feel strongly. Now phrase a question to guide future discussions of this problem. In most cases you will want to select a question of value (concerning the assumptions used to guide policy decisions affecting college or university life), or a question of policy (concerning how modifications or changes can be instituted to improve the quality of an aspect of college or university life). An example might be: "What recommendations can be made to improve the distribution of student government funds to student activities?" or "What recommendations can be made to improve the parking situation?" In either case, your task is to determine what information it is necessary to have before making any recommendations. Your task should be to collect as many facts, relevant opinions, and arguments as you can regarding the question posed. Make individual assignments and explain that during the next class meeting time will be allotted to hear individual group members' reports. You can collect information from local authorities, members of the student government, school records kept in the library, and perhaps by conducting a limited survey.

   During the next class meeting ask each group member to give an oral report concerning the results of her or his fact-finding. Enter all student reports into the group record. You now have a foundation on which to establish criteria (goals that must be included in a solution), to generate alternative solutions (regardless of whether they adhere to or meet the criteria), and to construct a final solution based on your analysis and recommendation.

During the third class meeting and based on the results of your assignment, present a formal oral report to the class. (Note: This exercise can be used in a three-day period or can be extended over two or three weeks, depending on the judgment of the instructor and the small group.)

Finally, conduct a debriefing session dealing with the quality of participation reflected by the efforts of group members in fact-finding and communicating within the group. How did the participation affect the quality of the group's decision-making? What recommendations could be made about improving the quality of participation for next time?

The second exercise is designed to show you the dynamics of role-taking and playing in your small group. Pay close attention to how the communication patterns of the participants affect your assessment of their role, character, and contributions to the group.

2. Assemble your small group. The purpose of this exercise is to use role-playing to demonstrate how conflict influences a group, and to determine how you make choices about participating in conflict which influence the results of disagreement within the group. Distribute to each member of the group one of the following roles printed on a 3 × 5 notecard. Ask each player to read the instructions, think about the character she or he is playing, then determine a strategy for enacting the role in the group.

J. J.: You are the leader of the problem-solving group charged with the responsibility for making a recommendation about instituting Quality Circles in this hospital. You are not quite sold on the idea, but you are willing to try anything that may help reduce the high turnover of salaried employees, especially nurses and nurses' aides. You are an administrator of the hospital with five years experience here. To you the most important aspect of this problem will be the ability of the Quality Circle concept to assure a lower turnover rate.

M. T.: You are a head nurse at the hospital. You have twenty-three years experience here, and you are a firm believer in a strong hierarchy of authority and power within the hospital organization. You take your orders from the nursing administrator, and you make sure they are carried out, no matter what. You think this Quality Circles idea is a bunch of ivory-towered hoopla that will accomplish nothing and cause a great deal of disruption among your nurses. To have young nurses share in management decisions sounds like chaos to you, and to say they have the same vote as anyone else sounds communistic. You want to decrease turnover by increasing the salary and benefits package, because you think money is the bottom line.

F. H.: You are a physician who serves on administrative boards only because someone has to and you are usually selected for this assignment by your peers. You would rather be tending your patients or sailing. The Quality Circles concept sounds interesting to you, but you are not ready to accept it until you find out how much time physicians will have to spend meeting with their Quality Circle groups. You think most of the problems in the hospital are caused by poor management (thus, you don't think much of J. J. who is an administrator) and a lack of respect for doctors.

D. C.: You are chief of maintenance for the hospital. You are the one who suggested the Quality Circles concept and are convinced it will work. You have seen it function at the other local hospital and have attended a training session on Quality Circles at your own expense to find out how to implement it. You have worked here for twenty years and have a deep affection for M. T. However, you know she is stubborn, and that if she is to join your side in this dispute, you will have to demonstrate the benefits of the idea to her nurses. You will tell her that financial rewards and benefits may still be improved, that this is not an either/or issue. You are convinced that most of the problems in the hospital are caused by poor communication among the various divisions: administrators, physicians, nurses, maintenance crews, and professional staff. Quality Circles will result in better communication and thus improve the operation and efficiency of the hospital.

G. K.: You are a physical therapist with two years experience and much enthusiasm for Quality Circles. You are in touch with the other local hospital and know how well the use of Quality Circles has worked out there. You are also aware of the problems caused by strict hierarchies in your hospital, and you don't really get along very well with M. T. or J. J. because of it. Everybody knows you are very bright and highly skilled, but by and large you think they still treat you like a kid. This may be your golden opportunity to show them that you have maturity and skills that they can use. You want to resolve any conflicts that emerge in the discussions and to keep your temper.

Conduct the group discussion. When you have arrived at consensus, go back and review how the vested interests in the group influenced the nature of the conflict. What was the evidence presented by the participants? Experience? Authority? Testimony? Statistics? Examples? Personal power? How was the conflict resolved (if it was)? What could have been said or done that might have improved the group's chances of resolving the dispute without "bloodshed" or "tyranny?"

5 Leading the Small Group

Introduction

What is leadership?

Leadership is at least partially a set of behaviors you recognize when you confront them. Leadership does *not* always consist of an identical set of behaviors, however, a fact that makes the study of leadeship and the development of leading skills difficult. For example, there are times when you want a strong leader to direct the activities of the group. In these circumstances you may respond favorably to an individual who tells you what to do, who does not encourage much discussion, and who operates in an autocratic style.

If you change these circumstances you may also need to change the style of leadership. When small groups are exploring alternative solutions to a problem, the autocratic style of leadership may impede progress. Instead, you may want a leader who encourages diversified discussions on a variety of issues, who listens to group members exchanging ideas and opinions, rather than directing them, a person who operates in a more democratic style. In O'Connell's (1979) terms, this leader uses a problem-solving approach to interaction, rather than the arbitrary style characterized by the autocrat.

Between these two extremes of the leadership style continuum there are other choices about behaviors affecting group interaction. You may desire a leader who possesses a keen sensitivity to the needs of group members, who responds not only to what they say and do, but also to how they *feel*. You may want a leader with special skills in conflict resolution. You may prefer someone who acts more like "one of the gang" instead of a "leader." Requirements for leadership are as varied as the situations and contingencies to which leaders must be able to respond (see Scheidel, 1987; Fisher, 1986).

Thus, leadership is not simply one set of behaviors. We respond to other characteristics of leaders besides their talk and actions. Often we feel more comfortable working in a group directed by a proven leader, someone with expertise and experience in group interaction. We may also be affected by the sex of the leader. Women have long regarded the attainment of leadership positions in organizations as a desirable goal. As women began acquiring leadership roles, men had to learn how to adapt their behavior to the presence of a woman in this position. It was not that women led groups differently, but rather that an unprecedented change was occurring, and the sex of the leader was the most obvious characteristic of this change. We also respond to the physical and psychological attractiveness of a leader. These are some of the traits affecting our perceptions of and responses to leaders.

This chapter addresses the question of leadership in small groups. I call it a question, because the leader's ability to make effective choices requires the ability to ask and to answer a variety of relevant questions about group members, the task to be accomplished, the situation, and the history of the group. The question of leadership also necessitates acquiring a variety of interpersonal and group skills; these range from calling meetings to order and planning agendas to resolving disputes between and among group members. Finally, the question of leadership demands that we be able to implement our answers to these challenges effectively, efficiently, and consistently.

First, you will examine a brief history of leadership research. Second, you will discuss the strengths and weaknesses of the adaptive approach to leadership by asking questions about the leader in relation to other group members. Third, you will consider the skills associated with leadership. Fourth, you will explore some of the problems associated with leading small groups, from ways of solving leadership problems through adequate preparation for group meetings. Following the chapter references are exercises designed to reveal some of the critical issues concerning leadership in small groups. Before you begin your exploration of leadership, consider the following statement made by a corporate executive about leaders.

William McA., 55   Leadership ability is very important to any organization. We tell our recruiters how to spot leadership potential in candidates for entry-level positions. Once someone is hired, we train him, often spending as much as a quarter of a million dollars over fifteen or twenty years developing leadership skills. So we expect a great deal from our leaders. We know a leader has to be able to take heat from both sides: from superiors in the organization who constantly demand more and better results, and from subordinates who blame the leader for anything that goes wrong. That is simply part of the job. I guess the bottom line is this: can a person handle the responsibilities of being a leader without showing signs of cracking up? We've lost some of our best managers to drugs, especially alcohol. We've lost others to bad marriages, bad love affairs, bad feelings with other managers, and so forth. You know what's sad? These kids come here looking for a good job after college. They're smart, they're trainable. They all say the same thing, "I want to be a leader." If they only knew what that meant I bet most of them wouldn't want it at all.

Leadership is not a responsibility or a personal commitment to be taken lightly. If developing leadership skills is important to you in your professional career, this chapter can only begin to teach you what you will need to know.

A Brief History of Leadership Research

The idea of leadership, what it is, what it means, what it takes to be a leader, has a long and distinguished history. Virtually every major thinker has addressed the subject of leadership, usually to discuss the role of a leader in politics or religion. Plato, and later Aristotle, established the tone for most later works on the subject, emphasizing the personal traits of leaders: knowledge, skills, ability to rule fairly. Aristotle was the first philosopher to discuss the relationship between leaders and a class of discourse used to describe them, praise or blame (i.e., epideictic rhetoric; see *The Rhetoric,* chapter III). Machiavelli (1516; 1561) and Castiglione (1528; 1561) provided instruction for potential leaders, again relying on the traits associated with success in political matters, and the kinds of praise or blame ascribed to effective and ineffective leaders. These works expanded the idea of leadership to include *private* as well as *public* interactions, thus laying a significant foundation for all future texts on the subject (see Sennett, 1978).

Trait Approach Modern scholarly investigation of leadership began with "scientific" approaches. Although claiming to be scientific in their study of characteristics associated with leaders, these early twentieth century researchers essentially succeeded in confirming what essayist Thomas Carlyle believed in the early nineteenth century: that leaders are people who possess certain innate qualities which others do not have. From 1927 to 1940, leadership research concerned itself with discovering what these "innate qualities" were, eventually listing seventy-nine of them (Bird, 1940). Unfortunate uses were made of these early studies. For example, while much of the credit (or blame) for Hitler's "Superman" theory of the Aryan race is attributed to German philosophers and British statesmen, some of the traits associated with Hitler's views were supported by what were then described as scientific research practices. Thus, it was claimed that tall, blond haired, blue-eyed males were "born" leaders, destined to be great.

Recently some researchers have taken a different approach to identifying traits associated with leadership (for a review, see Cragan and Wright, 1980, p. 202). For example, Janet Yerby (1975) discovered a relationship between gender and leadership style which suggests that the sex of a leader is a significant trait when the attitudes of group members toward the gender of the leader affect the group's behavior. Bormann, Pratt, and Putnam (1978) simulated a corporate setting and discovered that males had difficulty adapting to female group leaders. It would be unwise to conclude from these studies that women make poor group leaders. A safer conclusion might be that gender may affect how leaders are chosen and how leaders are perceived by other group members (see Bunyi and Andrews, 1985). After all, sex is not how people lead; gender is only one aspect of leadership which must necessarily be considered in relation to the expectations of group members, the task to be accomplished, the behaviors associated with leadership in the particular group, the history of the group, together with the ability of the leader (male or female) to adapt language to the needs of the situation and of the other group members.

What became a major influence on leadership research began in 1939 with Kurt Lewin's studies of ten year-old boys in YMCA camps. Dissatisfied with the traits approach to studies of leadership, Lewin initiated an approach based on his belief in social forces. By manipulating three different styles of leadership, autocratic, democratic, and laissez-faire (or leaderless), he found that both democratic and authoritarian styles of leadership were *quantitatively* productive, but that only the democratic style produced higher *quality* decisions. The laissez-faire groups produced neither quantitatively nor qualitatively superior results. Also, Lewin found that group members were more satisifed with democratic leaders and reported being happier with the outcomes of their groups. Autocratic groups reported hostility between group members, apathy toward outcomes, with no real sense of involvement in decisions. In laissez-faire groups, the members reported liking the association with each other, but feeling they did not accomplish very much (which was true). As a result of his research, Lewin concluded that democratic leaders were most effective in group situations. Phillips, Pedersen, and Wood (1979), in reviewing Lewin's work, believe he may have been heavily influenced by national prejudices at the time of his studies. With the threat of Hitler's Germany a daily concern, there might have been a need to establish the superiority of a style of leadership reflected in our government's democratic beliefs.

Recent research toward this "styles" approach to leadership combines psychological awareness with behaviors of leaders. For example, Kwal and Fleshler (1973) discovered that high-esteem group members share leadership responsibilities better than do low-esteem group members. Their research suggests that democratic styles of leadership are most effective when group members feel good about themselves and their ability to accomplish the task. Sargent and Miller (1971) listed the differences between autocratic and democratic leaders, and concluded that a principal difference is the amount of participation encouraged by the leaders. Autocratic leaders tend to encourage less participation than do democratic leaders. Rosenfeld and Plax (1975) and Rosenfeld and Fowler (1976) investigated leadership style and personality characteristics. Their findings suggest there may be an "authoritarian personality" and a "democratic personality" which can be developed by both women and men. Also, in the later study, democratic males were found to possess a more forceful and analytic approach to leadership, while females were found to be more open-minded and nourishing. Care must be taken in interpreting the results of these studies for their meaning in any given case; scientific findings are capable of generating only *tentative* conclusions.

A third major influence on our thinking about leadership appeared around 1948. Dissatisfied with previous manipulations of leadership positions in groups, Ralph Stogdill investigated how leaders emerged in groups. In what has become known as the "situational" approach to leadership, Stogdill postulated that behaviors and innate qualities associated with leadership will depend on the nature of the task and the situation. For example, being physically attractive and possessing a degree in advertising may be more important to a fashion-consulting group than to a committee assigned the task of establishing criteria for college-admission standards. According to Stogdill (1974), some people may have more leadership potential than others; but the nature of the situation and the task to be accomplished will influence whether or not their potential is developed by the group.

Researchers following Stogdill's lead reached a variety of interesting but somewhat flawed conclusions about the influences generated by situations and tasks. For example, Howells and Becker (1962) studied the seating arrangements of small groups with different leadership styles. They concluded that leaders tended to be seated centrally in group discussions. This finding may have been true of the groups they studied, but in situations where circular seating arrangements are used, centrality would be determined by the eye of the beholder. Perhaps the best research concerning this situational approach to leadership was done by Downs and Pickett (1977). They concluded that three interrelated variables affect the emergence of leaders: leadership style, group compatibility, and nature of the discussion situation.

Functional Approach A fourth major element in leadership research concerned the functions performed by people in leadership positions. Chester Barnard's work, *The Functions of the Executive* (1938) may have laid the groundwork for studies developed during the 1950s and early 1960s. In the last chapter I described the roles of group members using Benne and Sheats' (1948) classification schema. Essentially, researchers were interested in identifying the functions performed by group members, especially by group leaders functions, which could then be taught to others who aspired to leadership positions. The functional approach is perhaps the most radical alternative to the traits approach because the former assumes that the tasks or functions performed by the leader are more important than are any innate characteristics.

The major finding of this line of research was a delineation of two types of functions performed by group leaders: (1) *task functions,* such as calling a meeting to order, circulating agendas, asking for and furnishing information, summarizing ideas, etc., and (2) *maintenance functions,* like encouraging participation from group members, resolving disputes, relieving tension, seeking compromises, etc. According to the functional approach, the ideal group leader is able to balance task and maintenance goals.

Gouran (1970) concluded that the functional approach to leadership research would prevail because it provided the most promising avenues for studies of the communication characteristics associated with leading. Gouran's conclusion seemed appropriate at the time. But the 1970s launched a new era in leadership research which radically altered our understanding of how traits, styles, situations, and functions affect group interaction. In retrospect you can understand how this development occurred by considering some of the important work done by management theorists during the 1950s and 1960s.

During the 1950s two major universities were involved in studies of leadership which dramatically affected later research. I have already discussed the situational interpretation of leading as developed by Stogdill and his associates at Ohio State University. By focusing on the *behaviors* exhibited by leaders, rather than on innate characteristics or personality traits, Stogdill demonstrated how leadership appears in action. It was this line of research that culminated in the separation of task and maintenance functions by other theorists. While Stogdill and his associates were working at Ohio State, at the University of Illinois, another team of researchers, led by Fred Fiedler, was developing what came to be known as the "contingency theory" of leadership.

Fiedler was primarily interested in the products or output of leaders. Measuring productivity in terms of output or performance, he studied the performance of high school basketball teams, air force combat crews, chemical research departments, hospital wards, health teams, cadets at West Point, and other groups. While other researchers were interested in both productivity and group satisfaction generated by the leader, Fiedler was only concerned to measure the success of a group by its performance record. For example, a basketball team was evaluated on the basis of number of games won during competition. Like the Ohio State group, Fiedler also found that he could separate task-motivated leaders from relationship-motivated leaders. Fiedler also observed that when task-motivated leaders gain control over their group's ability to perform the task satisfactorily, the "will relax and be concerned for the satisfaction and feelings of subordinates" (1974, p. 66).

As Fiedler continued his work through the 1960s and 1970s he became concerned about the effect of situation on the style of leadership. Here is where the term *contingency* became important to his work. He found that in highly structured situations (e.g., basketball teams, bomber crews, etc.) task-motivated leaders seemed to perform best. However, in moderately unstructured situations (e.g., where tasks are loosely defined and group members enjoy more autonomy) relationship-motivated leaders seemed to perform best. Depending on what the situation calls for and the contingencies the leader must respond to, either a task- or relationship-motivated leader may be needed. The key to effective management was not simply the situation, the style of leadership, or the leader's experience as a leader but *what the leader has to respond or react to* within the group in order to maximize performance.

Fiedler's work attracted the attention of behavioral scientists interested in the *motivation of group members* in response to a leader. The result of these studies is what is now referred to as "expectancy theory." Included in this theory are two approaches to leadership based on what management specialists refer to as "path-goal analysis" (see Hampton, Summer, and Webber, 1978, pp. 608–10 for overview). Before examining two major approaches to path-goal analysis, let's consider the assumptions of expectancy theory:

1. Human beings are goal-oriented. We establish goals and work toward them in systematic ways.
2. Human beings are reasonable. We will be motivated to perform a certain action because we expect (predict) the action will lead to a payoff. Either we will gain a pleasurable payoff or avoid a painful one.
3. There are two kinds of payoffs. First, we are motivated by *basic payoffs* such as satisfaction of physiological needs, security, self-esteem, friendship, and love. Second, we are motivated by *instrumental payoffs,* such as money, promotions, and praise, which we perceive as means of obtaining desired basic payoffs. In path-goal theories of leadership, the instrumental payoffs are the *paths* to the *goals* of need fulfillment.
4. Human beings seeking goals will tend to choose the path most likely to gain the desired payoff with the least amount of effort and expenditure of time.
5. Human beings have different goals. Consequently, it is very difficult to predict how paths are chosen in relation to the goals to which they lead.

Using the above framework for understanding how leaders can develop strategies for motivating group members, you confront two models of path-goal analysis designed to explain successful leadership.

Path-Goal Approach   Evans (1968) used the earlier work by Ohio State researchers to identify three characteristics of leadership used to develop strategies for effective group performance:

The leader should *show consideration* for other group members.
The leader should *structure group meetings* by clarifying goals and tasks.
The leader should *make rewards contingent* upon group members' achieving the goal of the meeting or the objective of the organization.

Evans proposed the following statement as the core of his path-goal theory of leadership: *If* the leader acts in a considerate way toward group members, providing structure in a way the group members can use to achieve their own personal rewards (instrumental and basic payoffs), while at the same time informing group members that their rewards are contingent upon their performing the task, then both the motivation and the productivity in the group will increase. Unless the group leader can link rewards to performance, she or he will not motivate group members to find their own instrumental payoffs.

The second theory utilizing path-goal analysis was proposed by House (1971) and House and Mitchell (1974). Instead of using three characteristics of the effective leader, House and Mitchell defined four styles of leadership which could be used to match leaders with group members' expectations. The four types of leaders are (House and Mitchell, 1974, p. 83):

1. *Directive leaders:* Let subordinates know what is expected of them, give specific guidance as to what should be done and how it should be done, make their (leadership) role in the group clearly understood, schedule work to be done, maintain definite standards for performance and require that group members observe standard rules and regulations.
2. *Supportive leaders:* Show concern for the status, well-being, and needs of subordinates. Such leaders do little things to make the work more pleasant, treat members as equals, are friendly and approachable.
3. *Participative leaders:* Consult with subordinates, solicit their suggestions and consider these seriously before making a decision.
4. *Achievement-oriented leaders:* Set challenging goals, expect subordinates to perform at their highest level, continuously seek improvement in performance, and express a high degree of confidence that the subordinates will assume responsibility, put forth effort, and accomplish challenging goals.

As you can see, organizations following House and Mitchell's theory attempt to match leadership styles with the expectations and needs of group members within a particular division. The problem with this approach to leadership is that no two situations are exactly alike. Moreover, it may not be practical to move effective leaders in and out of various small groups to carry out assignments. The House and Mitchell approach identifies two contingency factors that make it practically impossible to implement their otherwise sound theory. First, the people in the group may be "internals" (e.g., find satisfaction and reward in their own ability to control the outcomes of situations), or "externals" (e.g., find satisfaction and reward in the ability of other people and environments to influence what happens to them, sometimes believing in luck or chance rather than in active choice of behavior). The second factor is *ability.* The leader who attempts to use path-goal analysis with group members who lack confidence in their ability to carry out the task will fail. Since both of these factors involve the *personalities* of group members and the leader, rather than specific behaviors performed, it becomes difficult to match leaders with groups. Perhaps even more damaging, however, is the fact that these theories do not allow for individuals to *change* their leadership styles to meet the needs of new group members and situations.

Although these approaches to leadership are flawed, they provide significant and useful information about the role of a leader, as well as the considerations that must be made when explaining the effectiveness of a particular leader with a given group. Consider the following testimony provided by one of the major leadership theories:

> Most research in the leadership area is conducted in laboratory settings, with each group seen as an independent unit. In real life, task groups are almost invariably subunits of larger organizations. These groups have a history as well as a future. They also have a boss who plays a very vital and important part in the lives of the group members but who is nearly always ignored in laboratory studies. It is not too surprising, therefore, that none of the major leadership theories has come out of the laboratory, nor are the most cited leadership theorists known for their elegant laboratory experiments (Arygris, Fiedler, Fleishman, Hollander, House, Likert, McGregor, Stogdill, and Vroom). We simply do not know enough about the universe in which leadership interactions take place to build the relevant variables into our laboratory studies.
> From Fred E. Fiedler, "Leadership Effectiveness," in *Small Group Behavior* 1981, pp. 630–31.

The studies reviewed above, and Fiedler's statement, lead to a similar conclusion: The effective leader must be able to adapt to the nature of the situation by understanding the needs and expectations of group members, and his or her own communicative style.

It is this conclusion which provided the idea for what is now called the "adaptive theory" of leadership.

The Adaptive Approach to Leading: Strengths and Weaknesses

Dissatisfied with previous theories of leadership focusing on the ability to predict and control the behavior of group members, Julia T. Wood (1977) began looking at small groups as unique human situations in which people *learned* how to treat each other while participating. From her studies of actual small groups, Wood developed the pragmatic basis for the adaptive approach to leadership, which is explained in her work with Phillips and Pedersen (1979, pp. 78–95).

Wood focuses on two interrelated aspects of leadership which affect any small group: (1) analysis of members and situation, and (2) behavioral flexibility. Both the strengths and weaknesses of her approach to leadership can be observed by separating these two concepts for the purposes of analysis and understanding.

Analyzing the Group Members and the Situation
You cannot be a group leader unless the members of the group are willing to respond to your leading. To establish a leadership role, you need to develop an appreciation for the *unique* needs and expectations of each member of your small

group. Like the contingency approach to leadership, the adaptive approach postulates that a leader must be able to (1) analyze the goals and rewards of each group member, (2) show appreciation of this analysis by treating group members with respect and consideration, (3) structure group meetings using agendas that clarify precise goals and outcomes, while sanctioning behaviors leading to the accomplishment of the group's objectives, (4) make rewards contingent on group members' performance during the meetings, and (5) consistently reassess the changing dynamics of the group in relation to its task to revise strategies as needed.

Analyzing the group and situation is a continuous task for any group leader. People change, and the effective leader must respond to these changes when they occur. Forcing group members to adhere to a pre-established notion of what ought to happen during group meetings, without taking into account their goals and feelings, may mean that no matter what rewards are offered, the group will not be able to obtain them effectively and efficiently. The more group members rebel against the methods of the leader, the less effective the group will be. But the more able the group leader is in defining objectives for the group and explaining how individual goals can be met while satisfying the objective, the more effective the group should be. Consider Herb's experience:

Herb W., 40   I grew up in this organization. Mostly I worked for the same guy, a very autocratic leader who told you what he wanted, and that was it. Either you accomplished the task he gave you, or you didn't. No middle ground. I guess I learned how to be a leader from watching him operate. When I was promoted and became a group leader I adopted his ways, at least at first. I couldn't understand why everyone hated me. I just figured I was being a good manager, you know, weeding out the talent from the goof-offs. But then I lost Helen. Helen had been my most productive worker, always on time, always willing to go the extra mile to complete a project. She was swell. When I was told she resigned I couldn't believe it. I asked to see her. I thought she had been given a better offer by another company and I was willing to top it. But that wasn't it. She was leaving because she couldn't stand the way I "bullied" people, that is exactly what she said. She laid it on the line that afternoon and I've never forgotten it. I was hurt. I didn't know you could choose how to act in a group setting, nobody ever told me that before. I didn't know how to be a leader, I just knew I was in the position and had to be one. So I behaved on the only model I knew and made the same mistakes he did. Only I lost Helen. Since that afternoon I have made real changes in the way I treat people. I only wish I had known how sooner.

Like most of us, Herb learned by experience. Unfortunately, in his case he lost a valued worker before the experience made any sense to him. Unless you know how to examine experience for meaning, it is difficult to learn from it. All the experience in the world will not make you a better leader unless you perceive the need to *learn how to lead*.

The adaptive approach to leadership advances the proposition that you can learn how to lead if you are taught what to look for when analyzing group members and situations. There are four areas in which effective leaders should prepare themselves (Phillips, Pedersen, and Wood, 1979, p. 82):

1. *The issues or agenda must be foreseen.*   A group leader should prepare an agenda for each group meeting, then circulate it among group members. If group members wish to modify the agenda, they should be able to do so by contacting the leader and explaining the need for the change. Thus, the group will have a *public agenda* to guide interactions. The leader should also have a *private agenda*. Prior to the group meeting, the leader should prepare a list of probing questions to generate interaction among group members on each of the issues to be considered during the group meeting. After the meeting, the leader can use this outline to check her or his effectiveness.

2. *The group and the individual members must be analyzed.*   Any human group is composed of individuals with strengths and weaknesses, skills, experiences, and personal goals. The effective leader develops the ability to determine what each of these qualities or deficiencies is for each member of the group. Furthermore, the leader should then prepare for group meetings by thinking through the agenda in relation to the needs and expectations of the group members. By learning to ask questions about how the issues might affect each individual in the group, the leader can prepare for possible problems. Who may be most directly affected by this discussion? Who has the most to gain (or to lose) by this decision? Who with experience in this subject can we use? How can I induce this person to become more involved in the interaction; what motivates him or her? These are some of the questions group leaders need to raise and to answer prior to attending group meetings. By "psyching out" the group members and situations before the meeting, the leader can better analyze his or her own behavior after the meeting. How well did I accomplish my objectives with each individual in the group? This should be the guiding question in analyzing performance during the meeting.

3. *The physical situation in which the group will meet must be anticipated.*   The group leader is usually responsible for setting the time of the group meeting and arranging for any and all group interaction aids, including the conference table, chairs, chalkboards, flipcharts, ashtrays, ice water and cups, etc. The effective leader will ask for suggestions from group members about their special needs and try to meet them. For example, some people are seriously distressed by cigarette, cigar, or pipe smoke in a closed room. The leader should establish a smoking policy appropriate to the members of the group.

The size of the group must be considered when arranging for tables and chairs. Use of a long conference table capable of seating fourteen when you have a small group of five may make group members uncomfortable. Do not schedule large rooms for small groups nor small rooms for large groups. The comfort of the group members should be the guiding consideration of leaders in preparing the physical setting.

4. *The leader's personal style must be appropriately selected.* In addition to analyzing the needs and expectations of group members, leaders must also analyze themselves. What are my needs and expectations? What are my strengths and weaknesses? What does my past experience contribute to this problem or decision? By asking questions about your own ability to participate in the group interaction, the effective leader prepares for the meeting through self-analysis. Leaders must be aware of their own personal prejudices in leading behavior; am I generally autocratic, democratic, or laissez-faire in my approach? Which of these styles is most appropriate for this group and this situation? Are we pressed for time or can we set a leisurely pace for our activities? What obstacles have to be overcome with this group? Are there members present who desire to be the group leader? How can what I know whether past interactions shape my performance in the present situation? Are there likely to be disputes between group members? How can I overcome these obstacles? What specific behaviors must I choose to guide the group toward the accomplishment of its objective at each meeting? The effective leader not only understands the value and importance of choosing among available strategies the one most likely to gain the desired outcome, but also is able to implement the strategy in the given case. For the effective leader knowledge and action are inherently interrelated.

These four areas for leadership preparation should guide the selection of useful strategies to help the group attain its objective. However, in the adaptive approach there is a second major aspect of learning how to lead: *behavioral flexibility*.

Behavioral Flexibility

The key to success in the adaptive approach to leadership is what happens during group meetings. All the preparation made by a leader must pay off in actual performance. To attain this goal of effective performance in group meetings, the effective leader will learn how to *adapt behaviors* to the needs and expectations of group members. To adapt behavior successfully in the given case requires appreciation of the value of behavioral flexibility, as well as considerable skill in employing it.

Behavioral flexibility means developing an extensive repertoire of self-presentations which can be used in any given group situation. The best way to use any one of the self-presentations is formulating an appropriate *response* to

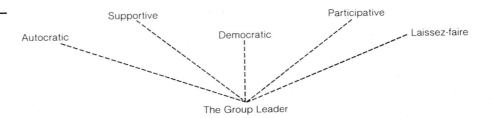

Figure 5.1. Styles of Behavior for Leaders

the messages of group members. Recall that one of the criticisms of previous leadership theories was their inability to take into account the changes in leadership style. Once an autocratic leader, always an autocratic leader. A more effective way to perceive leadership style is to consider that a *range of available styles* are present in any group situation. Figure 5.1 provides examples for behavioral leadership styles.

The second step in developing flexibility is to use *contingency approaches* to leading. Some leadership styles will work better than others, depending (or contingent) on the nature of the group, the task, and the situation. The effective group leader is able to adapt the most appropriate style to the contingencies operating in any group meeting. For example, when pressed for time, the flexible group leader may choose a more autocratic leadership style to attain the objective. When exploration of alternative courses of action requires much detailed discussion, the effective group leader may adapt to the setting by choosing a more participative or even laissez-faire style of leading.

Furthermore, the style of leading may change during the course of a single group meeting. If the group leader believes that the group is reaching consensus too quickly under a supportive style of leadership, then she or he may need to adapt to this contingency by switching to a more participative style. A final objective in effective leadership is the ability to induce group members *to follow your lead*. When the style of leading changes, the group should recognize the change and adapt to it.

The third step in developing a flexible leading style is to convince group members of *the legitimacy and honesty of all self-presentations*. This does not mean we change our basic personalities. It means that we can temporarily modify selected behaviors to respond to urgent circumstances. This goal may be the most difficult for most people to attain. We are seldom equally comfortable with different styles of behavior; we usually prefer one or two patterns of behavior to several others. Group members learn to *expect* these preferred patterns of behavior from group leaders. If the leader changes style abruptly or is not convincing when shifting from an autocratic to democratic style, members of the group are likely to become suspicious of the leader's motive for the change. Consider the following statement:

> **Marcy M., 27**   . . . Then my boss went away on one of those "management training" weekends. When he came back he tried to act like a different person. Where he had been supportive, he became "Management By Results" oriented. He was pretty funny, to tell the truth. No one knew how to behave

around him because we all knew what he was really like. The change didn't fit. I guess he picked up on how we were responding to him because it didn't last more than a week. Then he was back to his old self.

Marcy's statement is important for two reasons. First, it indicates how people learn to expect certain behavioral patterns to occur, and when these patterns change, people resist it. Second, Marcy's case is a good example of how a change in behavior can be negated by group members. Her boss returned to his old style of leading because the new style was not paying off.

Effective changes in behavioral flexibility do not occur overnight, or even over a weekend. It takes time for group members to accept changes, especially if they seem insincere. Had Marcy's boss said "Look, I went to a really interesting training session last weekend and I want to try to implement some new ideas from it in our group," he might have been more successful. You need to *prepare* people for changes. Simply changing your behavior and expecting others to accept the change runs counter to human nature. For changes to be effective, they must take place slowly.

The purpose of understanding behavioral flexibility is to prepare the leader for effective leading. If a leader is new to a group, the group probably will provide useful information about the choices of behaviors, as well as their individual responses to the leader's choice of style. If the leader has previously been a member of the group, then the group will expect similar patterns of behavior during the transition from participant to leader. In either case, the responses you receive to leadership styles should be considered primary sources of information about how to make choices in the future. Do not just "try something new" without first considering how the change may affect the group, based on your past experiences with them.

The adaptive approach to leadership emphasizes preparation for group meetings and the ability to be flexible in choices of communication behaviors. One of the major strengths of this approach is the presumption that management of your own communication may help to achieve optimal group outcomes. Another strength of this theory is its reliance on performance in the given case. No matter how well a leader prepares for leading, if the objectives are not met, if contingencies are not met, then the leadership has not been effective. A third strength of the adaptive approach is that it emphasizes learning communication skills used by leaders to influence group outcomes and goals. The adaptive approach implies that these skills can be learned by almost anyone, and that they can be improved by informed experience in small group settings.

The adaptive approach to leading is not perfect. Unfortunately, this approach assumes that leaders will be motivated to learn how to maximize the outcomes of group activities. Like Herb, there are managers who do not know that alternative forms of leading exist, therefore, they are not motivated to change their style unless something dramatic affects them, like his loss of a valued worker.

Herb felt Helen's departure. Even in this respect he may be different from many managers who would have simply chalked her up as a loss without asking why she no longer wanted to work for the organization. A second weakness of the adaptive approach is its reliance on preparation. As many management theorists have pointed out, there may not be time enough to plan adequately for all group meetings. Today's average manager spends about 60–90% of her or his time in group meetings. Very often this manager may be a leader in one or two groups, and a participant in three or four other groups. The time required to prepare for all of these group meetings would probably prevent the manager from doing anything else. Although it is certainly laudable to encourage the kind of preparation advocated by the adaptive approach, it may be a goal that is more *desirable* than *viable*. Finally, the adaptive approach involves an optimistic assessment of human ability to change. Though it is true that leaders *ought* to have several styles of leadership available to them, in practice many leaders are limited in their ability to choose. As I pointed out, when leaders suddenly alter their behaviors, group members become suspicious. It may be easier for some managers to rely on past patterns of behavior to lead groups, because they do not know how to prepare the group for their changed approach.

Despite these weaknesses, the adaptive approach to leading promises the most for individuals concerned to learn how to become effective leaders of small groups. Rather than viewing human behavior as static, shaped by the environment or situation, or the result of innate characteristics, the adaptive approach expresses what is most noble about human beings: our ability to adapt to our surroundings, to act in response to situations and others in order to promote useful change. Perhaps the greatest advantage of employing the adaptive theory is that *you can learn it*. Now that you have reviewed the history of leadership research culminating in the adaptive approach, you are ready to look more closely at specific communicative behaviors and functions that effective leaders should master.

The Skills of Leading

Up to this point I have concentrated on how a leader prepares for leading, stressing the importance of mental preparation in making plans for group meetings and in the selection of possible self-presentations. However, as important as mental preparedness is, group members will not be able to read your mind. The decisive aspect of leading is what you *do,* the skills you apply as group leader. In this section you will systematically examine what a group leader should do, from the time group members are selected until the leader debriefs him- or herself in preparation for the next group meeting.

Selecting Group Members

Organizations differ in their approach to group selection. Some organizations allow division leaders to name group leaders who, in turn, select the individual group members. Some organizations assign people to groups. In other organizations membership in groups is at least partially voluntary. Since organizations differ in how members are selected it is difficult to generalize about any "one way" to select group members.

Assume that you have been appointed the leader to a newly established small group. You are told by your superior to choose six people to serve with you. What do you do? Whom do you choose? If possible, group selections should be based on *demonstrated competencies*. For example, if your group will be solving a problem you need experienced problem-solvers on board. If the problem you are to solve concerns the design of a new industrial plant, you need people trained and experienced in design, industrial engineering, plant supervision, and security. If you have the option of making the choice of group members, your first consideration should be demonstrated competency in the areas relevant to your objective.

A second consideration is *experience*. It is generally a good idea to have an older organizational person included in your group. Preferably, this individual will possess some special skill or expertise needed by the group. This person should be familiar with the organization's history, how previous decisions were made, and what their results were. He or she may also have chosen working relations with people at all levels within the organization, and know whom to ask about issues as they arise during interactions.

A third criterion should be *availability*. In most large organizations it is difficult to coordinate people's work schedules in making group selection decisions. You may not be able to obtain the assignment of all the people you want, because of conflicts in their availability for group work. You may be able to work out an exchange agreement with another group leader or to offer a reciprocal arrangement sometime in the future to obtain whom you want. But there will be times when you will have to make other choices. Make sure you check group members work schedules before assigning them to your group. If an individual is presently engaged in three other group activities, it is probable that she or he will not have much time to work on your project. Be sensitive to individuals' capacity for work.

A fourth criterion should be *communication style* (see Schultz, 1986). You want group members who can work well together as a group. If two strong and opposing personalities are in the same group, this may have a damaging effect on discussions. The presence of individuals hostile to each other may impair the group's ability to deal rationally with a decision or problem. Find out what you can about each potential group member's past history of communication with other possible group members. This is a time-consuming activity, especially if you are unfamiliar with the people, but it is an absolutely essential task. You should *not* be looking for individuals who will always agree with what you say and do ("Groupthink!"); rather, your purpose should be to find knowledgeable, skilled, competent, experienced people who possess no initial biases against each other. Try to imagine a group meeting with your choices present. Who would say what to whom with what effect? Who would have power? Who might be reticent? Who has a territory to protect from some other group member? How would these factors affect the group interaction?

Figure 5.2. Objectives
for Group Leaders

Productive Objective	Poor Objective
By five o'clock the group will reach consensus on how the question should be phrased.	By the end of the meeting we will know what we are doing.
By three o'clock we will have written a draft of the final report.	We will have completed the report.
By twelve o'clock we will have resolved the three disputed issues left over from our last group meeting.	We will all agree on what the real issues are.

These four criteria should be used in selecting group members. Do not make Mike's mistake:

Mike P., 32   When I was promoted to project manager I made good on a lot of promises I had made to friends along the way. I assigned my friends to my group. What a mistake! You cannot lead your friends unless you want to end up friendless. You also bring all that history with you to meetings. Everybody knows every dumb thing you've done since high school. You lose credibility. I'll never make this mistake again, believe me.

Planning the Group Meeting

Earlier I discussed four areas of preparation for group meetings:

1. The issues or agenda must be foreseen.
2. The group and individual members must be analyzed.
3. The physical situation in which the group will meet must be anticipated.
4. The leader's personal style must be appropriately selected.

Now take a closer look at *how* you plan a meeting.

First, the leader must *formulate an objective for the meeting.* The group leader must know what the outcome of each group meeting should be to plan ways of reaching the objective. If you are using Standard Agenda, which phase of communication are you presently in? If you are not using Standard Agenda, what must be discussed during the meeting, and what should the outcome be? Figure 5.2 provides examples of productive and poor objectives. What will be accomplished by the end of the group meeting? Be as precise as possible in your use of language. For example, what is a "real issue"? The more precise your statement of objective, the more likely you will know when you have reached it.

Second, *list the items or issues to be discussed in an order leading to the accomplishment of the objective.* Do not encourage spontaneous talk. Group members will have opportunity to modify the agenda, once it has been prepared and circulated. Your responsibility is to provide direction for the talk. Find an order or procedure that will permit the group to reach its objective in the time specified. For example, your list may look like Figure 5.3.

The advantage of preparing a list of topics is that it allows the leader time to think about the group meeting and to plan for any contingencies that may

AGENDA FOR GROUP MEETING

AUGUST 28, 1989

Figure 5.3. Agenda for
Group Meeting

OBJECTIVE: By two-thirty we will have completed our fact-finding reports and circulated the individual documents among group members.

TOPICS:
1. Review of old business
2. Proposed changes in today's agenda
3. Roberta's report on the history of the problem
4. Ron's report on the present status of the problem
5. Lew's report on what CDC did when they faced a similar problem
6. Belinda's report on available resources to solve the problem
7. Michelle's report on what the strategic planners say about it
8. Discussion
9. Circulation of the individual documents
10. Assignments for next time
11. Adjourn.

affect the group's operation. The leader may review the list and decide that the group cannot attain the objective in the time specified. The leader may then modify the list or change the objective for the meeting. If the list appears reasonable, the leader is ready to proceed to the next stage.

Third, the leader should, if possible, *circulate the agenda,* since it is usually desirable to prepare group members for what should happen during the meeting. Thus, the leader is responsible for preparing and circulating the agenda for the member's inspection. I recommend the agenda be distributed at least *two days* prior to the meeting to give group members an adequate opportunity to peruse it and consider how they may best participate. The leader should also make provision for any changes to be made in the agenda prior to the meeting. Listing your phone number on the agenda may encourage group members to call you to discuss changes before they are announced at the meeting.

> **Mable S., 24**   I let my group members know that I prefer to be consulted about agenda changes *before* they bring them up during the meeting. I have seen too much time wasted deciding changes, when the time could have been more productively spent on the problem. I always list my phone number and times when I will be in on the agenda sheet. I find people do call, and we can discuss the changes more personally. I know it sounds like I control what is discussed during the meetings, and I don't deny it. But my groups always get their work done on time, and that has made me respected in this organization and liked by the group members as well. In my opinion, that's the best of both worlds.

A fourth consideration for group leaders is to *review the four areas of preparation.* Have you analyzed the group and the individual members in relation to *this* meeting and *this* objective? Have you chosen a style of leading appropriate to the agenda? Have you prepared for the physical setting? Is there anything else you need to do prior to the meeting to ensure its success?

Opening the Meeting	The leader is always responsible for opening the group meeting. Five tasks should be accomplished during the initial stages of any group meeting, and usually they can be done in the following order:

1. *Call the meeting to order on time.* If you establish a precedent for being punctual, group members will learn to expect and adhere to it. If you do not establish this precedent, the individuals who do arrive on time will resent it, and those who do arrive late will grow in number. When you call the meeting to order, simply say "Let's begin," or "Are we ready to begin?" Do not engage in a private conversation with another group member and expect the group to drop what they are doing to watch.

2. *Take the roll.* If you want to encourage people to attend group meetings, keep a record of attendance. Usually the leader will appoint a recorder or secretary to keep minutes of the meeting; this should include a record of attendance. If a group member is absent and has previously informed you of it, announce this to the group. "Larry's not here today because his kid's in the hospital. He called this morning. Tom, will you be sure to call him this evening at home to let him know what we did today?" If the group member is absent without giving notice, you might ask the group if anyone knows where she or he is.

3. *Announce the agenda.* It is not enough to simply circulate the written document. The effective group leader will announce the agenda at the beginning of each group meeting. This serves two important functions: (a) it provides a common source of information for all group members to use, and (b) it allows group members to correct the sidetracking behavior of other group members who lead the group away from the agenda.

4. *Ask for modifications to the agenda.* Do not assume because the group members did not inform you of any changes that there are none. Some group members may not have read the document until just before the meeting. It is considerate for a group leader to ask for any modifications of the agenda at every group meeting.

5. *Review any old business.* Before initiating any discussion, a group leader should ask for any new information. Since the last meeting, has anything happened that may bear on the group's decision-making or problem-solving? Also, if issues from the previous meeting were left undecided, it is generally a good practice to resolve them prior to discussing any new business. The effective group leader does not encourage group members to consider subjects other than the issues or topics at hand.

The above five tasks are the responsibility of the group leader. Opening a meeting successfully is a good sign. If a leader uses the same format for openings, the members will come to expect it, thus establishing an important precedent in their shared experience.

After opening the meeting, an effective leader manages the talk of group members. By *manages* I do not mean "controls" or "manipulates." Managing refers to the ability of the leader to maintain orderly procedures for equitable exchanges between and among group members. While managing the meeting the leader should not be the focus of attention, nor the person to whom arguments are addressed. The effective leader presides over the meeting, using seven basic skills identified by researchers from the "functional" approach, and most recently modified by Sandra O'Connell (1979, p. 161):

1. *Initiating goals and procedures.* The effective leader helps group members to organize discussion so as to accomplish objectives. The leader establishes and maintains an orderly progression of talk by preparing the agenda and circulating it prior to the meeting, by announcing the agenda and requesting any modification, and then by adhering to the agenda during the meeting.
2. *Seeking information.* The effective leader is adept at asking members key questions that may clarify a point, lead to consensus, or reveal strengths and weaknesses in an argument. While preparing the agenda, the leader should also write out tentative questions to ask individual group members. While at the meeting, the leader should refer to those prepared questions to make sure they are answered. As the leader develops experience with a particular group, his/her ability to ask questions quickly adapted to the needs of situation and others should improve.
3. *Giving information.* The effective leader provides useful information to the group. He or she is also a productive participant in group interactions, creating and carrying out essential assignments, and reporting to the group the results of research efforts. Leaders must be careful not to abuse their role by providing biased information selectively developed to support their own views.
4. *Clarifying ambiguous terms and elaborating ideas.* The effective leader constantly strives to reduce ambiguity in the messages of the group. The leader must be able to recognize abstractions, ask questions designed to identify behaviors, goals, tangible means and ends, while detecting the characteristics of ambiguous terms and phrases. He or she should be especially sensitive to the uses of jargon and technical language within the group. When the group prepares public documents, they should, for the sake of clarity, eliminate technical terms, jargon, or in-house language. The leader should also be capable of developing the ideas of others, adding to them by references to previous group decisions, information, or experience.
5. *Summarizing different points of view.* The effective leader maintains order in discussions and is able to summarize the essential points of agreement and disagreement among group members. Leaders must always strive to present *balanced* summaries; the strongest and weakest points of each person's argument should be

included. Do not favor any one group member's position, or the ability to maintain order through the use of summaries will be seriously diminished. Also, a leader must make judicious use of summaries, must not interrupt a speaker to make a summary, or attempt to summarize until all the arguments have been presented.

6. *Consensus-checking.* The effective leader knows when to ask the group whether or not they are in agreement or disagreement. This does not mean to force the group to reach or achieve consensus. A leader must reveal sensitivity to the needs of group members to continue or exhaust arguments, while observing the overall group need to maintain a pace of interaction necessary to cover the items on the agenda. An effective technique for consensus-testing is the question: "Are we ready to decide about this issue now?" or "Are we in agreement?" Generally it is better for the leader to ask a consensus-testing question than to make a consensus-assuming statement.

7. *Giving assignments or directions.* Toward the end of each group meeting the leader should sum up the work of the group and make assignments or give directions for next time. Assignments should be equitably apportioned among group members; if possible they should be based either on prior experience or on expertise in a particular informational area. The leader should also be responsible for making "devil's advocate" assignments, should seek out new sources of potentially conflicting evidence or ideas to test the strength of the group's work. Assignments should be made publicly. The group leader who makes private assignments may gain personal loyalties at the expense of group cooperation.

These seven tasks are the leader's guidelines to successful meeting management. Effective leaders usually keep a chart of their progress with a group. By using these seven task areas as a guide, develop your own checklist of leading skills. You may want to use the format in Figure 5.4.

Preparing for and Monitoring Nonverbal Communication within the Small Group

Although I purposefully place great stress on managing verbal communication within group settings, there are also valuable nonverbal characteristics which the effective leader should possess. In this section you will be introduced to some useful research findings about the effects of choices in connection with nonverbal communication and perceptions of leading ability. To begin, consider the following statement summing up much of what we know about nonverbal communication and leadership.

Veronica L., 24: You spend a lot of time watching people in group meetings. I know you are supposed to be listening to what they are saying, but sometimes you become more interested in what they are wearing, or how they are sitting,

Use the following checklist to help assess your ability to carry out managing tasks and functions during group meetings. Your evaluation should be based on (a) your ability to *perform* the task or behavior, (b) your ability to *adapt* the task or behavior to the needs of the situation and others during the meeting, and (c) your *willingness and ease* in performing the behavior. Use the scale 1 (low) to 5 (high).

Figure 5.4. Self-Assessment of Leading Skills

Task Behaviors	1	2	3	4	5
1. Initiating goals and procedures to help group organize performance.	___	___	___	___	___
2. Seeking information, getting the opinions of group members.	___	___	___	___	___
3. Giving information, providing your own views on the subject.	___	___	___	___	___
4. Clarifying terms, reducing ambiguities, leveling abstractions.	___	___	___	___	___
5. Summarizing different points of view among group members.	___	___	___	___	___
6. Checking for consensus, determining areas of agreement and disagreement.	___	___	___	___	___
7. Giving assignments or directions for the next meeting.	___	___	___	___	___

Areas needing improvement: *Goals for the next meeting:*

_____

_____

_____

_____

_____

From *The Manager as Communicator* by Sandra E. O'Connell. Continuing Management Education Series, edited by Albert W. Schrader. Copyright © 1979 by Sandra E. O'Connell. By permission of Harper & Row Publishers, Inc.

or the movement of their eyes. At least I know I do. Anyway, let me tell you about Sam. Sam is a middle-aged guy from southern Georgia. He went to Vanderbilt. He is kind, courteous, sincere, and just a little bit decadent. Anyway, Sam was our group leader for awhile. He was so "laid back" he put people to sleep. It was his style, I guess. I mean he took forever to get a point across, and there would be times when silence seemed eternal while he figured out what his position would be. He was a meticulous dresser, and I often found myself admiring his clothing, especially the silk ties and elaborate vests. But he had no energy, no real enthusiasm, or at least that's how he looked when he tried to lead the group. He would sit there at the head of our conference table with his hands folded, his eyes curiously focused off in space somewhere, and he would talk slowly and syrupy. He put more action into lighting his pipe than he did into leading the group. He was a very nice man, but I would not want to work in a group under him again.

Veronica's story points out some of the essential characteristics (in her case, deficiencies) of a group leader's nonverbal communication.

You know that the exchanges of talk with a group are designed to be persuasive. A group leader should be able to persuade the group to reach a consensus, to monitor its talk, to summarize diverse positions, and so on. This individual should also be able to persuade the group members to accept him or her as their leader. Mehrabian and Williams (1969) found that individuals trying to persuade others will typically exhibit a high frequency of facial activity, gestures, and head nodding. Although theirs was not a study of small groups, the characteristics of nonverbal communication which they isolated as concomitants of persuasive messages seem relevant to small groups.

Nonverbal Behaviors Associated with Leading O'Connor (1971) studied four categories of nonverbal communication as related to the emergence of leadership in small groups. These categories were:

1. *Dynamism:* Use of hands and arms while speaking.
2. *Alertness:* Facial expression and head movement while participating in discussions.
3. *Involvement:* Body posture while listening or speaking, particularly leaning forward.
4. *Participation:* Mouth movement, verbal participation in the discussion.

Of these four categories, O'Connor found that participation and dynamism were positively correlated with leadership emergence. This would seem to indicate that persons seeking leadership positions within small groups should be both verbally and nonverbally active during group meetings.

O'Connor's observations were given additional support by a similar study by Baird (1977). He found that of all categories of nonverbal communication, hand gestures and arm movements (dynamism) seemed to indicate emerging leadership. While it would be simplistic to assert that if you move your arms and gesture your hands while participating in small groups you will become a leader, it seems to be reasonable to assume that leaders are perceived as being more dynamic in their nonverbal communication than are nonleaders.

We also know that a leader's style, incorporating both verbal and nonverbal components, influences the choices of behavior among other group members (Sadler, 1970). Earlier I discussed the importance of understanding the norms or rules within a particular group. If you assume that a leader exerts influence on the group's choices of behavior, then you can observe how nonverbal norms established by a group leader may influence choices about nonverbal behavior among group members. Consider the following statement:

Rodney E., 26 The first group meeting alerted me to a whole host of standards used to determine how well you fit into the group. My group leader was a man who had worked for IBM in the 1950s and who still adhered to the white shirt, dark tie, dark pants, and polished shoes dress code. I came to the meeting in a pink shirt with a white tie, faded jeans, and desert boots. He looked at me as if I was a visitor from a distant planet. I looked around the room and saw conservative suits everywhere, even among the women. I also noticed that our leader would stand up and pace while arguing for a particular point. While no one else in the group would stand up, or pace, they all used their hands when they talked, and they all sort of, I don't know how to say this but, kind of imitated him, the sound of his voice, the tone of it, you know. Now look at me. No more pink shirts! I am the straight man all the way. And in that room with that leader, I guess even I sound something like him. He is very domineering, though, and even though we may imitate him, there is still only one George.

It is difficult to generalize about nonverbal communication norms. The best advice I can offer is to be sensitive to the nonverbal style of your group. How do they dress? How do they sit at the table? How do they gesture? At whom do they look when they are speaking? One important idea to remember is that the only good reason to adapt to the group's nonverbal norm is to establish a sense of group identity. If they are less than effective nonverbally, if they are more like Sam than George, you may choose to be different to produce a needed change. If there is little dynamism in the group's nonverbal communication, you may find positive response given to your use of gestures, facial expression, and body movement. You may be able to exert positive influences on the group's ability to accomplish their objectives by demonstrating nonverbal communication effectiveness to complement your verbal effectiveness.

Leaders of small groups must be able to develop considerable skill in the resolution of conflicts. When people work together in groups tensions develop; arguments about issues and agendas may escalate into arguments about personalities and ego-involvements. Because productive use can be made of conflict, group leaders do not want to prevent disagreements, but they need to learn how to *manage* them effectively.

Identifying and Resolving Conflicts

A leader must be able to identify the source of conflicts. Many small group disputes erupt because of previous interpersonal difficulties. Unless the group leader is able to perceive how the past influences the present, she or he is likely to mistake a conflict about an interpersonal problem for a conflict over an idea. Consider the experience of Jane:

Jane S., 27   Talk about blowing it! I was the leader of a group charged with calculating the trajectories of a new missile for the Army. I should have known better than to put Phil and Nat in the same arena with Cindy. Both of them had dated her, both of them were still vying for her attention, and the group setting simply proved to be a testing ground for them. In almost every meeting these two guys would create disagreements. These would begin with a technical dispute, then move to personal insults, and by the time I stepped in both of them were fuming. I think Cindy enjoyed the attention. She knew they were fighting over her. Finally, after wasting about a month of our time and falling behind on the schedule, I got my supervisor to place Cindy in another group. Phil and Nat stopped using my meetings for sparing matches, and we got along much better. The odd thing about this situation was my own ignorance. I should have known better than to mix business with love. There are times when you need to see people as human beings instead of just members of groups.

Jane's experience with conflict indicates the need for group leaders to be cognizant of interpersonal disputes *outside* of the small group. In any organization there are sources of interpersonal conflicts which may directly affect work in any small group. While other group members should share the responsibility for alleviating conflict (when it is destructive) or managing conflict (when it is productive), the ultimate authority rests with the group leader.

There is no formula for a group leader to deal productively with interpersonal or group conflicts. Leaders will develop their own personal style of handling disputes, based on the information they gather about group members and the issues at hand. However, some common techniques can be used to resolve disputes in small groups; these usually follow this basic procedure:

Procedure for Dealing with Group Conflict

1. *Identify the source of the conflict.* The leader should halt interaction when conflict develops and ascertain the cause of the dispute. Do not allow communication about any issue to continue until the conflict is resolved. One unresolved misunderstanding about the meaning of a term, a group's charge, or a disputed fact or interpretation of a fact, can lead to escalation of the conflict.
2. *Ask each disputant to present a brief statement concerning the end to be achieved by the conflict.* Do *not* ask the participants in the conflict to talk about their perceptions of the *problem.* No one ever agrees about what the problem is; instead, focus on the *outcome* to be achieved. To what end or purpose are the arguments presented?
3. *Seek common ground between the two positions stated.* Disagreements may exist at the level of (a) *attitudes* toward issues, objects, or persons; (b) *values* held about what is right or wrong, good or bad, appropriate or inappropriate; and (c) *beliefs* about causes for praise or blame. A group leader should examine the disputant's arguments for common ground at any or all of these levels. Once such common ground can be identified, the leader should encourage the disputants to use the initial agreement as basis for additional agreements, finally leading to resolution of the conflict.
4. *If common ground cannot be established, then say so and move on to the next item on the agenda.* Usually conflicts can be resolved by finding common ground, then reworking the dispute on a cooperative basis aimed at reaching the common goal or end specified. However, there are times when disputes cannot be immediately resolved. When this occurs, the group leader should admit it and get on with the work

of the group. In these cases it is advisable to arrange a private meeting with the disputants and find some workable compromise which may then be reported to the group at the next meeting.

Most people believe one sign of leadership is the ability to manage conflict in groups. Although it is very difficult to generalize about what technique may work best for you or the groups you lead, the foregoing suggestions should help you better understand some available communication behaviors from which to choose. Again, a leader must be able to adapt to the peculiar needs of a group situation and group members. It takes time, effort, and communication skills to know how to accomplish this.

In the last chapter I discussed the importance of developing a *process* orientation to group work. A leader must see the connections between group meetings and events. To encourage the development of process thinking, group leaders should set aside a time following each group meeting to review what was accomplished and to prepare for the next meeting.

Preparing for the Next Meeting

> **Karl W., 34** I have made it a practice to spend at least one hour between group meetings in review and preparation. I have found it is not a good idea to prepare for the next group meeting immediately following the last one. Let some time go by, clear your head of the burning immediacy of what has just transpired. Usually I meet once a week with my team as a group, on Mondays. So my time for review and preparation is Thursday or maybe Friday. This way I keep in touch with those group meetings on a regular basis. I believe it helps me lead the group.

Leaders differ in their approach to review and preparation time. Some leaders use standardized forms to check their progress. Other leaders prefer a more informal debriefing session; they casually think back over the meeting, try to isolate key statements, questions, and events. With this base of information they try to formalize specific plans for the next meeting. In either case, the result of this time spent in reflection should be a plan or strategy for the next group meeting.

You have now reviewed the skills of leading. In the final section, you will study some ways of overcoming potential leadership problems in the small group.

Overcoming Leadership Problems in the Small Group

The theme of this chapter is the need for leaders to learn how to adapt to the needs of group situations and group members. An effective leader is an individual who possesses the desire to lead, an understanding of the leadership role and functions, as well as the ability to demonstrate competency in the skills of leading others while striving to attain objectives. Failure in any one of these three essential areas may lead to problems of leadership which will adversely affect the group.

As I pointed out earlier, a leader must be aware of his or her own strengths and weaknesses as a leader; he or she should also be able to develop an understanding of the strengths and weaknesses of individual group members. The underlying principle of effective leading, then, has been the same since the earliest sages wrote about it: *know thyself.*

Self-analysis is essential to effective leadership. Self-analysis is crucial in developing behavioral flexibility, the will to choose among the available behaviors and styles of leading the ones most likely to obtain the desired results. Self-analysis is vital in learning how to monitor your own behavior in groups. The skill of learning how to observe and interpret your own actions and statements from the perspective of other group members is not easy to develop. But a leader must be sensitive to *how behavior is perceived* in the group, recognizing that each small group develops its own standards of meaning. The goal of self-analysis is action directed at systematically overcoming one's perceived weaknesses as a leader without sacrificing perceived strengths. The successful group leader knows there is always room for improvement.

The best way to learn leadership skills is to develop *questions* aimed at improving the responses made to others in group situations. As experiences in small groups develop over a period of time, these questions reveal deeper and deeper levels of meaning. When the need to adapt to new situations and others arise, additional questions should suggest themselves. Here are some important ones to get you started.

Questions to Ask

1. *What is the goal of my group?*
   —How does this goal relate to the organization's objectives?
   —Who will determine whether or not we have reached our goal?
   —Have I provided the group members with an adequate awareness of our goal and the tasks needed to accomplish them?
   —Are there any obstacles that may prevent us from reaching our goal?
   —What can be done to overcome these obstacles?
2. *What are the goals of the individual group members?*
   —How do these goals enhance our ability to attain the objective?
   —How might these personal goals conflict with our ability to attain the objective?
   —How can I overcome these potential or real sources of conflict?
   —What factors outside of the immediate group setting may influence the statements or actions of my group members?
   —Are there hierarchical or territorial problems that may affect our discussions?
   —Are there interpersonal problems that may affect our discussions?
   —What can I do to help overcome these potential sources of difficulty?

3. *What are the patterns of influence generated by my group?*
   —Who says what to whom with what effect?
   —What are each member's sources of personal power?
   —How do these sources of power conflict? How may they be coordinated?
   —What is my authority with the group?
   —What are my sources of power within the group?
   —How do the individual group members perceive my authority and power? How do they respond to it?
4. *What are the equities and inequities within this group?*
   —What rewards are pursued by individuals in the group?
   —What punishments are meted out by or to individual group members?
   —What are my group's standards for apportioning resources among members?
   —Who regularly feels distress during group meetings? What is the source of the distress?
   —How can I be instrumental in alleviating the distress of group members?
5. *How effective are the agendas and procedures used by this group?*
   —Are group members well prepared for group meetings?
   —Do group members have an active role in shaping the agenda?
   —Do I provide adequate understanding of the uses of the agenda and procedures involved in making decisions and in solving problems?
   —What can be done to improve the efficiency of the group?
   —How can I be instrumental in improving the efficiency of the group?

Realistic Goals for Leading

Although I encourage an adaptive approach to leading, no leader can be all things to all group members. Leading does not mean dominating; it means organizing the actions of group members to accomplish the tasks specified by the charge. Effective leaders are adept at delegating responsibility to able group members, and directing the activities of the group when the members need direction.

The style of communication developed by the group leader is vital in overcoming difficulties. Condemnations should be avoided. Criticism and censure should be used only when directions are needed and time is short. "Selling" is an acceptable skill for any group member when arguing for a point of view, but group leaders must be careful not to "oversell" a group. I advocate a problem-solving approach to choices about the communicative style of all group members, and especially of group leaders. The problem-solving style of communication encourages input from group members and engenders a spirit of cooperation in the group. When disputes arise among group members, the leader should approach the dispute as a problem to be resolved, not as a personal affront.

Communication is both a means and goal of leadership. In an atmosphere where talk is encouraged, participation usually becomes more active and group members are more satisfied with the outcome. Effective leaders are necessarily effective communicators. The choices made about behaviors are communicated to group members when the behaviors are enacted. The choices made about leadership styles are communicated to group members in the statements, questions, and actions of the leader. When I ask you to monitor your behavior in groups, I am requesting you to note what and how your behavior *communicates* to other group members. When I ask you to adapt to the needs and expectations of situations and of other members of the group, I am asking you to adapt your *communication* to the needs and expectations of situations and of others.

Every leader faces problems of leadership. People may challenge you for the leadership role, engaging in conflicts that damage egos and the attitudes of group members. At times the agenda will remain unaccomplished and the goals of the group may be jeopardized. To be a leader is to understand that no matter how hard we try, inevitably there will be times when we fail. Given this fact, the process of learning how to lead includes a frank acknowledgement of imperfection.

Summary

This chapter addresses the challenge of leadership of small groups. The theme of this discussion is adapting to the needs of group members and to situations of leadership by developing the ability to ask probing questions about preparation, and flexibility in leading.

First you examined the history of leadership research. I identified seven approaches to the study of leadership prevalent prior to the development of the adaptive approach. The *trait* approach assumed that leaders were born, not made. There were said to be identifiable innate characteristics of leaders, such as size, coloring, and sex which predetermined an individual's ability to become a leader. The *styles* approach assumed the existence of three basic styles of leadership (autocratic, democratic, laissez-faire), and that the democratic style was superior to all situations. The *situational* approach claimed that leadership style depended on the responses made to environmental urgencies. The *functional* approach postulated the existence of demonstrated competencies as the bases for leadership, and found that two functions, the task and maintenance of positive group relations, were both important for leaders. The *contingency* approach argued that the effectiveness of any style of leadership was dependent on the nature of the group situation and the tasks performed. The *expectancy* approach asserted that human beings are goal-oriented, that they will look for instrumental ways and means of attaining their goals. The expectancy approach generated two varieties of illustrating how ends and means were coordinated: the *path-goal* approaches to leading. None of these seven approaches presupposes that leadership skills and behaviors can be learned, although each provides important insights into the nature and components of leadership.

Second, you examined the strengths and weaknesses of the adaptive approach to leading. I discussed two interrelated assumptions of this approach: (1) the need to analyze group members and to discuss the situation, and (2) the need to develop behavioral flexibility. I emphasized that there should be a balance between a leader's preparation for leading and actual demonstrations of competence in the small group setting. I advocated an adaptive approach to leading.

Third, I discussed the skills of leading, identifying six categories essential to effective leading: selecting group members, planning the group meeting, opening the meeting, managing the meeting, identifying and resolving conflicts, and preparing for the next meeting. In each category you examined the specific skills and communicative behaviors which leaders should develop so as to demonstrate competencies.

Finally, you examined ways of solving leadership problems in small groups. I discussed the importance of self-analysis as a necessary prerequisite to all decisions expressing effectiveness as a leader. I developed the bases for pragmatic questions which leaders can use to further develop their own ability to adapt to situations and others. I discussed the importance of selecting an appropriate communication style, and concluded the section with a review of the need to recognize that effective communication practices are the key to effective leading.

References

Aristotle. *The Rhetoric and the Poetics.* Edited by F. Solmsen. New York: The Modern Library, 1954.

Baird, J. E. "Some Nonverbal Elements of Leadership Emergence." *Southern Speech Communication Journal* 42 (1977): 352–61.

Barnard, C. *The Functions of the Executive.* New York: Harper Bros, 1938.

Benne, K. D., and P. Sheats. "Functional Roles of Group Members." *Journal of Social Issues* 1, 4 (1948): 41–9.

Bird, C. *Social Psychology.* New York: Appleton-Century-Crofts, 1940.

Bormann, E. G., J. Pratt, and L. Putnam. "Power, Authority, and Sex: Male Response to Female Leadership." *Communication Monographs* 45 (1978): 119–55.

Bunyi, J. M., and P. H. Andrews. "Gender and Leadership Emergence: An Experimental Study." *Southern Speech Communication Journal* 50 (1985): 246–60.

Castiglione, B. *The Book of the Courtier.* Translated by C. S. Singleton. Garden City, New York: Doubleday-Anchor, 1959.

Cragan, J. F., and D. W. Wright. "Small Group Communication Research of the 1970s: A Synthesis and Critique." *Central States Speech Journal* 31 (Fall 1980): 197–213.

Downs, C. W., and T. Pickett. "An Analysis of the Effect on Nine Leadership Group Compatibility Contingencies Upon Productivity and Member Satisfaction." *Communication Monographs* 44 (1977): 220–30.

Evans, M. G. *The Effects of Supervisory Behavior Upon Worker Perception of Their Path-Goal Relationships.* Diss. Yale University, 1968.

Fiedler, F. E. *A Theory of Leadership Effectiveness.* New York: McGraw-Hill Book Co., 1967.

Fiedler, F. E. "The Contingency Model—New Directions for Leadership Utilization." *Journal of Contemporary Business* 3, 4 (1974): 65–79.

Fiedler, F. E. "Leadership Effectiveness." *American Behavioral Scientist* 24 (1981): 619–32.

Fisher, B. A. "Leadership: When Does the Difference Make A Difference?" In *Communication and Group Decision-Making.* Edited by R. Y. Hirokawa and M. S. Poole. Beverly Hills, Ca: Sage, 1986.

Gouran, D. "Response to the Paradox and Promise of Small Group Research," *Speech Monographs* 37 (1970): 218–19.

Gouran, D. "Group Communication: Perspectives and Priorities for Future Research." *Quarterly Journal of Speech* 59 (1973): 22–29.

Hampton, D. R., C. E. Summer, and R. A. Webber. *Organizational Behavior and the Practice of Management,* 3d ed. Glenview, Ill. Scott, Foresman, and Co., 1978.

House, R. J. "A Path-Goal Theory of Leadership Effectiveness." *Administrative Science Quarterly* 3, 16 (September 1971): 321–38.

House, R. J., and T. R. Mitchell. "Path-Goal Theory of Leadership." *Journal of Contemporary Business* 4, 3 (Autumn 1974): 81–97.

Howells, L. T., and S. W. Becker. "Seating Arrangement and Leadership Emergence." *Journal of Abnormal Social Psychology* 64 (1962): 148–50.

Kwal T., and H. Fleshler. " The Influence of Self-esteem on Emergent Leadership Patterns." *The Speech Teacher* 22 (1973): 100–106.

Lewin, K., R. Lippitt, and R. K. White. "Patterns of Aggressive Behavior in Experimentally Created 'Social Climates'." *Journal of Social Psychology* 10 (1939): 271–99.

Machiavelli, N. *The Prince.* Edited by T. G. Bergin. New York: Appleton-Century-Crofts, 1947.

Mehrabian, A., and M. Williams. "Nonverbal Concomitants of Perceived and Intended Persuasiveness." *Journal of Personality and Social Psychology* 13 (1969): 37–58.

O'Connoll, S. *The Manager as Communicator.* New York: Harper & Row Continuing Management Education Series, 1979.

O'Connor, J. "The Relationship of Kinesic and Verbal Communication to Leadership Perception in Small Group Discussion." Diss. Indiana University, 1971.

Phillips, G. M., *Communicating in Organizations.* New York: Macmillan, 1982.

Phillips, G. M., D. J. Pedersen, and J. T. Wood. *Group Discussion: A Practical Guide to Participation and Leadership.* Boston: Houghton Mifflin Co., 1979.

Rosenfeld, L. B., and T. G. Plax. "Personality Determinants of Autocratic and Democratic Leadership." *Speech Monographs* 42 (1975): 203–8.

Rosenfeld, L. B., and G. D. Fowler. "Personality, Sex, and Leadership Style." *Communication Monographs* 43 (1976): 320–24.

Sadler, P. J. "Leadership Style, Confidence in Management, and Job Satisfaction." *The Journal of Applied Behavioral Research* 6 (1970): 3–19.

Sargent, J. F., and G. R. Miller. "Some Differences in Certain Communication Behavior of Autocratic and Democratic Group Leaders." *Journal of Communication* 21 (1971): 233–52.

Schultz, B. "Communicative Correlates of Perceived Leaders in the Small Group." *Small Group Behavior,* 17 (1986): 51–65.

Scheidel, T. M. "The Study of Leadership." Inaugural Lecture in Honor of B. Aubrey Fisher, University of Utah, 1987.

Sennett, R. *The Fall of Public Man.* New York: Vintage Press, 1978.

Stogdill, R. "Personal Factors Associated with Leadership: A Survey of the Literature."
    Journal of Psychology 25 (1948): 35–71.
Stogdill, R. *Handbook of Leadership.* New York: Free Press, 1974.
Wood, J. T. "Leading in Purposive Discussions: A Study of Adaptive Behavior."
    Communication Mongraphs 44 (June 1977): 152–65.
Wood, J. T. "Leading as a Process of Persuasion and Adaptation." In *1976 Group
    Facilitator's Annual Handbook,* edited by J. W. Pfeiffer and J. E. Jones, 132–35.
    Lajolla, CA: University Associates, 1976.
Yerby, J. "Attitude, Task, and Sex Composition as Variables Affecting Female
    Leadership in Small Group Problem-Solving Groups." *Speech Monographs* 42
    (1975): 160–68.

Exercises

The best way to prepare for the role of leading a small group is actually to lead a small group. Depending on how your class is organized, you probably have already experienced the leadership role or are about to. Unlike the exercises presented in earlier chapters, those included here are not designed to have you demonstrate the skills discussed in the chapter. You will have that opportunity in your group at the discretion of your instructor. Instead, I want you to expand your analysis of the leader's role by understanding how your group members view effective leadership. The first exercise is intended to help you analyze the communication skills of successful leaders.

1. Assemble your group. Ask each group member to assess the strengths and weaknesses of each of the following candidates for the position of leader of your group. After each member has completed that task, your group should engage in a consensus-seeking discussion designed to: (a) determine which one(s) of the following candidates best fits your group's idea of a potentially ideal leader, and (b) the common characteristics of an "ideal" leader, based on your discussion of a leader's strengths and weaknesses.

   Alice Q., Ph.D. candidate in Art Education, 30, 5'9" 130 lbs., married, no children: Five years teaching experience in art schools, two years of college level teaching experience, part-time work as graphic artist for a computer science firm. Known to be very competent, hard-working, and sincere; good performance appraisal reviews, but consistently ranked low by peers in social skills: acts aloof and removed from others, somewhat obnoxious to persons who are less educated. Experience leading groups is limited to teaching small groups of art students basic drawing and graphics skills.

   Jerry T., B.A. in History, 23, 6' 190 lbs., single: Two years experience as salesperson for computer software firm where he topped all salespersons in output. Known to be very aggressive salesperson, but not hard to get along with. Possesses keen insight and a good sense of humor, but tends to become bored if subject under discussion doesn't interest him. Experience leading groups limited to Sunday-school sessions.

Karen R., part-time undergraduate majoring in English; full-time employee of engineering firm as technical writer, 24, 5'5" 120 lbs; married twice, one small child: Two years experience as technical writer with average performance appraisal reviews, occasionally thought neurotic by peers because of constant complaints about insomnia and back pains. Also considered very bright and fairly easy to work with. Experience leading groups as coordinator of the technical writing staff at the engineering firm, familiar with Standard Agenda.

Robby W., full-time undergraduate majoring in business administration, 20, 5'10" 155 lbs., single: Honor scholar all semesters at the University, independently wealthy from family trust, highly motivated to succeed on his own. Thought bright but high marks usually attributed to long hours and hard work, social life somewhat mysterious, some consider him gay. Never complains, always punctual, expects others to be the same way. Sharp tongue when angered. Experience leading groups since the age of 16 in a variety of settings, usually related to family businesses. Familiar with Standard Agenda, Delphi technique, adept at public speaking and technical writing.

Vivian S., full-time undergraduate majoring in accounting, recently accepted at premier law school, 21, 5'4" 110 lbs, single: Honor scholar all terms, very bright and very hard worker. Won national prize for poetry as a freshman. Exceedingly shy, but able to work well with others, always polite, sometimes too much so. Some peers consider her insincere. Experience leading groups limited to one term course in small group communication in which she received her usual "A".

The second exercise asks each group member to compose an agenda for the next scheduled group meeting in class. Ask your instructor for information about the assignment if you are unsure.

2. Write an agenda *anonymously,* turn it in to this session's group leader. The group leader should then ask the instructor to make a copy of each agenda for every member of the group. Hand out one copy of each agenda to each group member for evaluation. Rank the agendas, based on their (a) completeness, (b) accuracy, and (c) neatness. Engage in a group discussion designed to establish criteria for an "ideal" agenda. Use the results of this discussion to guide the preparation of agendas for future group meetings.

Introduction

Organizations are only as good as the decisions they make. In most organizations, decision-making tasks and responsibilities are used to plan, direct, and control all of the various functions performed by individuals employed by the company. These decisions are usually made by small groups operating under a specific charge, a limited budget, a time constraint, and also the knowledge that individual group members' jobs may be on the line if the decisions do not meet with the approval of the boss. The ability to render consistently effective decisions in organizations marks an individual as a leader and a valuable asset to the company. Inability to acquire decision-making skills poses a serious threat to any individual's career in business and industry.

The quest for decision-making skills begins with an understanding of what it means to make a decision. *A decision is a recommendation for action made after careful and systematic deliberations concerning alternative ways and means of attaining a specified goal.* This definition of a decision challenges you to explore the process of decision-making.

First, a decision is a recommendation for action. People make decisions resulting in one of three kinds of outcomes:

1. *Change the present system:* A decision to change the present system may be made when all other ways and means of bringing about the desired outcome through modification or repair have been exhausted. To change anything in an organization means to change the organization itself, because the basic structure of the company shapes the functions performed by individuals and groups within it. For example, when Thomas Watson took over a loose alliance of three small companies known as C-T-R (Computing-Tabulating-Recording Company) in 1914, he made decisions about the future direction of the companies which resulted in a change from what was then the present system. Ten years later the company changed its name to IBM; despite the fact that most of the company's employees remained the same, every aspect of their lives within the organization changed.

Watson's decisions did not simply modify an existing operation; they literally changed the internal and external dynamics of the organization. What were these decisions? Surprisingly, three of the four decisions dealt with how individual employees would be treated by the management of the company (Watson, 1963):

—The company will strive to guarantee life-long employment to its workers.

—The company will strive to promote and maintain respect for the individual.

—The company will provide the best customer service of any company in the world.

—The company will not settle for anything less than a superior effort in everything it accomplishes.

Major changes in an organization are rare. By nature, most organizations are conservative in their approach to change. Decisions recommending a change in the present system are, therefore, only possible when all other ways and means of achieving the goal have been demonstrated to be either ineffective or inefficient.

2. *Modify the present system.*   A decision to modify the present system may be made when the goal can be reached by alternative ways and means which do *not* require major organizational changes to ensure success. Modifications are the source of most organizational decision-making, and depend on the ability of the group to recognize and articulate alternatives from which a decision can be made. One example from IBM's corporate history demonstrates how modifications can be instituted without disrupting the entire organizational system. During the 1930s and 1940s IBM grew and expanded at a rapid rate. Thomas Watson's belief in respect for the individual worker led him, as early as 1914, to establish an "Open Door Policy," which meant that any employee of the company could have a private conference with him at any time. Because of the rapid growth of the organization, it became impossible for Watson to see every employee who had a problem. However, Watson believed in the idea of the Open Door Policy and refused to change it. He met with his division managers to discuss possible solutions; as a group they made a significant decision requiring modification, but not change, in the policy. This modification assured to every employee of the company the right to a private conference with Watson *when all other avenues had been exhausted.* Under this new policy, workers who perceived that they had been wronged or who felt mistreated could appeal to line managers, regional managers, and finally divisonal managers, all of whom had authority to make the desired modifications if the situation warranted it. By creating a hierarchy of appeal, Watson maintained the integrity of his Open Door Policy, but allowed the modifications to ease his personal schedule.

Modifications in organizations are routine. Because any organization must respond to changes in the marketplace and in the values of their workers, decisions requiring modification in the present system must be made. These modifications are actually *more* important to the organization than are complete changes in the present system precisely because if the modifications work, the organization becomes more efficient at much less cost (both human and fiscal) than may be required by major overhauls.

3. *Maintain the present system.* A decision to maintain the present system without modification or change is always one practical alternative that groups must consider when making decisions. The group should determine whether the desire to modify or change something within the organization's operation is *really needed at this time.* Although most organizations must be altered to meet existing market conditions, to expand operations, or to increase productivity, the proposed alterations must be demonstrably superior to the present system. One important question facing decision-makers is: "What will happen if we do nothing?" Often the companies that refuse to change their ways despite external and internal pressures to do so, survive and prosper long after other companies that made the changes have failed. IBM has often been cited as an excellent example of the ability to maintain a consistent philosophy despite cultural and social pressures to change.

The determination to maintain the present system is a decision. It is not a hedge against making a decision, nor a stall to prevent decision-making. To decide to continue "as is" requires just as much time, effort, and group deliberation as recommendations for modification or major change.

These three alternative recommendations for action should always be considered in a decision-making process. Failure to analyze and discuss each of them may lead to bad decisions. In most organizations, there is very little tolerance for bad decisions; they may cost you your job.

Second, a decision should be made after careful and systematic deliberations concerning alternative ways and means of achieving a specified goal (Hirokawa, Ice, and Cook, 1988). Moreover, decision-making is an orderly process. A charge is given to the group, who must formulate an appropriate agenda to guide their deliberations. Such deliberations should focus on the content of alternative propositions, the nature of the facts, and the best available conjectures about how the alternative recommendations may affect the company. The deliberations should strive to impose order on the decision-making process so as to enable the group to attain its goal.

This description of decision-making will guide the presentation of material in this chapter. You will begin with an introduction to how decisions are made in small groups. Second, you will explore some procedures for implementing a decision-making process in small groups. Third, you will investigate how communication affects decision-making, as well as developing standards for participants and leaders to use when evaluating the effectiveness of the oral communication in the group. Fourth, you will examine some potential problems affecting decision-making in small groups, and note how systematic observation and evaluation of the group decision-making process can provide solutions to these problems. Following the summary and references, you will consider two exercises, which can be used to train groups in decision-making skills.

The Nature of Decision-Making in the Small Group

I have already defined the three alternative types of decision that can be made by small groups in organizations: (1) to change the present system, (2) to modify the present system; and (3) to maintain the present system. In this section you will examine *how* these three kinds of decisions are made. Specifically, you will examine the structure of the decision-making process to understand the need for a procedure to guide communication in the process. Since the emphasis in this chapter is on the *structure* of the decision-making process, you will consider the phases of decision-making as interdependent units which may be accomplished during individual group meetings. Research has consistently shown that regardless of the nature of the decision (e.g., whether to modify a design specification for a rocket booster or to change a company procedure), the phases of decision-making remain the same (Scheidel and Crowell, 1964; Fisher, 1970; and Poole, 1981).

First, you need to examine the *general* aspects of decision-making. Based on research by Fisher (1974), these phases describe decision-making processes in terms of the communication occurring in groups.

Phase One:
Orientation

When a decision-making group initially meets, two kinds of verbal exchange usually occur: (1) talk about the reason for the group meeting and the nature of the task to be accomplished, and (2) discussion among the group members which is designed to reduce tension and improve understanding of who we are and why we are here. Fisher calls this phase of decision-making "orientation" because group members communicate to understand each other and the nature of their task.

> **Rebecca W., 37** By now I know what will happen when we get together as a group for the first two or three meetings. In a way it reminds me of cocktail party conversation. You know, people greet each other, exchange basic information about who they are and why they are here, and then move on. Some people don't think this kind of talk is important, but it is extremely important because what we find out about each other allows us to figure out how we ought to approach each other. In a sense I think of initial group meetings as opportunities to provide my instincts about people with better information. I decide whom I can trust, whom I need to know more about, and who might cause me trouble. Oh sure, we all play politeness games and pretend to like each other and be cooperative, but really we are gaining information.

Rebecca's statement is useful because it reveals the emphasis humans tend to place on getting to know each other in a group setting before accomplishing a task. Beebe and Masterson (1982, p. 109) believe that the orientation phase of decision-making is significant, since it tends to develop *trust* among the group members. Trust is not conceded instantly; it is the result of repeated interactions during which we assess the character and motives of the other group members. Ideally, a group characterized by a high degree of interpersonal trust should function more efficiently than a group characterized by a lack of trust; but trust does not, of itself, promote effectiveness in group discussions.

The orientation phase of decision-making is "officially" terminated when the group leader announces the charge and the group begins deliberating about the nature of its goal and the members' responsibilities. However, this is an artificial line of demarcation. Most people require more time to form opinions about other group members; although they may act like a decision-making group after the task begins, in reality they are usually still adjusting to each other, becoming more acquainted, and continuing the process of orientation (see Poole, 1983 for commentary).

Phase Two: Conflict

The second phase of decision-making is characterized by verbal exchanges seeking to establish and to argue persuasively for a position or perspective regarding the task. Usually groups move into the second phase of conflict during the first group meeting when a specific task must be accomplished. For example, if a group uses Standard Agenda, they may become oriented during the session when the charge is stated. Their next task is to phrase a question to guide discussions; this task requires efforts of mutual persuasion characterized by taking a position and trying to support it. Ideally, a spirit of cooperative competition will characterize the conflict stage; however, I have pointed out how conflicts can impair the ability of the group to obtain its goal.

> **Larry A., 28** I have learned to prepare for group meetings. When I go in, I know what my position is, how I intend to support it, and I also have a fair idea of who will argue against me. I used to get mad when somebody would argue against my position, but I have learned to accept it as a natural part of working in a group. So long as my character or integrity isn't the focus of the attack, I keep cool. You have to accept criticism of your arguments when you work with others. That's how you learn.

The premise of productive conflict in small groups is the assumption that if all sides are given an equal hearing, the truth should prevail. It is natural for group members to disagee with each other, to ask for more or better information, and to dispute claims. If the group enters the conflict stage with an appreciation for the merits of conflict, their chances for completing this stage with improved understandings and commitment to the consensus attained will be substantially increased. Furthermore, research indicates that argumentatively competent persons tend to directly influence group outcomes (see Schultz, 1982).

Phase Three:
Emergence

The third phase of decision-making is called emergence because it is during this time that the group shifts from conflicts aimed at establishing positions, facts, and information, to encounters seeking how best to formulate a final recommendation for action, and what this recommendation must include. Literally, the decision "emerges" from the exchanges of words between and among group members. As various alternatives are tested against criteria, as new possibilities are exposed to doubts and critical judgment, consensus about the recommendation slowly begins to merge.

> **Alice G., 34**   . . . You should have seen how it happened! First we rejected Tom's solution because it cost too much. Then we rejected Paul's solution because we still didn't know whether or not it would really solve the problem. Then we combined what I had recommended with what Jane was recommending, and one by one everyone agreed that was the decision. When it was all over we were exhausted, but we had done it!

Decision emergence is a critical time for group members. Because your ego naturally comes with the recommendations you make or favor, you can be hurt when they are rejected or substantially revised by other group members. However, if trust has been established and care has been exercised as to how conflicts are managed in the group, this phase of decision-making can allow each group member to "save face" when her or his recommendation is thwarted. Furthermore, research by Hirokawa and Pace (1983) demonstrates that the quality of talk during this phase of decision-making tends to distinguish ineffective from effective small groups.

Phase Four:
Reinforcement

The fourth and final phase of decision-making is usually characterized by an intense spirit of unity and cooperation among group members. The decision is put into final form, the last assignments regarding how the report or verbal expression will be given are made, and group members exhibit a high degree of cohesiveness in the statements they make, about both the decision and the other group members (Alderton, 1982). Conflict seldom occurs during this phase of interaction unless inequities have developed within the group, or the group members are not yet satisfied with their decision.

> **Richard E., 31**   I look forward to the last of the group meetings much more so than to the first ones, but not because it means I won't have to attend group meetings anymore. I look forward to the last meetings because it has been my experience that people strive to become the best of what they are during those times when what we've accomplished is finally dawning on us. We stop bickering, we forget old tensions, and we work together. To me, that's job satisfaction!

The above four phases of decision-making represent what usually happens in small groups when no special training in decision-making procedures has been presented to them. These phases, then, are *natural* manifestations of our ability to use communication to make decisions. By superimposing procedures on these phases you can increase the effectiveness and efficiency of the decision-making process.

Procedures for Implementing a Decision-Making Process

Why tamper with a "natural" process of decision emergence? Why not simply take for granted that groups will arrive at consensus as their talk flows from orientation to conflict to emergence to reinforcement? Or, as some authorities have done, why not provide detailed instruction in how to use each one of these phases by improving communication in them (Beebe and Masterson, 1982; Fisher, 1974)?

You study communication to improve what you know about communication processes and to improve your competency levels. Just as the natural and exact sciences produce information that may be translated into useful technologies, so too the social and behavioral sciences seek to establish better ways of understanding human behavior and, when possible, to improve it. Our technologies include better methods of writing, speaking, and listening; better ways of solving problems and making decisions; better ways of organizing individuals and groups in a productive society. Discovering what is "natural" to human beings is a logical first step in searching for ways and means to improve those natural processes.

For example, we know that Standard Agenda is a technology based on John Dewey's discoveries about how the mind solves problems. Dewey was interested in uncovering the natural processes of decision-making and problem-solving; group researchers who followed him were more interested in adapting his findings to the ways in which groups solve problems and make decisions. As a result, you are better able to learn systematic, productive group procedures which have helped us to achieve critical advances in society.

Now that you understand how decisions emerge naturally in small groups, you can use this information to develop a better way of approaching decision-making. You now need to investigate how communication may be productively guided as the group evolves. In this section I will discuss two basic decision-making procedures you may find useful in guiding and directing the work of groups. First, we will examine the Delphi Technique, an approach to group decision-making which de-emphasizes oral communication until consensus is attained. Second, we will examine the Standard Agenda, an approach to group decision-making that emphasizes a way of organizing the verbal exchanges or communication used to make decisions.

The Delphi Technique As we have noted, the Delphi Technique (Dalkey, 1969; Thomas, 1979) refers to the use of a small group of experts to make decisions or solve problems without face-to-face communication or the benefit (disadvantage?) of knowing who the members of the group are. The purpose of Delphi is to exclude "personalities" from group processes, to offset differences in verbal communication skills, communication styles, leadership behaviors, diversity in status, and other potential problems caused by face-to-face interaction in small groups. Ideally, the result of these exclusions is the powerful coalescence of anonymity and knowledge. The ideal product of a decision made by a Delphi group would be based solely on the information available and the group members' abilities to express their ideas, opinions, and arguments in writing. This is how Delphi Technique, in its original form, was designed:

1. *A group is selected by a charging authority.* Only the charging authority knows the identities of the group members. She or he is responsible for informing all group members that they will be participating in the group, as well as to define their task and goals.
2. *A memorandum is given to each member, stating the nature of the situation or problem.* Each group member reads the memorandum, thinks about the issue, and formulates a position relative to the question. This position is written down and returned to the charging authority. During this first round of contact with the issue, the positions taken by each group member are known only to the charging authority and the individual group member. No communication is allowed among the group relative to their positions.
3. *The charging authority then writes another memorandum, detailing the positions taken by each of the group members.* During this second round of contact with the issue, the identities of the group members remain anonymous and only their positions are stated. Each group member may then modify his or her original position, but the individual must furnish specific written reasons for departing from the position originally stated. The result of this second round is then sent back to the charging authority.
4. *This procedure is continued until all group members arrive at consensus about the decision or solution to the problem.* At no time are the identities of the group members revealed.

Since its inception, Delphi Technique has attracted the attention of a variety of scholars and corporations. Today there are a variety of Delphi Techniques, each one adapted to the particular needs and situations of the companies using them or the researchers studying them.

You can examine the merits of the Delphi Technique as a decision-making process by comparing what happens during the Delphi process with what happens in Fisher's decision-making schema:

1. *Orientation:* The urgency to make a decision about something is felt by someone or some group within the organization. A charging authority then selects group members, based on their qualifications and experience to deal with the decision. Then the group is given a written formal charge. The group members are asked to think through the issue, to write out the questions they believe need to be answered before any decision can be reached.

2. *Conflict:* The person giving the charge to the group is responsible for collecting the initial written responses and producing a written document (usually a memorandum) in which the positions are stated. This document is then transmitted to one group member, who writes his or her second responses to it on the same form. Then this group member sends the memo to the next group member, who also responds to what is written on the memorandum. This process is repeated until all group members have made their second responses to the charge.

   Conflict occurs because each group member can read what every other member has written concerning the issue and the charge. Questions raised by one group member may be answered by another, whose solution can then be reviewed by a third and fourth group member, each one able to agree or disagree with it. Usually the memo must be circulated among all group members at least three times before preliminary consensus begins to emerge. As the document circulates, additional written material may be added in the form of appendices. In this way, all group members participate in the decision-making process by providing useful information. By working alone and together, the members have the advantage of private thought and public responsibility for their thinking. Instead of forcing productive thinking to occur in a limited time format (e.g., the one-hour group session), the Delphi Technique encourages independent thought and action in extended time frames (e.g., a group member may keep the memorandum up to three days before transmitting it back to the group leader.

3. *Emergence:* After the original memo and appendices have been circulated three or four times, group members have generally reached preliminary consensus on most of the central issues pertaining to the decision. When one group member agrees with the other, he or she stamps the memo with a symbol used by the group to indicate

consensus. Emergence of the decision using Delphi Technique is based on an assumption concerning the value of written documentation and the ability of the group members to share meanings about what they read. Proponents of this method argue that because ideas are preserved in writing, they are easier to understand, to recall, and to analyze. However, unless the group members are skilled writers, Delphi Technique may cause confusion rather than avoid it.

4. *Reinforcement:* Group members who have used the Delphi Technique tend to behave much as group members who rely on oral interaction during the last phase of decision-making. As consensus is achieved and the stamp of approval imposed, there is usually a spirit of cooperation and a shared belief in the value of their task and commitments to it. Because goodwill usually increases as group members contribute to the decision, and the emergence of preliminary consensus areas contributes to a shared belief about cooperation among members, group members reinforce each other through written displays of appreciation, through written statements of cooperation, and through a cooperative desire to complete the task.

After the decision attains final consensus, the group must assign one or more persons to complete the formal report. In most cases, this also will be a written document to which the original memo and appendices are attached.

The uses of Delphi Technique have been consistently demonstrated in American organizations. By combining the advantages of privacy for reflective thought with group inputs centering on a common issue or problem, Delphi Technique is especially attractive to scientific and engineering firms; moreover, substantive uses of this technique have also been made by other business concerns.

The Standard Agenda

In Chapter 2 you were introduced to the procedure known as Standard Agenda. I explained Standard Agenda as a procedure widely used in business and industry to guide small groups. The purpose of this method is *to influence the kinds of communication taking place during group meetings.* By establishing what the goal of each meeting is and by carefully explaining the responsibilities of leader and members to reach the goal, Standard Agenda improves the natural process of decision emergence because the broad phases of decision-making can be broken down into systematic steps, each with identifiable goals for discussion and communication.

Standard Agenda and Natural Phases of Decision-Making

Here are the seven steps of Standard Agenda in relation to Fisher's model of decision-making:

Phase One: Orientation

Step 1: Understanding the Charge. When a small group is initially assembled for the purpose of reaching a decision about anything, there are four issues which must be settled: (a) what is the goal of the group; (b) who formed the group and why; (c) what resources are available to the group, including financial, material, technological and human support; and (d) when must the group make its final report, what form the report must take (oral or written), and to whom the report is to be made. Communication during the initial group meeting should be directed toward attaining consensus about these four issues.

Step 2: Phrasing the question. During the second meeting the group must achieve consensus on exactly what the issue requiring a decision is. The issue must be phrased as a *question* to guide all future discussions. There are three goals to be accomplished by interaction during this meeting: phrasing the question (a) to assure maximum utilization of resources available to the group; (b) in a way which enables the group to reach its desired outcome; and (c) to prepare the group to enter the next step of decision-making. Communication during this meeting should be directed toward achieving consensus about these three aspects of phrasing the question.

By the end of the second group meeting, assuming that the goals have been accomplished, the orientation phase should be completed. Group members not only should have acquired a substantive understanding of the group task, they should also have come to know each other in a *productive* way, by limiting the content of disclosures to information about personal perceptions of the task and methods of accomplishing it.

Step 3: Fact-finding. There are two goals to be attained by the group during fact-finding: (a) to collect as much relevant information about the issue as possible, and (b) to exchange the collected information among all group members. To reach these goals, interactions must focus on (a) presentations of the facts collected by individual group members; (b) critical examination of these facts by all group members; (c) assessments of the effects of the data on the phrasing of the original question and the ability of the group to carry out the task given to them; and (d) assessments of whether or not enough information has been gathered to warrant moving on to the next step. These four issues must be discussed, *in order,* and consensus reached, *in order,* before the group should enter step four.

Step 4: Establishing criteria for a decision. The goal of this step is to produce a set of carefully worded statements to guide the group in the making of a final decision. These statements must be designed to allow the group to recognize acceptable decisions and to reject decisions which may not accomplish this task. Communication should focus on (a) the nature of an ideal decision (What would it look like? What would it necessarily include? What would it do for the organization?); (b) the several elements in the ideal decision which could allow the group to find a reasonable, but less-than-ideal decision (given the constraints of the group, including financial, material, and human limitations); (c) the standards to be used for constructing a final decision, and (d) any limitations on the group's decision, including financial, material, legal, moral, logistical, and suasory constraints which may impair it. These four issues should be discussed *in order,* and consensus attained, *in order,* before moving on to step five.

The second phase of Standard Agenda encourages conflict among and between group members. Arguments about the nature of evidence, the existence and reliability of facts, the retention or change of the original question, the statements of criteria and limitations, should be contributed by all group members. As I pointed out earlier, conflict is a neutral term. If managed properly, the results of the conflict phase of decision-making can lead the group to productive, creative outcomes. Hence, all group members must understand that conflict is a vital part of the group process of decision-making and strive to manage it appropriately.

Phase Three:
Emergence

Step 5: Generating alternative decisions.   The goal of this step is to present as many alternative decisions to the group for inspection and analysis as possible. However, during this step the group should *only* attempt to generate the alternatives, *not* inspect and analyze them. To accomplish this, the interaction should (a) use the "brainstorming" technique to discover real and imagined possibilities and (b) establish some way of recording these alternatives for later analysis. During this step, group members' discussion must be constrained by the goal of the interaction; this is not a time for analysis of the facts, or comparison of decisions on the basis of criteria and limitations established earlier. Regardless of how absurd an alternative may seem, it should be recorded without comment. Consensus must be reached by the group to end the brainstorming session before moving on to step six.

Step 6: Testing the alternative decisions against the criteria.   The goal of this step is to find, if possible, the best decision relative to the original issue. If this goal cannot be reached by testing the various alternatives against the criteria, then the group must try to combine parts of less desirable decisions to construct a "best" solution-decision. To accomplish this, the group should (a) isolate each of the alternatives proposed; (b) consider the merits and limitations of each alternative by comparing it to the criteria; (c) rate each alternative based on its ability to satisfy the criteria; and (d) recommend how the final decision should be constructed. These four tasks should be accomplished *in order* before moving to the final step.

One major advantage of implementing Standard Agenda for decision-making is to systematize the ways in which possible decisions can emerge during the group interactions. Instead of relying on instincts or chance, Standard Agenda encourages small groups to follow an orderly procedure for the enunciation of decisions and discussions of their merits and limitations.

Step 7: Formulating the final decision and preparing the final report.
The goal of the final step in Standard Agenda is to present a convincing argument to the proper authority in the organization. To accomplish this goal, the interaction should (a) review all the steps in the process of decision-making; (b) carefully scrutinize the group's selection of a final decision *or* carefully prepare a final recommended decision based on consideration of the other alternatives; (c) make assignments to individual group members for the preparation of the final report on the decision; and (d) assemble the final report and (if necessary) rehearse the final group presentation. These four phases must be discussed, and consensus reached, in order for the group to accomplish its task.

Phase Four: Reinforcement

I have already discussed what happens during the "reinforcement" phase of decision-making. An advantage of using the Standard Agenda is that it often *encourages* the spirit of cooperation and commitment vital to the success of the group.

Combining Delphi Technique and Standard Agenda to Make Decisions

Your exploration of decision-making techniques may seem to suggest that there are only two recognized methods for improving small group interaction: Delphi Technique and Standard Agenda. However, when you think this way you risk incurring the same lack of creative choice which characterized early approaches to decision-making procedures. By approaching these methods as mutually exclusive, thus regarding decision-making as something to be accomplished *either* by Standard Agenda (when group interaction is preferred) *or* by Delphi Technique (when privacy and written communication are preferred) you limit and unnecessarily constrain your options. There is no good reason to suppose that you cannot combine the strengths of these two divergent methods to produce a new, integrated approach to decision-making in organizations.

The question becomes: How? How can you successfully combine Delphi Technique and Standard Agenda? Let's reexamine the phases of decision-making and see how we make productive use of a combined method:

As you know, the orientation phase of decision-making is intended to (1) introduce group members to the nature of the task, and (2) provide an opportunity for group members to know each other. Often these two tasks can be accomplished with equal facility by group members. However, in many cases, group members either

Phase One: Orientation

concentrate their energies on understanding what they are expected to do or on trying to create relationships with each other. Consequently, valuable time and effort may be lost while the group becomes oriented.

Standard Agenda's orientation phase consists of two steps: (1) understanding the nature of the charge, and (2) stating the discussion question. Delphi's orientation phase consists of the selection of group members and initiation of the memorandum. Because people may work better as a group after they have some information about each other as individuals, the following steps can be implemented, *in order:*

1. *Selection of group members:* The charging authority determines the composition of the group, then notifies each group member in writing. A convenient date, place, and time is established for the first group meeting.
2. *Understanding the charge:* During the first group meeting the members are given their task and the reasons for their inclusion in the group. All resources available to the group are stated in detail, and the appointed leader explains how the group is to proceed.
3. *Individual conceptualization of the task:* Following the first group meeting, the individual members return to their workplaces and think through their charge. The group leader will circulate a memorandum with the charge, the resources, and any other information about the group's operation. Each group member will read the memo, respond to it, and send it to the next person as indicated. Responses to the charge may be ("I still don't understand what Ed wants us to accomplish"), to the resources ("Can we really accomplish this task in two months?"), or to the operation of the group ("I need more information about how this circulation of memos is going to work").
4. *Phrasing the question:* During a second group meeting the individuals are briefed concerning any new information regarding their task or operation, based on the questions raised by their memos. Then a discussion about how to word the question should be conducted. Using the guidelines given in Step Two of Standard Agenda, the group should arrive at consensus about the question used to guide future discussions.
5. *Individual conceptualization of the question:* Following the second group meeting, the leader will circulate a memo with the agreed upon phrasing of the question, for examination and comment by each group member. Members are encouraged to respond to this phrasing, raising any objections or questions which they may have about the task. If no serious issues or objections emerge from circulation of the memorandum, the group leader should make individual assignments to each member concerning research about the issue.

The advantages of combining Standard Agenda and Delphi Technique during the orientation phase of decision-making include:

Use of interactions to provide direction about the task and reasons for each group member's appointment to the group;

Use of written statements to determine how each group member is responding to the task and the group's approach to it;

More time for thought about the task and about other group members;

Better accountability for agreements reached by the group;

Better assurance that individual group members will participate actively in the group.

A major disadvantage is the loss of anonymity, a condition that may introduce status rivalries and personality constraints within the group.

You know the conflict phase of decision-making is designed to (1) provide information about the task to the group for critical examination, (2) provide assurances to group members of the appropriate opportunities to express their own ideas about how facts may be interpreted, and (3) furnish group members with a way of working through various interpretations to arrive at consensus about which facts may be productively used by the group to make a decision. You also know that conflict can cause anxiety in individuals and ill will within the group if not properly managed.

Phase Two: Conflict

Standard Agenda's conflict phase consists of two steps: (1) fact-finding, and (2) establishing criteria. Delphi's conflict phase consists of the continuous circulation of the original memo until preliminary consensus is reached on most major issues related to the decision. The strengths of both methods can be used by the group if the following plan is carried out, *in order:*

6. *Fact-finding:* A third group meeting is arranged by the leader. During this meeting individual assignments regarding fact-finding are given. Group members are told that a memorandum will be circulated by the leader and that relevant facts should be typed on this form and initialed by the person responsible for recording them. There are two constraints on individual fact-finding missions: (a) research must be conducted in an orderly fashion and completed within the alloted time, and (b) each group member must limit recorded information *only* to the information that she or he has been asked to locate (this constraint will be altered later).

7. *Individual research on assigned topic:* Following the third group meeting, the leader circulates a memo on which the phrased question is stated. Each group member receives the memo, records pertinent data on it, and sends it to the next group member. (*Note:* No time limit is specified here. This decision depends on the nature of the task

and how long it should take to find the relevant information. However, the group leader must make sure that each group member understands the time limits for fact-finding for each group project. Once time limits are established, they must be strictly enforced!)

8. *Continuous circulation of the memorandum:* After the memorandum has been circulated and pertinent data recorded, the group leader receives the document and is responsible for organizing it. The organization of facts should be *topical;* it should only reflect what the data naturally suggests. It should *not* be modified to fit preconceived notions about what the facts should mean or how they should be interpreted. After the facts have been organized, the group leader again transmits the memorandum to the group for continuous circulation and commentary, according to the procedures described in the discussion of Delphi Technique. The document should circulate among group members at least three times before the leader calls the next group meeting. During this period, any issues related to the facts recorded *by any group member* should be subjected to doubt, criticism, and if necessary, challenged.

9. *Establishing criteria:* After preliminary consensus is achieved about the nature of the facts to guide future discussions, the leader should arrange for a group meeting. The purpose of this meeting is to review the fact-finding stage and prepare for establishing criteria. During this meeting, problems that still prevent the group from reaching an agreement about the facts should be resolved. After these problems have been discussed and consensus reached, the group leader should explain the procedure to be used for establishing criteria.

10. *Individual conceptualization of the criteria.* Following the group meeting, the group leader circulates the memorandum on which the *question* and the organized *facts* are stated. Each group member receives the document and lists statements that she or he believes may be useful as criteria to reach a decision, or as a limitation on how the group can make a decision. (Note: Again, no time limit is specified here. Time limits must be established by the group leader and explained to the group.) As the memo circulates group members should register any objections to statements of the others. After preliminary agreement is achieved about most of the statements, the group leader should call another meeting.

11. *Consensus on establishing criteria and limitations:* After the group reaches preliminary consensus, the group leader should arrange for a formal group meeting to review the criteria and limitations. During this meeting, outstanding objections to any statements of criteria or limitations should be resolved. At the end of this group meeting, the leader should explain the process of "brainstorming," and prepare the group for it.

Advantages of combining Standard Agenda and Delphi Technique during the conflict phase of decision-making include:

Use of group interactions to resolve conflicts and promote argument about the issues;

Use of written statements to reveal how each group member is responding to the task and the group's approach to it;

More time for research and thought about establishing criteria;

More time for research;

Better accountability for facts collected and agreements reached by the group;

Better assurance that individual group members will participate actively in the decision-making process.

You know that the emergence phase of decision-making is designed to (1) use brainstorming techniques to generate ways of making decisions and what the decision should include, (2) test the proposed alternatives against the statements of criteria and limitations, and (3) begin formulating a decision that will satisfy the charge and elicit the commitment of all group members. Emergence is a busy time in small groups; group members may, in the rush of activities, sacrifice quality in decision-making. At this point in the process, the decision may appear to be "perfect" and hence reduce the opportunities for questions and criticisms to be raised against it. Groups must maintain an "objective" approach even when they feel certain that the best decision is "obvious," because experience attests that it seldom, if ever, is obvious.

Phase Three: Emergence

Standard Agenda's emergence phase consists of two steps: (1) generating alternative decisions and ways of reaching them, and (2) testing the alternatives against the criteria and known limitations to find the most acceptable one. The emergence phase of the Delphi Technique usually consists of arguing about remaining difficulties with the decision. This is how you can combine the methods to form an integrative approach to decision emergence:

12. *Brainstorming:* Each group member arrives at the group meeting prepared to generate as many alternative decisions as he or she has considered since the last group session. The group leader must arrange for recording of the "brainstorming" session. Normally these sessions last no longer than one hour but should seldom last less than thirty minutes. During this period it is imperative that the group not be interrupted. After the group leader calls the meeting to order, group members begin the process of "brainstorming." Usually the privately (individually) generated alternatives will emerge first, then the group will begin developing new ways of making the decision and formulating additional alternatives. When the group exhausts the possibilities, someone should call for consensus to end the "brainstorming" session. "Brainstorming" should continue until all group members agree to abandon it.

13. *Individual review of the "brainstorming" session:* After the group meeting, the group leader should circulate a memorandum on which (a) the question, (b) the organized facts, and (c) a list of the proposed alternatives are stated. Each group member should review the information, registering reactions to the proposed alternatives before passing the memo to the next group member. When the group leader discovers most of the alternatives have been discarded, and the group seems to be concentrating on two or three alternatives, the leader should then arrange for a group meeting.

14. *Testing alternatives against criteria and limitations:* During this group meeting the leader should review the memorandum alternatives already rejected by the group, and provide (or ask for) brief explanations. Then the leader should list the remaining alternatives and ask those who support them to furnish arguments in their favor. (Note: Statements of criteria and limitations should always be referred to in presenting arguments for or against alternatives during this step.) Then the group leader should ask for objections and give them a fair hearing. Following these brief presentations and refutations, the group should be able to discuss the alternatives with the objective of finding the best decision.

The advantages of combining Standard Agenda and Delphi Technique during the emergence phase of decision-making include:

Use of group interactions to generate alternatives and make final decisions about them;

Use of written statements to guide the decision-making process;

More time for reflection about various alternatives;

Better accountability for the process of decision selection;

Better assurance that individual group members will actively participate in decision-making.

Phase Four: Reinforcement You know that the reinforcement phase of decision-making is designed to (1) find a decision to which the group can be committed, (2) assign the composition of the final report (oral or written) to competent group members, and (3) prepare for any group performances related to completing the task. Reinforcement is usually a happy time for group members, who feel a sense of accomplishment for the task and who share a commitment to its fate. There is likely to be a substantial expression of comradery during this phase; but group members should be reminded that even the best decision will do no good (and win no favor) unless it is competently submitted to the charging authority. Therefore, group members and especially the leader should exercise care to assure the timely completion of the task.

Standard Agenda's approach to reinforcement includes (1) construction of a "best decision", and reasons for it, (2) assignment of the final report among group members, and (3) preparation for any final performance of the project. The Delphi Technique's approach to reinforcement usually includes only a written review of the decision by group members, together with preparation of the final report. This is how these two methods may be combined:

15. *Group construction of the decision:*   After the "best" decision is selected by the group, the leader should arrange for another meeting to *construct the presentation of the decision.* The group may need to make individual assignments of portions of the final report. For example, one person may be selected to review the decision-making process; a second person may be assigned to collect and review the pertinent facts; a third person may be asked to collect the results of the "brainstorming" sessions; and a fourth person may be asked to make a list of the criteria and limitations used by the group. Consensus about these assignments and how they should be completed should be reached before the group meeting is adjourned.

16. *Individual work on the final report:*   Following the group meeting, each member should complete his or her task as quickly and as thoroughly as possible. Group members may want to consult with each other during this time. When each group member completes the task, she or he should contact the group leader. When the group leader receives notification from all members, the leader should then arrange for a final group meeting.

17. *Final group meeting:*   The purpose of this meeting is to "see" the final report in its oral and/or written forms. After the group is satisfied with its product, the decision-making process is completed and the group work is done.

The advantages of combining Standard Agenda and Delphi Technique during the reinforcement phase of decision-making include:

Use of group interactions to determine who is best prepared to complete an aspect of the final report;

Use of written statements to present a review of what the group accomplished;

Better accountability for the process of decision-making;

Better assurance that individual group members will actively participate in decision-making.

In this section you have seen how Standard Agenda and Delphi Technique may be combined for the decision-making process, a combination whose advantages I have stressed. However, there are disadvantages that may accrue if care is not exercised. For example, unless the task is sufficiently large, complex, and demanding, a combination of these two methods may only lengthen the process of decision-making, rather than improve it. If group members become bored with reliance on procedures-for-their-own-sake, the group process suffers. Unless there are very good reasons for lengthening the process by joining these two methods, the group should elect one or the other method.

Now you have reviewed the *methods* of decision-making. You are ready to consider the role of communication during decision-making interactions.

Decision-Making Communication

I have consistently stressed the idea that communicating is *how* people participate in small groups. Chapter 3 developed a theory of how communication *should* operate in groups, and what happens when failures, misperceptions, or breakdowns in communication occur. In Chapter 3, I also suggested that equity is a goal of all human groups, and that equity may be achieved through fair exchanges of goods, services, sentiments, and time among group members. Hence, communication is the substance of equity in groups, because it is through communication that exchanges are made between and among group members.

You realize that equity does not "just happen" in small groups. You must adapt a developmental view of how exchanges occur and shape meaning over a period of time. As relationships develop within the group, individuals begin to sense "who does what to whom with what effect." Too often, you learn this principle just as Karen did:

> **Karen S., 21** I guess it was about the fourth or fifth group meeting before I realized that it was what I had said and done in the first two meetings that prejudiced the group against me. Had I known then what I learned about the others' view of design specs, I would never have denigrated the use of Army methods. It took me a long time to realize what had happened and even longer to understand how people used those initial impressions to make long-lasting judgments about me, and maybe the best I can say about it is that we have to learn from our mistakes, right?

Learning from experience is often painful, especially when the experience from which you have to learn was a major mistake. The point of Karen's example is this: *we seldom consider the importance of what we say and do until it gets us into trouble.*

Because of the critical functions served by decision-making groups in organizations, there is little tolerance for inept communicators. Remember, communication is how you form an identity. When people hear or see you make mistakes they seldom attribute those mistakes to problems of communicating; they usually ascribe them to deficiencies in your character, training, or intelligence. No matter how faulty these judgments may be, they nevertheless occur.

In this section I wish to investigate how choices about communication effectiveness can be made in decision-making groups. Reading through this section will not make you a better communicator, but it may improve your understanding of what needs to be done before, during, and after group meetings with respect to what you say and do in them.

Previously you investigated the roles of group members and the rules that guide decisions about how to behave in those roles. I suggested that one way of improving group effectiveness is for each group member to understand what he or she is supposed to bring to the group (role) and what norms or standards are used by the group to determine the worth of individual contributions (rules). Let's examine these standards of effectiveness more closely.

Standards for Effectiveness

First, you need to understand how group processes influence your developmental view of communication in the group. Initial interactions among unfamiliar group members are like casual meetings at parties: you exchange basic information about yourself (perhaps enhancing it for rhetorical appeal), observe how the information is received and responded to by the other parties, then make a decision about how you should act in the presence of these new people. However, because of the *task* orientation of decision-making groups, the comparison to party behavior ends here. When your job and career depend on working with other people, you tend to be more *protective of yourself,* of your identity, and more *demanding of others*. You may be polite and responsive, but you are also wary. You have a job to do.

Consequently, communication during early phases of group development should be *carefully monitored*. Prior to group meetings, think through what you know about the task, other group members, and what you can contribute to the group's operation. Here are some useful guidelines for talk at initial group meetings:

Guidelines for Communication During the Orientation Phase

Safe Topics	*Potentially Dangerous Topics*
Names	Deeper biographical information such as marital status, hobbies, perceptions of family and co-workers, and career aspirations; In-depth discussions of any of these topics may provide cause for bias against you; Complaints about any of these topics may be offensive; unless you know to whom you are talking and their allegiances, you may risk more than you know.
Occupations	
Reasons for group membership	
The weather	
Recent news/sports events	
Where you reside	
Where you went to school	
Previous jobs held	
When the meeting will start	
Who is the leader	
Names of other group members and reasons for their inclusion in the group	

All potentially dangerous topics may become "safe" *after* you get to know your listener. Never assume you are speaking to a friend until the friendship has been seriously tested (Phillips and Goodall, 1983).

Most people expect the quality of talk before and during initial group meetings to be rather dull. If this is the expectation, any attempt on your part to improve its quality may either reflect positively or negatively on you. Do not assume it will reflect positively on you; recognize that there is at least a 50–50 chance of failure every time you risk communication. The "harmless" joke may offend people who view humor as an index of low character. The loyalty you may feel toward the Atlanta sports teams may not be shared by your listener. In fact, unless your listener has expressed an interest in sports, the mention of loyalty to a team may be interpreted as "pagan." Recall the "jock" stereotypes and the degree of hatred for them expressed by certain members of your high school class. You should not miss the point of the following story:

> **Cynthia N., 34** We had a big party, invited all the brass, and some people from Tom's company (her husband) as well. We spent over a month planning it, down to the last detail. The food alone cost me nearly a month's pay. Anyway, we thought people would appreciate all the work that went into it, and believe me, almost everyone did. Well, about half way through the evening this guy comes up to me and says, "Gee, I really hate these kind of dull parties, don't you? I mean, look at all the waste! Who are these people trying to impress, anyway? The little fishy hors d'oeuvres are rotten, and the band stinks. I'll bet you someone is just bucking for a promotion." He went on and on. I just listened to him until he finally turned to me and said, "Hey, I didn't introduce myself—I'm Paul W.—who are you? I smiled as viciously as I could and said very clearly, "I'm Cynthia N., your host." You talk about turning red! This guy couldn't apologize enough on his way out the door. But it didn't matter, everyone else was having a wonderful time and I knew Tom would appreciate hearing this story about one of the people who worked *for* him.

The classical dictim for intelligence is "know thyself." However, given the importance of communication in your daily lives, you should be equally well-versed in "knowing thy audience."

Initial group meetings are, as you have learned in this chapter, orientation sessions. People get to know each other and their responsibility to the task. *How* and *what* they learn about each other and the task will influence their ability to reach consensus (Gouran, 1969; Knutson, 1972; Kline, 1972). Your choices about what to say and do during these initial phases of decision-making should be carefully planned and executed. If this sounds mechanical, consider what some of the possible consequences may be if spontaneity overcomes reason. Remember, you are a member of a decision-making group assigned to accomplish a specific goal. Your success in the organization well depend primarily on your performance as a group member, not on how well you impress people with personality. If people learn to rely on your judgment and character they may then learn to appreciate your more vivacious traits. Reversing the process, particularly in a pragmatic work environment, is a dangerous, if not an unnatural, act.

Communication during the conflict phase of decision-making should be characterized by the rules of argument: state your case and attempt to prove it; listen carefully to the refutations provided by your hearers and determine the merits of their position before responding. Communication during the conflict phase can contribute to the relationships you develop with other group members as well as to your own identity within the group. Competence in argumentation usually leads to favorable judgments about you, even when group members disagree with the content of your ideas. Remember *equity* should be the goal, and *exchange* must be the method of attaining the goal. Do not treat someone who opposes your argument as an enemy, or else you can expect them to reciprocate in kind when you least expect it, or least need it.

One team of communication researchers (Poole, McPhee, and Seibold, 1982) concentrated its energies on developing an understanding of how communication determines the quality of decisions made by small groups. Their findings strongly suggest the need for looking very carefully at the *influences* generated by arguments which group members advance during the conflict and emergence phases of decision-making. Specifically, they distinguish three interrelated levels of analysis for any message communicated by group members (1982, p. 6).

1. *The valence of the message.* Refers to the degree of positive and negative sentiments expressed about any alternative proposed by any group member. For example, within a group deciding policy about orientation for new company employees, several alternatives may be offered. How each group member voices agreement and disagreement with the alternatives suggests the sentiments they feel toward them. What is spoken will count as the valence of the message.

2. *The quality of the message as argument:* Refers to the ability of any group member to state a case and provide reasonable support for it. For example, using the above decision group, a group member may argue for a two-day session based on experiences she or he had in another company. Another group member may argue for a one-day session on the grounds that less time will be spent conducting the orientation and the company will save money. Yet another group member may argue for a week long session and attempt to justify the expense in terms of a long-range savings because properly oriented employees will make fewer logistical and procedural errors. How the group makes the decision will be based, in part, on the quality of the individual arguments. What is stated will also count as the message's argument content.

3. *The influence-strategy employed by the message:* Refers to any attempt to induce cooperation with a position, using techniques of equitable exchange ("side with me on this issue and I will try to help you get your idea accepted next time"), persuasion ("look at all the evidence we have concerning this issue and there is no way you can't see the need for a new policy . . ."), coercion ("if you don't side with us I will recommend your removal from the group"), and so forth.

How the group arrives at a decision will be based, in part, on the influence strategies employed by the individual group members. What is spoken will demonstrate the influence strategy.

From examining Poole, Seibold, and McPhee's research findings you can infer the importance of making productive choices about words and actions within decision-making groups. What you choose to communicate attains meaning and relevance at three interrelated levels, all of which directly influence the decisions made by the group. Their model further implies the importance of statements concerning the feelings which group members have toward decision options. Of the three levels of analysis of any message communicated by group members involved in making decisions, the expressed *valences* (sentiments) may account for as much as 75% of the variance in group decisions. This does not mean that sentiments are more important than information, evidence, or argument; it only suggests an important role of sentiments or feelings about options in the formulations of group decisions. Here are some guilelines:

Guidelines for Communication During the Conflict Phase

1. Be courteous to all members of the group.
2. Listen to opposing points of view before making any comments or refutations. Do not interrupt anyone who is speaking.
3. Organize your ideas before speaking. State your claim, provide support for it, adapt your message to the needs and expectations of your listeners.
4. Express sentiments about other group members' ideas.
5. Do not talk too much; do not monopolize the floor. Limit your words to the essentials of argument; if more information is needed it will be requested by the other members of the group.
6. Know when you have won or lost an argument. Do not labor the point after it has been settled. If you consistently oppose the will of the group you will only encourage them to oppose your ideas and work against you.
7. Do not transform arguments about facts or interpretations of facts into disputes about the character, integrity, values, or beliefs of your opponent.
8. Strive to develop a reputation for fairness. Do not try to acquire a reputation as a star debater, a "motor mouth," or a trouble-maker.
9. Always give credit to those who have helped you. Do not claim credit for an idea that was given to you by someone else.
10. Ask for responses to your ideas. Solicit feedback even if you believe the group agrees with you.

Your choices about talk during the conflict phase of decision-making are very important. Too often groups suffer because enemies are made over conflicts. Problems also occur when conflicts are repressed by authoritarian leaders or group members. Remember, you can disagree with someone's ideas and express the disagreement courteously; you do not have to express malice or ill-will to convince others.

Communication during the emergence phase of decision-making is characterized by more cooperation and less conflict. There may also be a tendency in groups characterized by developing relationships for communication to concentrate more on the interpersonal than on the task aspects of the decision. Group members may express more openly their feelings about the decision and how it may affect others. As people begin to trust each other, and to rely on their perceptions of the group based on experiences shared with them, communication may also make productive use of commonplaces. Hence, the group's communication may appear to an outsider as a strange kind of shorthand; a word or phrase whose meaning is clearly recognized by group members may represent an extensive background of shared experiences. Here are some guidelines for talk during the emergence phase of decision-making:

Guidelines for Communication During the Emergence Phase

1. Encourage group members to express their feelings about issues and approaches to the decision.
2. Rely on shared experiences and examples to guide arguments used in support of, or against, alternative propositions.
3. Monitor the effects of talk on group members. Strive to adapt to their needs and expectations.
4. Strive to articulate clearly and precisely the several alternatives and criteria. Much time can be lost through overlapping ideas.
5. Do not persist in allegiance to one or two favored proposals. Be open to the alternatives and try to find merit in them.

Your choices about talk during the emergence phase are important because they reflect your perception of the group and its members, while also revealing your level of commitment to the group's decision. By this time the group has shared experiences that allow individuals more freedom to express ideas in a context of acceptance; however, this privilege must not be abused. Every group member should still monitor his or her communication efforts, always striving to adapt the message to the needs and expectations of the audience. Remember, *appropriateness* is also a standard used to evaluate talk.

Communication during the reinforcement phase of decision-making is often more pragmatic, more precisely goal-oriented, than in any other phase of the process. During this time the work of the group is the formulation of the decision, and its presentation to the charging authorities. There are assignments to be completed, details to be checked, and rehearsals to be scheduled (if the group is to present

Guidelines for Communication During the Reinforcement Phase

an oral report). In many cases the activities of the group during this phase resemble a cast before opening night: hectic and harrassed individuals who express great optimism and pessimism in the same breath, and who share a commitment to the quality of the performance. Here are some guidelines:

1. Do not overreact to statements made by others. Remember that the tension and anxiety prior to the submission of a final report or a group presentation will influence what is said and done by group members. When people are nervous or anxious they tend to be more or less communicative than usual.
2. Perform your task! The group effect will proceed more smoothly if everyone accomplishes what he or she is supposed to accomplish. Do not volunteer to help someone until your task is completed, unless you cannot complete your task until you receive information from the other member.
3. Believe in your final product. Express this commitment in statements you make about the group's work.
4. Thank the people who help you and be courteous to those who seem to be in your way. Do not let the group process suffer because at the last minute you suddenly unleash a series of emotions.

If communication within the group is effective and efficient, so also will be the decision, provided the group has acquired and properly processed the information necessary for the decision-making. If you observe the communication occurring within a decision-making group over a period of time, you will generally note these tendencies:

1. As the group process develops, talk becomes less constrained by roles and rules;
2. As group members come to know each other, communication becomes more personalized and better adapted;
3. Talk becomes more open and honest as the group develops closer interpersonal relations among its members;
4. Nonverbal communication becomes easier to interpret as the group progresses;
5. Initial prejudices, fixations, and anxieties gradually yield to more cooperation and unity.

These five tendencies occur in groups that rely on procedures to generate the content of talk during group meetings. There is less reliable data about groups who function without strict adherence to procedures for decision-making. The use of procedures seems to assure better communication, while better communication, in turn, seems to produce better decisions.

On this note of optimism, you are ready to examine some potential problems which affect decision-making groups.

Problems in Decision-Making Groups

A colleague once observed that there are probably as many different kinds of problems affecting small groups as there are fingerprints of people participating in small groups. When you "see" a problem in a group setting, it is always personal and immediate. You perceive the problem as a result of specific statements (or lack of them) and actions (or lack of them) by identifiable group members. The problems that *you* face in small group decision-making always seem beyond the wisdom or counsel furnished in textbooks. They are "your" problems, unique to your settings and the people in them.

As a result of study about group communication, it is possible to list some of the ways problems affecting group decision-making can be conceptualized. For example, you know some difficulties occur because of the group's *inability to establish a decision-making procedure* (Hirokawa, 1988). I advocate the use of established procedures such as Standard Agenda, Delphi Technique, or a combination of the two methods when making decisions in groups. By using a procedure, you reduce the ambiguity of the situation and improve the ways in which choices about communicating can be made. In fact, virtually all problems associated with decision-making groups stem from a lack of inappropriate use of a decision-making procedure. So critical to the performance of a group task is the implementation of a procedure to guide talk that I urge any group to make it the first order of business. Here are some problems resulting from a lack of procedure:

1. Lack of group cohesiveness
2. Lack of leadership
3. Lack of motivation to complete the task
4. Lack of participation in decision-making activities
5. Lack of coordination in decision-making activities
6. Lack of role specification
7. Greater anxiety among group members regarding the task
8. Greater anxiety among group members regarding each other
9. Greater cost to the organization
10. Greater opportunity for conflict escalation

The above list is based on data obtained from observations of small groups and interviews with personnel in organizations that have had to function in group settings that lacked a procedural orientation. Admittedly there may be decision-making groups that operate successfully without strict adherence to procedures. However, the chances for problems to arise in groups without specified procedure seem to be far greater than in groups that use Standard Agenda or Delphi Technique.

As groups develop they may alter the rigidity of procedures affecting their operation; i.e., they may modify the present system. These modifications usually do not adversely affect the operation of the group, so long as each group member understands how the modification affects his or her role and responsibilities. However, the best advice is to make judicious use of an established procedure for decision-making.

Summary

This chapter addressed decision-making in small groups. I began by defining a decision as "a recommendation for action made after careful and systematic deliberations concerning alternative ways and means of obtaining a specified goal." I then specified the three possible goals of decision-making groups: (1) to change the present system, (2) to modify the present system, and (3) to maintain the present system.

I addressed the nature of decision-making in small groups, explaining four phases natural to any decision-making process: (1) orientation, (2) conflict, (3) emergence, and (4) reinforcement.

I then described the procedures used to implement decision-making processes. In this section I reviewed the steps of Standard Agenda and Delphi Technique in relation to the four phases of decision emergence. I then suggested the two methods could be combined to produce advantages for groups seeking to make major or complex decisions. I detailed what procedures would be used to combine effectively the strengths of both methods.

I then addressed communication in decision-making. I reviewed each phase of the decision-making process and the requirements for effective communication in each one. I explained how the developmental view of groups allows us to predict how communication will change as the group acquires experience, providing guidelines for effective communication in each one of the decision-making phases.

Finally, I discussed some of the problems affecting group decision-making. I argued for a systematic view of group problems, in contrast to a lack of procedures or inappropriate uses of procedures, as guides in the decision-making process. I stressed the need for groups to use an orderly procedure to guide decision-making, because such procedure will aid choices about communication.

References

Alderton, S. M. "Locus of Control-Based Argumentation as a Predictor of Group Polarization." *Communication Quarterly* 30 (1982): 381–87.

Beebe, S. A., and J. T. Masterson. *Communicating in Small Groups: Principles and Practices.* Glenview, Ill.: Scott, Foresman, and Co., 1982.

Dalkey, N. C. "The Delphi Method: An Experimental Study of Group Opinion." Rand Corporation Memorandum RM 5888–PR, June, 1969.

Fisher, B. A. "Decision Emergence: Phases in Group Decision-Making." *Speech Monographs* 37 (1970): 53–66.

Fisher, B. A. *Small Group Decision-Making.* New York: McGraw-Hill, 1974.

Gouran, D. "Variables Related to Consensus in Group Discussions of Questions of Policy." *Speech Monographs* 36 (1969): 387–91.

Gouran, D., R. Y. Hirokawa, and A. E. Martz. "A Critical Analysis of Factors Related to Decisional Processes Involved in the Challenger Disaster." *Central States Speech Journal* 37 (1986): 119–35.

Hirokawa, R. Y., Ice, R., and J. Cook. "Preference for Procedural Order, Discussion Structure and Group Decision Performance." *Communication Quarterly* 36 (Summer 1988): 217–226.

Hirokawa, R. Y., and R. Pace. "A Descriptive Investigation of the Possible Communication-Based Reasons for Effective and Ineffective Group Decision-Making." *Communication Monographs* 50 (1983): 363–79.

Kline, J. A. "Orientation and Group Consensus." *Central States Speech Journal* 23 (1972): 44–47.

Knutson, T. J. "An Experimental Study of the Effects of Orientation Behavior on Small Group Consensus." *Speech Monographs* 39 (1972): 159–65.

McPhee, R. D., M. S. Poole, and D. R. Seibold. "The Valence Model Unveiled: A Critique and Reformulation." In *Communication Yearbook 5,* edited by M. Burgoon. New Brunswick: ICA-Transaction Books, 1982.

Phillips, G. M., and H. L. Goodall, Jr. *Loving and Living.* Englewood Cliffs, N.J.: Prentice-Hall/Spectrum Books, 1983.

Phillips, G. M., D. J. Pedersen, and J. T. Wood. *Group Discussion: A Practical Guide to Participation and Leadership.* Boston: Houghton Mifflin Co., 1979.

Poole, M. S. "Decision Development in Small Groups I: A Comparison of Two Models." *Communication Monographs* 48 (1981): 1–24.

Poole, M. S. "Decision Development in Groups II." *Communication Monographs* 50 (1983): 206–32.

Poole, M. S., R. D. McPhee, and D. R. Seibold. "A Comparison of Normative and Interactional Explanations of Group Decision-Making: Social Decision Schemes versus Valence Distributions." *Communication Monographs* 49 (1982): 1–19.

Scheidel, T., and L. Crowell. "Idea Development in Small Discussion Groups." *Quarterly Journal of Speech* 50 (1964): 140–45.

Schultz, B. "Argumentativeness: Its Effect on Group Decision-Making and Its Role in Leadership Perception." *Communication Quarterly* 30 (1982): 368–75.

Thomas, L. *Medussa and the Snail.* New York: Viking Press, 1979.

Watson, T. J. *A Business and Its Beliefs.* New York: McGraw-Hill, 1963.

Exercises

This chapter addressed decision-making in small groups. Because many decisions made by small groups in organizations are undertaken to solve organizational problems, the following exercises attempt to simulate this basis for decision-making. As you will see, each exercise is actually a case study of an organizational problem. Using whatever decision-making technique you prefer, your task is *to render a decision to each one of the following problems.* At the discretion of your instructor you may be asked to deliver a formal group report detailing the decision-making procedure and its outcomes.

1. Applied Technology Innovations (ATI) is a medium-sized R&D company incorporated in the mid-South. The company is less than ten years old but already has gained a solid reputation for innovative technology designed to improve the routine operations of modern organizations. Recently the CEO of ATI received a report urging the immediate development of a computer-assisted group selection software package. The package would be an aid to mid-level managers who face the burden of assigning professional persons to work groups and then listening to them groan about the others they must work with to accomplish the task. The report indicated that academic research in the disciplines of speech communication, social psychology, and organizational behavior was replete with information about how to make better group selection decisions. Unfortunately, this information had not yet been adapted for use by organizations.

One possible tool is the SYMLOG field map (see Robert F. Bales and Stephen P. Cohen, SYMLOG: A SYSTEM FOR THE MULTILEVEL OBSERVATION OF GROUPS. New York: Free Press, 1979), which purports to be a valuable aid in determining how group members get along in problem-solving or decision-making settings. If such a system could be adapted to a simple-to-use, flexible, user-friendly software package, the market could be captured, because at this time there is no competition. This report further urged that a group be assigned the task of investigating the feasibility of such a software package. YOU ARE THAT GROUP. YOUR TASK IS TO INVESTIGATE THE FEASIBILITY OF MARKETING A SOFTWARE PACKAGE DESIGNED TO AID THE GROUP SELECTION PROCESS. Notice that you are *not* responsible for actually developing the software, but only for determining the feasibility of marketing such a product. Who would the market be? Does the need for such a package actually exist? How could the package meet the needs? What would it have to include? How could it be made "user-friendly?"

2. XYZ Corporation is a California-based manufacturing firm specializing in widgets (never mind what a widget is!). Recently some messy personnel situations have developed because of a lack of guidelines concerning how performance appraisal reviews should be used to determine merit raises in pay. Under existing guidelines each section manager/ supervisor is responsible for recommending merit increases following the six-month appraisal review. In seven cases reported since the last review cycle, individuals have received outstanding appraisals but no merit pay increases. When they asked their supervisors/managers why not, they were told the company could not afford to give merit increases at that time. Because XYZ is financially sound and continues to expand, the employees are disgruntled. Rumor has it that the company is trying to avoid giving any merit increases because the high national unemployment situation suggests any employee can be easily replaced, and usually at a lower cost to the company. The only pay increases since the last appraisal cycle have gone to employees in the professional categories, persons who would be more difficult to replace because retraining would also be necessary. The line workers are upset, and the result is a lower morale among employees, suspicion between the ranks of skilled workers and professionals, and poorer quality control for the widgets.

Clearly there is a problem. YOUR GROUP HAS BEEN ASKED TO LOOK INTO THIS PROBLEM AND TO RECOMMEND A SET OF GUIDELINES CONCERNING MERIT PAY INCREASES FOR OUTSTANDING PERFORMANCE REVIEWS. However, the problem is not easily solved. Corporate headquarters does not now use a standardized evaluation form, nor do they have any policies regarding what percentage of the company's profits can be channeled into merit pay increases. You will have to do some substantive research concerning these vital issues. You should have no trouble designing a standard evaluation form for a small manufacturing concern (even one that makes widgets) using the following data:

a. The average worker can produce twelve widgets an hour. The average work day is eight hours. Overtime is mandatory for all line workers when the production schedule demands it. During the past two years of operation overtime has been required for all workers in time which translates to 57.35 hours per year, per worker. There are 175 full-time line workers, 60 part-time (20 hours per week).

b. Quality Control inspects the completed widgets. On the average they reject 1 widget out of every 27. However, since the negative rumors started, QC reports they reject 1 widget out of every 14.

c. Line workers are hired in at $4.85/hour, and receive time-and-one-half for all overtime hours. Workers with good performance records generally receive a $.10/hour pay raise every three months, or $.40/hour per year. The man with most seniority is John Williams, who has been with XYZ for 22 years and refuses to be made a supervisor (he also refused to enter officer candidate school in the Army). John makes $12.75/hour, the top money payable to a line worker, and a salary equivalent to a third-year supervisor.

d. XYZ expands its line work force according to need, but for the past five years it has expanded by 8–12% per year.

e. Line workers receive the following paid benefits from XYZ: paid medical insurance (no dental or eye care), paid worker's compensation, and a matching contribution to any IRA or similar retirement account up to $75/month.

f. XYZ is a non-union shop. There are no paid vacations nor annual sick leave for line workers.

g. Evaluations are done by the supervisors. There is one supervisor for every thirty-five line workers. In the past supervisors wrote out or dictated one-paragraph assessments of each worker. Here is an example of a typical one: "Harriet C. is a good, reliable worker. She is never late for work, and has only missed a couple of days during the past six months. She produces about 14 widgets an hour, on the average, with an occasional rejection. She is well liked and well respected, but tends to get foul-mouthed about overtime. She wants to be with her kids." As you can see, these informal evaluations emphasize subjective assessments of workers and do not provide any standards for merit pay increases.

3. Your University/College is trying to improve its curriculum. YOUR GROUP HAS BEEN CHARGED WITH THE RESPONSIBILITY FOR DESIGNING A NEW DEGREE PROGRAM IN *HIGH TECHNOLOGY MANAGEMENT.* Your report must be given to the Vice-President for Academic Affairs in one month's time, and it should contain the following items:
   a. An assessment of the need for the new degree program, including a statement of its mission or purpose, and a rough estimate of the number of students who will choose it during the first two years of implementation.
   b. A complete sample curriculum for the degree program, using existing and proposed new courses.
   c. An evaluation of existing campus resources for the proposed degree program, including library holdings, faculty, computer resources, and classroom space.

To accomplish your task you will need to conduct informational interviews with various campus authorities (administrators, deans, department chairs, knowledgeable faculty, etc.), as well as investigate similar degree programs at other institutions.

Use factual information drawn from your school.

Implementing Decisions 7

Introduction

Organizations survive by solving problems. No organization, large or small, can avoid having problems; the world and its markets constantly change, requiring quick and efficient responses from organizations serving them. Despite the prevalence of problems affecting all human organizations, any study of corporate histories reveals that some organizations prosper under conditions of stress while others collapse. Authorities have attempted to identify characteristics of the survivors. Although there seem to be many different contributing factors ranging from "creativity" in executives to sound economic contingencies, one consistent finding is the capacity of an organization to inspire confidence in its employees and its customers. These organizations successfully implement decisions made by small groups.

This chapter addresses the implementation of decisions made by small groups. First, you will examine a method frequently used for implementing group decisions: The Program Evaluation and Review Technique (PERT). Second, you will examine a discussion of how a decision-making group can combine the strengths of Standard Agenda and PERT to unify the decision-making and implementing processes, using a new procedure called MAT (Modified Agenda Technique). Third, you will examine communication processes during group problem-solving. Fourth, you will investigate potential problems arising during the implementation process and ways of resolving them. Following a chapter summary and references I provide an exercise designed to help you apply the material in this chapter.

Program Evaluation and Review Technique

Groups responsible for implementing decisions are like decision-making groups because both require the use of a standard operating procedure to guide communication, define roles, and aid the group in orderly conduct of argument. In the last chapter I discussed the uses of Standard Agenda and Delphi Technique, and demonstrated how they could be combined when groups attempt to make complex decisions. In this section I will detail the use of a widely used implementing procedure—PERT (Program Evaluation and Review Technique).

PERT is a technique originally developed during the 1950s by the United States Navy to assist the Polaris missile program (Federal Electric Corporation, 1963). Phillips (1965) then presented a detailed application of PERT combined with the decision-making technique of Standard Agenda. He indicated PERT could be most useful for working out details of a complex plan of action. Since that time PERT has been a popular technique of group problem-solving, with wide applications in business, industry, and the Federal government.

PERT is an easy technique to explain. Essentially PERT involves determining all events and activities that must take place to carry out a decision and then drawing up a sequential diagram of those activities, using an hour-by-hour, day-by-day, week-by-week plan. For each event or activity, all resources (human, financial, material, or technological) needed to complete the task are listed, and provisions are made for having those resources available at the appropriate time and place.

PERT requires the small group to use a step-by-step procedure for constructing a plan of action (Phillips, 1965; Bormann, 1975):

1. Determine the goal of implementing the decision.
2. Determine the events and activities necessary to reach the goal.
3. Order the events and activities in the best way possible.
4. Determine the duration of the activity or event.
5. Divide the activities and events into small sub-activities and sub-events.
6. Allocate priorities to each activity and event.
7. Determine resources for each activity and event.
8. Arrange a diagram specifying the flow of activities and events.
9. Begin putting the plan into action.

As you can see, PERT allows a group to organize talk toward the achievement of nine goals which together produce the solution to the problem. Like Standard Agenda, PERT operates as a constraint on communication between and among group members so that consensus on *one issue at a time* may be reached.

Andy S., 42   The thing I like about PERT is how it tells you exactly what you have to accomplish. With the administration of government programs, we need to know what everybody even remotely connected with the project is doing on a day-to-day basis. PERT makes us to do that, and believe me, you appreciate it when something goes wrong and you need to contact people. All you have to do is go look at the PERT chart—immediately you find out the who, what, when, where, and how of any aspect of the program. Some people call it more bureaucracy, but I think it is necessary.

Two authorities have discussed the use of statistical procedures within a PERT group (Brilhart, 1978; Bormann, 1975). Because of the need to create a workable plan of action, large quantities of information regarding the time required to complete a task, the cost of time and material resources, and a variety of other concerns that may be expressed in mathematical formulas and data, may be necessary for the group's work. As you can see, PERT is a sophisticated, highly systematic procedure for group problem-solving, amenable to discussion involving interpretations of complex data in the construction of a systematic plan of action.

The role of the leader in PERT interactions is largely defined by the nature of the specific task to be accomplished during the meeting. In Chapter 5 you observed how a leader can gain the confidence of group members by (1) announcing an agenda and circulating it among group members prior to the meeting, (2) calling the meeting to order and asking for any modifications in the agenda, (3) providing for some way of keeping a permanent group record, (4) reviewing and summarizing material when necessary, (5) intervening in conflict situations when necessary, (6) asking for consensus, and (7) making assignments for the next group meeting. All of these responsibilities can be logical components of a PERT group problem-solving process; the designated leader should use the nine steps as guides to effective action.

Role of the Leader and Participants in PERT

    The role of group participants in PERT interactions is identical to responsibilities in any other effective small group. Members must come to the meetings prepared to raise questions relevant to the agenda, to answer questions related to their expertise, to ask questions to help clarify or resolve conflict issues, and to move in an orderly fashion toward consensus. Most discussions in PERT groups are intended to *systematize* all aspects of a program. Consequently, group members usually spend considerable amounts of time discussing how activities should be ordered, numbered, classified, assigned priorities, or divided into smaller units. Good reasons for positions taken must be found and articulated; conflict will be a natural part of the process.

You will encounter PERT in American business and industry. If you obtain a position with the Federal government, you will undoubtedly use PERT for all contract work. If you enter a career in the health planning or maintenance fields, you will use PERT to implement planning decisions (see Arnold, 1966). In this section I will outline how PERT functions in a small group. I will chart a PERT process that was used by a defense subcontractor to implement a decision concerning the design of special aircraft windows for high technology fighter planes. What you will read is a step-by-step account of how PERT was used to implement a decision.

An Example of PERT

1. *Background of the decision:* The group consisted of nine individuals drawn from three divisions of a major defense subcontracting organization. Three design engineers were selected because of their expertise in the technology of design for aircraft windows; three sales personnel were chosen because of their involvement with the contract and previous experiences with the particular defense unit's specifications; two individuals were drawn from the technical staff (one person who was a draftsman and would be responsible for the

Figure 7.1. Inter-Office
Memorandum

To: Members of the TS-1000 Group

From: H. Wilson

RE: Transition Meeting 6/14/9_

Please attend this meeting. The following agenda has been established and I welcome any additions to it. If possible, let me know by Friday.

Agenda:
Explanation of the deadline
Report from design engineering about their time framework
Report from sales about their time priorities
Report from accounting about the cost of the program and our operating budget
Discussion of objectives based on the design decision
Discussion of the individual tasks
Scheduling of future meetings
Anything else???

See you then.

final drawings, and one person from the accounting section, who was responsible for cost estimates and other financial matters); and one person was appointed from management to serve as group leader/ coordinator (this person's expertise was in electrical engineering).

This group used Standard Agenda to make the decision about the design of the window and how the recommendation should be made to the defense unit. The decision-making process required two months work, and included three separate negotiations with the defense contractor concerning design specifications. The group's recommendation was made in the form of two written reports (one detailing the design of the windows, the other detailing the pricing of the program); these were reviewed by the defense unit contractor before an oral presentation was made. The contract was awarded to this subcontractor on a competitive basis.

2. *The transition from deciding to implementing the decision:* Once the contract was awarded, the leader of the decision-making group met with and congratulated the group members responsible for the contract (in this case the award was in excess of $30 million over the next ten years). The group leader debriefed the members of the project and then announced the need to decrease the size of the original group to implement the decision. The group was reduced from nine to five members (two design engineers, one sales person, one accounting person, and the group leader). The other group members were formally released from participation with this assignment.

The leader scheduled a meeting on the following Monday to plan the transition to implementation of the original decision. A memorandum was circulated (see Figure 7.1).

During this meeting the leader explained how the project should develop, given the defense unit's priorities and budget. Some minor

To: Members of the TS-1000 Group

From: H. Wilson

RE: PERT Chart Meeting 6/28/9_

Figure 7.2. Inter-Office Memorandum

Please arrange to be at the above scheduled meeting. I expect all of you to have completed your assignments by then. I have arranged to have use of the front and rear overhead projectors to draw initial PERT activities. We will also use the large board to complete the final diagram. I have asked Susan Elliot from drafting to serve as diagrammer during this group session.

Agenda:
Review of our responsibilities and deadlines

Report from design engineering concerning plant priorities and supplies

Report from sales concerning any modifications from the defense contractor

Report from accounting on our budget expenditures to date and projected costs for the program.

Discussion of any potential problems

Diagram of the PERT chart based on current information

Assignments for the next meeting.

problems were foreseen concerning how supply channels for the electrical work might cause delays in shipment. Certain contingencies were established to ensure confidence in the time framework. The objectives for the project were listed:

—To complete the shipment of the contract material (windows) by December 1, 1990.

—To comply with all contract specifications as detailed in the original proposals.

—To set aside 15% of the contract material prior to the shipment in case of any damage to the shipped windows. These additional units could then be immediately shipped to comply with the contract; if they were not needed, they would be transferred to storage for routine re-supply.

—To remain within the specified budget for this project.

   This meeting was adjourned after the leader made individual assignments to all group members (including himself). These assignments were to be completed by the next group meeting (two weeks) and would serve as the fact-finding foundation for the design of the PERT chart.

3. *The development of the PERT chart.*   During the interim two week period all group members were responsible for carrying out their assignments. Four days prior to the next scheduled meeting, the group leader circulated an agenda for that upcoming meeting (see Figure 7.2).

During the second group meeting the reports were given and there was again the discussion of supply channels for electrical systems (heating and cooling) to be installed in the windows. The group designed the following PERT chart (see Figure 7.3).

Figure 7.3. PERT Chart for the TS-1000 Group

Date	Activity	Resources Needed
7/6/89	Transfer of design specifications to the plant manager at 8:30 a.m.	Design specs Ms. Timms (carrier)
7/12/89	Meeting with plant manager at 10:00 a.m. to discuss scheduling of the project.	All group members
7/16/89 (opt.)	Meeting with plant manager to resolve any potential problems in scheduling.	All group members
7/26/89	Meeting with shipping department supervisor to establish deadlines and procedures (tentatively set for 9:30 a.m.).	Mr. Wilson
7/27/89	Meeting of all group members to discuss progress thus far and to plan for any contingencies.	All group members
8/2/89	Plant begins manufacturing procedures to be verified by group leader.	Mr. Wilson
8/4/89	Group meeting to review progress thus far.	All group members
8/16/89	Meeting with plant supervisor on this project to evaluate progress and plan for any potential problems.	All group members
8/20/89	Meeting with shipping department supervisor to evaluate scheduling requirements based on the plant's operation.	All group members
8/31/89	Group meeting to discuss any problems encountered on the project thus far.	All group members
9/6/89	Group meeting with supply personnel from ECTA to settle shipment schedules for electrical components.	All group members Mr. Jones (Plant supervisor)
9/20/89	Group meeting to discuss any problems encountered thus far.	All group members
10/5/89	(Tentative supply deadline of electrical components) Meeting to check on progress thus far.	All group members Mr. Jones
10/18/89	Tour of the plant to ensure quality control of the contract material.	All group members Mr. Jones
10/19/89	Group meeting to discuss any problems encountered thus far.	All group members
10/25/89	Group meeting to report on all activities related to the final stages of the project including transfer of samples to Quality Assurance for testing.	All group members Mr. Jones Ms. Edwards (QA)
11/1/89	Tentative date for transfer of samples to QA for testing. Mr. Wilson to be present for delivery and initial inspection of the samples.	Mr. Wilson

Figure 7.3.—*Continued*

11/3/89	Group meeting on progress thus far; contingencies discussed if necessary.	All group members
11/15/89	Group meeting to announce results of QA testing.	All group members Ms. Edwards
11/17/89	Group meeting to plan contingencies, if necessary.	All group members
11/22/89	Mr. Wilson meets with Mr. Jones, Ms. Edwards, and the shipping supervisor to detail final delivery procedures.	Mr. Wilson Mr. Jones Ms. Edwards Shipping supervisor
11/26/89	Group meeting to report on progress thus far.	All group members
11/29/89	Final check out of all operations related to shipment of contract material.	All group members Mr. Jones Ms. Edwards Shipping supervisor
11/30/89	Final group meeting prior to shipment of contract material.	All group members
12/1/89	Shipment of contract material.	—
12/6/89	Group meeting to report on delivery and government inspection of contract material.	All group members Ms. Edwards
12/31/89	Final group meeting to debrief the project.	All group members

As you can see from Figure 7.3, the PERT chart essentially details the work of the small group during the implementation process. Of course, this chart is for use only by group members. It allows them to plan meetings, establish due dates and deadlines, and coordinate their work with other divisions within the organization.

Most organizations using PERT charts to guide group implementation of a decision employ a PERT detailed chart. These charts contain all of the procedures, personnel, and resources to be used by all divisions within the organization to carry out the decision. In this case, the defense subcontracting group arranged to make PERT charts for the whole of the operation. This chart was computer-assisted and was 157 pages long, so that I will not reproduce it here. It accounted for every hour, every woman and man, every detail, every procedure, every checkpoint, and every deadline to be accomplished so as to complete this project. Figure 7.4 presents an exemplary excerpt taken from the Master PERT Chart for this project.

Figure 7.4. Example from the Master PERT Chart

11/2/89

Time:		Activity:	Resources:
8:00		Check-in of personnel for QA responsible for testing the TS–1000 project material.	Ms. Edwards, Mr. Rubie, Mrs. Thomas, Mrs. Jacoby, and Mr. Freeno
	8:15	Phone Mr. Wilson to acknowledge START of QA Testing.	
8:30		QA test #1.1 (Contract specification for size of windows).	Mr. Freeno, Ms. Edwards
	9:15	Submission of report to secretary.	Procedure SAM; all measurement equipment.
9:30		QA test 1.2 (Contract specification for weight of windows).	Mr. Rubie, Ms. Edwards
	10:15	Submission of report to secretary.	Procedure WAM; all weighting and scaling equipment
10:30		QA test 2.1 (Contract specification for glass).	Mrs. Thomas, Ms. Edwards
	11:15	Submission of report to secretary.	Procedure GLASS TEST; all GLASS TEST equipment

PERT is a logical adjunct to Standard Agenda used by small groups responsible for both making and implementing a decision. Central to the implementation of a small group decision is the development of PERT charts, such as the ones detailed above. The major tasks of a decision-implementing group should be:

Review of PERT

1. To complete all PERT charts before implementing the decision;
2. To monitor communication during all group meetings to ensure goals are accomplished;
3. To use the PERT charts consistently to check on the progress of work toward accomplishing the goals of the project;
4. To plan for the contingencies that may be necessary if problems arise using the original PERT charts.

Now you have reviewed the use of PERT to implement decisions. You have seen how PERT can be used in conjunction with Standard Agenda to coordinate all work involved in implementing the decision. In the following section you will be introduced to a procedure based on Standard Agenda and PERT, which may be used to guide a decision-making and implementing group.

Modified Agenda Technique

Development of the Technique

MAT (Modified Agenda Technique) is an integrated, systematic approach to group decision-making, and combines the strengths of Standard Agenda with the precision of PERT. First used by this author in training sessions with university administrators and later with high-technology groups, MAT is a process relying on the use of key questions to guide group meetings. Like Standard Agenda, MAT requires a group to follow a reflecting-thinking model of decision-making; like PERT, MAT requires a group to create a systematic plan for carrying out decisions. However, unlike either technique, MAT assumes that each group meeting can be guided by formulating a single, critical question that must be answered before the group can move on to another issue. The questions are:

1. Why are we here?
2. What are we supposed to accomplish?
3. What must we know in order to accomplish it?
4. How will we know when and if we have accomplished it?
5. What are our alternatives?
6. What is our recommendation?
7. What actions/events need to be performed to carry out the recommendation?
8. How can these actions/events be diagrammed?
9. How must resources be allocated to complete each task?
10. What is our purpose after accomplishing the task?

The purpose of asking these questions is to guide group communication. Each group meeting deals with a question, and normally a group should not attempt to answer more than *one* question per meeting. In this way all attention and information are directed toward achieving consensus on a particular issue. Also, no one issue or question becomes more or less important than any other. All questions require the same concentration of attention, and all are allotted the same amount of time. Preliminary research using MAT indicates it is most effective when:

Group members are selected because of their experience/expertise with the problem;

Group leaders are designated on the basis of seniority *and* previous success leading problem-solving small groups;

Group meetings last no longer than one hour (60 minutes);

Group leaders circulate agendas at least two full days before the meeting;

Group members actively seek to constrain talk to the limits prescribed by the question.

MAT can be understood in terms of the communication exchanged by group members:

The group leader calls the meeting to order and explains the charge given to the group. Each group member then provides a brief biographical sketch and reasons for being selected for the group. If two or more group members' areas of experience or expertise overlap, the group leader must explain why they were chosen.

Question 1: Why Are We Here?

Following this exchange of information, the group begins a discussion designed to achieve consensus on how the problem will be approached. *The result of this meeting should be a brief, written document containing a statement of purpose and method.*

Question 2:
What Are We Supposed
to Accomplish?

The group leader circulates an agenda with this question written on it, at least two days prior to the group meeting. If desired, the group may use a modified Delphi operation at this stage, asking each group member to write down his or her views about what is to be accomplished to achieve preliminary consensus. The purpose of this group meeting is to *phrase a single question* that succinctly describes the problem faced by the group. Group members must determine (1) the kind of question it is (fact, value, policy); and (2) how the question enables them to fulfill their obligation as set forth in the group charge. *The result of this meeting should be a carefully phrased question to guide future interactions.*

Question 3:
What Must We Know in
Order to Accomplish It?

The group leader circulates an agenda at least two days prior to the group meeting, with this question written on it. The purpose of the group meeting is to determine what information and resources are necessary to accomplish the task, and to make individual assignments about collecting data for the group. *The result of this meeting should be a list of information and resources required by the group for problem-solving, and a corollary list of individual research assignments.*

Question 4:
How Will We Know
When and If We Have
Accomplished It?

The group leader circulates an agenda at least two days prior to the group meeting with this question written on it. The purpose of the meeting is to answer the question by (1) specifying a goal based on the available information presented by group members, (2) specify a timetable for attaining the goal, based on the available resources and information presented by group members, and (3) specify a final report mechanism (written/oral report). *The result of this meeting should be a written set of answers to these issues.*

Question 5:
What Are Our
Alternatives?

The group leader circulates an agenda at least two days prior to the group meeting with this question written on it. The purpose of the meeting is to answer the question by using "brainstorming." Each group member should articulate his or her solution(s) to the problem, without detailing events or activities needed to accomplish the solution. *The result of this meeting should be a list of possible alternative solutions to the problem.*

Question 6:
What Is Our
Recommendation?

The group leader circulates an agenda at least two days prior to the group meeting with this question written on it. Group leaders are encouraged to use available criteria to determine the worth of the alternatives, and to achieve consensus on one recommended way of solving the problem. *The result of this meeting should be a formal, written recommendation of a solution to the problem.*

The group leader circulates an agenda at least two days prior to the group meeting with this question on it. Group members are encouraged to use available information and resources to provide descriptions of the events and activities necessary to implement the solution. *The result of this meeting is a list of steps for implementing the solution.*

Question 7:
What Actions/Events
Need to Be Performed
to Carry Out the
Recommendation?

The group leader circulates an agenda at least two days prior to the group meeting with this question on it. Group members are encouraged to present alternative ways of drawing a schematic representation of how the solution will be implemented (e.g., using functional, matrix, or other schematic devices). *The result of this meeting is a diagram of the solution.*

Question 8:
How Can These
Actions/Events Be
Diagrammed?

At least two days prior to the group meeting the group leader circulates an agenda with this question on it and a copy of the consensus diagram. Group members are encouraged to list what resources (human, financial, material, etc.) will be needed to complete each event or activity, given their area of expertise or experience. *The result of this meeting is a complete final report of the implementation of the solution.*

Question 9:
How Must Resources
Be Allocated to
Complete Each Task?

The group leader circulates an agenda at least two days prior to the group meeting with this question on it. The purpose of the discussion is to determine whether the group should serve on the project in any further capacity. *The result of this meeting is a decision about the future of the group.*

Question 10:
What Is Our Purpose
after Accomplishing
This Task?

You have now reviewed how PERT and MAT work. By using either technique, a group improves its chances of success in the decision-making process. You are now ready to consider communication processes during group decision-making.

Communication in the Decision-Implementing Process

All acts and actions in the decision-implementing process, from articulating the nature of the decision to determining ways and means of carrying it out, are acts of communication. Skill in communication will determine the quality of the group's problem-solving efforts. Unless a question can be accurately phrased, it will not guide the group in a productive way. If research cannot be systematically reported and catalogued, the results of fact-finding may not aid the group. Unless the group members can divide events and activities into smaller units and agree how work should be accomplished, PERT may not ensure a successful operation.

No matter how much you emphasize the structure of group work and the use of specific decision-implementing techniques to guide the group, it is the process of human communication that will ultimately determine the results. PERT and MAT do not guarantee good solutions; they are artificial devices developed to help groups implement decisions. Communication among group members will generate the decision, focus group attention on it, divide the necessary labor, establish power and equity, and finally, determine how well or poorly the group reaches its goal. Or, to put it Lisa's way:

> **Lisa A., 27** You can tell me about Standard Agenda and PERT and any other technique for small groups. In the end it is what is said and done by the people. No method is better than the people implementing it, right?

The question becomes "what types of communication characterize successful decision-implementing groups?" Throughout this text I have emphasized an *adaptive* approach to small group communication, explaining that it is urgent to adapt words and actions to the needs and expectations of the situation and listeners. Wood (1977) studied problem-solving groups and concluded that adaptive patterns of interaction produced the highest levels of satisfaction among group members and were significant ingredients of successful group decisions. In adaptive groups, systems of equity guide the group's treatment of individual members, help the group members to monitor the effects of their own talk and that of others, allowing the group to develop norms for controlled communication. Using a procedure for decision-making and implementing the decision, the group members restrict what they introduce to the group for discussion.

Decision-implementing groups are purposive groups. Since they are formed to implement a decision already reached, they need a shared sense of purpose and a structure within which to operate. Effective and efficient communication is characterized by a shared sense of purpose and the maintenance of a group structure, both of which are reflected in statements made by group members about their task and each other.

Transcript of Decision-Implementing Group:

Ed: . . . well, we appreciate that information, Louise. You sure have done your part! (Pause) What do the rest of you think?

Mike: I think Louise has done a good job of defining the design problem, and Willy got the specs on the solenoid. I'm still not sure we can meet the deadline for Rockwell. I'm concerned about the time it will take to manufacture a new rotation arm for the triggering device.

Louise: Mike's right. The sooner we can make our report, the sooner we can begin manufacturing the new piece. Our concern should be the deadline, now that we've essentially solved the design and specifications problems. What do you think?

Ed: I agree.

Mike: I agree.

Willy: I agree, too. But—and I know what Louise will say—the solenoid is still a problem. No matter what we do with the new triggering device or the rotator, we still don't know if the solenoid will act up. We only *think* we can solve the problem with the new piece. We don't have enough data yet.

Louise: How about if we make a contingency recommendation?

Ed: Huh?

Louise:	How about if we recommend the manufacturing of the new piece, *and* get the testing people to do another run on the solenoid? That way we save time. If Willy's right, we will need a new solenoid design as well. If I'm right, we are capable of meeting the deadline.
Mike:	What's the harm? I think she's got it.
Willy:	Yeah, me too. I'll contact Frank in testing and get him to start up immediately, if not sooner.
Louise:	Good. In the meantime, I'll get my secretary to type up the report.
Ed:	I think we're all in agreement. Let me review what goes in the report before we leave. . . .
Mike:	Let's do it!
Ed:	Okay (pause, reviewing notes). Let's see . . . first we need to explain how the rotation arm failed to meet the temperature and humidity tests. We'll use the test data for support. Then we need to talk about how we isolated two possible causes: the misaligned solenoid and the triggering device. We'll say we believe the problem is the triggering device and recommend the use of the revised specs to manufacture a new part. Then we can make Louise's contingent recommendation to re-test the solenoid. We have the data on the original run, right?
Willy:	Right, got it.
Louise:	Okay, sounds good to me.
Mike:	Don't forget the stuff about deadlines; make sure the report indicates our need to act fast. Otherwise the cost accountants will be breathing down our necks.
Ed:	Okay, anything else? (Group members shake their heads). Okay. Louise, here's the information for Liz. Let's meet again on Thursday to read over it. In the meantime, let's get that new piece and re-test the solenoid.

The above transcript provides evidence of adaptive communication. For example, although Ed is the leader of the group (notice how he maintains control by summarizing?) the other group members *talk to each other;* they do not just direct their comments to him. Each group member is courteous, polite, and unwilling to interrupt another speaker. Each group member addresses one issue at a time. Every statement is purposive. Every response is adapted to the needs and expectations of the situation and listeners.

One way to examine communication in successful small groups is to find out what is *missing*. What don't you see (or hear) in the conversation of group members? Here are some guidelines:

Guidelines for Effective Decision-Implementing Communication

1. *There is a general absence of personal talk.* Group members address the problem and its solution, rather than discussing each other's personal lives, habits, or character.
2. *There are few, if any, "politeness" errors.* People do not interrupt each other, nor do they articulate vanity, profanity, or a desire for personal gain.

3. *There is no non-substantive haggling.* Conflicts are issue-oriented, not person-oriented. Arguments are given, received, and refuted according to their merits and the availability of data to support them.
4. *There are no attempts to break down the group's sense of order.* Group members do not waste time arguing about who should be the leader or who isn't taking notes, etc. Power conflicts are managed either away from the group's activities or within the boundaries of the specified task.
5. *There is a lack of public speaking (no monopolizing the floor).* Group members *interact, discuss, ask or answer questions,* and produce *arguments;* they do not make isolated speeches to the group.

The goals of adaptive communication practices, including the need to exclude the five negative characteristics of group talk listed above, are learned by practice. They do not "just happen" when you are in a "good" group. Each group member can contribute to the adaptive goals by striving to make his or her communication PERTINENT:

1. *P*repare for group meetings.
2. *E*stablish goals for talk and actions.
3. *R*espond to the communication of other group members.
4. *T*ake responsibility for the effects of communication on listeners— strive to monitor words and actions.
5. *I*ndividualize your style of communicating.
6. *N*otice emerging conflicts and strive to manage them.
7. *E*xpress your intentions and plans before acting on them.
8. *N*egotiate disputes with reasoned argument and a spirit of cooperation.
9. *T*ake the initiative for improving the group's communication practices.

Using these guidelines for effective communication in group interactions should improve the quality of the group's activities and the level of satisfaction of the group members. Remember, *communication itself is a goal.* The choices you make about words and actions in groups develop your skill in reaching the goal of "having communicated."

Now that you have reviewed the role of communication in decision-implementing groups, you are ready to consider some potential problems affecting these groups.

Some Problems in Decision-Implementing Groups

Absence of Procedures

Decision-implementing small groups encounter difficulties similar to those confronted by decision-making groups. One major cause of these difficulties is the *failure to establish a procedure.* For example, organizations familiar with the

PERT method sometimes assume that group members understand the procedure. Instead of receiving an explanation, the group forges ahead with its own ideas, or lack of them. They may forget to complete a charting task, or fail to break down work into manageable units. When the error is discovered, the group works feverishly to correct mistakes or omissions, often wasting time and money.

Decision-implementing small groups also encounter difficulties peculiar to their particular organization. It should be noted that decision-implementing groups are used to implement a decision *already made*. Because information must be exchanged between the decision-making and decision-implementing groups, the chances for errors increase. The group leader of the implementing group must take special precautions to assure accurate exchanges of information between the two groups. Also, group members who must rely on information previously generated by the decision-making group should assume the responsibility for checking it out.

Information Exchange

> **Mary W., 30**   . . . So when we got to the serious business of finding a way to distribute the cash bonuses, I made the critical mistake of assuming that the data I had been given was accurate. I didn't ask for the information, I didn't check the calculations, I didn't do anything except pass on a quarter of a million dollars in real money to our employees. I was only about one hundred thousand dollars off. Nobody laughed. Our group leader was fired, the rest of us were given stern reprimands, and I finally got even with the people who gave me the data, but it wasn't until about a year later. And I never thought I was one to hold a grudge. . . .

Mary's mistake was the result of an assumption she made about the accuracy of the data she received from another small group. (Incidentally, notice how she blamed the other group and not herself for the error!)

A third problem confronting decision-implementing groups is related to the concept of information *load*. By "load" I mean the amount and complexity of information an individual or group must receive to complete a task. In Chapter 3 I discussed the special problem of communication overload, which is caused by having *too much* information to receive in a given period of time. Individuals in organizations encounter this problem frequently (Farace, Monge, & Russell, 1977). Here is a typical example:

Information Overload and Underload

> **Ed Q., 27**   Every morning I arrive at my desk to find work left over from the night manager. Just as I am sorting through it, the phone rings. About that time a guy will come in with a problem. I put the phone on hold, the guy tells me his problem, another guy comes in to tell me the crew is late. Another call comes in on the other line. This first guy is still telling me his problem. Am I listening to any of it? Nope. Do I feel abused? Yep. What am I going to do about it? Pretend I know all and understand all and hear all. Nothing much gets accomplished, but most of the guys think I'm swell.

Now imagine five to seven members of a small group who have all had mornings like Ed's. They arrive for the decision-implementing session, the group leader begins with the agenda, and. . . . The problem of having too much information causes most people to "turn-off" all incoming information, or to neglect less important messages in favor of more important ones.

Information overload also arises when groups get noisy. If communication is not properly controlled and if interruptions are allowed, a group can sound like one long, syncopated roar. When too much information is given at the same time very little information is actually exchanged. Semantic, physical, and hierarchical sources of noise interrupt with message reception and interpretation. But groups need to be orderly; there is no substitute for maintaining order during any group interaction.

The inverse of information overload is *information underload*. Information underload refers to a situation in which an individual group receives *too little* information. Boredom, a feeling of ineffectuality, or a lack of assigned work can produce bad results for the organizational employee who desires a challenging task and the information to accomplish it. However, decision-implementing groups may also experience information underload when their use of procedures becomes monotonous, mundane, or tediously ineffective. For example:

> **Donna R., 25** We had worked together as a small group for the past three years on a regular basis. We always were called in to implement a decision, and our task was to use CPM (Critical Path Method—another term for PERT). Fred was always our leader, and it got to the point that I could mimic him word-for-word in group meetings. He always said exactly the same thing! Our meetings became so boring that Wilma usually fell asleep. Curt used to make little drawings of animals in swimsuits. Nobody listened. Nobody cared. If you ask me whose fault it was, I'd have to say it wasn't really anybody's fault. It was just that Fred was so damned rigid in his beliefs about CPM that he wouldn't admit we already knew what we had to do. He *explained* us to death. "This is how we need to do this," and "Using this charting technique we should be able to do that,"—it was a real drag. Fred wasn't such a bad guy. He just didn't know any better. But, like you say, part of the responsibility was ours. We didn't try to persuade him to change, either.

Dealing with Information Underload

When groups lose their sense of purpose and drive, when the monotony of the task interferes with group productivity and creativity, information underload may be the problem. You know what to do when information overload occurs: you simply reduce the amount of information you receive. But what can be done when information underload adversely affects a group?

Depending on how the organization is arranged, it may be feasible to dissolve the group and select new members who will approach the task with more energy and determination. Sometimes people simply tire of doing the same task again and again. This appears to be more true of white collar employees than of blue collar workers (Gooding, 1972). If little can be done to change the task or the method of accomplishing it, it may be necessary to assign responsibility for carrying out the task to other members of the organization. A group leader must be sensitive to the *needs and expectations* of the group and be prepared to adapt to them.

A second possible way of resolving information underload is to revise the way the task is accomplished. For example, if PERT is causing the problem because it has become too routine, a group may decide to implement an alternative technique (e.g., MAT). As long as the task can still be accomplished, group members should be allowed some freedom of choice about the methods which they use to complete their work. Most government projects require the use of PERT, or evidence of it in written reports. However, MAT essentially achieves the same ends; and written reports can still be completed using the information generated. Caution must be exercised, however, whenever a change in the group's standard operating procedure is contemplated. There is purpose in sacrificing a good system for one that may not produce desirable results. Be sure that the change is needed and that the group can implement the new procedure without seriously interrupting their work.

These three problems, (1) the inability or failure to establish a decision-making procedure, (2) the failure to verify information received from other groups, and (3) information overload and underload, may cause difficulties for the decision-implementing small group. In each instance the problem is directly related to a *communication* failure. Decision-implementing procedures must be articulated before they can be successfully accomplished; failure to verify data received involves an assumption that accurate communication has taken place, when it has not; information overload and underload express opposite extremes of failure to properly manage the amount and complexity of information communicated among group members. Because these problems are created by communication failures, their solutions must be found in what can, should, or must be communicated. The substance of group interaction is talk. What occurs or does not occur in the group is a function of the communication within it. Just as a decision-making group is heavily dependent on its ability to phrase an appropriate question to guide interactions, so also the solutions put into effect by a decision-implementing group will only be as sound as the communication among group members.

Summary

This chapter addressed the problem of how to implement decisions using small groups. I began by pointing out that organizations survive by virtue of their ability to solve their problems. Although all organizations experience difficulties, some are better at solving them than are others; the former organizations typically make productive use of decision-implementing procedures.

You investigated two valuable decision-implementing procedures. PERT is a widely used method of implementing decisions. PERT requires group members to construct a sequential diagram of all events and activities which must be carried out on a day-to-day, hour-to-hour basis to complete the task. One advantage of using PERT is the inclusion of statistical techniques within a PERT operation. For this reason, PERT is adaptable to a variety of decision-implementing situations in which quantifiable data may be obtained and used by the group.

MAT is an integrated systematic approach to group decision-implementing, combining the strengths of Standard Agenda with the precision of PERT. MAT is based on the group's ability to raise and answer ten questions to guide the group through to completion of its task. Each group meeting may be devoted to answering one, and only one question. Using MAT, each group meeting also has an identifiable result.

You then investigated communication practices in the decision-implementing process. I stressed that simply implementing PERT or MAT will not ensure the group of success. Any group's decision-implementing skills are directly related to choices made about communication within the group. You reviewed the tenets of the adaptive approach to communication in groups; and I suggested that one way to analyze and evaluate the effectiveness of group communication is to find out what is missing from group interactions. I listed five specific communication activities usually absent from successful groups: (1) personal talk, (2) politeness errors, (3) non-substantive haggling, (4) attempts to break down group order, and (5) public speaking. I concluded this section by explaining the PERTINENT approach to effective communication in groups.

Finally, you reviewed some problems affecting decision-implementing small groups. I listed three sources of potential difficulty: (1) inability to implement a procedure; (2) failure to verify data received from other groups or individuals; and (3) information overload and underload. I suggested ways of overcoming these problems, and explained how each solution depends on effective communication.

Following the references you will find an exercise designed to help you put into practice what you have learned in this chapter. Remember: this text will only help you if you are willing to practice the skills and understandings contained in each chapter. As Martha Graham once put it: *Discipline is liberation.*

References

Arnold, M., ed. *Health Program Implementation Through PERT.* San Francisco: American Public Health Assoc., 1966.

Bormann, E. *Discussion and Group Methods: Theory and Practice,* 2d ed. New York: Harper & Row, 1975.

Brilhart, J. K. *Effective Group Discussion,* 3d ed. Dubuque, Ia.: William C. Brown Company Publishers, 1978.

Farace, R. V., P. R. Monge, and H. M. Russell. *Communicating and Organizing.* Reading, Mass: Addison-Wesley Publishing Co., 1977.

Federal Electric Corporation. *A Programmed Introduction to PERT.* New York: John Wiley & Sons, Inc., 1963.

Gooding, J. *The Job Revolution.* New York: Walker, 1972.

Phillips, G. M. "PERT As a Logical Adjunct to the Discussion Process." *Journal of Communication* 15 (1965): 89–99.

Wood, J. T. "Leading in Purposive Discussions: A Study of Adaptive Behavior." *Communication Monographs* 44 (June 1977): 152–65.

Exercises

The following problem asks you to investigate ways or means of implementing a policy decision already made. Using PERT, MAT, or an agenda of your own design, see what you can do with the following information.

The Appraisal Problem

SPC is a medium-sized manufacturing operation located in the mid-south. The company employs nearly 2500 people, most of whom are engaged in the line production of the product. There are about 135 mid- and upper-level managers responsible for personnel, finance, planning, marketing, and consumer affairs. The company has a strong history of dedication and resourcefulness among all its employees, and enjoys a solid popular reputation in the community.

Recently the personnel manager has heard a lot of grumbling among other managers who have been with the company for three to five years. They are complaining that newer managers are being hired at equivalent, and in some cases, higher salaries than they receive. The problem seems to be caused by inflation, which has driven up the cost of production and at the same time "compressed" salaries of the managers. The line workers continue to enjoy regular increases based on merit, but this is in part because they have a strong union. Within the past thirty days, 25 mid- and upper-level managers have given notice. These were *not* people SPC wanted to lose.

Your group has received a charge to resolve this problem. You are supposed to implement a new *performance appraisal review* system for mid- and upper-level managers which will allow SPC to offer bonus incentives and other inducements to those who do well. The decision has also been made that due to inflation, no across-the-board increases in pay can be given at this time. The key seems to be revealed in the following memorandum given to your group by the company Vice-President for Personnel:

TO: TASK GROUP ON PERFORMANCE APPRAISALS

FROM: V.P. PERSONNEL

RE: FINDINGS OF THE DECISION-MAKING GROUP

Our group consisted of six people from each of the major areas in our company. After careful fact-finding and deliberation, we determined that we are in danger of losing about fifty percent (50%) of our seasoned managers if we don't overcome this problem. Here is what we found:

1. *There seems to be an inequity in salaries.* New managers are being hired in at between $25,00–$30,000 depending on experience and qualifications. In many cases their salaries equal or exceed the salaries of managers with three to five years experience who were hired in when times were better. For example, we used to be able to hire recent college graduates with business degrees and work experience at $14,000–$21,000. This trend has changed in the past eighteen months.

2. *There seems to be a need to increase job enrichment in some areas.* The managers most directly affected are talking about the dullness and routine of their work. When I hear this kind of complaining, I know we need to do something to make their work more personally satisfying. There is a lot of literature out there in trade journals and magazines about how to do this, so find it and do something.

3. *If we don't solve the problem, we will be in real trouble.* We are in danger of losing practically all of our mid-level work force, people with three to five years experience who know the plant and who have shown a dedication to it. We may be left with the new guys and the older guys, and nothing in-between. That's no way to run a business!!

4. *The next performance review is scheduled six weeks from now.* You need to have your system in place by then. Use MAT to come up with recommendations (REMEMBER: WE CAN'T AFFORD SALARY INCREASES!), and use PERT to demonstrate how we can use your solution in the performance review.

5. *I will expect a written report and an oral presentation when you have completed your task.* The written report should be no longer than ten (10) double-spaced, typed pages. The oral presentation will be given to the assembly of managers one week prior to the beginning of the performance reviews.

Good luck!!

Here is some additional information about the managers in SPC:

	Salary Breakdown					
Number of years experience	*14K*	*16K*	*19K*	*21K*	*25K*	*30+K*
1	2	3	3	1	0	0
2	0	5	3	3	1	0
3	1	5	6	3	1	0
4	0	10	5	5	3	1
5	0	4	7	11	9	3
5 +	0	1	7	12	5	2

Here is some additional information supplied to your group from the decision-making group:

TO: TASK GROUP ON IMPLEMENTATION

FROM: DECISION-MAKERS

RE: SUMMARY OF COMPLAINTS MOST OFTEN GIVEN BY
           MANAGERS IN SPC

We collected data for a two-week period. Essentially, we asked supervisory staff to list the complaints being made. There has been no effort to use any statistical manipulations of this data to count the categories. Here is what we found:

1. *"I don't ever get to exercise my own judgment on the job."*   We found thirty-eight statements of this kind on the reports. In most instances, they were from managers with five or more years experience. However, the statements were being made to managers with two to four years experience. May create a domino effect.
2. *"Nobody appreciates what you do around here."*   We found twenty-seven of these statements on the report. In most cases they were followed up with examples of how other companies in the area give news releases about good work, promotions, or new projects. In some cases these statements were made by people who disliked the closing of the company newsletter last year.
3. *"I could make more money going back to school and getting my degree all over again. It just isn't fair."*   We collected one-hundred and five of these statements in a two-week period, however, there were several instances of the same statement being repeated daily by some managers. These statements were typically made by people with three to five years experience.
4. *"I don't have much to do during slack times."*   This statement was found on twelve reports. The statement seems to be made by managers with two to three years experience in areas which routinely have slack times.

5. *"The company ought to make it more attractive to stay than to leave."* This statement was found, in a variety of formats, in about fifty of the reports. Clearly, the statement is being made by managers with three to five years experience, and very often in the presence of younger managers.

The above five statement types were characteristic of the complaints. There were also the usual reports of absence, tardiness, and no pay for overtime in salaried positions. We didn't pay much attention to them, because you hear them everywhere.

Good luck!

Hints:

You may want to read over the literature on Equity Theory for possible causes of the problem and predictions about what might happen.

You may find it useful to investigate work done on job satisfaction among managers in *Personnel Journal, Academy of Management Journal,* and *The Harvard Business Review.*

You may want to contact businesses in your area for reports about salary expectations among managers with three to five years experience.

You may wish to read over the material on performance appraisal design and implementation. Your instructor can provide additional sources.

Strategies for Improving Your Communication in Small Groups

8

Introduction

You have observed the small group in an organization as a collection of individuals who interact regularly to make decisions, solve problems, implement decisions. In the case of informal groups, the group also functions to make friendships and pass time. You have examined small group processes and functions, communication, leadership, participation in groups, and you have also investigated procedures for decision-making and decision-implementing. Throughout your exploration I have consistently stressed the need to *adapt choices about talk and action* to the requirements of the given situation and the other group members. I have emphasized that group outcomes are the results of group inputs, and that you can control the inputs by learning how to make better choices about what you say and do.

This chapter addresses the use of strategies for improving your group communication. I begin by explaining the term *strategy* and showing how rhetorical strategies can benefit *and* harm the group. Second, I examine strategies available to members of small groups, furnishing attitudinal and behavioral profiles of the possibilities. Third, I investigate how to choose from the available strategies the ones most likely to elicit the responses you seek. Fourth, I examine more closely the role of communication in building strategies. Following the summary and references, I provide an exercise designed to help you use the material and procedures covered in this chapter.

Before beginning your examination of strategies, you need to consider carefully the objection most frequently raised about the ethics of strategies:

Wallace B., 19   I think talk is best when it is spontaneous, free-flowing, and honest. I think using "strategies" or "plans" is basically wrong because they prevent you from being yourself. I mean, so what if you offend someone by being honest? Whose problem is it, anyway? I say it's *their* problem—if they can't handle it, tough. I wouldn't want to be around them anyway. Look, the only way we are going to improve our lives is to say what we mean, mean what we say, and tell it like it is. Strategies are dishonest, man. Strategies are evil.

Wallace's statement is similar to a number of others I have heard when I advocate the use of a rhetorical approach to small group interaction. His objection stems from a belief that there is an inconsistency, a contradiction that exists between being *honest* and being *rhetorical*. Yet, since antiquity the study and practice of rhetoric has always valued the honest statement, the reasonable argument, the appropriate use of emotional appeals. No dichotomy exists, except for those individuals who choose to *mis*use rhetoric, to argue on behalf of an evil cause. Rhetoric is a method, not a cause. An understanding of how to persuade can and does lead to moral and ethical goals *as well as* to immoral or unethical ends. The choice of good or evil is in the mind and heart of the speaker and hearer, not in the method used to reach those ends.

Wallace's statement also reveals a preference for spontaneity and free flowing talk rather than strategic communication. You have already noted the impossibility of talk being "spontaneous" because of your mind's need to impose order on everything. However, there are people who seem to talk without thinking, who say whatever comes to mind without attempting to adapt their talk to the needs of the audience and the situation. You normally believe these people to be "rude," not "spontaneous," or perhaps worse, self-centered, narcissistic, and insensitive to the needs of others. The person who believes as Wallace does, who thinks that being offensive in a group is acceptable if it's honest, that the problem is not with the speaker's words but with the ability of the audience to "handle" it, is essentially being insensitive. Behaving according to Wallace's credo is very much like behaving as a spoiled child.

In place of spontaneity, a rhetorical approach to group interaction relies on courtesy, integrity, and an understanding of the needs and values of others. Adapting to what others are interested in, planning to address their attitudes, values, and beliefs, organizing messages for ease of comprehension, can only enhance the opportunities for productivity and success in the group. Failure to adapt to situation and others, combined with a belief in the philosophical purity of free, spontaneous expression, does not contribute to the group's well-being. And for this reason, you should reject it. Consider Lacy's testimony:

Lacy B., 41: I grew up as a "flower-child" of the 1960s and believed in the values of who were then called the "hippies." We were to be open and honest and free; we were to love everyone and accept everything, so long as they agreed with us and satisfied our needs. I honestly behaved this way until sometime in the mid-1970s, when I discovered, much to my own surprise, that I didn't trust anyone and I wasn't making anything out of my life. I mean, you can't sit around listening to the Allman Brothers Band all day long forever. I was not really involved in anything beyond myself. I had no civic activities, no place in society. All I had was me—and of course, my freedom. Big deal. It had been fun, but. . . . So I went back to school and studied business administration, can you believe it? I received my MBA and was hired by my present company as a manager. Essentially this meant to select people for group work and to organize their activities. From time to time I still wanted to slip back to the "old me," the flower child. I craved spontaneous interaction, the freer attitude I assumed I had left behind. But you know what? I was wrong. I didn't leave it behind, I just adapted it to new surroundings. I still treated people honestly, and I think I am more open than most. There are a lot of us around, although you may not recognize us by our uniforms. We look like business people. We make money. We live in the suburbs. What we learned to do is make plans and act on them with a sense of purpose. What we learned to become was responsible for our own lives.

Part of what I am doing in this chapter is to encourage a view of choice-making about strategies. A strategy is not something to be taken lightly; it should be based on a choice you make among alternatives, a choice designed to gain the responses you seek in an honest, ethical, and responsible way.

What Is a Strategy

A strategy may be defined as a detailed plan designed to reach a goal or to gain an advantage. When you play chess or checkers, you usually employ some strategy to decide how to make your moves and how to respond to the moves of others. You may use strategies to gain the attention and affections of someone else, as when you plan to ask someone out on a "date." Organizations have strategies for improving their operation, their share of the market, and their image with the general public.

Strategies should be *contingent*. The best chess players, the most successful organizations, and those who display skill in making friends and having lovers know the value of responding to the urgencies of the given case. No matter how well thought out a particular strategy may be, it should be capable of alteration if circumstances require it. This is what is meant by contingencies; you have a particular goal, but you plan several different ways of reaching it. The best strategies are those which take into account the changing nature of human reality.

Strategies should be *productive*. You don't just "have a strategy." You select from available strategies one or more that seem most likely to elicit the desired response. A strategy is a plan you make to bring something into existence or to modify something already in existence. A strategy must have a purpose, a goal, some end in sight. For example, a group member who initially is in conflict with another person's position may decide to "go along" with it to build a sense of goodwill which may later be useful. A group leader may reward a particularly aggressive group member with a responsible assignment to re-establish authority by letting the group member know it is the *leader* who still controls the group. The choice of a strategy carries with it the implication of intent.

Strategies should be *detailed*. A choice of strategy should encourage further decisions about specific statements, responses, and actions. It should be noted, however, that a strategy is a partial plan requiring a sequence of steps to enact. This sequence may look like this:

Creating a Strategy **Goal:** To gain acceptance for my proposal about the performance review process. **Strategy:**

1. During the first half of the meeting, I will remain silent unless asked a direct question. I will take careful notes on all other proposals and think them through.
2. After John and Phyllis have argued their cases and the group comes to a standstill, I will ask for the opportunity to speak.
3. I will present my proposal. First I will review what we have already decided about the need for change. Then I will briefly outline my plan, after which I will compare my plan to their plans in relation to the group's criteria. Then I will ask for any questions and try to answer them clearly and concisely.
4. I will invite John and Phyllis to offer any minor amendments to my proposal, based on the strengths of their plans.
5. I will ask for consensus in the group.

The person composing this strategy not only knows what she or he wants to accomplish during the meeting, but also has a good idea of how to accomplish it. The details show a sequence of steps which, if followed, should lead to the desired outcome. However, for this plan to respond to the needs of the situation and of others, it should also allow for certain *contingencies*. For example, what will this person do if Phyllis' proposal is sound and gains group acceptance? What should be said if the group leader wants to limit the discussion to two alternative plans, but John and Phyllis have already made it known that they have come prepared for a discussion of their proposals? You should always prepare for contingencies, as Harold knows so well:

Harold F., 24   I'll never forget the time I went into a meeting with what I believed to be a fool-proof plan of action. I wanted to make the best report on fact-finding of anyone in the group. I wanted to show them how competent I was. I knew they thought I was just a kid out of school, and I had a lot to learn, you know what I mean. Well, I presented my report, handed out copies for everyone in the group, and felt great until I saw the expressions on the group member's faces. The chairman cleared his throat and said, "Harold, that was a fine report, and I'm sure we all appreciate the information and work you've done, but we aren't supposed to have reports until next week. We haven't defined our problem yet." I had forgotten about that. In my desire to do well, I only succeeded in showing everyone that I was, after all, just a kid out of school with a lot to learn.

Harold's unfortunate experience illustrates a major concern. Because strategies can be used for both productive and unproductive ends, you need to consider how selection of a particular strategy may influence the group's outcomes. Gouran (1982) discusses one common manifestation of the use of strategies under the heading "mixed-motive interaction." Drawing on previous research by Nemeth (1972), the mixed-motive interaction involves "a motive for cooperation in order to reach a mutually agreeable solution, and, simultaneously, a motive for competition to gain at the other's expense" (Gouran, p. 196). This phenomenon frequently ccours when there are perceived inequities among group members (Walster and Walster, 1976). Expressed concisely, the strategies used by the group members are developed in response to their own perceived goals *and* to the group's designated task.

Although this broad definition of mixed-motive interaction could be employed to discuss a variety of situations in which personal and group goals are sought (this would include virtually all group interactions), there are four characteristics of mixed-motive interaction which separate it from other, similar circumstances (Gouran, 1982; p. 187–88):

1. Two or more people who must function collectively have incompatible personal goals or incompatible views concerning how best to achieve common goals.
2. An individual perceives inequity in his or her relationships with others and seeks redress from the responsible agent.
3. A conflict that has persisted over some period of time requires resolution, and:
4. Two or more parties, as a result of legal or social constraints, are obliged to negotiate their disagreements or to redefine prior contractual relationships.

Characteristics of Mixed-Motive Interaction

You can see how a mixed-motive interaction could interfere with the group's productivity. The two or more people with incompatible goals would choose strategies designed to further their own causes. The articulation of these strategies would cause disruption within the group setting, producing interpersonal and group conflict. Harold's experience cited earlier is a minor manifestation of this problem: he simply made a mistake that could easily be corrected. Consider the following case:

Harriet H., 32   Here is what happened. I had not liked Dave even before we had to work with each other on the project. He always seemed so cocksure and egotistical. He also was rising in the company, you know, the kind of guy who will actually be vice-president by thirty-five. Part of the problem, of course, is that he was getting some of the rewards I also wanted. I knew that, even though I may not have admitted it. So, anyway, I was in this group meeting and I was determined to get even with Dave. I knew I had to contribute my share to the group, but I looked for every opportunity to point out his errors.

He soon saw what I was doing and retaliated. The group became a very unpleasant experience. Sometimes we would end up calling each other names. Sometimes we would stall the group until one of us gave in. You know what I mean. So, in the end what did we accomplish? Nothing. The group's final report was rejected by upper management, and we had to do the whole task over again from scratch. I still had to work with Dave and everyone in the group knew it. During the first meeting of the group after we were reassembled, our group leader, Ann, simply told us to resolve our personal disputes outside of the group or she would see to it that we were fired. So Dave and I both shut up and did our part. But the bad feelings were still there. In fact, they still are.

Ann's management of the conflict between Harriet and Dave was not particularly successful. Although they ceased quarrelling with each other in public, the group still had to suffer their heated presence. Ann, using her position as group leader as legitimate authority, simply forced the conflict into hiding. No resolution of the differences was sought. No negotiation of a settlement between them was considered. Ann's strategy was not an appropriate one for the given case. Neither was Dave's nor Harriet's.

In the above case you see how three group members can become involved in a mixed-motive interaction. Each one chooses a strategy designed to seek immediate gratification of personal goals at the expense of the group's task. However, rather than resigning from the group, or seeking resolution of the quarrel outside of the group setting, these individuals enacted their strategies within the group. The result was a *group* problem that transcended the individual inequities. The group experienced inequity greater than the sum of the individual inequities, thus reducing the group's outcomes and raising the costs of participating. Choice of a "bad" or unproductive, self-serving strategy can have serious negative consequences for the group.

What can be done by group members when a mixed-motive interaction begins to take place? Before any actions can occur, the mixed-motive interaction must be clearly recognized and identified. Here are some guidelines to the identification of this problem:

Guidelines for Identifying Mixed-Motive Interactions

1. *The content of talk between two or more group members shifts from the issues or ideas being considered to personal evaluations of motives or character.* When a group interacts, talk should be consciously restricted to the issues or ideas at hand. Conflicts arise when arguments deteriorate from considerations of the issues to considerations of the character of the persons advancing them.

2. *Group members witnessing the troubled interaction perceive evil or injurious intent.* Conflicts are an inevitable part of group interaction. As I pointed out earlier, disagreements between and among group members can be productive. However, when group members have the feeling that there is more to the dispute than differences over the quality of the ideas can account for, some maneuver against the mixed-motive interaction may be necessary.

3. *Personal goals overtly replace or supersede group goals.* When the mixed-motive group members begin using personal *pronouns* (e.g., "I," "me," "mine"), personal *references* (e.g., "I said so, that's why"; or "I want it this way."), or take personal *credit* for group ideas, there may be a hidden purpose behind their words. Another manifestation of this problem appears when a group member cites personal concerns as being "more important" or "more worthy" than group concerns. Although there may be legitimate problems in his or her life, these do not supersede group concerns. One person's personal problems can cause imbalances for the entire group.
4. *Old issues and ideas are consistently rehashed by the two or more persons involved in the conflict.* Though it is necessary that a group have an awareness of its history which can be used to guide communication and to recall past actions, the use of history for negative or unproductive purposes may indicate a deeper problem.

These four guides to identifying a mixed-motive interaction should alert group members to the use of inappropriate strategies. The question then becomes "what can we do about it?"

First, the problem should be stated by a group member or the group leader. If there is convincing evidence of a mixed-motive interaction, and its occurrence is disrupting the group's performance of the task, there is just cause to acknowledge it within the group. One tactful way to accomplish this goal is to put the problem in *question* form:

Resolving Mixed-Motive Problems

"Is there something troubling you two we should all know about?"
"Excuse me. Could you point out the relevance of this discussion to the issue at hand."
"What can the rest of us do to help you solve this dispute?"

Whatever strategy is chosen to point out the problem, care must be taken not to escalate the dispute. Avoid blaming the individuals or commanding them to obey. Do not bring up old issues or conflicts about which they previously have disagreed, ask for evidence about why they are disagreeing on this occasion.

Second, ask each disputant to state his or her case. If the parties to the dispute respond by attacking each other's motives or character, interrupt them and ask them to limit their remarks to the issues involved in the group's discussion. Sometimes this strategy will only reduce the argument and the arguers to silence. This does not mean the problem is solved; *it merely means they do not want to have it solved for them.* When this happens, the group leader should arrange to meet with each of them outside of the group setting and discuss how the problem can be resolved. If the arguers wish to state their cases, allow them to speak without being interrupted by other group members.

Third, try to determine the source of the dispute in relation to the issue or idea before the group. Usually this method of intervention will allow the group to identify and resolve quickly any real disputes involved in the mixed-motive interaction. However, these overt disputes may only be superficial causes of the problem. They may be resolved and the group may continue its deliberations, but the disagreement will remain. If this is the case, the group leader may need to meet with the arguers (together, not separately) outside of the group.

Fourth, when the source of the dispute is identified, seek a pragmatic solution: Ask what can be done about the problem. Try to establish some pragmatic goal to guide the discussion. Do not belabor the source of the dispute, or admit its complexity but attempt no resolution of it. If a real problem has been isolated, solve it before moving on with the group's discussion.

These four guidelines for resolving mixed-motive interactions usually allow a group to avoid or eliminate some of the unpleasantness associated with the problem. However, no prescription for conflict resolution can solve all possible forms of the problem. When a well-planned strategy is involved in the dispute, it is difficult to predict the success of any intervention.

In this section I have defined a strategy as a contingent, productive, and detailed plan of action. You have examined how strategies can be useful to the group, and how they can create mixed-motive interactions which often reveal or contribute to inequities within the group. In the following section, you will investigate some of the common forms which strategies may assume in small groups.

Strategies-In-Use: Some Attitudinal and Behavioral Profiles

Choices of behavior can be guided by information. What you know about previous interactions helps you make better predictions about future communication needs and goals. The responses you receive from other group members shape your opinions about them and determine how you obtain more acceptable responses from them. When you consider the available kinds of strategies people employ in group settings, you confront a seemingly endless variety of tactics and ploys. Obviously it would be impossible to catalog all of these available strategies, for they are as various as the fingerprints of the people using them. However, you can make productive uses of some very generalized categories of strategies which are encountered typically in most organizational groups.

The strategies discussed in this section are based on my personal observations of small groups over a number of years. They are also derived from discussions of some common attitudinal and behavioral types found in organizations. Please understand these descriptions are not exhaustive, nor can claims about their empirical reliability be advanced. They represent some *possibilities* for strategies. I present them to you at this time to help you better understand some of the choices available to you and to demonstrate how you can interpret some strategies used by others in small groups. The behavior profiles include the following types: the Good Soldier, the Altruist, the Prince, the Courtier, the Power-Broker, the

Facilitator, the Servant of the Masses, the Friend, the Friendly Enemy, the Shy Person, the Narcissist, the Gameplayer, the "Yes" Sayer and the "No" Sayer, and the Angry Young Wo/man.

The "Good Soldier" strategy is based on the "go along, get along" philosophy of small group behavior. The Good Soldier is a company man or woman content to obey the policies and rules of the organization. The "Good Soldier" is typically a conservative person, a church-goer, a member of few (if any) social or political clubs, and may present a passive appearance. In group settings the Good Soldier may volunteer to keep the group's records, or, if she or he is a long time employee, may be assigned the task of group leader (which usually makes the Good Soldier somewhat uncomfortable). This person can be relied upon to do what she or he is expected to do. Assignments will be carried out on time and to the given specifications. There may be little creativity or personal expression found in any of the Good Soldier's assignments, but such individuals will virtually always be technically competent.

The Good Soldier strategy is designed to gain positive, acceptable responses from others; he or she rarely aspires to high status positions within the company, and will virtually never do or say anything controversial in the group. The Good Soldier is a team-player, a reliable person, and a solid worker. You need these people in any organization, although you may not need to know their names. If you see yourself as a Courtier, a Power-Broker, a Prince, a Narcissist, a "No" Sayer, or an Angry Young man or woman, then the Good Soldier presents a problem. On the one hand, you need the support of the Good Soldiers to successfully implement your strategy; on the other hand, the Good Soldier may present a threat to you because she or he does not share your aspirations or propensity for risk-taking. No matter what happens to you, the Good Soldier will always have a valued place in the organization and especially within the group.

The Good Soldier

Altruistic behavior refers to the doing of good deeds at the cost of personal risk or sacrifice. Sociobiologists are usually confounded by the presence of altruism because it represents a difficult problem for the science of genetics (Wilson, 1979). Why would a person sacrifice so much for someone else when the result of the sacrifice is limited or negligible personal gain? Although you may feel honored by someone else's sacrifice, it also usually makes you feel somewhat uneasy. If you use the Equity Theory as a model, self-sacrifice in groups is likely to cause an inequitable situation. The Altruist, therefore, is likely to present a problem to the organization or group.

Altruists actually exist. They tend to be limited in number, but you know one when you see her or him. The Altruist in contemporary times tends to be either very liberal or very conservative, and to profess a strong belief in God. In many cases the belief in God may be used as a reason for the altruistic act. "My

The Altruist

reward is in Heaven," or some similar statement may be used to justify the sacrifice. The Altruists are conspicuous in most organizations, primarily because there are so few of them and because their actions tend to attain an almost mythical quality. "Do you remember when Al worked forty-four hours straight on that project to protect the boss's reputation? And he wouldn't even accept a bonus for it?" The Altruist is seldom motivated by standard rewards. The promise of more money or greater status does not seem to matter. If anything, the Altruist tends to be a loner; even inclusion in the affections of the group or opportunities for greater affiliation with other people may not serve to motivate him or her.

The altruistic strategy, if indeed it is a strategy, is not easy to master, since there is a substantive difference between *altruism* and an altruistic *act*. An altruistic act performed by the Good Soldier may be rewarded in standard ways, and equity restored to the group. Altruism itself is virtually impossible to reward, and therefore presents special problems for the group. Other group members may think of the Altruist as a "do-gooder," the one who elicits participation from the Shy Person or who takes the blame in a conflict situation, even though she or he does not need or deserve to. Like Jesus Christ, the Altruist may be crucified by friends who are more motivated by secular rewards.

The Prince

The Prince strategy is based on Machiavellian approaches to gaining and using power. The Prince may think of himself or herself as a "political realist," whose actions are dictated by circumstances and the desire to obtain positive outcomes. In fact, in many cases, the approach used by the Prince is the familiar "end justifies the means" strategy. Very often the Prince aspires to positions of power and authority within the organization, and considers membership in the group as an opportunity to gain favor with people in power. If such places of power and authority are sought, they are almost always the "top" positions within the company. The Prince does not like to obey the orders of others, and will usually circumvent them if there is any political advantage to be gained.

The Prince may be thought of as the inverse of the Altruist. While the Altruist does the right things for the right reasons, the Prince usually does the right things for the wrong reasons, if you assume that personal gains should be seen *in relation* to group goals. Moreover, it is difficult to find rewards for the Altruist, but easy to find them for the Prince. The difficulty is that you may not want to reward the Prince because you fear what may happen if he or she arrives at a position of power.

The Prince is both advantageous and disadvantageous to the group. This person may be advantageous to have around because of intense awareness of and responsiveness to political considerations affecting the group's decision-making or decision-implementing function. It is good to have a "realist" on board, so long as this person does not sink the ship. On the other hand, the Prince may be disadvantageous for the group because personal goals do supersede group goals. The Prince is looking for personal gain; whatever happens to the group is at best a secondary consideration, since for him/her the group itself is merely a means to an end. Beware of the Prince. He or she may be very attractive, intensely seductive, well-spoken, and overtly concerned for the group's welfare. But beneath this slick veneer lies a very cold, calculating, self-centered being.

Princes tend to seek affiliation with others, particularly with people who can "do me some good." For this reason Princes tend to lure Good Soldiers, Courtiers, Friends, and "No" Sayers into their ranks. But do not count on being rewarded for your efforts, because the Prince is more fickle than firm.

The Courtier

The Courtier strategy relies on ingratiating behavior in the presence of people in positions of authority or power. In 1547 Baldassare Castiglione wrote *The Book of the Courtier,* an early attempt to identify those attitudes and behaviors which would help a young person gain a position at Court. Hence the term *courtier.* The Courtier tends to be self-centered and concerned with personal advancement, but not to the degree evidenced by the Prince, nor with the malice of the Narcissist. The Courtier is mostly a "good person who desires to please," yet who is often discussed in much less favorable terms by other people in the organization.

The Courtier is a master strategist. By not offending anyone and by simultaneously gaining the favor of higher-ups in the group or organization, the Courtier usually rises to positions of prominence. But the Courtier is usually known by the friends he or she keeps. When they lose power or position in the group or organization, so does the Courtier.

Courtiers tend to be physically attractive, mentally alert, and highly verbal. They are quick to learn and skilled in adapting to the needs and expectations of others in virtually any situation. In many ways, the Courtier is an ideal communicator, rhetorically sensitive and behaviorally flexible. The Courtier wants to please, and will sacrifice to obtain that end. In group settings, such a person will complete assignments on time, and these will usually be very well done because the Courtier gains favor by words and deeds. Displaying technical and aesthetic competence, the Courtier becomes an informal group leader long before she or he is a formal leader. A Courtier can be counted on to perform well consistently.

Courtiers tend to gain allegiance from Good Soldiers, Power-Brokers, aspiring Princes, Friends, and occasionally from Shy People. The Courtier is usually held in contempt by Narcissists, Servants, "Yes" and "No" Sayers, and Angry Young Wo/men. If you choose the "Courtier's strategy, you will probably have as many friends as enemies in the group and organization. People may like and admire what you produce, but they may dislike you.

The Power-Broker

The Power-Broker uses a strategy based on a desire to control or directly influence the outcomes of everything. Power-Brokers tend to be older members of groups or organizations, because it takes time to acquire the information and degree of influence needed to shape destinies. Power-Brokers tend to be conservative males with expressed liberal tendencies (the incidence of male "Power-Brokers" may be owing to the fact that there are simply fewer women in status positions in organizations). Power-Brokers tend to be less physically attractive than Courtiers or Princes, but equally skilled in rhetoric. They also tend to want to operate alone, limiting their contact with strangers unless the stranger can provide assistance or service to them. For this reason, Power-Brokers and Courtiers tend to become allied until such time as the Courtier reaches a position of power which no longer requires obedience or service to the Power-Broker.

In small group settings the Power-Broker tends to downplay his or her power. They like to hear people make reference to them and their abilities to control what happens, but they defer politely when approached about the subject. They do not say very much unless addressed directly, but they love to be addressed directly. They may "doodle" or otherwise appear distracted during group meetings, but do not be deceived by appearance: the Power-Broker always knows the score. Power-Brokers also tend to be mean when engaged in conflict. They may play "dirty," or accelerate the conflict so that it involves questions of personal character or motives. Power-Brokers do not engage in conflicts they do not plan to win. They are seldom content to win without destroying the credibility of their opponents. For this reason, you must be very careful about disagreements with Power-Brokers; they may be ruthless and vindictive.

Power-Brokers often are disliked, but always respected. Usually it is not possible to become a Power-Broker unless you have the necessary skills and information; for this reason Power-Brokers can be sturdy additions to any small group. However, there should never be two of them in any one group.

The Facilitator

The Facilitator strategy is predicted on the beliefs and attitudes of the humanistic psychology movement of the 1960s and early 1970s. Spokespersons for this movement use the term *facilitator* instead of *group leader*. The Facilitator helps the group be open and honest when dealing with issues and ideas. The Facilitator is "attuned to" the "feelings and fantasies" of the individual group members, and perceives the group situation as a place where personal development should and must occur.

It is difficult to be a Facilitator unless you are a group leader, because so much of the strategy is based on how you direct the activities of the group. However, there are group members who use this strategy to induce others to self-disclose, or to reveal their "true feelings" about the issue at hand. You will notice that Facilitators almost never reveal *their* "true feelings" or engage in self-disclosure. This is a strategy used to gain potentially hazardous or sensitive information from and about others. If this involves a direct question about another person's feelings, the Facilitator will most likely deflect the question, or turn it around so that the questioner has to answer it. For example:

Questioner: "So how do you feel about this issue?"
Facilitator: "I don't know, exactly. How do you feel?"
Questioner: "Well, I think that . . . "
or:
Questioner: "So how do you feel about it?"
Facilitator: "I think I hear you saying that you are displeased with the data presented thus far. Is that accurate?"
Questioner: "Well, yes. In fact, I think what we ought to do is. . . ."

The Facilitator strategy appears, on the surface, to be open, honest, and friendly. For this reason, Facilitators usually make allies among Good Soldiers, Servants, Friends, Shy People, Narcissists, and Gameplayers. However, Facilitators are usually distrusted by Princes, Power-Brokers, Courtiers, Friendly Enemies, "Yes" and "No" Sayers, and Angry Young Wo/men. The Facilitator strategy is mostly based on learning certain verbal techniques. For example, Facilitators tend to say:

"How do you feel?"
"Tell me something about yourself?"
"Let's be honest about this, okay?"
"I'm not sure. What are your feelings?"
"Let's all be together on this, all right?"

And so forth. Beneath this external projection of verbal openness and honesty, there are usually consistent attitudes of the "laid-back and cool" variety. Facilitators tend to express liberal concerns and to adhere to the dictates of liberal fashion. They want to "experience" groups rather than "maximize outcomes." They want to "encourage communication" rather than "participate." And they always want to "facilitate interactions," rather than "construct arguments."

Facilitators tend to be loners who express a desire to be involved with a large number of people. They appear to value friendship and affiliation more than power and status, yet they often seek power and status at the expense of friendship and affiliation. If they hurt a friend or abuse an associate, they will usually attribute the blame to the other person: "He or she just couldn't handle the situation." Facilitators and Narcissists have a great deal in common.

The Servant of the Masses is a strategy employed by people who find themselves in positions of power or authority and want others to know they are only there to serve them. The Servant of the Masses strategy is most often used by successful politicians, and for this reason should be considered the logical counterpart to the Prince.

The Servant of the Masses

The Servant is usually a good listener. She or he will invite new ideas and proposals, gather as much available information as possible on a subject, and then ask the group to make the decision or solve the problem. The Servant is usually true to his or her word. He or she will *serve* the group and organization, not lead or actively participate in it.

The Servant tends to be courteous and exceedingly polite. Conflicts often make the Servant uncomfortable because they interrupt routine and sometimes cause hard feelings. The Servant can be a useful member of a small group, but will usually be an ineffectual leader. Servants tend to associate with Good Soldiers, Altruists, Facilitators, Friends, Shy People, and persons who habitually say "yes." They tend to be less successful socially and professionally with Princes, Courtiers, Power-Brokers, Enemies, Narcissists, Gameplayers, "No" Sayers, and Angry Young Wo/men. It is very difficult to dislike the Servant, but you may find it equally difficult to get a straight answer out of him or her.

The Friend	The Friend is a person who wants to help you, in exchange for favors to be granted in the future. The Friend is trustworthy, loyal, helpful, courteous, kind, sometimes obedient, always cheerful, and fun to be around. The Friend is amicable by nature and inclination, enjoys people. Not necessarily motivated by power, status, or hard work, the Friend is someone who will complete a task simply because she or he "wants to do something for you." However, you never know when a Friend will ask for a favor in return.

There are usually three kinds of Friends. First, there are "Just Friends." In organizations these people tend to be acquaintances; you may know their name and position in the company, but little else about them. When you meet, you greet each other and walk on. There is a lot of smiling among "Just Friends," and little conversation. When conversations do occur, they tend to be superficial and very polite. "Just Friends" may as readily be Friendly Enemies, but it is hard to say, because you seldom see them as they really are.

The second category of Friends is "My Friends." "My Friends" are people you have known and associated with for a long period of time. You tend to be possessive toward and about them. You can ask them for help, but you are not sure you would like it if they helped me. These Friends are sometimes called "True Friends," which means the friendship has been tested. It is both pleasant and painful to work in a small group with Friends. Constrained by your relationship, it is difficult to have productive, honest conflicts. When you feel restricted by the nature of the task, it is difficult to treat them as a Friend. In fact, Friends (second category) who work with each other in small groups may be risking their friendship. It is better to work with relative strangers than with "My Friends."

The third category of Friends is "My Best Friend." These Friends are rare and precious. If you have "My Best Friend" in an organization or small group, she or he can be a great comfort to you. You can argue honestly and heatedly with a Best Friend without risking the friendship. You can be led by or lead a Best Friend without invoking feelings of inferiority, superiority, or anxiety. After the age of thirty men tend *not* to have a Best Friend (Phillips and Goodall, 1983). Women tend to have one lifelong Best Friend through thick and thin. If you have a Best Friend working with you, you are a very fortunate person.

Friends (all categories) tend to be attractive in every possible way, at least to you. They may have shortcomings, but they are "worth it." For this reason, Friends can pose a threat to the cohesiveness of the small group. If there are two Friends you have a conspiracy, three or four Friends become a clique, four or more Friends may constitute a party. It may be difficult to accomplish your task when Friends are around.

The Friendly Enemy	The Friendly Enemy is a person whose strategy is based on the desire to *appear* friendly while masking an evil intent. The Friendly Enemy smiles a lot, seems polite, seems very interested in *your* well-being and happiness, and cares very much how *you* complete your task. Watch out. The Friendly Enemy is almost always with you, in every organization and virtually every small group. It is difficult to unmask the Friendly Enemy, but well worth the effort.

Friendly Enemies may dislike you for reasons of envy, jealousy, greed, lust, despair, or for no reason at all other than the fact that you exist. So intense is the feeling about you that the Friendly Enemy will go to extremes to make you look the fool. The really adept Friendly Enemy will then console you, expressing what may pass for real sorrow at your ineptness. Because the Friendly Enemy looks and acts very much like a Friend, you may take him or her into your confidence at your own expense.

Friendly Enemies usually associate with Friends, Servants, Facilitators, Courtiers, Good Soldiers, and even Altruists, on the surface. Their deeper allies, however, are Narcissists, Gameplayers, "No" Sayers, Power-Brokers, and Angry Young Wo/men.

There are two kinds of Shy People. The bona fide Shy Person is one who suffers tremendous anxiety about any speaking situation and almost never says anything unless directly addressed. This genuinely Shy Person is usually very bright, very creative, and simply lacks speaking skills. Such a Shy Person may find the group setting intolerable unless some conscious effort is made to help him or her overcome shyness (Phillips, 1981).

The second kind of Shy Person is the *strategically* Shy Person. This individual uses the *guise* of shyness to mask poor work, lack of preparation, or unwillingness to participate in the group. Although there are many legitimately Shy People in the world, the use of shyness as a way to gain positive responses from others is generally not their usual pattern of behavior. The Shy Person strategy is most often used by people who could participate actively, but who have found it easier to claim shyness instead. The Shy Person may do very well in ordinary social activities, but then clam-up during group meetings. The Shy Person would rather let the other group members do the work; he or she is not really concerned about the final product of the group.

There are more strategically Shy People around these days. Perhaps one reason for this explosion of shyness is the great amount of literature on the subject: in books, magazines, newspapers, etc. In an attempt to create a supportive atmosphere for the legitimately Shy Person, speech professionals may have unwittingly encouraged a host of Shy People to use the strategy. These people tend to associate with everyone, from Prince to Gameplayer; and this is precisely how you can separate a genuinely Shy Person from one who is using the Shy Person strategy. The bona fide Shy Person associates with virtually no one; you seldom even know he or she is there. But the Shy Person is consistently acknowledged because she or he says, "I am shy."

The Shy Person

The Narcissist is a person who uses the "me first" or "me only" strategies, based on a high level need for self-centeredness. Much has been written about the Narcissist since Christopher Lasch's *The Culture of Narcissism* (1979). Although there are elements of narcissism in all of us—even our understanding of Equity

The Narcissist

Theory is based on the assumption that "individuals will try to maximize their outcomes"—there are important differences between a healthy concern for one's own affairs and the Narcissist strategy.

The Narcissist sees the organization as an opportunity to further personal goals, and perceives the group as the mechanism to seize that opportunity. The Narcissist is not interested in the group's goals, its productivity, its well-being and cohesiveness. The Narcissist is interested only in how the group can reward "me." Hence, this person tends to accept only those assignments that will further his or her personal goals or reveal his or her efforts in a favorable light. The Narcissist does not usually aspire to positions of leadership or authority, unless those positions allow more time for self-glorification. The Narcissist is not a teamplayer, and cannot be relied upon to contribute consistently to the group.

The Narcissist *uses* other people. This person may be very attractive and rhetorical, a seducer who gains entrance to other group member's lives and exploits what she or he finds there. The Narcissist usually presents an outwardly charming appearance and may be socially polite and involved; but the purpose of every action is to attract attention and admiration for him or herself. The Narcissist is a very destructive force in any small group.

The Gameplayer

The Gameplayer strategy is revealed in a variety of ways. Just as there are a number of different interpersonal and group "games" that can be played, so also there are a number of distinct strategies for the Gameplayer. Eric Berne's *The Games People Play* (1964) provided the first account of these strategies; it is a useful guide to understanding the motives behind the actions of the "Gameplayer."

The Gameplayer tends to be of no particular personality type; he or she plays the game best suited to individual character and talents. For example, there are some people who play "The Child," a strategy based on unwillingness to accept responsibility. One can also play "The Adult," a strategy based on complete willingness to accept responsibility and to guide the lives of others. One can play the "I'm OK—You're OK" game with people who want reciprocal acceptance of their pasts through present interactions. Or one can also play the "Golden Boy/Girl" game, in which all activities are designed to elicit "oohs" and "aaahs" from audiences. There are also games, such as "Mr./Ms. Nice Guy," played by individuals who want everyone to like them; or "No More Mr./Ms. Nice Guy," played by individuals who are tired of people liking them. And so forth.

The Gameplayer is recognized by a casual, extroverted manner that seems to suggest vulnerability and lack of depth. This type of individual is most attractive to people who are also playing games, though usually not of the same variety. Gameplayers tend to be disruptive in groups, but are somewhat valued in organizations. They are disruptive because they interject a full range of unnecessary talk based solely on a desire to gain acceptance of their game-playing style or of the game itself. They tend to be somewhat valued in the organization because many people assume that games are supposed to be played in organizations. There are even guides to what games ought to be played. See, for example, Michael Maccoby's *The Gamesman: The New Corporate Leaders* (1976).

One problem with the strategy of the Gameplayer is that it takes at least two people to play the game. Unless the Gameplayer is sufficiently skilled in finding other people to share the game, she or he becomes sullen and often dangerous. Also, the Gameplayer who loses at his or her own game is likely to become an Enemy, even if you had little to do with the loss. For these reasons, the strategies of the Gameplayer are usually bad news for the small group. Gameplayers tend to disrupt group activities, especially agendas; they do not contribute to the group's cohesiveness. Perhaps the best that can be said about the Gameplayer is that she or he can make valuable contributions in a devil's advocate role, if he or she is willing to play that part.

These two strategies are used by people who have very low tolerances for either (1) the ambiguity brought on with disagreements or conflicts, or (2) the opinions of people who disagree with them. In the former case we have a "Yes" Sayer; in the latter case a "No" Sayer.

The "Yes" Sayer and the "No" Sayer

The "Yes" Sayer is a person who agrees with anything that is said by anybody, but is especially willing to go along with the leader. "Yes" Sayer behavior is usually a strategy used by weak or ineffectual people, who find comfort and acceptance through expressing agreement with others. They may harbor deep resentments toward those with whom they agree, but they probably will convince themselves that they have good reasons for agreeing. "Yes" Sayers also come in different varieties. For example, there are "Yes" Sayers among those who wish to do well in the group or organization, and believe "doing well" is directly related to agreeing with the group leader or boss. These "Yes" Sayers may resemble Courtiers; but Courtiers will use disagreement to win favor, while "Yes" Sayers will virtually never be heard to disagree with anyone about anything. Another variety of "Yes" Sayers is the person who is committed to the expediency of a position or an issue. This kind of "Yes" Sayer is akin to the Narcissist; but while the Narcissist is interested only in achieving his or her own goals, the "Yes" Sayer may believe expedient action is really in the group's best interests. "Yes" Sayers tend to be a problem in groups because they often help produce "Groupthink" condition.

The "No" Sayer is a person who disagrees with everything except those who agree with her or him. This negative person may be the Narcissist or the Angry Young Wo/man in other situations, but during group meetings the "No" Sayer demands summary agreement from everyone. This individual is very disruptive in the group because she or he tends to dominate discussions, act as bully in confrontations, and destroy the cohesiveness of the group. If the "No" Sayer is also the leader, the group is in for a very rough time. Most "No" Sayers secretly aspire to leadership positions, although they will deny the charge. Because they are generally disliked by others, they do not do very well in groups or organizations. Hence, they tend to become more disagreeable with age.

Whereas "Yes" Sayers tend to like association with people, responding affirmatively to the needs and expectations of others, "No" Sayers tend to be loners who seem not the least bit concerned with the needs and expectations of others. These are the strategies of *absolutes;* but most reasonable people who find good and bad in every issue, avoid either extreme.

The Angry Young Wo/man

This strategy combines the self-centeredness of the Narcissist with the cunning of the Gameplayer and the aspirations of either the Courtier or Prince. The Angry Young Wo/man is usually impatient or disgusted with the organization, tired of the rules and procedures used to guide the group, and ready for immediate change. This strategy is followed most often by people who use the group or organization as something to rebel against, and who enlist other people as instruments of their rebellion.

The Angry Young Wo/man is likely to be highly emotional in times of conflict, and to be barely able to contain emotion during other interactions. One of the purposes behind these actions is to induce the feeling in others that the Angry Young Wo/man is just about to explode and should be treated with extreme caution. In some instances this behavior inspires fear and trembling; in other cases it is merely laughable. However, the origin of the Angry Young Wo/man's behavior is usually a desire for acceptance and power. Most Angry Young People believe that they are being repressed, they are wasting away doing menial tasks while their creativity suffers.

This strategy usually does not work well with Good Soldiers, Altruists, Courtiers, Power-Brokers, Facilitators, Servants, Friends, or Shy People. To be generally distraught is unpleasant; to be *purposefully* distraught is the finer art of the Angry Young Wo/man.

The above strategies are likely to be encountered in any organization, and in many group situations. Some of the strategies are useful; Good Soldiers, Courtiers, Friends, and even Gameplayers can make substantive contributions to the group while seeking their own personal rewards. Power-Brokers and Princes, Servants and Friendly Enemies are typically present in group situations; they often provide a balance of power for the group. The more self-centered strategies tend *not* to promote cohesiveness or effectiveness in the group; but I present them to you so they can be more easily recognized.

These strategies are described in very generalized terms. Within each category listed here there are particular, detailed, purposive maneuvers used to gain precise responses from the group and its individual members. I believe an appreciation of these general strategies can prepare you to deal with them in group situations. *I also believe most of us are capable of using almost all of them.* What we see in the behavior of others often tells us a great deal about ourselves.

You are now ready to investigate how to choose a strategy designed to improve your communication in small groups.

How to Choose a Strategy: Considerations and Consequences

In the previous section you reviewed a variety of possibilities from which specific strategies may be developed. In this section you will explore a method for *inventing, managing,* and *evaluating* the effectiveness of a strategy used for a specific reason in a given case. I will present a series of questions which can lead you from considerations about possible strategies to performance of a particular one. This method is based on a description of how to improve communication, and can be examined in greater detail elsewhere (see Goodall, 1983).

Talk is purposive. Before you can choose a productive strategy for the given case you must first know what you want to accomplish. Here are the questions you need to ask to establish a goal for talk:

Inventing a Strategy

1. *What is my goal?*   What, specifically, do you need to accomplish in this group meeting? What kinds of responses are you seeking from other group members?
2. *What is the nature of my group?*   What is your purpose in this discussion? What urgencies are likely to be manifested by other group members? How will they respond to your statements and questions? What does your group history tell you about your record of success and failure? Are there any other considerations regarding your group which can help you choose a strategy?
3. *What are the available strategies capable of helping me reach my goal in the given case?*   Are there any aspects of history you can recall which may help you make a choice? What choices are actually available to you? How does your group view your participation? What are your communicative strengths and weaknesses? What limitations do the general nature of the group and the task to be performed place on your selection of a strategy? What are the specific limitations constraining your selection of a strategy by the individual group members? What are their strategies?
4. *What is the best available strategy to reach my goal in the given case?*   Out of the cluster of possible strategies, which one is most likely to gain the desired response for the right reasons? Which strategy is likely to increase your credibility with the group? Which strategy has the probability of improving your relations with other group members? Which strategy is best calculated to help you reach your group and your personal goals?
5. *What contingencies should I prepare for?*   What will you do if the strategy you plan to use cannot be carried out? What other communication plans will help you make progress toward attaining your goal? What might be the probable responses from other group members toward these contingencies?

These five questions should result in a clear idea about (1) the best strategy for the given case, and (2) the available contingencies which can be employed if circumstances prevent you from using the chosen strategy. Consider how the above information can be used to invent a strategy.

Example of Inventing A Strategy

My goal is to gain consensus in the group for two statements of criteria which I will propose during our next group meeting.

> I also would like to gain acceptance for my role as a team player.
> I also believe that reaching consensus on these criteria would enhance my posture within the group and perhaps increase others' trust of me.

My group is composed of six other people, each drawn from a different department within the organization. We are using Standard Agenda to decide on a new employee benefits package.

> The other group members are anxious about our proposal. Three of them have been involved in unpleasant union contract disputes and want to avoid these problems this time. The group leader is mostly interested in completing the task on time. The other two group members are people I don't know very well, but they seem to be willing to go along with well-thought out ideas.
> I think these group members will respond favorably to my proposals. Problems could arise if there are competing propositions, but I can argue for my position on the basis of our fact-finding and use those statements as support.
> Our group history is limited. We have only known each other for three weeks, and although I know Sally and Wayne outside of the group, I do not know much about them as group members. Thus far everyone has been considerate and motivated to complete the task. I can use these ideas to confirm my recommendations.
> The only other consideration may be power. Wayne is power-hungry and may need to be consulted about this proposal before the meeting.

I could use the Good Soldier, the Courtier (with Wayne), the Altruist, the Servant, or the Friend, all of whom I have identified at times in the group.

> I can recall two aspects of history that may help me: (1) our discussion about the need to remain objective, and (2) our response to the fact-finding reports.
> In view of what I know about the group and myself, I do not think I could use the Altruist, the Servant, or the Friend strategies. I am both a Good Soldier (as a result of our fact-finding history) and a Courtier

(based on my reputation in the company) to the group. I can use these strategies because they are believable.

I am a fairly strong arguer, especially good in presenting organized messages. My weakness is a tendency to become emotional in defense of my own position. I also make mistakes, speaking without thinking, but nobody in the group seems to hold that against me.

General limitations have to do with my previous record of participation in the group; specific limitations have to do with how Wayne will respond to what I say, and whether or not the group leader will try to out maneuver and overcome us with her opinion. Their strategies will be Courtier (Wayne) and Prince (group leader).

Probably the best strategy is the Good Soldier. If I try to interfere with the power dispute between the group leader and Wayne I will only confuse the issue.

The group will have increased respect for me and for my arguments if I do not become involved in a power-play. The group leader will let me speak and will agree with me if there are no better proposals. Wayne will let me speak because he is my friend and because I will talk to him before the group meeting.

By making my proposals I will be able to help the group reach its goal. They are well thought out and sensible. If the group accepts them, I will also achieve my personal goals.

The contingencies in this situation are dependent on how my conversation with Wayne shapes up and how the group leader acts during the meeting.

I may also need to pay special attention to those two group members I don't know much about. They may use this meeting to assert themselves; they may have their own proposals.

I may also need to watch the time. If I wait until the other proposals are made, I may not have enough time to accomplish my purpose.

The second phase of creating a strategy is referred to as the "management" phase. During this stage the purposive details of the choice are developed. Specifically, the group member should be concerned with how talk will be organized to reach the goal in the given case. Here are the questions:

Managing the Strategy

1. *How can I organize my basic message for presentation to the group?* Nothing is worse than listening to a disorganized speaker, especially in a group situation where others expect to have their turn to talk. Your concern should be how to state the case clearly and concisely, and support it. Usually it is advantageous to present your *conclusion*(s) first, then provide the *reason*(s) for it.

2. *How can I generate the appropriate appeals in my message?* Using what you know about the past history of the group, the individual needs and expectations, what forms of support for your claims are likely to gain approval? Are there vivid, persuasive examples available to you, to which your group will respond positively? Are there logical arguments, based on precedent or reasoning, which can help the group see why you feel as you do? Can you rely on the credibility of witnesses or authorities to help you gain acceptance of your proposal? Try to find one or two supports for each claim which you advance; then think about how your listeners will react to them. *Who* will be influenced by *what?* Remember to take *all* group members into consideration.

3. *How can I prepare for possible objections and counterarguments?* Presenting your case is only the beginning of group communication. In most instances the group will ask you to defend your position. They will ask questions, raise objections, provide counter-data or conclusions, or present alternate testimony of witnesses or authorities. How can you plan for these contingencies? What additional information do you have that can be used to counter their objections or to respond to their questions? It is important to plan the strategic use of these additional supports: what material can be most effective in countering what other kinds of claims or objections?

These three questions should help you to prepare for your presentation within the group, and to respond to questions or objections raised at that time. Here is an example:

Example of Managing a Strategy

I can organize my message this way:

First, I will preview what I want to say (e.g., "I have three statements that I think we can use as criteria . . . ").

Second, I will state each criterion succinctly.

Third, I will restate each criterion and supply examples, arguments, and testimony necessary to gain acceptance for each.

My appeals will be based on previous experiences within this group.

When I provide the first criterion, I will be relying on the principle of remaining objective, and will say so.

When I furnish the second criterion I will be using the testimony of two authorities on union contracts, both of whom have been quoted in our fact-finding session.

When I present the third criterion I will use an example based on the illustration that Wayne used when he presented his report last time.

I am prepared for objections, questions, and counterarguments:

I have more information about each criterion: how I arrived at it, how I think it can help us, and why we ought to consider using it.

I have additional support in the form of statements made by witnesses, together with reasoned arguments which I can use to counter specific objections.

I have all of this material organized on note cards, and I have reviewed my strategy well enough to know exactly how to proceed.

The third phase in planning a strategy is to determine how you will know whether or not you reached your goal in the given case. To accomplish this end, ask these questions:

Evaluating the Effectiveness of the Strategy

1. *How will I know if I reached my goal?* What responses must you receive from other group members to let you know whether you were successful? What, specifically, will they say or do? How long are you willing to use your strategy to gain these responses?
2. *How can I save face if I fail to reach my goal?* What responses must you receive from other group members to let you know you were unsuccessful? What will you do if this happens?
3. *How can I improve my effectiveness next time?* Following the group meeting, you should assess the effectiveness of your strategy. If you did not reach your goal, why? What can be done next time to improve your performance? If you did reach your goal, was it for the reasons you thought? What can be learned about this group meeting to help you prepare for future sessions?

These three questions should help you evaluate your effectiveness in the group. In any group situation there is information available to the critical group member that can assure improvement next time. Regardless of how well or poorly you perform in a given case, one major goal should be to find ways and means to become a more productive and satisfied group participant or leader.

Communication and Strategy

Remember: there is a difference between presenting a public speech and communicating in a small group. You can present a public speech without interruption from beginning to ending, then invite questions and other forms of responses. When you communicate in a group setting, however, you are constrained by the fact that several other people will also want (and expect) to speak. No matter how well thought out your strategy is, it will fail if you attempt to dominate a group discussion. You must be concise. You must limit what you say, how you say it, and always be mindful of the fact that your primary goal is to complete the group task.

Strategic interaction in a small group is a learned skill. When people begin studying group discussion, they tend to be less prepared and more verbal than they need to be. As they learn to develop skill in presenting arguments and responding to the words and actions of others, they begin to *adapt* their behavior to the needs of the situation and other group members. As these skills develop, they gradually increase in effectiveness. Individuals also create better strategies. Strive constantly to improve your strategic skills, paying very careful attention to the responses you receive from others, and monitoring the communication plans of more successful group members.

Communication is how strategies are created, managed, and evaluated. No matter how well thought out your strategy may be, unless you spend time rehearsing its presentation to the group and planning responses to possible objections, your strategy may fail. Group members respond to what is *said and done,* not to what is well thought out. The only way group members will know the quality of your thinking and planning is through what is revealed to them in the given case. *How* you talk is just as important as *what* you talk about. Before closing this chapter, you may learn from Gordon's example:

Gordon D., 25   I wanted to do so well in the group that I spent all night writing out my approach, my arguments, and my refutations. I drank a gallon of hot coffee, ate two dozen donuts, and ran a mile in the brisk morning air before going to work. I did not even try to get some sleep. The room was hot, my mouth was dry, and the meeting seemed to go on and on and on. I would have been okay had I not fallen asleep before my fact-finding report. When Ben had to wake me up, I was embarrassed, but so deep was my sleep that I could not pull it together. I sounded like a real idiot. My words were slurred like some drunkard, my arguments were only half remembered, and in the end I lost a good deal of the credibility I had worked so long and hard to achieve. In one group meeting I virtually ruined my reputation with the other members. It took nearly a year to make up for it. Everyone thought I had been out all night boozing, and I don't think anyone would have believed my story about being up all night working. I can't blame them. I remember it all through a haze, but the embarrassment is very, very clear. Nothing matters unless you can deliver the promised goods on time. From the receiver's point of view, that is all that is important.

As Gordon learned the hard way, a strategy is only as good as the way it is communicated.

This chapter addressed strategies for improving communication in small groups. I began by pointing out the need for an *ethical* approach to the development of rhetorical strategies. I explained that rhetoric is a tool which can be used for good or evil purposes. The rhetorically sensitive communicator always strives to maximize outcomes for the group and for the individual members. Rhetoric is the core of the adaptive approach to group interaction.

Second, I discussed the idea of rhetorical strategies. A strategy should be *contingent, productive,* and *detailed.* You investigated how strategic interaction can produce a mixed-motive problem in which two or more participants attempt to satisfy their personal goals at the expense of the group's goal. I concluded this section by providing a summary of recommendations about overcoming the mixed-motive problem in small group settings.

Third, you investigated some possible, generalized strategies that can be used to prepare for and to interpret the behavior and attitudes of others in group situations. I listed the Good Soldier, the Altruist, the Prince, the Courtier, the Power-Broker, the Facilitator, the Servant of the Masses, the Friend, the Friendly Enemy, the Shy Person, the Narcissist, the Gameplayer, the "Yes" and "No" Sayers, and the Angry Young Wo/man approaches to small group communication. I explained that this list is not exhaustive, but includes some of the general characteristics of people who are commonly encountered in organizational groups. I concluded this section by pointing out that these are strategies which most of us use at some time in group situations. They represent possibilities for planning talk.

Fourth, you examined the considerations and consequences of choosing a detailed strategy. In this section you reviewed the three basic stages of rhetorical strategy-building: invention, management, and evaluation of talk. For each stage, I developed a list of questions that can be used to guide the selection, implementation, and evaluation of a strategy in a given case. I concluded this section by pointing out that you can learn how to improve your effectiveness in groups by systematically examining how others respond to your strategies, and how you respond to theirs.

Finally, I discussed the role of communication in the development and use of any strategy. I argued that effectiveness in building strategies is a learned skill requiring careful concentration and adaptation. I concluded this section, and the chapter, by repeating the major premise of this book: communication is how you reveal the substance of your strategies. No matter how well you prepare for a group communication, what ultimately matters is how you perform in the situation.

Summary

This chapter addressed strategic interaction in small groups. The goal of this chapter was to show you a systematic method for improving the responses you receive from others in small groups. In the next chapter you will examine methods for improving the performances of *others* in group settings.

References

Berne, E. *The Games People Play*. New York: The Grove Press, 1964.

Goodall, Jr., H. L. *Human Communication: Creating Reality*. Dubuque, Ia.: William C. Brown Publishers, 1983.

Gouran, D. S. *Making Decisions in Groups: Choices and Consequences*. Glenview, Ill.: Scott, Foresman, and Co, 1982.

Lasch, C. *The Culture of Narcissism*. New York: W. W. Norton, 1979.

Maccoby, M. *The Gamesman: The New Corporate Leaders*. New York: Simon and Schuster, 1976.

Nemeth, C. "A Critical Analysis of Research Using the Prisoner's Dilemma Paradigm for the Study of Bargaining." In *Advances in Experimental Social Psychology*, vol. 6, edited by L. Berkowitz, 203–34. Englewood Cliffs, N.J.: Prentice-Hall/ Spectrum Books, 1981.

Phillips, G. M. *Help for Shy People*. Englewood Cliffs, N.J.: Prentice-Hall/Spectrum Books, 1981.

Phillips, G. M., and H. L. Goodall, Jr. *Loving and Living*. Englewood Cliffs, N.J.: Prentice-Hall/Spectrum Books, 1983.

Walster E., and G. W. Walster. "Interpersonal Attraction." In *Social Psychology: An Introduction*, edited by B. Seidenberg and A. Snadowsky, 279–308. New York: The Free Press, 1976.

Wilson, E. O. *On Human Nature*. Cambridge: Harvard University Press, 1979.

Exercises

This chapter dealt with strategies for improving your communication in decision-making groups. The following exercise is designed to help you develop strategies, try out new strategies, and investigate the differences between effective and ineffective strategies. The core of this exercise is the problem of a veteran employee, Mr. L. M. Enopee. Here is the problem:

1. *Mixed-Motive exercise:* The class should be divided into seven teams. The instructor will then give each team a strategic identity (e.g., Prince, Good Soldier, Gameplayer, "No" Sayer, etc.). The identities will be handed to the groups on pieces of folded paper; these identities must *not* be revealed to the other teams. Then the groups will be formed. The instructor will choose one member from each group. The groups will be assigned discussion areas in the classroom. After the groups are seated, the instructor will announce the nature of the task to be completed:

   a. A company employee has been found guilty of misrepresenting evidence in a decision-making small group. The group reported the problem to a duly-elected grievance committee who reviewed the situation and passed judgment. If the employee is fired, she or he will suffer the consequences of this decision for life. If the employee is retained, it might weaken company morale. Your group must decide what to do with this employee. Based on the role assigned to you by the instructor, you must conduct a group discussion designed to resolve this problem. Here is the information you may need:

NAME OF EMPLOYEE: L. M. Enopee

Department: Production

Years of service: 11

Record:

L. M. Enopee joined our company after graduating from high school. First employed as a line assembly worker, L. M. was promoted to line foreman after completing college through a night extension program (six and one-half years later). L. M.'s degree was in Business Administration with a major in management and a minor in marketing. L. M. has consistently done well in performance appraisal reviews, although L. M. does show signs of tiring with the present job. L. M. expressed a desire to go back to school for an MBA during the last review. Because the company does provide tuition assistance for these programs pending approval of the department head and an overseeing committee, L. M. was encouraged to apply. L. M.'s application was rejected by the department head and never reached the committee.

---

    b. A department head seems to be standing in the way of subordinates' promotions and raises, according to the records submitted by the personnel office. This department head is in production, and the most recent case involves a line foreman named L. M. Enopee. Enopee applied for tuition assistance for an MBA program and was rejected by the department head. Enopee has a B.S.B.A. (Management and Marketing) and eleven (11) years of service with the company. Performance appraisals have been consistently good, but Enopee is showing signs of boredom in present position. Personnel feels that Enopee is a valuable employee and should be encouraged by the company via the tuition assistance program. There is nothing in the record to disqualify Enopee except the rejection of the application by the department head. This is the fourth straight application so rejected by the department head, and in at least two previous cases the applicants quit their jobs and are now employed by competitors. Your group must decide what to do about this department head. But first you will need some information about him:

NAME OF DEPARTMENT HEAD: William Milgram

Department: Production Department Head

Years of service: 24

Record:

    Mr. Milgram joined our company after graduating from high school. He was promoted to line foreman after seven years of service, during which time he completed a college degree in management. He expanded the production department over a period of five years and increased productivity during this time approximately 400%. He is a very valuable member of the company with extensive experience in and understanding of the whole operation. His performance reviews were among the highest ever given until about two years ago. At that time Mr. Milgram was denied a company Vice-Presidency, which was given to a younger man with an MBA. Mr. Milgram expressed no bitterness, but was obviously dissatisfied with the decision. Since that time his reviews have been satisfactory. He is still very much involved with the operation of the production department, but he seems less interested in the people who work for him. Rumor has it that he has been drinking very heavily off-the-job.

---

    c. Your group is a special overseeing committee charged with developing guidelines for a new policy concerning the tuition assistance program. For the past ten years our company has offered full tuition to any employee wishing to further his or her education provided (1) the employee's application is approved by the department head; (2) the employee's application is approved by the overseeing committee; (3) the employee's educational goal is directly related to his or her task in the organization; and (4) the employee maintains at least a B− average. Many employees (over two hundred) have taken advantage of this program and the company is satisfied with it. However, there have been problems. For example, if the department head does not approve an application, it never reaches the committee. Recently four employees' applications were disapproved by a single department head, and as a direct result two of them resigned from the company. Another problem is to determine what is meant by the educational objective being "directly related to" the employee's task. Does this mean a line worker cannot be approved to study for a management degree? Does a person working as a typist in the personnel department not have the right to earn a degree in personnel administration? The third problem is concerned with what happens after the employee receives a degree at company expense. In about twenty cases during the past five years, employees who have received tuition assistance from the company have resigned their jobs upon completing the degree to work for a competitor. Clearly we need some assurance that we are helping people who plan to remain with us, at least for a while.

d. Your group is a special grievance committee. Recently you had to decide on the case of an employee (L. M. Enopee) who misrepresented factual information about the production department to a decision-making group. Your charge was simply to determine his or her guilt or innocence in this case. You found that L. M. Enopee was clearly guilty. However, during the hearing you discovered that L. M. Enopee was trying to get revenge against the production head who had recently turned down his tuition assistance application. There was good reason to believe the production head acted unfairly, but this problem was beyond the scope of the specific charge given to your group. Now the production head, William Milgram, has brought a charge against L. M. Enopee, and the matter is before your group. The charge is that of misrepresenting production department information to a formal decision-making group. Mr. Milgram believes Enopee should be terminated without recommendations. Your group has sought special powers in this case from the Vice-President for Personnel and the Vice-president for Production. You have now been formally given those special powers, which include rehearing the case and making a recommendation about action.

To accomplish your task, you will have to receive the reports of three other groups who have been working on related aspects of this case.

After each group (except the "d" group) makes its decision or recommendation, they should appoint one spokesperson to report them at the "d" group hearing. The "d" group hearing should be an open, public discussion in which the remainder of the group members serve as the audience. *Remember to remain in your assigned role.* You now have a mixed-motive situation and several issues to resolve. Good luck!

2. *Question for Discussion/Debrief:* Try to isolate each one of the roles played by group members. What specific attitudes and behaviors were revealed by them that contributed to your opinions? How did the roles played by the group members influence the decision reached by the groups?

9

Strategies for Improving the Communication Skills of Others in Small Groups

Introduction

Small groups provide you with opportunities to sharpen leadership and participation skills. You can learn to make better choices about your own behavior, to choose words and actions that are more appropriate and adaptive to the needs and expectations of the given case. But there is the principle of reciprocity to consider. While you try to adapt your presentations to the needs and expectations of other group members, you expect them to adapt to yours in return. Equity in the group depends on a balance of giving and getting, of choosing effective communication strategies, and on the responses made to what is communicated.

Despite your ability to understand the principle of reciprocity in groups, and to adapt your choices to unique situations and to others, you still confront difficulty when these tacit, internal agreements are violated by group members who refuse, for whatever reason, to cooperate with you. Consider the following case:

> **Carol R., 29** We were a good group until Allan came up for promotion. Before that happened Allan was about as group-minded as the rest of us were, and he was considerate. But when he found out he was being recommended for senior project analyst, he flipped. Almost overnight he changed from the good group member ready to cooperate, ready to perform his duties, to an obstinate, high-minded, egotistical jerk. He came late to group meetings, he sat back and daydreamed, yawned loudly, interrupted people, made silly comments, you know, the whole, "I am better than you are" routine. What could we do? We were stuck with him. We needed his expertise on the project but we didn't need his grief. I tried to talk to him away from the group but it didn't work out. He wouldn't listen. A couple of the others tried to ridicule him during group meetings, but he just laughed. The leader, Vera, tried to intervene on several occasions but he knew if he was promoted she would be technically his subordinate and didn't pay her any mind. That experience turned me against small groups. You know what happened? He got promoted and just continued to get worse. Vera quit, one guy transferred to Montana, and I returned to school. So let me ask you, professor, what do you do with someone like Allan?

This chapter addresses problems associated with *other* group member's choices about communication behavior in the group. First, you will examine the role of education in the small group. Second, you will investigate participant's responsibilities in educating each other. Third, you will explore the leader's responsibilities in educating wayward group members. Fourth, you will look at some of the problems associated with giving advice in small groups. Following the chapter summary and references you will find three exercises designed to implement material covered in this chapter.

The Role of Education in the Small Group

Let us begin this exploration with an assumption: *The outcomes of any small group are directly influenced by choices made by group members about what to say and do.* Hence, group members are responsible for group outcomes, because in every word they utter, in their every movement, they are actively determining what those outcomes will be.

Let us further consider how this "group reality" can be created. If the group begins with the shared assumption that whatever happens in the group is the result of influences beyond their control (e.g., the physical environment is too constraining, the budget for this project is too small, the leader has an abrasive personality, etc.), then the *value* of making adaptive choices decreases, because no matter what choices individuals make, the result will be more influenced by factors beyond their control than by their own behavior. This is a fatal assumption for a group, but it accurately characterizes one negative approach to group work in modern organizations. You can see that by making this assumption the group reality would be essentially *unrewarding* and *unproductive*. It would be unrewarding because there would be little sense of shared purpose and very slight reason to compliment helpful behaviors. It would be unproductive because the group doomed itself from the start to its own uselessness; no matter what was attempted, there would be little hope of its ultimate success. The end product of this kind of thinking is a group that does not (1) encourage active choice-making among members, (2) sanction the use of agendas to guide interaction, or (3) provide a shared spirit of cooperation and purposefulness.

How do these problems occur in a small group? How does such a negative attitude become established? The answer is found in the *early statements* made by the group leader or group members. For example, if, during an initial group meeting the leader says, "Well, I don't really know why we are meeting about this because there is really nothing we can do about it," the establishment of a negative group reality is already underway. This statement may arouse similar feelings and attitudes in other group members who would rather be elsewhere doing other work or for whom the experience of group work seems unrewarding. Within the short span of a few minutes the group can be effectively defeated; there will be no sense of purpose, no need for equity, no inducements for good work.

The Influence of Early Statements on Group Outcomes

Now let us consider an alternative group reality. Suppose that a group begins with the assumption that whatever happens in the group will be the result of the members' choices and actions. The *value* of those choices about actions increases dramatically, because all individual decisions directly affect the group and its purpose. This assumption provides the group with (1) a sense of shared purpose, (2) a need to establish equity, (3) a need to find an agenda that can guide interaction, (4) a system of rewards and punishments, and (5) a need for careful preparation for all group meetings. Operating under this assumption, the group has an awareness of the importance of choices about behavior and an understanding of the processes necessary to carry out the group charge.

How does this happen in a small group? How does a group establish such a positive attitude? The answer is found in the early statements made by the group leader or group members. For example, if during the initial group meeting the group leader says, "I am counting on each one of you to contribute to our task, and I believe we can accomplish this task effectively and efficiently if we all remember to think before we speak," then she or he encourages productive communication among group members. If the leader then institutes an agenda, explains how it will impact individual's tasks and the timetable for decision-making, a second inducement for effective communication is provided. Other inducements may include a brief exploration of initial attitudes toward the issue (which provides each group member with the opportunity to receive vital information from other members about their views and possible priorities), and an introduction of the group members, with some information about why they have been chosen for the group.

Consider these two opposing views of how the group constructs its reality. In both cases the initial statements made by the group leader induce members to respond in particular ways, and the choices made about what to say and do influence other group member's decisions about what they will say and do. In both instances the meaning of the initial interaction is determined by the choices made about behavior in the group. While I am dichotomizing reality construction in the group, you can see how these two opposing views provide starting points places for the group's attitude toward its task and toward itself. Choices about behavior, even something as seemingly insignificant as an initial statement, influence the group's outcome. Hence, the better (e.g., more adaptive, more purposeful) the choices made about group behavior, the more likely the group will construct positive outcomes.

Purposeful Education   This example reveals the role of education in the small group. Education is not something that "just happens." Instruction and training among group members about how to interact as a group, how to treat each other as individuals, how to approach the group task, is a purposeful, goal-oriented activity. It is the responsibility of all group members to contribute to this process by making statements reflecting a positive group attitude, by monitoring communication between and among group members, and by making productive choices about what to say and do. The group "learns" how to act.

Mark W., 28   I'll never forget what happened when we were assigned to a team with a leader who had been trained in small group communication. Everything was different from the start. She began by explaining our charge and then told us how she viewed the role of talk in the group. Can you imagine? The engineers were very skeptical at first and the tech writers were dumbfounded. Here is this woman, a senior project engineer, actually *training* us in how to operate as a small group. She convinced us that what we talked about determined how successful and productive the group was. We were all a bit shaken up by it, but I don't think any of us has forgotten her. Let me tell you what else she did. There were times when conflict would emerge. She would intervene, explain how conflict operates in groups, and then encourage us to see what was happening as a problem we all needed to help solve. Blew away the whole group! Another time she was making assignments for our final presentation and someone argued with her. Instead of getting mad—this is what I would have done—she listened to the argument and then began asking questions. The guy answered them, and before we knew it they had agreed. I'll tell you something, it was pretty interesting. I know some guys thought she was full of herself, but as we learned more about her we began to see how right she really was. And the best thing was that our group completed the project in record time. We all got bonuses, and that's when we really began to appreciate her ability to educate us. That's right, *educate* us. She taught us to work as a group.

This is an atypical example. The point being made is *not* that it takes a special person to lead a group, but instead that *how the group learns to operate is the result of the information given to group members by each other.* If the group leader wants to encourage the group to value its choices about behavior, then the leader needs to say so. If the group members want to establish a sense of equity within the group, then someone needs to bring up the issue and explain how equity operates in a small group. Nothing happens unless someone makes a statement or asks a question. Through communication of an idea or an objection to an idea, the group contributes to the mutual construction of its own reality and outcomes.

Education about group roles, group processes, the importance of choices about actions, and the importance of choices about communication are integral parts of any group situation. Whether the group attitude toward itself and its work is negative or positive, education will occur. The goal should be to make education work *for* the group, toward attaining more productive outcomes. Now that I have established the need for education within the group and the ways in which a group reality is developed, let's examine specific tools for group education and reality construction which are available to participants and leaders.

Participants' Responsibilities in Educating Each Other

You know that individuals bring to group situations unique histories, characters, goals (personal and group), personalities, and ways of communicating. You *know* this to be true, but you may seldom act as if this understanding was directing your choices about behavior. Instead of recognizing and responding to the *uniqueness* of individuals, you may often categorize, group, or stereotype them. Although the way you stereotype others indicates more about you than it does about them, you probably do tend to treat others as representatives from stereotyped groups.

The Negative Influence of Stereotypes

"Oh, you're from Engineering. I see. . . ."

or

"Lisa, so glad to meet you. You're from the Personnel Office, aren't you? I've always had good dealings with people over there. I'm sure we'll get along."

As you gain information about others you tend either to (1) reinforce the original stereotyping, or to (2) begin to respond to them as individuals. This behavior is the result of a conscious choice you make about your attitude and approach toward other people. Very often this decision is heavily influenced by your personal goals for the situation, but it can also be the result of a *conscious effort to treat people as individuals.*

Methods for Overcoming Stereotypes

How can this be accomplished? First, you need to reinforce the value of responding to others as individuals. When you treat people as respresentatives of stereotypical categories you essentially *de*humanize them. You strip them of their personality, their history of interactions and relationships, their goals, their ambitions, their unique drives and needs, and so forth. You respond *only* to the stereotype. You "leave out" much more information than you "take in," because your perception of them is distorted by prejudice and judgment. You tend to think of them in "all or nothing" terms: either you like them or you dislike them, you agree with them or disagree with them, they are your friend or your enemy. Yet to treat others as representatives of stereotypes is to violate the rule of reciprocity in human relationships. If you treat them as a representative from "X," then they can treat you as a representative from "Y." If you are willing to respond to them in an "all or nothing" fashion, then you should expect the same treatment from them when you speak. What you hold against them can also be held against you.

You can understand how stereotyping can cause difficulty between people working in small groups. Since it is necessary for you to be able to adapt to the needs and expectations of others, you require more information about them than stereotyping can provide. A second way this goal may be accomplished is to implement the values of effective communication. Most people believe they know how to communicate; it is equally evident that they don't always try hard enough. You have seen how important effective communication is in small groups, and I have consistently made the point that communication must be learned. We become educated in the arts of communicating with each other when we interact over a period of time in small groups. We learn to recognize and respond to individual characteristics, adapting to unique turns of character or personality. By recognizing the importance and value of effective talk, you encourage yourself and others to avoid treating people as "types," and instead reaffirm their basic individuality and uniqueness.

A third method of assuring conscious effort to treat others as individuals, concerns how you elicit responses from them. When you don't care about others, when you are content with your stereotyping and judgment of who others are and what they are "worth" to you, you tend *not* to ask them for feedback. Who cares what *they* think, anyway? Consequently, they do not ask you for responses to their ideas either. The result is a stalemate of a dangerous kind. In small groups, where so much of what happens depends on *inter*action, the failure of individuals to elicit responses from each other can seriously impair the group's efforts. You need to be aware of the goals of *behavioral flexibility,* and to formulate your goals with others in mind. You need to adapt your talk to them in the given case. You need to elicit responses from them. You need their cooperation with your plans.

Communication Style

In the last chapter I discussed the urgency of being able to adapt to the needs and expectations of others, to respond to their motives as well as their ideas. Let's expand that statement. Let's go one step further, from what others say and their reasons for saying it to their *style of communicating* (Norton, 1983). Because what you "see" and "hear" is what you respond to, you need to be conscious of how your responses to the behavior of others can be influenced by the characteristics you associate with their communicator style. After all, if you want to improve the communication of others within the group, you should know how you have arrived at decisions about their need to improve. Consider Table 9.1.

This table was developed by Paul Mok and Associates. Mok is interested in how people respond to the *behavior* of others. A strong tradition in social and clinical psychology, mostly derived from the perspective of Carl Gustav Jung, indicates that most communicative behavior can be described in relation to "personality" characteristics (see Knapp, 1978, pp. 281–83 for review). If you have biases for or against a particular style of behaving, then you usually attribute your prejudices to the person's personality or character. *It is essential that you make a conscious effort to know what you are responding to when you respond to other's behavior.* Here is a way of thinking about each one of the styles presented in Table 9.1 (Knapp, 1978, p. 281):

Intuiting: Speculating, imagining, envisioning, daydreaming, creating, innovating. Wordy, but aloof. Impersonal. Challenges statements with the ubiquitous "why?" Can go off on a theoretical tangent. Often has fresh ideas and novel approaches to things.

Thinking: Rationally deducing, analyzing, ordering facts, identifying and weighing options, reflecting. The fact gatherer. Systematic, organized, and information-centered. Businesslike. Speaks in specifics. Has an ordered and measured manner. Often works from an agenda. Unemotional.

Table 9.1 Effective and Ineffective Styles in the Behavioral Styles Theory of Effective Communication

Primary Communicating Style	Characteristics Associated with the Communicating Style	
Intuitor	*Effective Application*	*Ineffective Application*
	original	unrealistic
	imaginative	"far-out"
	creative	fantasy-bound
	broad-gauged	scattered
	charismatic	devious
	idealistic	out-of-touch
	intellectually tenacious	dogmatic
	ideological tenacious	impractical
Thinker	effective communicator	verbose
	deliberative	indecisive
	prudent	over-cautious
	weighs alternatives	over-analyzes
	stabilizing	unemotional
	objective	non-dynamic
	rational	controlled and controlling
	analytical	over-serious, rigid
Feeler	spontaneous	impulsive
	persuasive	manipulative
	empathetic	over-personalizes
	grasps traditional values	sentimental
	probing	postponing
	introspective	guilt-ridden
	draws out feelings of others	stirs up conflict
	loyal	subjective
Sensor	pragmatic	doesn't see long-range
	assertive, directional	status seeking, self-involved
	results-oriented	acts first then thinks
	objective-bases opinion on what	lacks trust in others
	he actually sees	domineering
	competitive	arrogant
	confident	

Feeling: Empathizing, perceiving, associating, remembering, relating. Warm, friendly, and supportive. Informal. Injects humor and personal anecdotes into conversation. Talks a lot and animatedly.

Sensing: Acting, doing, relying on sensory data, combating-competing, striving for results, living in the here and now. Abrupt. Sits on the edge of the chair. Gets to the point and expects others to do the same. Controls the conversation. Trusts and believes in action. Does what he or she believes in and believes in what he or she does.

REMEMBER: THESE ARE ONLY CATEGORIES!! They provide you with a way of describing some of the behavioral characteristics of other people (and yourself), but they do *not* define what these people should *mean* or *be* to you. They are helpful when analyzing our responses to how others behave. They are less helpful when used to describe how "all" others "are." Use them to begin the analysis of how you respond to others and why; they are useful starting places, not final destinations.

These four basic styles of communicating are used by all of us. To be a truly effective communicator, you need to be flexible in your choices of behavior. To adapt to the needs and expectations of others in the given case you need an *inventory* of available styles to choose from. You also need consciously to recognize that *others* are capable of using alternative styles of communicating. You should, therefore, allow individuals the freedom to choose from among their inventory the most effective, efficient style of communicating in a given case. To accomplish this goal means you must provide them with information about how their choice of style influences your responses.

Methods for Improving Your Responses to Style

Finally, you should be able to make adjustments to others over a period of time. You know that as groups spend time together they develop more information about the task and about each other. You realize that the more you are around other people, the better you seem to know them. And the better you know them, the better capable you become in making effective choices about how to communicate with them. But this requires *time*. It is essential that you become aware of the tentative nature of your judgments about other people, based on what you claim, at any given time, to "know" about them. As you acquire new information you should be able to adjust your assessments of others.

These methods of improving the effectiveness of others in small groups depends on *your* willingness and ability to respond to them as individuals. As a participant, you can exert control over *your* choices, *your* behavior, and *your* motives or goals for the situation. By becoming more flexible in your styles of communicating, by responding to the overt or subtle changes in the communicative behavior of other group members, you encourage a sense of communicative competence within the group. People will respond to what you say and do, according to how you respond to or treat them. If you wish to improve the ways in which group members respond to you and your ideas, then you first need to improve your style of responding to them and to their ideas. You may be surprised at how effective other group members can be if you encourage them.

Up to this point you have considered your attitude and approach to others in the group as important indices of how you will behave toward them. I have recommended the idea of making a *conscious effort* to improve what happens in the group by improving the ways you respond to and treat other group members. But, as we all know, the best laid plans of mice and men can go awry. It is not enough simply to *choose* to improve the effectiveness of others in the group; you must also find ways of *behaving* which reflect your choices. Now we will examine some of the behaviors associated with effective communication, especially as they relate to improving the communication of others in groups.

Goal-Oriented Methods of Reducing Ambiguity

You cannot divorce a person's communication skills from the goals that the skills are intended to serve. You know that individuals have personal goals and organizational or group goals, and that often these goals differ from one another. You are familiar with the case of the person who uses the group for personal gain and thus causes hard feelings among group members. You are also familiar, to a lesser extent, with people who sacrifice everything for the good of the group, thus causing feelings of guilt and admiration in others. These two extremes are clearly defined, but they do not identify a whole range of other possibilities for goal-orientations within the small group.

What I wish to do in this section is to examine goals in relation to the *process of communication* within the group. I will assume, for the time being, that you are capable of treating others as individuals, and further, that you have made a conscious decision to improve the effectiveness of communication within the group. Now the question is: *How?*

The Primacy of Language

Many of the problems in small group communication are the result of *ambiguity*. You may misinterpret what someone else says or vice-versa. You may "assume" you know what someone else is referring to when actually you do not. You may attribute a motive to a statement or action that is more descriptive of *your* goal for the situation than of the speaker's. You may want to have more information about a particular aspect of your group's problem but not know how to ask for it. These are typical communication problems which are the result of ambiguity. The language you use to talk about "it" is abstract, vague, confusing, or simply inappropriate; the language used by other group members to respond to "it" is equally ambiguous. You may begin to feel alienated from the experiences of other group members, as if you were the only person capable of understanding what "it" is about. Hence, ambiguity in group communication often leads to nonproductive conflict.

There are some very practical methods to reduce ambiguity. Each of these techniques assumes that *the individual responding to the ambiguity does so with the goal of reducing it.* Consider this statement for a minute. Most people respond to ambiguity as if it was an "error" on the part of the *speaker,* not a *problem* to be solved by the *group.* Thus, you may "blame the victim" by attacking the statement as being what it so obviously is: vague. You may turn your attention away from the statement entirely, indicating to its speaker your lack of interest in pursuing it. You may laugh at it, you may make a joke out of it, or you may become aggravated because of it. All these responses only arouse hostility or further confusion in the speaker, and ultimately, in the whole group. They do not solve the problem. They way to solve the problem is to define it as a problem and then to investigate it further.

Once the statement has been defined as a problem there are six techniques for reducing ambiguity:

Six Techniques

1. *Supportive Feedback:* After the ambiguous statement is made, respond to it supportively. That does not mean support the ambiguity; it does mean *support the integrity of the speaker* expressing the ambiguity. Describe the specific aspects of the statement or action

that affect you: "You used the term *inadequate* to describe our understanding of the problem, and I am confused about what *inadequate* means to you." This encourages the speaker to elaborate, thereby providing more information about her or his interpretation of the term. The idea of supportive feedback is to reinforce the goal of cooperation between and among group members. To reach this goal, all group members must support each other psychologically and emotionally, to "validate" their experiences. To point out that someone is wrong or idiotic is to deepen the gap between you, and to deny the cooperative purposes of human communication. To point out the need for further clarification by offering supportive responses to ambiguity when it occurs is to use communication as a bridge to understand each other's interpretations.

2. *E-Prime Language:*   A long held truth among General Semanticists is that one major problem with our use of language is the verb form *to be*. E-Prime Language refers to the *absence* of the words *is, are, am, was, were, shall be,* and *will be*. When you use these terms you "fix" reality; you report something that is always changing as if it never changes. You attribute certainty to possibility, and you dichotomize situations that are not, by themselves, dichotomous. This is not simply a trick of language usage; it has serious consequences for communicators. For example, when someone in the group says "This *is* the most viable alternative to our problem," she or he is inviting a personal attack without meaning to. Consider how you could respond to the statement. You could agree *or* disagree. By "fixing" one alternative as a certainty, the speaker dichotomizes the possible responses of other group members. To break this habit is difficult. We are accustomed to using the verb form *to be*. One very effective technique seems to be to replace *is* with *seems to be*. The statement becomes less certain, more tentative, and more open to purposeful argument among group members. It removes the temptation to attack the speaker by eliminating the dichotomizing, "either-or" tone of the statement.

3. *Paraphrasing the Speaker's Statement:*   You may find yourself responding to a statement *before* you know what the speaker means. As you discovered earlier, there are barriers to effective listening, one of which is to begin formulating an answer to a statement before you "hear out" what the speaker is actually saying. To overcome this problem, you need to develop and practice good listening skills and to use the technique of paraphrasing. After hearing what the speaker has to say, try to paraphrase the message to her or him. "Let me see if I have this right. You are saying that we need to improve the plant's safety division to gain government approval for our contract?" Paraphrasing allows the speaker to receive feedback or responses about how the message was interpreted and thus reduce or eliminate ambiguities in the interpretation before they lead to conflict.

4. *Providing Descriptions of Feelings:*   Too often we fail to let others know how we *feel* about what they have said. Or, we tell them how we do feel, but make it sound as if it is *their* fault. "!@ ###!!, there isn't anything stupider than to display anger like that!!" only provides information about the anger, not its source, nor what can be done about it. "I am feeling very agitated because I think we need more time to think through this final solution" is a better statement, because it describes the feeling as well as the reason for it. It is also necessary to specify *who* is actually having the feeling. Rather than saying, "You make me ill," it is better to say, "I am feeling very hostile toward you right now."

5. *Asking Questions:*   A major problem with ambiguity occurs when you do nothing to help the speaker emerge from an abstraction. You should learn how to ask questions which can reduce the ambiguity. The goal of asking questions should not be to embarrass or ridicule the speaker; instead, the purpose of asking questions should be the productive resolution of the ambiguity. "Ann, I do not understand the current status of the marketing division report. Could you provide some clarification for us by describing how these projections were made?" This kind of response tends to direct the focus of attention away from the speaker's ambiguities and toward the resolution of the problem.

6. *Asking for Discussion:*   When an ambiguity surfaces, the group must deal with it. If the speaker seems unable to provide a less ambiguous response, then someone in the group should ask for discussion of the problem. "Frank, we seem to be having trouble with your report. Can we open it up for discussion by the group?" invites Frank to cooperate with the discussion, and diverts talk away from him as the cause of the problem.

The object of all these techniques is to resolve the ambiguity without threatening the integrity of the speaker or producer of the problem. These procedures all require clear definition of the problem confronting the group (not the speaker), and an honest attempt to get at the meaning of the issue without trying to damage the character of the speaker.

To improve the effectiveness of others in the group requires patience, understanding, and techniques for reducing the ambiguity of their talk. By encouraging them to communicate more effectively, you invite them to respond more favorably to your statements and questions.

Goal-Oriented Methods for Resolving Conflict

Conflict is the opposite of problem-solving (Filley, 1975). Conflict among group members should be perceived as a neutral event which, if managed properly, can result in productive, creative solutions to difficulty. In this section I will discuss how a participant in a small group can manage conflict.

The goal of resolving conflict should be (1) to arrive at a consensus decision about the issue, and (2) to reduce tension between or among the participants in the conflict. Often these two goals seem to produce conflict because of their interdependence, as when someone asks for a vote to be taken, and the majority "wins" despite the ill feelings of the out-voted minority. Consider the following approaches to conflict resolution (Filley, 1975):

1. *Win-Lose Methods:* Often a group seeks an expedient means of resolving a conflict. These expedient methods are:

    Three Approaches to Conflict Resolution

    a. *Authority:* Use of status or office or position in the organization to win an argument.
    b. *Mental or Physical Threat:* Covert or overt pressures are put on group members to conform to the rule of the majority.
    c. *Failure to Respond:* If a group member offers a suggestion, and the other group members refuse to address it, the group member offering the suggestion "loses" and the rest of the group "wins."
    d. *Taking a Vote:* The majority "wins" and the minority "loses." Each one of the above "win-lose" methods is likely to resolve the conflict, but at a high cost to group cohesiveness. Bitter feelings toward the winners and a determination to seek revenge may follow. Win-lose methods are expedient, but are seldom worth the effort.

2. *Lose-Lose Methods:* Often a conflict so divides a group as to warrant *compromise,* in which case each of the opposing sides in the dispute sacrifices part of what they originally wanted. This is known as the "lose-lose" method, because while the conflict may be resolved, neither side achieves its goals. There are several varieties of the lose-lose strategy:

    a. *Overt Compromise:* Occurs when the two opposing sides agree to each "give in" to restore consensus. Compromise usually has a positive connotation although it clearly has negative implications. The labor union that receives half of what it wants under this year's contract is likely to escalate its demands next year. A person who "compromises" integrity is said to have "damaged" his or her character. Compromise results in neither winning nor totally losing; but a vague in-between mix persists, in which both sides feel "compromised," and the problem is still there.
    b. *Favor Exchange:* Occurs when a solution is reached by agreeing to exchange the favor sometime in the future. The "losing side" gains an advantage but at the cost of the integrity of the original argument. The "winning side" never knows when the "losing side" will demand payment of the favor, thus creating an inequitable situation disguised as equity of exchange. This is characterized as a lose-lose situation because the conflict is resolved without the better argument prevailing.

c. *Calling in a Neutral Third Party:* Occurs when a group cannot resolve a conflict and submits the issue or problem to someone else for adjudication. This is also a lose-lose situation because the group renounces its decision-making responsibilities, thus establishing a precedent for such renunciations in the future. Although it may be easier to have someone else solve a problem, this usually means a decision will be made without the group's input.

d. *Resorting to the "Rules":* Occurs when a group reaches a stalemate in the conflict resolution process, and the decision is made because of an organizational "rule" or "policy" rather than because of the will of the group. Here again the group is relinquishing its decision-making responsibility and creating a dangerous precedent. This does not mean that decisions should be made without consulting company policy; it means that if the best decision requires changing or modifying the policy, it should be presented that way. Lose-lose methods do not really resolve conflicts; they postpone them. They choose the easy way out instead of the rational type of solution. Lose-lose methods are the worst possible forms of conflict resolution because nobody wins and usually nothing is actually accomplished.

3. *Win-Win Methods:* Notice that both "win-win" and "lose-lose" methods are based on disagreements about (a) the *causes* of the problem, or (b) the *ways and means* of solving the problem. They compel the group to argue about alternatives rather than focusing on the *goal* or *end* to be accomplished by the group. Win-win methods are based on the ability of the group to *specify what it wants to have happen as a result of the conflict.* In other words, the Win-win methods are goal-oriented ways of resolving disputes. Usually Win-win methods require that a procedure very much like Standard Agenda be implemented, but on a much smaller, less time-consuming scale:

a. Define the conflict.

b. Specify the goal or end to be attained by resolving the conflict.

c. If no clear goal can be established, there is no conflict, and the discussion should move on to the next point on the agenda.

d. If a goal can be specified, then real conflict exists and the group should be concerned about the *quality* of their decision and the *consensus* of the group, rather than simply finding an expedient solution.

e. The group must specify the points of agreement.

f. The group must formulate a resolution based on their points of agreement with the end or goal always kept in sight.

Win-win methods require open, honest, goal-oriented communication which places a premium value on the end to be achieved and agreements which make this end attainable.

Table 9.2 Common Characteristics of Win-Win and Lose-Lose Methods

Win-Win	Lose-Lose
1. We-versus-the-problem orientation.	1. We-versus-they distinction between arguers.
2. Energies directed toward the other party in a total victory atmosphere.	2. Energies directed toward the other party in a total defeat atmosphere.
3. Each party defines the problem from the perspective of mutual needs and goals.	3. Each party defines the problem from the perspective of its own needs and goals.
4. Emphasis of communication is on the *process* of attaining a viable solution.	4. Emphasis of communication is on the motives, causes, or symptoms of the problem and who is at fault.
5. Conflicts are depersonalized, seen as the group's shared difficulty.	5. Conflicts are personalized, seen as the individual's own difficulty.
6. A differentiation of conflict-resolving processes from processes associated with attaining the goal.	6. No differentiation of conflict-resolving processes from processes associated with attaining the goal.
7. The parties are relationship-oriented, emphasizing the long-term effects of their disagreement and how they might be resolved.	7. The parties are conflict-oriented, emphasizing the immediate disagreement and its effects.
8. Communication is goal-oriented and carefully monitored by participants.	8. Communication is spontaneous and not monitored by participants.
9. Talk is open, polite, and adapted to the needs and expectations of the listeners.	9. Talk is closed, discourteous, and not adapted to the needs and expectations of the listeners.
10. Consensus is used to resolve the conflict.	10. Voting or majority-rule is used to resolve or postpone the conflict.

Adapted from Alan C. Filley, INTERPERSONAL CONFLICT RESOLUTION (Glenview, Illinois: Scott, Foresman, and Company, 1975), p. 25. Reprinted by permission.

The key is to adapt to the needs and expectations of the group situation and each other, and the techniques of improving communication establish the bases for how the adaptations can be accomplished. In this section I stressed the concern for *reciprocity* in our attitudes and actions toward others when helping them improve their effectiveness as group members. I also stressed the need to *reduce ambiguity* and *resolve conflicts* by seeking goal-oriented approaches to communication, reflecting concern for individuality and accomplishment of the group's task. In the next section you will examine how group leaders can improve the effectiveness of participants.

Leader's Responsibilities in Educating Group Members

Although I have consistently stressed that group leaders are also group participants, there are some special responsibilities of leadership that differ from those of group participants. This is especially true when the group leader desires to improve the effectiveness of the communication of other group members. Although the techniques of effective communication for participants can be successfully implemented by a group leader, the idea of leading also carries with it more responsibility for planning, directing activities, making assignments, and influencing the communication within the group.

Planning

One of the most persuasive techniques used by successful group leaders is the creation of a workable plan for group interaction. I have discussed this plan as an "agenda," pointing out how essential making and keeping to an agenda is for the small group. Think of an *agenda* as an outline of a problem-solving or decision-making process, sufficiently structured to provide clear direction but flexible enough to adapt to the needs and expectations of group members and situation.

Making and keeping an agenda is only one method of planning available to group leaders. In Chapter 5 I discussed the need for leaders to design and prepare for each group meeting in terms of the *interaction patterns* that may occur between and among group members. By making productive uses of information gathered through observation and personal contact with group members, the leader can anticipate any problems that may arise and think through possible ways of overcoming them. The central question will always be: Who talks to whom about what and with what effect?

Directing Activities

An effective group leader is adept at directing the work of the group. The leader should have access to people within the organization who can provide information about upcoming events and circumstances, and he or she should serve in a liaison capacity between such information sources and the group. The leader should also be in touch with every aspect of the organization which has bearing on the successful/unsuccessful operation of the group. One way to perceive a difference between leaders and participants is in the quality of information about the organization which they have. A leader should have *access to other organizational leaders,* individuals whose decisions and activities may enhance or impede the functioning of his or her group.

The group leader should be the most *consciously goal-oriented* person in the small group, should know exactly the implications of the charge, the resources of the group, and have the ability to guide interaction to a successful conclusion. If a group leader acts in a purposeful way, if she or he will make productive use of goal-orientation to organize the work of the group and to help carry it out, then group members will respond to these leadership skills.

The group leader should also be capable of *inducing members to carry out their assignments on time.* As a leader you will understand the need to assess how long it takes each individual in the group to complete an assignment. You will also need to discover what assignments can best be completed by particular group members. The ability of the leader to differentiate among the qualities and limitations of each member is an essential part of being able to direct successfully their capacity for carrying out assignments. The central question must be: Who should complete this assignment successfully with a minimum amount of effort and a maximum gain to the group in the achievement of its task?

Making
Assignments

One of the most difficult tasks for new group leaders to accomplish is to make assignments without sounding domineering or guilty. Very often groups suffer because leaders either don't know how to make assignments or they refuse to do so. The result is usually inequity. The people who want to do the work or feel an obligation will assume responsibility for it; and those people who are unwilling or feel no need to contribute will go along with what the workers report. This is a fatal prescription for a small group and can be attributed in many cases to the group leader's unwillingness or ineffectuality in making assignments.

Making assignments should represent a balance between *ability of the group member* to complete the task successfully and *equity* among the group. It makes little sense to assign a task to someone who cannot complete it, although group members may volunteer for difficult assignments to gain favor. A leader must always be a keen evaluator of the strengths and weaknesses of each group member. This knowledge must be balanced with an appreciation of equity in the group. If one or two people consistently receive the difficult assignments because they are capable, they are likely to develop feelings of inequity as strong as the other group members who may read into the assignment-making a less positive assessment of their own worth to the group. If situations occur in which expedience outweighs justice, then it becomes the responsibility of the leader to explain the situation to the group. Communicating the necessity for temporary imbalance can induce members to accept it.

The successful leader should keep a record of assignments made to group members. This record may also include an assessment of their strengths and weaknesses in carrying out the task, an inventory that may be helpful during appraisal time. A leader should consult this record *before* making new assignments and should always ask the question: from the perspective of the group, who should complete this assignment and why?

Influencing
Communication
Within the Group

Leading by example is also leading by motivation. By force of example the leader who reveals communicative competencies induces other group members to improve their communication skills Conversely, the leader who does not monitor communication, does not prepare adequately for meetings, predisposes the group members to mediocrity.

Norman Maier's four styles of communicating are of special importance to group leaders (cited in O'Connell, 1979). *Blaming, telling,* and *selling* are communicative strategies that may work under the right conditions, but they almost always are inferior to *problem-solving*. The problem-solving style of communication should be the goal of most group leaders. The group leader who recognizes the value of approaching difficulties as problems affecting the whole group contributes to the members' abilities to do the same.

A leader establishes the *tone* of interaction. Whether discussions will be rigid or flexible, slow or dynamic, inclusive or exclusive, participative or autocratic, the group leader sets the pace and determines how talk will be exchanged among group members. This is indeed a heavy responsibility. Group leaders are just as susceptible to distraction and noise as are group members; it is difficult to be the "best and brightest" every time the group meets. One skill important to group leaders is *self-analysis:* the ability to be sensitive to one's own strengths and weaknesses and then respond to them appropriately. If you are having a difficult day, you should know when to let the stronger group members take charge, and be able to explain how you feel. If a group has a good leader they will probably make allowance for an "off" day now and then. It should be recalled, however, that a group without a fully functioning leader is like a body without a head. If there are serious problems affecting your operation as a group leader, then seek a permanent substitute. Do not allow the group's efforts to suffer because of your own obstinacy or ineffectuality.

Problems Associated with Advice-Giving

There are two basic alternatives for people receiving counsel in small groups. They can agree or disagree with the advice. If they agree with, you probably will motivate them to do what you want them to do. If they disagree with the advice, it is unlikely that they will act as you want them to.

However, because communication is complex, and semantic interpretation can either aid or impair the meaning of the message, there are other possibilities for responses to advice-giving. For example, the listener can agree with what she or he *thinks* you said, in which case that person may perform in ways not intended by the advisor although believing that he or she is acting as directed. Or, the other person may disagree with what he/she *thinks* you said, and thus may actually agree with you. But because of the distortion neither one of you will ever know the intention of the other; or there will be confusion as to the meaning of the advice and the person receiving it won't do anything at all.

Advice-giving is one of the most difficult communication competencies. Most people do not like to be "told what to do," nor do they respond favorably to others "butting into their business." Advice-giving in small groups is difficult because in addition to these human factors the advice-giver (whether leader or participant) must calculate the effect of the advice-giving on the group's operation.

Typical Situations for Giving Advice There are some standard situations in which counsel or direction are given in small groups:

1. During conflicts
2. During crises
3. During periods of stalemated discussion

4. During moments of perceived inequity
5. During times when no clear direction is being pursued
6. During meeting breaks, when one participant attempts to interpret the meaning of an action in the group
7. During private conferences between group leader and participants, when past difficulties are being ironed out or new relationships established.

As you can see, none of the situations in which advice is typically given could be characterized as "routine" or "comfortable." For most people the rule seems to be: *do not give advice to others unless absolutely necessary.*

Unfortunately, during conflicts, crises, moments of perceived inequity, and similar situations, the necessity for giving advice is often so compelling that it overwhelms your sensitivities to the human needs and expectations of others. You may "explode" or become angry, you may "yell, tell, and sell" the listener on the "rightness" of the advice; or you may hold the floor so long other group members become impervious to what you are saying. Obviously, all of these ways of giving advice are inappropriate to most small group situations. You gain little by violent displays of emotion, whereas the cost to you and to the solidarity of the group is usually very high. Consider Gene's experience:

Gene D., 32   We got along just fine in the group until Wilma started giving everyone advice. She meant well, but as we all know, the road to hell is paved with good intentions. The problem was her attitude. She gave advice like she had divine guidance, you know, a "know-it-all"? Finally, Jon got angry, I guess because he got tired of listening to Wilma's 'Hints on Successful Living.' He told her where to go. She looked pained, but she struck back with a venom I never knew she had. So that was the demise of our group. In the space of about sixty seconds we went from cohesiveness to ruin. We never regained it. Wilma and Jon pretended to like each other after that, but we all knew better. I learned something very important from the whole thing: the only person you can advise is yourself.

I disagree with Gene's last statement. You can learn *how* to give advice, but you must give it sparingly. Wilma displayed two errors which are common to givers of advice: (1) she was perceived as having a superior attitude toward the advisees, and (2) she consistently gave advice, even when the situation did not call for it. Because she was not sensitive to the needs and expectations of other group members, she was unable to adapt her advice to their needs, and she failed. Furthermore, the advice she was giving may have been "right," or even "good"; but because she failed to adapt to the communication needs of the group, her counsels were unproductive.

How can you know when to give advice?

Advice as Intervention   Think of advice as an interpersonal *intervention*. For example, an analogous situation might be giving advice to a close friend about his or her spouse. Because close relationships foster both risk and trust, you would be well advised to consider the potential effects of your advice on the friendship as well as on your friend's marriage. You should consider how productive your statements may actually be, taking account of your own motives for making the statements. Finally, and perhaps most importantly, you should then prepare to communicate the information. When will you bring up the subject? How will you approach it? What might your friend's responses be? How will you deal with those responses?

Now expand your conception of the intervention to the level of the small group. An analogous situation might be a social group or club to which you belong. Instead of a single listener and respondent, you have five to seven persons in your audience. Again, ask yourself how productive your statement might be. What are your motives? In view of these constraints how can you prepare to communicate the advice? What might be the response of the individual group members? What might be the total group's response?

Prepare for Responses   The best way to enter a group intervention with the goal of giving advice is to
to Your Advice   prepare for the responses to your counsel or statement. Most people who give advice encounter trouble because they believe what they have to say is so important, so valuable, so right that the listener should only respond with admiring acceptance. This is a source-oriented perspective on the communication situation; as such it is usually destined to fail. Always consider the audience or listener. Adopt a receiver-oriented perspective: what is most important is not your advice, but *your listener's response* to the advice. The purpose of your communication is to elicit desirable responses from listeners, not to impress them with your command of the situation.

Attempting to improve the group performance of others is difficult. Most people believe they know how to communicate effectively, and that they do in fact communicate effectively. Therefore they are not in need of advice from others, especially from others with whom they share a workplace and task. However, in virtually any small group setting, performance of group members and leader can be improved to the betterment of the group and its task. So you confront a paradox: what most needs to be accomplished may have the least likelihood of success.

Summary

In this chapter I have stressed the fact that groups construct their own symbolic realities through choices made about what they say and do. First, you examined the role of education in the small group, establishing the principle that it is the responsibility of all group members to share in the development of the group's reality. Choices associated with the early statements influence the attitudes and behavior of group members and can shape positive and negative outcomes. How the group operates is a result of the information given to group members by each group.

Second, you investigated the participant's responsibilities in educating each other. I advanced the proposition that people should make a conscious effort to treat others as individuals. Using stereotypes and other broad categories tends to dehumanize others. This practice induces us to omit important details that could lead to a more individualized concept of others. A second way to improve the performance of those we are dealing with is to implement the values of effective communication, to encourage adaptive approaches to choices made about words and actions. A third procedure for improving group performance is to become more aware of the responses you wish to elicit from others, making a conscious effort to know what you are responding to when you respond to the other person's conduct. I listed four types of behaving which characteristically lead to either positive or negative evaluations: intuiting, thinking, feeling, and sensing. I then explored goal-oriented methods of reducing ambiguity (supportive feedback, using E-Prime language, paraphrasing, describing feelings, asking questions, and asking for discussion, and listed approaches for resolving conflicts (win-lose, lose-lose, win-win). I concluded this section by explaining how to implement "Win-Win" methods of conflict resolution.

Third, I explained the leader's responsibilities of educating group members, discussing the need for effective leaders to plan, direct activities, make equitable assignments, and influence communication within the group. I examined the need for leaders to undertake a self-analysis of their own strengths and weaknesses and then to use this information to guide their choices about communicating. I concluded this section by explaining how the leader establishes the tone of interaction and how important it is for a leader to consciously attempt to induce quality performances in group members.

Finally I examined the problems associated with advice-giving in small groups. I explored situations related to the urgency to give advice (during conflicts, crises, periods of stalemated discussions, moments of perceived inequity, times when no clear distinction is being pursued, meeting breaks, and during private conferences). The nature of these situations complicates and aggravates the problems of advice-giving. You need to be able to balance the exigence to provide advice with an understanding of how the advice may affect the group members and the group's task. I recommended that you approach advice-giving cautiously, as if you were giving advice to your best friend about his or her spouse. I recommended the need to consider (1) the potential effects of the advice on the listener/group; (2) how productive the advice actually may be; (3) your motives for giving the advice; and (4) the best alternative for communicating the advice in the given case. I concluded this section by pointing out the paradox of advice-giving: when it is most needed it has the least likelihood of success.

References

Filley, A. C. *Interpersonal Conflict Resolution.* Glenview, Ill.: Scott, Foresman, 1975.
Knapp, M. L. *Social Intercourse: From Greeting to Goodbye.* Boston: Allyn and Bacon, Inc., 1978.
Norton, R. *Communication Style.* Beverly Hills, CA: Sage, 1983.
O'Connell, S. *The Manager as Communicator.* New York: Harper & Row, 1979.

This chapter addressed the special problem of improving other's group communication skills. In the following exercises, you are asked to make productive use of the information presented in the chapter to resolve these problems. You may want to assign a group member the task of role-playing Allan, Chester, and Reeba to enhance the simulation. Although it will be fairly easy to provide advice to these actors/actresses, try to make the role-playing as real as you can.

1. *Crisis Intervention:* Assemble your group. Assume you have the same problem Carol R. had (see p. 000 of this chapter) with a difficult group member. What alternatives suggest themselves to you as a result of reading this chapter? How would you deal with the problem? What could be done to lessen the negative impact of Allan's behavior on the group?

2. *Participant's responsibility for educating another group member:* Here is the situation. Chester B. is a recent college graduate who has joined your group. He seems to be anxious to please the leader, but less anxious to please the rest of the group. You have the impression that he is a sycophant. Construct a role-playing situation in which the group is threatened by his behavior, and other group members must take responsibility for educating him. Perform the role-plays in class with critique by class members.

3. *Giving advice:* Reeba S. is a valued member of a task group charged with writing a new company policy about annual leave. She is from the personnel division and has access to all the company information about incidences of leave by company employees. The problem is that she regularly misses group meetings, and when she does attend she appears to be poorly prepared. Construct a role-playing situation for the class in which advisories are given to Reeba about improving her group performance. Use the material in the chapter on evaluations of behavior, and provide at least three different ways of dealing with this problem.

Observing and Evaluating Small Groups 10

Introduction

In organizations the observation of individual and group behavior is an integral part of performance appraisals. Our work is observed and evaluated by superiors who have the responsibility of rewarding productivity and competencies, while also devising ways to modify or improve deficiencies. These appraisals are generally used to determine raises and promotions within an organization, as well as to weed out non-productive workers.

Observing and evaluating human behavior is a difficult task. As you have learned, there are many cultural, social, psychological, and personal influences on an individual's behavior, including those people charged with the responsibility for "objectively" observing and evaluating the behavior of others. The likelihood of an observer being able accurately to assess someone else's *motives* for behavior depends on information not generally available to the formal researcher or organizational manager. For this reason, most companies rely on simpler observational techniques based on what can be seen and counted rather than inferred.

The need to base evaluations of behavior on *performance* is often referred to as "management by results." Demonstrated productivity is a basic determinant. Consequently, groups and individuals who reach their goals, who help the organization attain its objectives, who encourage productive, efficient, and equitable behaviors in themselves and others, usually receive favorable appraisals of their work. Managers and others charged with the responsibility for conducting appraisals of performance usually begin with results obtained by a group and its individual members, then review the processes influencing the results (Asherman and Vance, 1981; Yager, 1981). But how is this accomplished?

The question immediately becomes: what are the observations and evaluations based on? When you are looking at a small group, what should be the bases and norms of the critique? Aside from finding out whether or not the group reached its goal, how should appraisals of the group processes and interactions proceed?

Managers appraising the work of small groups confront some of the same problems faced by small group researchers. Since the early 1950s managers have relied on advances made by academic researchers to form their observations and evaluations of small groups. One result of this collaboration has been steadily increasing reliance on statistical and computer-assisted technologies now regarded as essential to accurate measurements of the human complexities involved in group assignments (Dertien, 1981). Another result is the need of most organizations to employ highly specialized research personnel to design and conduct appraisals of the organization's structure and the effectiveness of its personnel (Goldhaber, 1985). Many large organizations rely on professional consultants to help them devise and implement procedures for improving their operation through observations and evaluations of people at work, especially people who work in small groups.

Even with the introduction of these advanced methods for conducting appraisals of group performances, however, the ability to observe and evaluate human behavior in organizations has *not* significantly improved. The more complex the appraisal design, the more chance of human error. The more an organization relies on quantifiable data to conduct appraisals of performance, the less likely it becomes that quality and productivity will increase (Ouchi, 1981). As more individual employees come to recognize the ease with which quantifiable data can be manipulated, the less they may be motivated to improve the processes which can assure more effective and *humane* outcomes (Goodall, Wilson, and Waagen, 1986). Until we can train the people responsible for conducting observations and evaluations of groups to become better critics of given-case behavior, more knowledgeable and process-oriented rather than concerned only about the quantifiable result, our substantial advances in technology will be incapable of improving our organizations. The instruments of appraisal are only as reliable as their human user (Bales and Cohen, 1979).

This chapter addresses the issues of observing and evaluating small groups. Its purpose is to provide an introduction to criticism of human behavior, and to reveal skills associated with applying an understanding of criticism to observations and evaluations of small groups. First, I will discuss the nature of criticism as a process of establishing reasonable standards used to evaluate human performance. Second, I will review some of the instruments of criticism available to *observers* of small groups. Third, I will review some of the tools of criticism available to *members and leaders* of small groups. Fourth, I will discuss the problems associated with observing and evaluating small groups, and will recommend methods to overcome them. Following the chapter summary and references, I will provide two exercises designed to help you apply the material covered in this chapter.

The Nature of Criticism

When you evaluate anything you are engaged in acts of criticism. The result of criticism is judgment; you determine the good or evil, correct or incorrect, appropriate or inappropriate characteristics of the object of criticism (Ehninger, 1974).

Criticism is always *comparative*. When you engage in criticism, you are comparing the object of criticism to some set of standards used to arrive at the judgment (Kwant, 1967). Therefore, the person making the evaluation should always strive to stipulate the norms used in making the evaluation. Unless these standards are stated and communicated, the critique is less likely to be understood.

> **Louise E., 29**   Our group receives quarterly reports of our progress, otherwise known as a performance review of our work. For the longest time we were given "average" ratings by our supervisor, although none of us knew what that meant. I mean, the term *average* means you are a little better than "poor," and a little less good than "above average," right? So finally, I asked her what the evaluations were based on. "Oh," she said, as if she had never thought about it before, "I guess they mean. . . ." and her voice trailed off. So we talked about it. What came out was that she was comparing our work to what she had done when she worked in one of these groups years ago. All that time she had been doing the evaluations she knew what she was comparing us to, but she never told us. Also, I personally didn't think it was fair to rely on her memory of her past experiences years ago. So we agreed to establish more concrete standards for the evaluations. Lately, we have done much better.

Criticism should strive to be *productive*. Evaluating the process of human interaction is itself a process. The judgment you arrive at on any given day should be tentative. You should use this judgment to improve performance. Yet you should resist the temptation to pass permanent judgment on human beings, because they are likely to change. Managers and supervisors responsible for evaluating the work of small groups should consider these guidelines:

Basic Rules for Evaluating Organizational Performance

1. *Provide standards for the evaluative process.*   Explain to the group what is being evaluated. For example, does *productivity* equate with reaching the desired goal or objective? Does *leadership* mean the ability to call meetings to order, direct talk, summarize conclusions, make group assignments, etc.? Does *participation* mean asking and answering questions, fulfilling assignments, arriving on time prepared for the meeting, etc.?
2. *Make evaluations of both positive and negative aspects of the group.* Some managers dwell on the negative aspects of critique, on what was done wrong or incompletely, rather than balancing their criticism to include praise of good work. Any group needs to know what it has done right, what it has done incorrectly, and what it should work to improve in the future. It would be difficult to know what *wrong* signified without knowing what *right* meant to the evaluator.
3. *Explain how the group can improve performance.*   The goal of criticism should be to improve the group process. What goals should the group strive to attain during the next evaluation period? How can the group overcome deficiencies in their operation? What suggestions can be made to help the group accomplish its objective? The evaluator should be as specific as possible when making recommendations for improving the group.

Criticism, like *conflict,* is a neutral term. If it is managed properly, the outcomes of effective criticism can be beneficial to the group. However, if it is managed poorly, the group may experience ill-will between and among members and toward the person doing the evaluating. Now that you have established a basic understanding of the nature of criticism, you will need to develop an appreciation for some of the alternative standards used to evaluate small groups.

Standards Used to Evaluate Groups
Organizations differ in their approach to evaluating the work of small groups. Consequently, the norms used in critiques of the groups within organizations also differ. For example, the purpose of a research and development small group in United Technologies differs from the purpose of a small group in Brown Engineering trying to solve a design problem in a space vehicle. Because the *purposes* of the two groups are not the same, there probably are differences in what is considered appropriate and inappropriate behavior within each group. Thus, the first consideration when establishing standards for criticism should be:

1. **What is the purpose of this small group?**

In practice, evaluations of small group activity are usually based on a simplistic division (not always accurate) between leadership and participation within the group. Characteristics of appropriate behavior for leading and participating are established, and criticism of each member's actions are made with reference to these standards. Let's begin with the behaviors ordinarily associated with participating in the small group:

2. **What is the level of participation by each group member?**
   a. Does he or she attend group meetings regularly?
   b. Attend group meetings prepared for discussion?
   c. Exhibit skill in asking relevant questions?
   d. Exhibit skill in providing useful information to the group?
   e. Accept assignments from the leader?
   f. Listen actively to other group members?
   g. Help the group attain its objectives?
   h. Promote good interpersonal relations in the group?

Under each of these headings several specific behaviors can be isolated to further enhance the value and ultimate effectiveness of the criticism. Now let's look at the habitual skills of leading:

3. **How effective is the group leader?**
   a. Does she or he demonstrate competence in preparing for group meetings?
   b. Show skill in formulating agendas?
   c. Strive to keep the group on track?
   d. Call the meeting to order?
   e. Announce the agenda and ask for any changes?
   f. Direct the discussions of group members effectively?

g. Resolve disputes among group members satisfactorily?

h. Provide useful information to the group?

i. Ask relevant questions to generate interaction?

j. Summarize when necessary?

k. Test for consensus when appropriate?

l. Make individual assignments equitably?

m. Exert appropriate influence over the group?

n. Have the respect and confidence of group members?

o. Develop good interpersonal relations with the group?

p. Help the group accomplish its objectives?

Again, under each one of these general headings specific behaviors can be listed to aid in the evaluation. Also, based on the nature of the group and its purpose, some additional headings may be listed, such as level of technical expertise or ability to manage the resources of the group.

After these general categories of behavior are developed, the evaluator should focus on the aspects of the group process which meet the requirements specified by the organization. To accomplish this purpose, the evaluation should include:

4. **Characteristics associated with adequate or satisfactory performance by the group.**
   To receive an "average" evaluation, the group must:
   a. Show adequate understanding of the charge and goals of the group.
   b. Strive to complete all routine assignments on time.
   c. Seek out information from authorities when needed.
   d. Follow a prescribed agenda.
   e. Demonstrate ability to interact effectively.
   f. Promote good internal relations among group members.
   g. Keep an accurate record of all group meetings.
   h. Be responsive to the directives given by the leader or supervisor.
   i. Show progress in meeting objectives.

5. **A description of exactly how well the group is meeting these objectives.**
   Using the above categories, the supervisor should write out observations of specific behaviors which demonstrated competence in the proscribed areas. When possible, the evaluator should also list the place, time, and circumstances of the observation.

Finally, the evaluator should list and explain areas of group performance requiring improvement in order to receive higher evaluations next time. To accomplish this goal the evaluator should:

6. **Describe areas needing improvement during the next reporting period.**
   Actions and conduct should be listed under the headings of *leader, participant, task goals, interpersonal goals,* etc. The evaluator should then provide specific behavioral goals which she or he believes can *reasonably* be accomplished by the group members.

These are the general standards used to evaluate small group behavior and performance. The effective manager or supervisor/evaluator will use these categories to develop a written critique form, the details of which will be presented later in this chapter. A final word: *The most effective managers arrange a conference with the group to explain the evaluation.*

Standards Used to Evaluate Communication of Group Members

Talk is the substance of group communication. Although it is possible to generalize about the skills of participating in and leading small groups, you must be careful to observe closely the talk of group members. Verbal expressions either contribute to or detract from the ability of the group members to evaluate the group and to help the group accomplish its objectives.

The most important characteristic of talk in groups is its *appropriateness*. "Appropriate communication" means saying the right thing at the right time in the right place in order to elicit the desired response (Phillips, Pedersen, and Wood, 1979). For speech to be appropriate it must be *adapted* to the needs and expectations of the situation and group. These characteristics of effective communication are very difficult for observers to recognize unless they have a historical knowledge of the individual group members. For this reason, I recommend that group members facilitate the evaluation process by keeping accurate record of their interactions that can be reviewed by the supervisor or manager. I also recommend that groups be given the opportunity to evaluate their own behavior and performance and that this evaluation be made an integral part of the overall group critique.

Group researchers have long recognized talk as the essential property of group performance (McBurney and Hance, 1936). In the development of understanding the categories of effective communication, progress has been made in a relatively short period of time. Consider the following group evaluation form devised by Robert Freed Bales in 1950 (Figure 10.1).

This form was developed to facilitate the systematic observation of human groups by *trained* evaluators (Bales, 1950; 1970). Evaluators were given specific behavioral clues to look for while the group was interacting, and either the group members displayed these behaviors or they did not. Bales' Interaction Process Analysis (IPA) form was the prevailing group evaluation mechanism for a generation of researchers and organizational theorists, and his early work inspired questions about improving the art and science of group evaluation. By 1979, Bales' original form evolved into a highly complex computer-assisted program known as SYMLOG (Bales and Cohen, 1979). Even under their newest and most stringent rules for systematic observation and evaluation of talk in groups, these authors admit that different trained observers arrive at varying conclusions about the categories and especially the *meanings* of exchanges among group members.

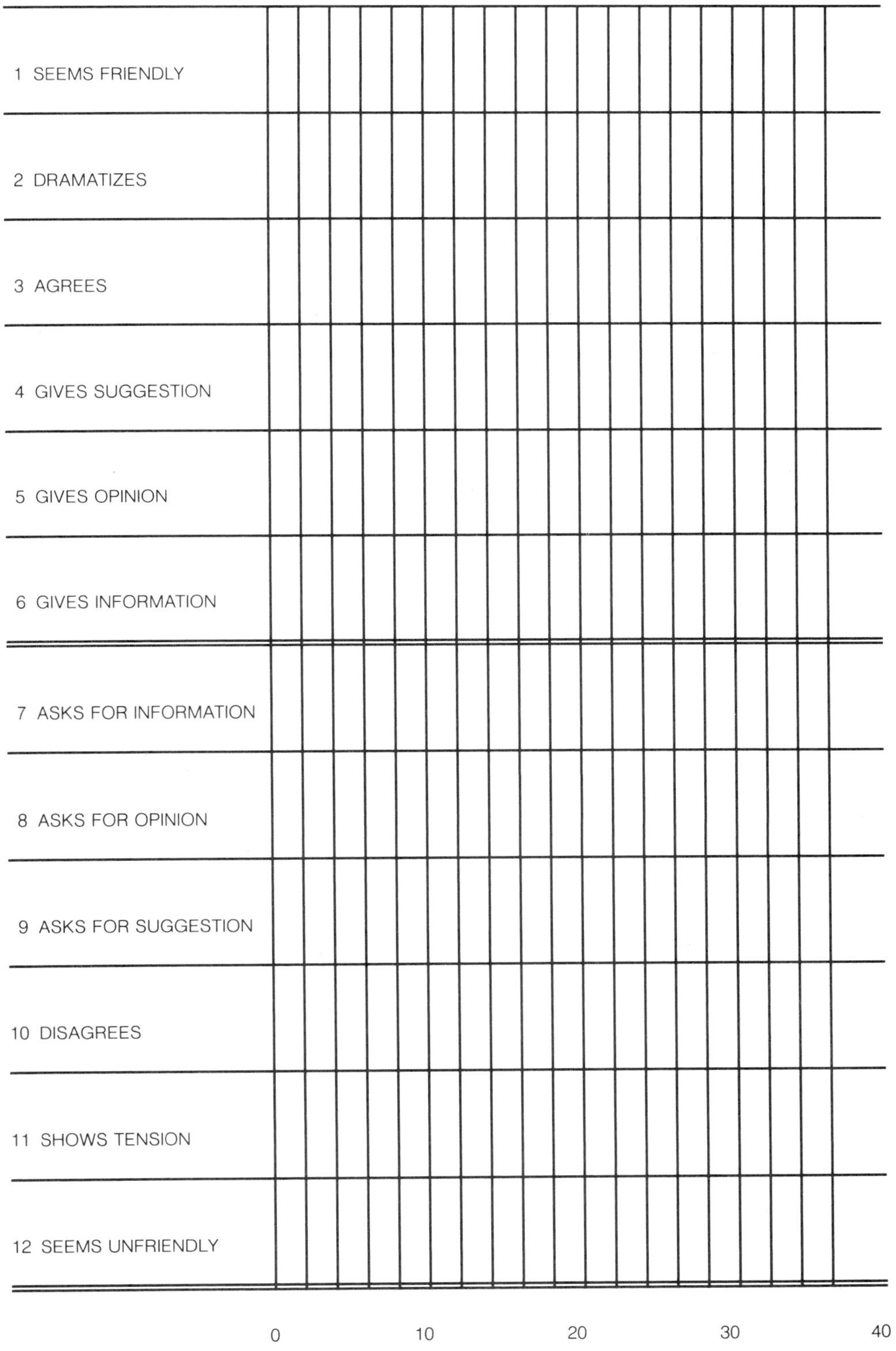

Figure 10.1. Interaction Process Analysis

1 SEEMS FRIENDLY

2 DRAMATIZES

3 AGREES

4 GIVES SUGGESTION

5 GIVES OPINION

6 GIVES INFORMATION

7 ASKS FOR INFORMATION

8 ASKS FOR OPINION

9 ASKS FOR SUGGESTION

10 DISAGREES

11 SHOWS TENSION

12 SEEMS UNFRIENDLY

0   10   20   30   40

265

In an attempt to categorize ways in which talk creates meaning in groups, one researcher listed 134 different classifications of talk, which could then be used to establish sixteen (16) categories of interactive experience, each capable of demonstrating four (4) levels of intensity (see LaForge, 1963). LaForge (and other users of this system) instructed the observers simply to check each item that accurately represented the behavior of the person being rated in the group. The researcher or evaluator would then collect all the interpretations and categorize them, using the sixteen classifications of talk, and the four levels of intensity. As a research tool, the LaForge checklist proved useful in helping to identify the kinds of talk exchanged by group members. As a pragmatic inventory for organizational evaluators, this method is much less useful because it describes what occurs only in *single* group sessions. There is no attempt to look at the *process* of interaction, and no way of avoiding subjective evaluations of individuals or groups (see Figure 10.2).

Such broad and generalized categorization schemas were enhanced by more specific checklists and rating forms during the late 1960s and throughout the 1970s. Researchers believed that more productive and less ambiguous results could be obtained by isolating one group variable (e.g., leadership, listening, feedback) and developing an evaluation form to measure it. Consequently, researchers devised a multitude of different approaches to criticism of groups based on which traits, skills, or characteristics they wanted to study (see Cragan and Wright, 1980, for work done during this period by speech communication researchers).

The difficulty with "variable analytic" approaches to group evaluations is simple: No one characteristic provides sufficient information to generalize about the overall behaviors or performance of any group. The *intent* of the research was to identify systematically the categories and behaviors of communication, *not* to provide checklists that could be used by business and industry. Some critics of the variable analytic method have pointed out the limitations of this form of generating understanding about humans in groups (see Bormann, 1980; Delia, 1976). Even if applications of this method of research to groups in organizations could be made, the picture of group communication that emerged would suffer from inability to reveal the interrelatedness of communication acts. People do not just "listen" or "consider the credibility of the speaker" or "lead" small groups; they do all of these things, sometimes simultaneously. Isolating one or two key factors does not produce an accurate assessment of what happens in the group.

While some researchers were developing variable analytic checklists and research methods, others were interested in establishing ways of characterizing *specific* small groups. One of the most widely used formats was developed by Hemphill (1956). His purpose was to formulate a questionnaire that could be used by observers as well as by group members to generate information about a given group in a given context. The questionnaire consists of 150 statements that may or may not apply to the specific group. Each observer or group member is

1. Able to give orders
2. Appreciative
3. Apologetic
4. Able to take care of self
5. Accepts advice readily
6. Able to doubt others
7. Affectionate and understanding
8. Acts important
9. Able to criticize self
10. Admires and imitates others
11. Agrees with everyone
12. Always ashamed of self
13. Very anxious to be approved of
14. Always giving advice
15. Bitter
16. Bighearted and unselfish
17. Boastful
18. Businesslike
19. Bossy
20. Can be frank and honest
21. Clinging vine
22. Can be strict if necessary
23. Considerate
24. Cold and unfeeling
25. Can complain if necessary
26. Cooperative
27. Complaining
28. Can be indifferent to others
29. Critical of others
30. Can be obedient
31. Cruel and unkind
32. Dependent
33. Dictatorial
34. Distrusts everybody
35. Dominating
36. Easily embarrassed
37. Eager to get along with others
38. Easily fooled
39. Egotistical and conceited
40. Easily led
41. Encourages others
42. Enjoys taking care of others
43. Expects everyone to admire him
44. Faithful follower
45. Frequently disappointed
46. Firm but just
47. Fond of everyone
48. Forceful
49. Friendly
50. Forgives anything
51. Frequently angry
52. Friendly all the time
53. Generous to a fault
54. Gives freely of self
55. Good leader
56. Grateful
57. Hard-boiled when necessary
58. Helpful
59. Hardhearted
60. Hard to convince
61. Hot-tempered
62. Hard to impress
63. Impatient with others' mistakes
64. Independent
65. Irritable
66. Jealous
67. Kind and reassuring
68. Likes responsibility
69. Lacks self-confidence
70. Likes to compete with others
71. Lets others make decisions
72. Likes everybody
73. Likes to be taken care of
74. Loves everyone
75. Makes a good impression
76. Manages others
77. Meek
78. Modest
79. Hardly ever talks back
80. Often admired
81. Obeys too willingly
82. Often gloomy
83. Outspoken
84. Overprotective of others
85. Often unfriendly
86. Oversympathetic
87. Often helped by others
88. Passive and unaggressive
89. Proud and self-satisfied
90. Always pleasant and agreeable
91. Resentful
92. Respected by others
93. Rebels against everything
94. Resents being bossed
95. Self-reliant and assertive
96. Sarcastic
97. Self-punishing
98. Self-confident
99. Self-seeking
100. Shrewd and calculating
101. Self-respecting
102. Shy
103. Sincere and devoted to friends
104. Selfish
105. Skeptical
106. Sociable and neighborly
107. Slow to forgive a wrong
108. Somewhat snobbish
109. Spineless
110. Stern but fair

Figure 10.2. LaForge Interpersonal Checklist

Figure 10.2.—*Continued*

111. Spoils people with kindness
112. Straightforward and direct
113. Stubborn
114. Suspicious
115. Too easily influenced by friends
116. Thinks only of self
117. Tender and softhearted
118. Timid
119. Too lenient with others
120. Touchy and easily hurt
121. Too willing to give to others
122. Tries to be too successful
123. Trusting and eager to please
124. Tries to comfort everyone
125. Usually gives in
126. Very respectful to authority
127. Wants everyone's love
128. Well thought of
129. Wants to be led
130. Will confide in anyone
131. Warm
132. Wants everyone to like him
133. Will believe anyone
134. Well behaved

A 1. Able to give orders
   2. Forceful
      Good leader
      Likes responsibility
   3. Bossy
      Dominating
      Manages others
   4. Dictatorial

B 1. Self-respecting
   2. Independent
      Self-confident
      Self-reliant and assertive
   3. Boastful
      Proud and self-satisfied
      Somewhat snobbish
   4. Egotistical and conceited

C 1. Able to take care of self
   2. Can be indifferent to others
      Businesslike
      Likes to compete with others
   3. Thinks only of himself
      Shrewd and calculating
      Selfish
   4. Cold and unfeeling

D 1. Can be strict if necessary
   2. Firm but just
      Hard-boiled when necessary
      Stern but fair
   3. Impatient with others' mistakes
      Self-seeking
      Sarcastic
   4. Cruel and unkind

E 1. Can be frank and honest
   2. Critical of others
      Irritable
      Straightforward and direct
   3. Outspoken
      Often unfriendly
      Frequently angry
   4. Hardhearted

F 1. Can complain if necessary
   2. Often gloomy
      Resents being bossed
      Skeptical
   3. Bitter
      Complaining
      Resentful
   4. Rebels against everything

G 1. Able to doubt others
   2. Frequently disappointed
      Hard to impress
      Touchy and easily hurt
   3. Jealous
      Slow to forgive a wrong
      Stubborn
   4. Distrusts everybody

H 1. Able to criticize self
   2. Apologetic
      Easily embarrassed
      Lacks self-confidence
   3. Self-punishing
      Shy
      Timid
   4. Always ashamed of self

I 1. Can be obedient
   2. Usually gives in
      Easily led
      Modest
   3. Passive and unaggressive
      Meek
      Obeys too willingly
   4. Spineless

J 1. Grateful
2. Admires and imitates others
Often helped by others
Very respectful of authority
3. Dependent
Wants to be led
Hardly ever talks back
4. Clinging vine

K 1. Appreciative
2. Very anxious to be approved of
Accepts advice readily
Trusting and eager to please
3. Lets others make decisions
Easily fooled
Likes to be taken care of
4. Will believe anyone

L 1. Cooperative
2. Eager to get along with other people
Always pleasant and agreeable
Wants everyone to like him
3. Too easily influenced by friends
Will confide in anyone
Want's everyone's love
4. Agrees with everyone

M 1. Friendly
2. Affectionate and understanding
Sociable and neighborly
Warm
3. Fond of everyone
Likes everybody
Friendly all the time
4. Loves everyone

N 1. Considerate
2. Encouraging others
Kind and reassuring
Tender and soft-hearted
3. Forgives anything
Oversympathetic
Too lenient with others
4. Tries to comfort everyone

O 1. Helpful
2. Bighearted and unselfish
Enjoys taking care of others
Gives freely of self
3. Generous to a fault
Overprotective of others
Too willing to give to others
4. Spoils people with kindness

P 1. Well thought of
2. Makes a good impression
Often admired
Respected by others
3. Always giving advice
Acts important
Tries to be too successful
4. Expects everybody to admire him

Figure 10.2.—*Continued*

asked to read the statements, and rate them: A = statement is definitely true; B = statement is mostly true; C = statement is equally true and false; D = statement is mostly false; E = statement is definitely false. These answers could then be tabulated and the results interpreted (see Figure 10.3).

Hemphill's format was useful in finding out how group members and observers *evaluated* small groups. Unfortunately, the instrument suffers from an inability to establish *how* these evaluations are arrived at by the observers or group members. For example, what specific communicative behaviors lead to the conclusion that "the objective of the group is specific?" What may be clear to an observer may be equally unclear to the group members. To be used effectively to critique group performance and behavior, the rating instrument must be able to *identify specific communicative behaviors* which can then be used to make an evaluation. To ensure appropriate evaluations, care must be taken to furnish data to support the evaluation.

Figure 10.3. Hemphill
Group Dimensions
Description Questionnaire

1. The group has well understood but unwritten rules concerning member conduct.
2. Members fear to express their real opinions.
3. The only way a member may leave the group is to be expelled.
4. No explanation need be given by a member wishing to be absent from the group.
5. An individual's membership can be dropped should he fail to live up to the standards of the group.
6. Members of the group work under close supervision.
7. Only certain kinds of ideas may be expressed freely within the group.
8. A member may leave the group by resigning at any time he wishes.
9. A request made by a member to leave the group can be refused.
10. A member has to think twice before speaking in the group's meetings.
11. Members are occasionally forced to resign.
12. The members of the group are subject to strict discipline.
13. The group is rapidly increasing in size.
14. Members are constantly leaving the group.
15. There is a large turnover of members within the group.
16. Members are constantly dropping out of the group, but new members replace them.
17. During the entire time of the group's existence no member has left.
18. Each member's personal life is known to other members of the group.
19. Members of the group lend each other money.
20. A member has the chance to get to know all other members of the group.
21. Members are not in close enough contact to develop likes or dislikes for one another.
22. Members of the group do small favors for one another.
23. All members know each other very well.
24. Each member of the group knows all other members by their first names.
25. Members are in daily contact either outside or within the group.
26. Members of the group are personal friends.
27. Certain members discuss personal affairs among themselves.
28. Members of the group know the family backgrounds of other members of the group.
29. Members address each other by their first names.
30. The group is made up of individuals who do not know each other well.
31. The opinions of all members are considered equal.
32. The group's officers hold a higher status in the group than other members.
33. The older members of the group are granted special privileges.
34. The group is controlled by the actions of a few members.
35. Every member of the group enjoys the same group privileges.
36. Experienced members are in charge of the group.
37. Certain problems are discussed only among the group's officers.
38. Certain members have more influence on the group than others.
39. Each member of the group has as much power as any other member.
40. An individual's standing in the group is determined only by how much he gets done.
41. Certain members of the group hold definite office in the group.
42. The original members of the group are given special privileges.
43. Personal dissatisfaction with the group is too small to be brought up.
44. Members continually grumble about the work they do for the group.
45. The group does its work with no great vim, vigor, or pleasure.
46. A feeling of failure prevails in the group.
47. There are frequent intervals of laughter during group meetings.
48. The group works independently of other groups.
49. The group has support from outside.
50. The group is an active representative of a larger group.

Figure 10.3.—Continued

51. The group's activities are influenced by a larger group of which it is a part.
52. People outside the group decide what work the group is to do.
53. The group follows the examples set by other groups.
54 The group is one of many similar groups that form one large organization.
55. The group's activities are approved by a group higher up.
56. The group joins with other groups in carrying out its activities.
57. The group is a small part of a larger group.
58. The group is under outside pressure.
59. Members are disciplined by an outside group.
60. Plans of the group are made by other groups above it.
61. The members allow nothing to interfere with the progress of the group.
62. Members feel honored by being recognized as one of the group.
63. Membership in the group is a way of acquiring general social status.
64. Failure of the group would mean little to individual members.
65. The activities of the group take up less than 10 percent of each member's working time.
66. Members gain in prestige among outsiders by joining the group.
67. A mistake by one member of the group might result in hardship for all.
68. The activities of the group take up over 90 percent of each member's working time.
69. Membership in the group serves as an aid to vocational advancement.
70. Failure of the group would mean nothing to most members.
71. Each member would lose his self-respect if the group should fail.
72. Membership in the group gives members a feeling of superiority.
73. The activities of the group take up over half the time each member is at work.
74. Failure of the group would lead to embarrassment for members.
75. Members are not rewarded for effort put out for the group.
76. There are two or three members of the group who generally take the same side on any group issue.
77. Certain members are hostile to other members.
78. There is constant bickering among members of the group.
79. Members know that each one looks out for the other one as well as for himself.
80. Certain members of the group have no respect for other members.
81. Certain members of the group are considered uncooperative.
82. There is a constant tendency toward conniving against one another among parts of the group.
83. Members of the group work together as a team.
84. Certain members of the group are responsible for petty quarrels and some animosity among other members.
85. There are tensions among subgroups that tend to interfere with the group's activities.
86. Certain members appear to be incapable of working as part of the group.
87. There is an undercurrent of feeling among members that tends to pull the group apart.
88. Anyone who has sufficient interest in the group to attend its meetings is considered a member.
89. The group engages in membership drives.
90. New members are welcomed to the group on the basis of the more the merrier.
91. A new member may join only after an old member resigns.
92. A college degree is required for membership in the group.
93. A person may enter the group by expressing a desire to join.
94. Anyone desiring to enter the group is welcome.
95. Membership is open to anyone willing to further the purpose of the group.
96. Prospective members are carefully examined before they enter the group.
97. No applicants for membership in the group are turned down.
98. No special training is required for membership in the group.
99. Membership depends upon the amount of education an individual has.
100. People interested in joining the group are asked to submit references which are checked.

Figure 10.3.—*Continued*

101. There is a high degree of participation on the part of members.
102. If a member of the group is not productive, he is not encouraged to remain.
103. Work of the group is left to those who are considered most capable for the job.
104. Members are interested in the group, but not all of them want to work.
105. The group has a reputation for not getting much done.
106. Each member of the group is on one or more active committees.
107. The work of the group is well divided among members.
108. Every member of the group does not have a job to do.
109. The work of the group is frequently interrupted by having nothing to do.
110. There are long periods during which the group does nothing.
111. The group is directed toward one particular goal.
112. The group divides its efforts among several purposes.
113. The group operates with sets of conflicting plans.
114. The group has only one main purpose.
115. The group knows exactly what it has to get done.
116. The group is working toward many different goals.
117. The group does many things that are not directly related to its main purpose.
118. Each member of the group has a clear idea of the group's goals.
119. The objective of the group is specific.
120. Certain members meet for one thing and others for a different thing.
121. The group has major purposes which to some degree are in conflict.
122. The objectives of the group have never been clearly recognized.
123. The group is very informal.
124. A list of rules and regulations is given to each member.
125. The group has meetings at regularly scheduled times.
126. The group is organized along semimilitary lines.
127. The group's meetings are not planned or organized.
128. The group has an organization chart.
129. The group has rules to guide its activities.
130. The group is staffed according to a table of organization.
131. The group keeps a list of names of members.
132. Group meetings are conducted according to *Robert's Rules of Order.*
133. There is a recognized right and wrong way of going about group activities.
134. Most matters that come up before the group are voted upon.
135. The group meets at any place that happens to be handy.
136. The members of the group vary in amount of ambition.
137. Members of the group are from the same social class.
138. Some members are interested in altogether different things than other members.
139. The group contains members with widely varying backgrounds.
140. The group contains white and black members.
141. Members of the group are all about the same age.
142. A few members of the group have greater ability than others.
143. A number of religious beliefs are represented by members of the group.
144. Members of the group vary greatly in social background.
145. All members of the group are of the same sex.
146. The ages of members range over a period of at least twenty years.
147. Members come into the group with quite different family backgrounds.
148. Members of the group vary widely in amount of experience.
149. Members vary in the number of years they have been in the group.
150. The group includes members of different races.

As you may imagine, various modifications of Hemphill's basic theme were made by researchers and organizational theorists during the 1960s and 1970s. Some researchers believed (some still do) that the best way to evaluate group behavior is to establish the categories and ask the group members or supervisor to fill in the blanks. Speroff's Conference Meeting Rating Scale (1959) is one example of this (see Figure 10.4).

Other researchers developed a different perspective on how evaluations of group behavior and performance should be made. Hawes (1977) and others (see Putnam, 1982 for review) recommend a method of conducting research about humans in groups based on data collected in naturalistic settings, and, if possible, using categories generated by the group members.

> Objectivists view reality as external to the individual; social phenomena are objective facts that occur independently of the individual. Subjectivists, in contrast, view reality as a socially created phenomenon, one that is interpreted by those who partake in the process. Social reality, unlike material phenomenon, does not exist independent of the events that create and maintain it.
> (From Linda L. Putnam, "Paradigms for Organizational Communication Research: An Overview and Synthesis," (1982), pp. 193–94.

Through interviews and self-reports, a researcher could collect information about how group members view important aspects of each other's behavior and performance. Using this naturalistic technique, the researcher avoids *imposing* categories on the respondents, but instead encourages them to talk freely about their experiences in the group. Pierce (1977) and others (Faules, 1982; Jick, 1979) believe that this approach to gathering data about humans in groups may lead to quantitative studies of the categories generated.

Regardless of the perspective of academic researchers, the practice of observing and evaluating group behavior and performance in organizations still relies more heavily on fill-in-the-blank, paper-and-pen, questionnaire-type rating forms. Managers using these forms usually recognize their weaknesses, though, and actively seek alternative ways of evaluating their groups.

Larry S., 34   Our company uses a standardized evaluation form on a semiannual basis. Because I am the manager, it is my job to administer the form to our employees. I never look forward to these times. The employees are always edgy; they know the results of these evaluations will be used to promote them, give them raises, or in some cases, to fire them. Everybody wants to be my friend during these times, which makes me sick to my stomach. You know, you work hard to promote good employee-management relations, and then evaluation time rolls around and ruins it. No, not all the time, but usually it does. And for what? I read over the forms and make my own comments. Then I have to schedule a meeting with each employee, go over the appraisal, argue with the ones who don't like it, short-change the ones who complain about it, and praise the ones who just accept it. It's awful. I've never received any training in this, either, which makes it harder on me.

Figure 10.4. Speroff
Conference Meeting
Rating Scale

Conference leader _____ Time start _____

Date _____ Time finish _____

Place _____ Delays or

Unit number or topic _____ interruptions _____

Number in group _____ Total time _____

I. Introductory Outcomes

	(+) 3	2	(−) 1

Conference Leader

	(+) 3	2	(−) 1
1. Has room and materials on hand and in readiness	___	___	___
2. Generates enthusiasm and interest in conference	___	___	___
3. Sets group at ease (creates group atmosphere)	___	___	___
4. Specifies objectives or problems to be considered for discussion	___	___	___
5. Stresses participation geared to *we* attitude and mutuality of purpose	___	___	___

Conference Group

	(+) 3	2	(−) 1
1. Feels and responds informally and freely	___	___	___
2. Feels a need or desire for fellowship and cooperation	___	___	___
3. Displays positive attitude toward group effort	___	___	___
4. Reacts favorably to group leader and discussion	___	___	___
5. Understands and accepts their role and function in the group (individuals)	___	___	___

II. Procedural Outcomes

Conference Leader

	(+) 3	2	(−) 1
1. Sequence of presentation logical and easy to follow	___	___	___
2. Visuals well integrated into presentation with meaningful transitions	___	___	___
3. Asks appropriate types of questions—allows for discussion and encourages personal opinions and views	___	___	___
4. Presents information, facts, data, and so forth, through use of appropriate channels—chart or pad, flannelboard, and the like	___	___	___
5. Presents realistic and practical problems, issues, and so forth, for group consideration and profit	___	___	___

Conference Group

	(+) 3	2	(−) 1
1. Understands and relates positively to the conference structure	___	___	___
2. Reacts favorably to visuals and transitions to content information	___	___	___
3. Accepts right to question, define, or delimit procedures or methods during conference	___	___	___
4. Feels responsibility for presenting information, data, and experiences in appropriate places and times	___	___	___
5. Accepts the informality, practicality, and atmosphere of the group's authority	___	___	___

Figure 10.4.—*Continued*

III. Process Outcomes

Conference Leader	(+) 3	2	(−) 1
1. Displays sensitivity to group needs, goals, and feelings	___	___	___
2. Avoids experting, antagonizing the group, and superiority attitude	___	___	___
3. Aids group in analysis and synthesis of problems	___	___	___
4. Allows for freedom of discussion and activity by group	___	___	___
5. Reacts successfully to group's progress in conference progress	___	___	___

Conference Group			
1. Feels freedom to participate in discussion	___	___	___
2. Derives benefit and value as a learning experience	___	___	___
3. Contributes a pool of experience and knowledge toward group effort	___	___	___
4. Has the ways and means of achieving results or furthering understanding	___	___	___
5. Affords opportunity for interpersonal growth, understanding, and development	___	___	___

IV. Summative Outcomes

Conference Leader			
1. Summarizes, clears up, or analyzes conference actions and reactions	___	___	___
2. Identifies, isolates, and refers for future consideration and discussion group problems, inadequacies, needs, and so forth	___	___	___
3. Affords group opportunity to suggest, reconsider, and act on common problems, interests, activities, and so forth.	___	___	___
4. Indicates the extent and amount of action required or needed to cope with and resolve undefined, inconclusive points or problems	___	___	___
5. Gets group acquiescence and/or support in conducting and concluding the conference discussion	___	___	___

Conference Group			
1. Feels definite worthwhile outcomes from discussion	___	___	___
2. Is allowed to participate in taking action when appropriate to do so and takes action	___	___	___
3. Presses for clarification or edification of obscure or non-comprehensible points, issues, and so forth	___	___	___
4. Feels a sense of accomplishment or achievement and purpose	___	___	___
5. Applies learning experience to job-related problems	___	___	___

Anyway, I do it. I have no choice. But I have learned my way around the damned form, believe me. I trust my own instincts. I ask the people I know about people who receive questionable evaluations, whether good or bad. Sometimes I observe people work, and pretend to just be thinking about something else. You've got to do it this way. No form can ever tell you what you really need to know about people.

In most organizations two forms of evaluation are used. First, an individual is given a personal appraisal of his or her work during the evaluation period. Second, each division or department within an organization is evaluated as a group. In this second category are the small group evaluations.

Summary of Approaches to Group Evaluation

Now you have reviewed the standards used to evaluate group behavior and performance. You have also reviewed some of the approaches to evaluation, including brief discussions of their comparative strengths and weaknesses. To summarize thus far:

1. Criticism is a comparative judgment based on the application of standards to the object of the critique.
2. Criticism should be productive. Rather than viewing criticism as a task to be performed, you need to encourage a process-orientation for making and giving evaluations. This means (a) providing standards used to make the evaluations; (b) making evaluations of both positive and negative aspects of the group; and (c) explaining how the group can improve performance.
3. The standards used in an evaluation are based on the *purpose* of the small group, and the *format* used to evaluate behavior.
4. General standards governing the evaluation of most groups in organizations include the (a) purpose of the group; (b) level of participation of group members; (c) effectiveness of leadership in the group; (d) characteristics associated with adequate or satisfactory performance by the group; (e) a description of exactly how well the group is attaining the objectives; and (f) a statement of how the group can improve performance during the next evaluation period.
5. General standards governing the criticism of communication by group members should be based on the *appropriateness* of talk and the ability of the speaker to *adapt* to the needs and expectations of the situation and of other group members.
6. There have been three basic methods of evaluating the communication of group members: (a) general categorical formats emphasizing *evaluation;* (b) general categorical formats emphasizing *description of specific communicative behaviors* (both variable analytic and general rating forms); and (c) naturalistic interviews and self-reports which can reveal *the meaning of group experiences.*

7. Despite their limitations most organizations still rely on basic questionnaires to conduct evaluations.

There is no "best" way to observe and evaluate group behavior and performance. Effective criticism of small groups is never an easy task to accomplish because individuals are complex and groups of individuals are even more so. The manager or supervisor desiring to improve the evaluative process within an organization should strive to (1) establish reasonable standards to make comparisons of behavior and performance, (2) construct an evaluation rating form in accordance with those standards, and (3) seek responses to the appropriateness of the form by the people charged with the responsibility for using it. Regardless of the format chosen, the manager or supervisor must be able to identify specific behaviors and skills to document the presence or absence of effective performance.

The Tools for Observing Small Groups

In most organizations there is less observation than evaluation of group work. Managers, supervisors, and other administrative personnel do not have the time nor the skills to watch group activities. Consequently, evaluations are usually based on the ability of the group to obtain *results* or *reach objectives*. The small group charged with the responsibility for decreasing the number and severity of accidents on the job within a company is evaluated on the basis of whether there is a reduction in the number of accidents and a decrease in their severity.

When "management by results" or "management by objectives" prevails, evaluation of group activities usually is based on *rating* or *ranking* scales (Yager, 1981; Baird and Weinberg, 1981).

Rating Scales

The rating scale is an instrument for determining the *results* obtained by the small group, or the *generalized impressions* of group members' work. Early rating scales were inadequate because they consisted only of checklists of nouns (e.g., initiative, ability, friendliness, cooperation, knowledge), without descriptions of behaviors as standards for rating. Today most organizations use behavior-based rating scales:

Figure 10.5 presents a rating scale designed to provide generalized indications of a group member's work. These scales are perhaps the most widely used instruments of appraisal in American business and industry. However, the use of this rating scale does *not* provide a picture of the individual group member as part of the small group. The characteristics noted here could apply more readily to someone working alone than to an individual working with a group. The use of rating scales to evaluate group work is more complicated.

Figure 10.5. Sample
Employee Evaluation
Form

Instructions: Read each item carefully. Select the response category which reflects this employee's performance. Limit your responses to the item mentioned.

Factor	*Superior*		*Average*		*Poor*
Appearance	_____	_____	_____	_____	_____
Dependability	_____	_____	_____	_____	_____
Cooperation	_____	_____	_____	_____	_____
Decisiveness	_____	_____	_____	_____	_____
Punctuality	_____	_____	_____	_____	_____
Efficiency	_____	_____	_____	_____	_____
Quality of Work	_____	_____	_____	_____	_____
Overall Performance	_____	_____	_____	_____	_____

Evaluate this employee's performance by comparing it to the performance level of employees with similar education, experience and skill levels.

0%	20%	40%	60%	80%	100%

_____

_____

Additional comments: Please describe any incidences of behavior which have been useful to you in evaluating this employee.

_____

_____

_____

_____

_____

NAME OF EMPLOYEE: _____

NAME OF EVALUATOR: _____

DATE: _____

SIGNATURE OF EMPLOYEE: _____

I have read and discussed this evaluation with my superior.

_____ Check here if you plan to file a grievance.

_____ Check here if you agree with the evaluation.

Group rating scales vary according to the type of organization; basically they fall into two categories:

1. *Numerical scales:* A type of rating scale in which the observer is asked to assign numbers to listed characteristics of group behavior and performance. For example, if we are interested in assessing the level of participation in group interactions displayed by each group member, we might construct this numerical rating scale.

   As you can see, one problem with the use of this type of rating scale is the *forced ranking* according to the listed characteristics. If the observer has no basis for evaluating certain characteristics, this format compels the evaluator to do so anyway. Usually the scores are averaged and a comparison is made among other group members.

2. *Likert-type scale:* Refers to a scaling technique designed by Rensis Likert in which an opinion is stated and the observer is asked to determine the extent to which she or he agrees with the statement. For example, if we are interested in rating the degree of cohesiveness among group members, we might use the Likert-type scale to gather impressions about cohesiveness.

Numerical Scale

Instructions: Rate how well (name of group member) kept up with the flow of the discussions. Use "1" to represent "excellent" and "10" to represent "poor."

Displayed awareness of topic area	_____
Asked relevant questions about major issues	_____
Paid attention to the directives of the leader	_____
Provided useful information to the group	_____
Did not stray from the topic during the interaction	_____
Arrived well-prepared for interaction	_____
Managed conflict appropriately	_____
Initiated new ideas for the group	_____
Responded enthusiastically to other group members	_____
Demonstrated an organized approach to discussion	_____

Observers using the Likert-type scale then assign numbers to the checkpoints and can thus arrive at statistical measurements of the assessed behavior and performance. One problem with the Likert-type scale is the lack of clear behavioral definitions or examples to guide the observer in making the ratings. What would constitute "agreement" or "disagreement" on any of the above items might vary from one observer to another.

Rating scales are widely used to evaluate the performance of individuals and groups. One serious drawback of using such scales is the limited amount of time observers in organizations spend actually watching the groups and individuals interacting. When these scales are used, the observer usually must rely on brief episodic remembrances of how members treated each other, impressions which may or may not be accurate assessments of their overall patterns of interaction. Yager (1981) points out that whenever a rating scale is used it reflects the *relationship between the rater and group member* rather than anything else.

Likert-Type Scale

Instructions: Respond to the following items by placing a check (✓) in the space which best describes your rating of the individual's performance.

He/She seemed to enjoy working with the group on the project.

/_____/_____/_____/_____/_____/_____/

| Strongly Agree | Agree | Neutral | Disagree | Strongly Disagree |

She/He behaved in a friendly manner toward other group members.

/_____/_____/_____/_____/_____/_____/

| Strongly Agree | Agree | Neutral | Disagree | Strongly Disagree |

He/She attempted to resolve conflicts in a productive, non-threatening way.

/_____/_____/_____/_____/_____/_____/

| Strongly Agree | Agree | Neutral | Disagree | Strongly Disagree |

Rating scales can be useful. However, they should not as a rule be used as the sole indicator of a group's performance, or an individual's behavior. Instead, rating scales used by an observer (or manager) should be employed, in conjunction with comparative ranking scales, self-reports, and group members' evaluations of each other.

Comparative Ranking Scales

This observational instrument is used to compare *individual group members to each other* and also to compare *groups with other groups* in organizations. Again, ranking group members comparatively only allows the formulation of generalized impressions about the group members. Care must be exercised not to add specific behavioral patterns to the generalized impression without first collecting solid observational data.

The standard format for comparative ranking scales is shown below:

The questionnaire would be completed for each group member, and an overall ranking would be obtained. In most organizations the comparative ranking scale serves a dual purpose. First, the manager may use the instrument to rank individuals and groups within a department or division. Second, the organization may use the instrument to compare how different managers rank their employees.

Although comparative ranking scales are usually reserved for observers or managers, they may also be productively used by group members to rank each other. When group members use comparative ranking scales, these may fall into one or more distinct categories (Baird and Weinberg, 1981, pp. 239–41):

1. *Simple ranking scales:*   These scales are used to evaluate the behavior of group members according to some standard or characteristic. (See page 000.)
2. *Paired comparisons scale.*   As its name indicates, this scale requires the observers to rank characteristics, behaviors, or members two at a time. (See page 000.)

    The advantage of this scaling method is that it compels the observers to consider comparisons between and among group members rather than considering each member in isolation.
3. *Dimensional ranking scales:*   This scaling technique is useful when specific characteristics of a behavior category (e.g., leadership or participation) are needed, and comparisons between and among group members are necessary to discover who did what.

Comparative Ranking Scale

Instructions: Answer the following statements by comparing <u>(name of group member)</u> to other members of the group.

This person's ability to generate new ideas and information

Is not as strong as most others in the group.   _____

Is comparable to most other group members.   _____

Is better than most other group members.   _____

Is far greater than most other group members.   _____

Exceeds that of all other group members.   _____

Simple Ranking Scale

Instructions: Rank the members of your group according to how much they contributed to the final phase of your decision-making (1 = least; 5 = most)

A. Man   _____

B. Cool   _____

C. Itoldya   _____

D. Licious   _____

E. Lated   _____

Paired Comparisons Scale

Instructions: Listed below are names of the members of your small group. Circle the number of each pair who provided the best alternative solutions to the problem during the brainstorming session.

1. A. Participant

2. B. Friendly

3. C. DeProblem

4. D. Solution

5. E. Zee

1–2   1–3   1–4   1–5   2–3   2–4   2–5   3–4   3–5   4–5

Instructions: Rank the following small group members according to the quality demonstrated of each behavior listed below. (1 = most; 7 = least)

Characteristics	Members					
	Carol	Paul	Chris	Lloyd	Carter	Roy
Preparation for group meetings						
Carrying out homework assignments						
Responding to other group members						
Following directives of the leader						
Initiating new ideas						
Resolving conflicts						

Comparative ranking scales, like rating scales, should not be the sole source of evaluations about group members. One difficulty in using any of these methods to observe and evaluate interactions is that most group members *resist* ranking each other because they are aware of how the evaluations might be used. A year's work in developing cohesiveness can be destroyed during the evaluation period. A second problem is the lack of time needed for skilled and consistent observations on the part of a manager or supervisor charged with the responsibility of making the evaluation. Rankings may be based on what the observer last saw happening in the group or on what the observer values seeing in the group. Finally, most employees feel that such evaluative techniques are used *against* them rather than to improve their performance. Because evaluations are too often used to justify raises and promotions, employees may see a sinister motive in them. Most organizational specialists agree that evaluations should be *separated* from considerations of rewards or punishments (see Yager, 1981). Unfortunately, this is not the practice in most organizations.

Since most managers know that they possess limited information on which to base appraisals of individuals and groups, they often seek additional data from the group members. In the following section you will examine some of the methods for developing effective criticism which can be used by group members and leaders.

The Tools of Evaluation Available to Members and Leaders of Small Groups

As pointed out in the previous section, many of the rating and ranking techniques used by observers of groups can also be used by the group members to appraise behavior and performance. However, there are additional ways to gain information about group processes and outcomes from the members and leaders of small groups. These methods of obtaining data include *interviews, self-reports,* and *collective appraisals.* In this section I will examine each one of these tools for strengths and weaknesses.

Interviews

The interview is a useful evaluative tool. Group leaders should use it when making selections of potential group members, and use the time to specify objectives, methods, and individual responsibilities, as well as to obtain the candidate's input about the project. Moravec (1981) believes that the selection interview should be used to establish goals for the evaluation period and to explain carefully the group leader's expectations relative to the group member's performance and responsibilities. Thus, the interview can be used effectively by group leaders to select group members more carefully.

The interview can also be used by group leaders to work out problems that occur during group sessions, but that cannot or must not interfere with the group's ability to meet its objectives on time. For example, if a group leader perceives a potential conflict developing between group members, the leader may request a conference with them, or schedule an interview to remove the difficulty. During these interviews the leader can obtain precise information about how group members perceive the group, its task, and their functions Consequently, the group leader should acquire access to more and better personal information about the group member, data that may be helpful in later assessments of the member's work.

A third use of the interview is as a debriefing tool. Following the group's completion of a specific task, the group leader may schedule interviews with all group members to exchange ideas and feelings about the progress of the group effort. In these interviews, the leader should allow the participant to do most of the talking, encouraging open and honest communication about perceptions of the task, the methods used to complete it, interactions among group members, together with any suggestions for improving the process next time. Consider the following statement:

> **Regina W., 26**   I have a practice of debriefing the participants of our groups. I find it useful to listen to their interpretations of what happened during the meetings, and to gain their impressions of my leadership skills. The important thing is to *listen.* During the group work we are usually too involved in the job to spend much time reflecting on how we work together, and when I get a chance to hear how the people think and feel and plan for these meetings, I gain what I consider to be really important information. I think the debrief has made me a much more effective group leader.

There are both advantages and disadvantages to the interview as a tool for collecting data about small group processes and outcomes. The advantages include gaining access to:

Personal interpretations of the group
Personal feelings about the group
Information about your leadership skills
Suggestions for improving the group process

The disadvantages of using the interview depend on the ability of the leader to avoid gossip, rumor, and viciousness. People may use interpersonal situations to disclose information about themselves which you would rather not know. The leader must take care to provide guidelines for the interview at the outset and to stop excessively negative talk when it occurs. If the word gets around that the leader only uses the interview to "spy" on group members, to form conspiracies, or to create empires within the organization, conflict will result.

Another methodological alternative to the use of observer-based rating and ranking scales is the self-report. Group members and leaders are asked to respond to questionnaires describing their group activities and individual perceptions of the group work. One of the earliest examples of a self-report questionnaire is the Seashore Index of Group Cohesiveness (1954) (see Figure 10.6).

Self-Reports

The Seashore Index combines the strengths of rating and comparative ranking scales. Each group member is asked to complete the questionnaire, and the manager may then compile data about how the individuals feel about the group.

Self-reports are generally used to collect information about attitudes toward the interpersonal or relational climate of the small group. Rarely are self-reports used to determine the task-related factors of group work. Another example of a self-report questionnaire developed during the late 1950s illustrates one way of determining how individuals feel about the group (Goldman, 1958) (see Figure 10.7).

Aside from the use of an older style of language, what characteristics of groups are revealed by the Goldman study? When you examine the statements people were asked to respond to, what topics naturally occur as being important to the morale of the group? Goldman used this index to discuss four key variables of group morale (from Baird and Weinberg, 1981, p. 267):

1. *Individual motives:*   A group is assumed to be more cohesive when there are opportunities present for satisfying individual motives related to group activities.
2. *Interpersonal relations:*   A group is more cohesive when opportunities are present to satisfy the need for interpersonal relations.

Figure 10.6. Seashore
Index of Group
Cohesiveness

Check one response for each question.

1. Do you feel that you are really a part of your work group?
   _____ Really a part of my work group
   _____ Included in most ways
   _____ Included in some ways, but not in others
   _____ Don't feel I really belong
   _____ Don't work with any one group of people
   _____ Not ascertained

2. If you had a chance to do the same kind of work for the same pay in another work group, how would you feel about moving?
   _____ Would want very much to move
   _____ Would rather move than stay where I am
   _____ Would make no difference to me
   _____ Would rather stay where I am than move
   _____ Would want very much to stay where I am
   _____ Not ascertained

3. How does your work group compare with other similar groups on each of the following points?

	Better than most	About the same as most	Not as good as most	Not ascertained
a. The way the members of get along together	_____	_____	_____	_____
b. The way the members stick together	_____	_____	_____	_____
c. The way the members help each other on the job	_____	_____	_____	_____

3. *Homogeneity of attitude:* A group is more cohesive if the members have relatively similar attitudes.
4. *Leadership:* A group is more cohesive if its leader(s) possess qualities valued by the group and if the group's dependence on the leader(s) is welcomed rather than resented.

Two problems arise with the use of self-reports, such as Goldman's. First, the questionnaire format limits the choices available to group members. For example, the items contained on the Goldman or Seashore questionnaire compel the respondents to answer *only* the questions deemed important by the developers of it. Perhaps a better way to administer a self-report questionnaire would be to

Instructions: Indicate the extent to which you agree with each one of the following statements. If you strongly agree with a statement, write SA (for strongly agree) in the space to the left. If you just agree with the statement, place A (for agree) in the space. If you neither agree nor disagree write in U (for uncertain). Write D (for disagree) or SD (for strongly disagree) if you either disagree or strongly disagree with the statement.

Figure 10.7. Goldman Study of Group Morale

_____ 1. I feel that what I am doing here gives me a chance to make friends.

_____ 2. I believe that all my associates in this group hold beliefs that are unreasonable.

_____ 3. Most of my associates here would help me if I needed help.

_____ 4. The leader of this group is out for his own advancement; he doesn't care about me.

_____ 5. The leader of this group can always be relied upon to do the right thing.

_____ 6. I just tolerate the people I associate with here.

_____ 7. All of my associates in this group are a dull lot and don't think seriously about important issues.

_____ 8. I feel that there is plenty of chance to get ahead in what I am doing now.

_____ 9. I would never make friends with any of my associates here.

_____ 10. The leader of this group is out to help me as much as he can.

_____ 11. I seldom pay attention to what other people say; I believe in making my own decisions.

_____ 12. I feel that I have made some lasting friends among my associates in this group.

_____ 13. I believe that the work I do now keeps me in a rut.

_____ 14. I feel that I can ask advice of most of my associates in this group.

_____ 15. Most of my associates in this group are stubborn; no amount of argument will change them.

_____ 16. Just a few of my associates in this group are open-minded; most of them have biased points of view.

_____ 17. The leader of this group got ahead because of his connections, not because of his ability.

_____ 18. Sometimes I like what I am doing here, but most of the time I hate it.

_____ 19. Most of my associates would risk their own security if it were necessary for the good of all.

_____ 20. I believe that most of my associates would stab me in the back if it meant they could get ahead that way.

combine the Goldman format with a list of short-answer essay questions to elicit natural responses. Consider the following example of how this might be accomplished:

Instructions: Write your own responses to each one of the following short-answer essay questions. Try to be as specific as possible.

1. Explain how you see your role in the group.

2. Explain how you feel the group members see your role in the group.

3. If you had the opportunity to make any changes in the group's activities, what might they be?

4. Compare this group to other groups you have worked with or for. What do you especially like or dislike about this group? How close do you feel toward other group members? How about the leader?

Asking the group members to write answers in *their* own language to the issues *they* think about should provide valuable information with which to re-examine the answers given to the standard questions. Using this combination self-report inventory and essay format, the *meanings* of the answers should become more clear.

A second problem associated with self-reports concerns their reliability. Do people actually respond to self-reports honestly? Do they answer the questions based on what they really think, or on what they believe the manager will want to read? Even using an essay format, it is difficult to know how reliable the answers given are. Some of the most important information individuals could supply about working in a small group may never be revealed because it may be too personal, or the individuals may fear repercussions. As I have stated consistently throughout this text, the best way to overcome any problems associated with understanding the meaning of any group is to develop effective relationships with them over a period of time. Only by getting to know the group members can a manager more accurately appraise the meaning of answers given to questions about the group. Consider the following testimony:

> **Shirley B., 31** Because I work in personnel administration I have to be sensitive to what the appraisal forms really mean. It is easy enough to dismiss the ones marked with Strongly Agree or Strongly Disagree straight down the page because you know no time was spent thinking through the questions. When I worked for the Army, they used a form that required the appraisers to write detailed reports for *any* answer other than "Average." So you know what happened? Almost all of the forms were marked "average." It takes too much time to write detailed reports. In personnel you learn to read into the evaluations. You have to get to know the appraisers and the ones being appraised. You'd be surprised just how much you can learn from getting to know people. For me, the forms are a necessary nuisance. I look at them, but I look at them *in relation to* a variety of other factors that come from knowing the people. It is when I don't know the people that I have to trust the forms, and that is a risky business.

Collective Appraisals

Recently a new method of obtaining information about group processes and outcomes entered some American businesses. In part, the method is derived from a Japanese corporate management style based on open communication between leaders and members of groups, as well as between managers and employees of companies (see Ouchi, 1981 for detailed treatment; see Hirokawa, 1982, for communication applications). The method is also in part derived from the work done in the 1960s and early 1970s by humanistic psychologists working with groups (see Friedman, 1978 for comprehensive review). The method is called by a variety of names, but we will refer to it as "collective appraisals."

The objective of collective appraisals is to encourage open and honest communication among group members about each other, the task, and the most effective and efficient ways of accomplishing it. When applied to communication practices the terms *open* and *honest* do *not* mean that you are using the group members as your own personal therapists or counselors. By *open and honest communication* I do *not* mean full self-disclosure of everything related to the personal joys and sorrows of group work. Willard Gaylin phrases this sentiment which he writes "I have never felt that people's inner feelings have some claim to public recognition" (Gaylin, 1979, p. 4).

Actually, open and honest communication refers to sharing ideas and feelings with group members (O'Connell, 1979). It does not mean using insensitive language when conversing with others, nor does it refer to simply saying whatever

Figure 10.8. O'Connell Self-Assessment of Building Open Communication

Check the extent to which you do each of the following.

	Very Little	Little	Some	Great	Very Great
1. I help others feel free to talk with me.	___	___	___	___	___
2. I understand how other group members feel about our task problems.	___	___	___	___	___
3. I encourage other group members to let me know when things are going wrong in the group.	___	___	___	___	___
4. I make it easy for others to do their best work.	___	___	___	___	___
5. I express confidence in the leader's ability to direct our activities.	___	___	___	___	___
6. I encourage group members to bring new information about the task to my attention, even when that new information may be bad.	___	___	___	___	___
7. Others feel the things they tell me are important.	___	___	___	___	___
8. I am willing to encourage argument and to give a fair hearing to all points of view.	___	___	___	___	___
9. I listen to all group members when they state things that are bothering them.	___	___	___	___	___
10. It's safe for my group members to say what they are really thinking.	___	___	___	___	___
11. I feel as though I understand the strengths and weaknesses of each group member, and attempt to adapt my communication to them.	___	___	___	___	___
12. I do not allow another group members position in the formal hierarchy of the organization negatively influence what I say in front of them.	___	___	___	___	___

From *The Manager as Communicator* by Sandra E. O'Connell. Continuing Management Education Series, edited by Albert W. Schrader. Copyright © 1979 by Sandra E. O'Connell. By permission of Harper & Row Publishers, Inc.

comes to mind about the group work. Throughout this text you have been made aware of the need for group members to *think about the effects of their words before speaking,* to consider the responses sought from others, and to determine how effective one approach to eliciting those desired responses might be in a given case. Open and honest communication is a *goal* for people in organizations; it does not "just happen." You must strive to reach the goal, but be satisfied with small steps toward reaching it.

O'Connell (1979, p. 139) offers a self-assessment form to help organizational members develop open communication practices (see Figure 10.8).

This form may be completed by each member of the small group. Then a group meeting should be scheduled to discuss ways of avoiding closed communication practices within the group. *It is absolutely essential that the talk shared among group members during this meeting should focus on the ends to be attained, rather than on the causes of group or interpersonal problems.* If causes are discussed they will probably reveal sources of conflict at the ego or value levels. When such conflicts appear within a group, they become burdensome to all concerned and virtually impossible to resolve in the short-run. Rather than focusing on personalities of the people "causing" the problem, group members should strive to concentrate on *behaviors* associated with the goals of the group. Group meetings should be productive aids to building better communication between and among group members. They should *not* be used to "roast" a particular group member or to point out the flaws in character of each group member.

Using the self-assessment form and the scheduled meeting to build open communication within the group is only *one* phase of evaluating the processes and outcomes of the group by using collective appraisals. Building open and honest communication practices should be an organizational objective, as much a part of the appraisal process as determining whether or not the group has accomplished its task. But collective appraisals must do more than merely help the group find better ways of working together; as an *appraisal,* this method must also find ways and means of assessing individual contributions to the group, and the success of the group as a whole.

Sample Agenda for Collective Appraisal Session

Time: Wednesday, 10 A.M.–12 Noon

Place: Room 007

Call the meeting to order.

Explain the purpose of the appraisal.

Hand out self-report forms:

    Goldman

    O'Connell

    Company Assessment of Performance Rating Scale

Collect self-report forms.

Open discussion of the goals of this group.

Open discussion of any improvements in our operation.

Summary.

Adjournment.

Here are some guidelines for using collective appraisals:

*Guidelines for Using
Collective Appraisals*

1. *A convenient time for the group meeting should be scheduled, and the agenda should be circulated among group members.* This is a group meeting and should be conducted as a group meeting, not as an encounter or a therapy session. Group members should be aware of the topics for discussion, the evaluations to be made, and the time needed to attain the appraisal objectives.

2. *The leader or manager should explain to the group the purposes of the appraisal.* Group members often feel threatened when they are asked to evaluate their own work and that of other group members. To reduce anxiety associated with evaluations, some specific guidelines concerning the purposes, uses, and methods of the evaluation should be explained to the group. Are members supposed to evaluate (a) their ability to accomplish the task, (b) their interpersonal relationships, (c) their leader, or (d) each other? To what use will these evaluations be put? Will they be used to determine raises and promotions? Will they be used to provide feedback to the group about their activities? Who will receive the evaluations? What will be done with them? What methods will be used to evaluate the group? Rating or ranking scales? Self-reports? Collective appraisals may make use of any or all of these methods, and group members should be informed of their strengths and weaknesses.

3. *During the meeting the group leader should act as a participant in the group, not its overseer.* For constructive criticism to take place, there should be a climate of open and honest communication. It would be unfair to other group members if the group leader directed the talk beyond simply managing the agenda.

4. *Establishing objectives for improving the operation of the group should be the final task accomplished by the group in the meeting.* Appraisals, like every other group meeting activity, require a sense of accomplishment. The goal of the appraisal is to articulate ways and means of improving the operation of the group. The group may decide to write out a list of suggestions for perusal by group members after the meeting.

In this section you have reviewed some of the appraisal tools and techniques available to small group leaders and members. Criticism of individual behaviors and group operations is seldom as simple as any questionnaire or form may imply. I recommend the use of collective appraisals where possible, inasmuch as they focus on the group's ability to coordinate observations and evaluations of all aspects of group work.

Problems Associated with Observing and Evaluating Groups

We spend a lot of time watching other people. We notice how they walk, talk, the way they dress. We compare people to each other and determine (at least tentatively) their personal worth and their value to us. We listen to them, attempt to discover their meaning, and provide them with responses indicating how they are coming across to us. In our minds we are amateur critics of all that surrounds us, especially the people with whom we interact. With this extensive natural background and training in criticism, we should enjoy the opportunity to observe and evaluate small groups.

A major problem associated with this necessary critical process, especially in organizations, is that most people do *not* enjoy evaluating others even when they have had ample time to observe them. Managers are reluctant critics. Like most of us, they prefer to keep their thoughts about others to themselves. When they are asked to complete a quarterly or annual report on workers they may suddenly act as if they have never had experience in criticism. What they privately think they may publicly conceal. But this problem reaches beyond managers. Members of small groups are also reluctant to pass judgment on each other. Even when the group has been cohesive and the work accomplished to the satisfaction of everyone, there is generally a shared anxiety about completing the questionnaires or using collective appraisals.

A second major problem concerns the lack of understanding of or training in evaluative techniques. Despite the fact we spend a large share of our daily lives engaged in acts of observation and evaluation, these acts seldom are approached systematically. Nor are they used to determine someone else's raises, promotions, or company records. Although many people agree about the inadequacies of standardized tests, forms, and questionnaires, these instruments are still widely used because they are relatively simple to complete and to quantify. For the person who does not enjoy criticizing, the use of a fill-in-the-blank form appears to solve many problems.

A third major problem is what to look at (or count) when examining group processes. Most large organizations begin with the "bottom-line," the ability of the group to attain its objective and the cost of reaching it. But the ability to attain an objective is only one small part of a group's activity. After all, objectives can be achieved by tyrants, or *not* achieved by the most conscientious, "democratic" small groups. There is no guarantee that the "best" group interactions occur in the groups which attain their goals. Other areas susceptible to evaluation in small groups include: the sequences of interactions, the hierarchies of group members, relationships between leader and participants, skills demonstrated by the group members, quantity and quality of individual contributions, the method used by the group to generate its outcomes, the time and resources used by the group, and the evaluations of what went on in the group meetings. When measured in terms of the desired results, the areas available for actual assessment of the group work far exceed the normal capabilities of a manager or supervisor.

In this section you will examine some of the specific problems associated with the observation and evaluation of small groups. All of them are related to the above three major difficulties; but the problems I have isolated can be solved by individual effort rather than by organizational change. The problems you will examine are (1) where to put the emphasis in evaluations; (2) the tendency to evaluate personalities rather than skills or competencies; (3) differences in communication style; (4) not understanding the special language (jargon, specialized vocabulary) of the group; (5) how disruptions within the group may trigger negative evaluations, and (6) how to combine "inside" and "outside" evaluations of group work.

Where to Put the Emphasis in Evaluations

Effective and equitable group appraisals present a balanced view of what occurred during group meetings. By *balanced* I mean there is no distortion of the evaluation toward (or away from) the responsibilities of the leader or participants, the task to be accomplished, or the processes and outcomes of the group. For example, the use of one questionnaire evaluating group cohesiveness seldom reveals important information about the processes and outcomes of the group. The use of a leadership or participant scale does not reveal essential information about the nature of the task or the way the group interacted. The use of all of these questionnaires does *not* solve the problem.

Managers must resist the temptation to see only what is reported. This is like valuing only what can be measured in numbers or quantified. People should not be compelled to live by numbers alone. What can be quantified as an outcome may not reveal much about the processes by which the outcome was generated. What can be "counted" about leadership skills may not reveal anything about the ability of the leader to adapt to new situations, changes in information, conflicts among group members, or the pressure of working with a deadline, on a limited budget. How can the significant information about group processes and outcomes be revealed on a scale of one-to-seven?

If you didn't know the leader of this group, if you never had the opportunity to observe that person leading the group, how could you possibly know what a "4" rating means? If you don't know how the members of the group interpreted the terms on the questionnaire (e.g., "static," or "dynamic," etc.), how could you be sure that they were all evaluating the same quality?

So what can be done?

Obviously, the best of all possible solutions would include equal consideration among all the variables affecting a group. This ideal solution to the problem of

Instructions: Place a check ✓ in the space which best describes your attitudes toward the leader of your small group.

	1	2	3	4	5	6	7	
Dynamic	/	/	/	/	/	/	/	Static
Positive	/	/	/	/	/	/	/	Negative
Good	/	/	/	/	/	/	/	Bad
Strong	/	/	/	/	/	/	/	Weak
Active	/	/	/	/	/	/	/	Passive

emphasis would also require an ideal evaluator who could be counted on to be fair and to see everything. Since these standards cannot be met, what can reasonably be accomplished? Here are some guidelines:

1. *Balance actual observations with training group members and managers in how to observe.*   Social psychologists have long known that people tend to see what they want to look for. In any given situation you "selectively" observe those objects, people, and actions which have meanings or convey meanings to you. Using this assumptive approach, it is easy to see how observations of what goes on in any group setting are likely to be heavily influenced by past experiences and prejudices. One way to offset this predisposition is to train people *how to observe and evaluate behavior and outcomes in groups.* Before the time for evaluations, managers should prepare group members for the experience, and if feasible, hold training seminars presenting and discussing the skills of group evaluation. Do not just ask people to fill out questionnaires without providing some basic knowledge to make valid evaluations.

2. *Balance consideration of outcomes with consideration of process.*   I have pointed out how easy it is to judge the worth of a group by the ends it achieves. Although the outcomes are essential in determining the success of the group's effort, outcomes are the *result* of communication. The group interactions, therefore, are just as important as the outcomes, because the outcomes would not have occurred without them. It is easy to assess outcomes: to find out what happened, to look at the final report, to listen to the group presentation. It is more difficult to assess processes. To accomplish this

Guidelines for Attaining Balance

you need to make judicious use of group-generated critiques and collective appraisals. Managers must learn to ask the group for input about the evaluations of *how* they achieve (or failed to accomplish) their objectives.

3. *Balance considerations of the leader's skills with considerations of the participant's abilities.* It is easy to blame the leader when the group fails to reach its goal. It is easy, in turn, for the leader to blame the group for not living up to its obligations. In either case someone is blaming the *victim*. Participaton and leadership are interdependent acts. To separate them, or to rely too heavily on one or the other as basis for a critique, is to bias the evaluation. You should ask the members of a group to evaluate their leaders and then ask the leaders to evaluate each of the participants. By examining both sources of the critique, you can better understand how the group views its leader as well as how the leader regards the group members. You should also be able to ascertain strengths and weaknesses in both camps, perhaps to suggest ways to overcome the weaknesses. It is imperative to collect information about the group from the group, and to balance the leader's responsibilities with the responsibilities of the participants.

These three guidelines should aid managers, group members, and group leaders in presenting a balanced evaluation of the group.

Avoiding "Personalities" While Examining Behavior

Earlier in this book I discussed the idea of "identity" in relation to group interaction. Essentially, we develop our group identities from the responses others make to us. Because we live within ourselves, we are prone to pass judgment on other people's inner selves as well. The common form of evaluating the inner self is known as psychology or psychiatry; the professionals trained in this field often use the term *personality* to describe their patients or subjects. Unfortunately, too often we make judgments about other persons' personalities, without our having the benefit of professional training for this task.

What is a personality?

This is a difficult question to answer, even for the most highly trained psychiatrist. The term is an abstraction indicating the sum total of an individual's attitudes, values, beliefs, and behaviors, as these traits constitute consistent patterns of behavior. For a psychiatrist to be able to understand another human being with this level of complexity requires about three years of intensive questioning and listening (Ogilview, 1977). To believe that most of us are capable of passing accurate judgments about other people's personalities is both inaccurate and presumptuous. Of course, when most people make these determinations, they do not intend them in a clinical sense. The personality of someone else is virtually always a ripe topic for informal discussion. We hear statements that sound like ways of collecting personal data about people's characters or personalities. The

Instructions: Read each item carefully. Circle the response which best describes your personal assessment of the member of your group whose name appears below.

Castor Oyle

Volume of Work Appraise only output and work load in the group.

/_____/_____/_____/_____/

| Insufficient output; slow; usually behind with work. | Output usually falls short of amount considered satisfactory. | Output meets job requirements. | Good capacity for work; often does more than is assigned. | Top worker; clearly does more work than expected. |

Quality of Work Appraise only standard of work, accuracy, skill.

/_____/_____/_____/_____/

| Excels in all work on all job assignments. | Work is accurate and skillful; complete attention to details; above the requirements. | Average quality of work and skill. | Improvement in quality needed; careless, incomplete and inconsistent contributions to group. | Absence of quality work or skill. |

approach to evaluations taken by the manager should be to acquire information about the group that can be used to improve performance and quality, thereby increasing the likelihood of rewards being given to the group members.

Second, specific behavioral guides should be included in any questionnaire administered to a group. Rather than using the weak "one-to-seven" rating forms already discussed in this chapter, organizations should design evaluation forms using more specific behavioral descriptions.

In the above example, notice the differentiation between *volume* and *quality* of work. Notice also the inversion of the evaluative scale—what counts as "good" and "bad" on the scale is reversed for every other question. Notice, finally, the descriptive expressions used to correlate the evaluations behaviorally. These considerations are desirable in the development of an appraisal form that seeks to evaluate behavior rather than personality.

Third, when collective appraisals are used, the leader should ask for clarification when terms such as *attitude, personality,* or other internally defined words are mentioned without descriptive behavioral support. If a group member says "I like Joan's attitude toward . . ." the leader should respond with the question "What do you mean by attitude?" or "What specific things did Joan do to create that impression?" Never assume the meanings others have for abstract terms will correspond to the meanings *you* have for those terms.

The above three suggestions should help substantially to improve the ability of the group members to specify and evaluate behaviors rather than personalities.

Differences in Communication Style

Most evaluations of participation and leadership assume that all group members have the same communication skills and an asexual style of communicating. For example, we expect reticent or shy people to be able somehow to eliminate their shyness while in the group setting, if for no other reason than because they have to in order to assure favorable appraisals of their group work. As research has consistently demonstrated, those persons who suffer communication apprehension (Burgoon, 1977; Burgoon and Burgoon, 1974) or reticence (McKinney, 1982) about communicating with others in groups not only have a potentially negative affect on the group; but they also receive significantly lower evaluations from other group members. Shy people do *not* appear to be able to simply "suspend" their shyness in order to improve their group evaluations.

Shyness

The problem of communication apprehension or shyness presents special difficulties to persons responsible for judging individual behavior in small groups. If shy people are evaluated on the same bases as non-shy people, then there would seem to be an inherent bias in favor of the non-shy. This is particularly true when using scales that place a premium on the *amount* rather than the *quality* of participation. The reticent individual may not speak often, but when she or he does speak the quality of his or her input may have real value. For example, in one study (Jablin, Seibold, and Sorenson, 1977), researchers found that apprehensive group members produced fewer ideas during brainstorming than did non-apprehensives, but the quality of the ideas could not be used to demonstrate differences in the productivity of either group. If a manager is interested only in the number of times a person speaks in a group setting, then shy individuals will undoubtedly rank lower than other group members. However, if a manager or the evaluator of group performance also can be made aware of (1) the presence of "communication apprehensives" or shy people within the group, and (2) the quality of their performance, then perhaps the standard scales can be used more equitably.

Of course, this procedure should not be used to encourage shyness. If too much attention and favor are accorded to reticent group members, it is possible that other group members may feel they are unfairly treated and seek restitution from the shy ones. Another potential problem concerns marginal group members who may find a new excuse for not producing quality or quantity work for the group when they see how timid persons receive special attention. Such individuals should be encouraged to become more active participants in groups (Phillips, 1981); their lack of confidence or communication skills are handicaps that can be overcome. If the shy person appears so *only* in group settings, the difficulty may be related to unclear role expectations (Smith, 1957), feelings of rejection by other group members (Pepinsky, Hemphill, and Shevitz, 1958), or defensiveness about contributions they make to the group. The sensitive group leader or supervisor should be able to investigate these problem areas and make substantive recommendations for modification or change.

A second area concerning the relationship between communication style and group *Gender* evaluations is the gender of the communicator (see Baird, 1976, for a comprehensive review of research). The problem arising from this relationship again involves to our assumption of equality among all group members and the asexual nature of talk. Unfortunately, most research clearly indicates differences between women and men in their communication style, a conclusion that suggests the need to reassess how evaluations of style are used in group settings. For example, a great deal of work has been done in the area of leadership and sex. The traditional perspective on this research would reveal that men as leaders of groups are generally (1) *more confident* about leadership (Maier, 1970); (2) *more dominant* in their approach to leading (Megargee, 1969); (3) *more skilled* at problem-solving tasks in groups (Milton, 1954); (4) *more achievement-oriented* within small groups (Bennett and Cohen, 1959); and (5) *more task-oriented* in group work (Rosenfeld and Fowler, 1976). On the other hand, women are reported to be generally (1) *more accommodative* in their style of leading (Bond and Vinacke, 1961); (2) *more socio-emotionally-oriented* as leaders of groups (Heiss, 1962); and *perhaps more democratic in choice of leadership behaviors* because of the socio-emotional orientation (Fowler and Rosenfeld, 1979). In some cases the differences between men and women as leaders of small groups reported by research has been used to imply that men are more competent and effective as group leaders. However, care must be taken in interpreting this latter statement, since traditional male attitudes toward women in leadership positions tend to devalue their performance (Bass, Krussel, and Alexander, 1971; Spence and Helmreich, 1972; Schein, 1973; and Bormann, Pratt, and Putnam, 1978).

There are two major problems with the research concerning sex and leadership of small groups. First, the research conducted has not been correlated with differences in leadership theories or styles of communicating (Baird, 1976; Fowler and Rosenfeld, 1979; Stogdill, 1974). For example, the adaptive approach to leading might favor females who are able to perceive the socio-emotional climate of group members and make choices about communication behaviors appropriate to the situation. Although this style of leading would be highly valued, given the adaptive theoretical orientation, it would be less valuable in a situational, trait, styles, or path-goal theoretical framework. Second, research about sex differences in general tends to reify attitudes, values, and behavioral orientations that are in the process of evolution. By *reify* I mean they tend to create theoretical categories, then treat these categories as if they were actual facts or behavioral expressions (Goodall and Phillips, 1981). The result is a static, even rigid view of a process that is undergoing rapid, and in some places, radical change. By analogy, this reification of sex differences is very much like viewing events rather than the processes of group communication. To understand how sex differences may influence judgments about leadership or participation in groups requires a historical and humane treatment rather than the ahistorical abstract approach that social science literature typically provides. For example, although men have been found to be more achievement-oriented in group-settings than women, one reason may be that women have to be careful about being overly achievement-oriented because such orientation might place them in direct and unfavorable competition with men with whom they must work. Also, we really do not know very much about the categories we describe in such facile manner. How would you know "achievement-oriented" if you saw it? Would a woman have to say she was achievement-oriented to warrant inclusion? Finally, you must be very careful about applying generalized research findings to the individual case. As you can see by statements made by women and men in this text, many individual women who have overcome these potential barriers to succeed in their professional fields. I have also encountered males who have suffered because of their inability to change when change was demanded.

Communication style differences between reticent or communication apprehensive persons and less shy individuals, as well as between women and men within groups, tend to make us more aware of the need for evaluation programs which recognize these differences rather than ignore them. By making use of personal interviews, collective appraisals, and self-reports, managers, supervisors, and group personnel can better account for these differences.

Understanding the Special "Language" of the Group

When "outsiders" are used to evaluate groups they very often confront the same problem: they do not know what the group members mean when they interact. Consider how you might evaluate the following excerpt from a group discussion:

Jolene: I think we oughta scope 'em . . .
Bob: Yeah, maybe. But first we need to get some facts about what happened before—
(*Laughter from all group members*)
Jolene: Bob, do you remember—
Bob: (still laughing) Boy do I ever!
Alice: Don't we *all!*
(*More laughter*)

Unless the observer/evaluator understood the meaning shared by the group members, this episode in a discussion would be senseless. The average evaluator (assuming there is such a person) would probably perceive this episode as a side-track to the discussion, something a leader should have halted, redirecting the discussion to the topic of the session. However, in this instance, the group *was* on track in their discussion; they were recalling an unpleasant incident that occurred the last time Bob asked for the facts in a similar case. It was useful for the group to remember the experience to avoid making the same error again. What the group would have seen as relevant to its operation, an outsider would have regarded as a deterrent to effective interaction.

Think of a manager or supervisor as an "outsider." Typically, a manager delegates work to small groups, then reappears later to hear their final report. Because the manager does not witness the group development, it is unlikely that he or she will understand the private meanings shared by the group members. In Chapter 2 you explored the idea of a small group's culture and history. It is virtually impossible for an outsider to comprehend what a group has experienced without being able to share in the experience. For a manager to say to a group, "Look, tomorrow I'm going to come by and watch your group perform" is probably not a good way to generate ideas about how the group interacts.

The special language of a small group is an integral part of its relational development. Unfortunately, what is important to the group members may seem unimportant to an observer not acquainted with the history, culture, or language of the group. This impediment poses serious problems for managers who want to both *observe* and *evaluate* groups. The solution to the problem depends on the situation. For example, if the manager has a history of communication with the group, and knows the details of its operation, then observing and evaluating a group performance and quality can be useful. An "outsider" can see problems, or suggest remedies that the group can't see. On the other hand, if the manager is not familiar with a group and does not share an appreciation of their history and culture, then the attempt of this leader simply to observe their operation in order to evaluate their performance is likely to fail.

How to Seek "Inside" and "Outside" Evaluations of the Group

Evaluations are a necessary part of group processes, and a vital element in organizational effectiveness. To acknowledge one's inability to make an evaluation is not an acceptable alternative, despite the obvious flaws in any system of examining human behavior. What can be done, then, to make evaluations more equitable and effective?

In any organization valuing appraisal techniques there should be a way to formulate at least three kinds of evaluations of group work:

1. *Evaluations generated by the group members.* This evaluation should focus on the processes used by the group to reach its objectives, together with the individual contributions of each group member, including the leader. Evaluations made by group members are useful sources of information about what actually happens during group meetings; as such, they can serve as informative guides about sources of power, equity, task, and relational structures contributing to the group's outcomes.

Three Types of Group Evaluators

2. *Evaluations generated by the group leader.* These should focus on the comparative contributions of each group member, the strengths and weaknesses of the group's operation, and self-criticism about how well or poorly the leading was done. Evaluations generated by the group leader should be the subject of private meetings between the leader and each group member to review his or her performance during the period. In turn, the group member's evaluations of the leader should be included in the discussion, and encouraged by the group leader.

3. *Evaluations by the manager or supervisor to whom the group reports.* This evaluation should accomplish two interrelated objectives: (a) determine how effective and efficient the group was in working toward its objectives, and (b) provide information about perceptions regarding the group, its membership, its leader, its tasks. This evaluation should be used by the manager to review the work of each group member and leader.

Once these three sources of information are collected, the organizaton can encourage collective appraisals on the part of group members, leader, and perhaps also the departmental manager or supervisor. During this meeting any problems which have arisen would be resolved to help improve the group's performance during the next reporting period.

All evaluations are documentations of the group's performance and behavior. As such, they are sources of information about the group and are the basis or evidence upon which evaluations can be made. It is a critical function of any group to make certain that all evaluations are as accurate as they can be.

Disruptions of the Group and Evaluation

In this section you have seen a variety of problems that can affect the quality of any evaluation. One problem you have not yet reviewed is the individual who disrupts the group. This may be the person who prevents the others from suffering "groupthink" or it may be an individual who consistently tries to prevent the group from accomplishing its task. The essential question for you to ask concerns the nature of the disruption, and how the disruption affects the group's ability to accomplish the task.

Leathers (1969; 1972) investigated how disruptions of the group process influence evaluations of the group's task, the quality of communication, and the ability to reach goals. Disruption does indeed seem to influence perceptions of the quality of communication within a group and hence may be used to evaluate the group members negatively and to reduce the ability of groups to accomplish goals. Accordingly, the nature of the disruption must be discovered if there is to be a productive assessment of the group. Here are some guidelines:

1. *Review the individual's self-report about group work in relation to the evaluations given the disruptive member by other group members.* If the individual cites the group's tendency toward premature consensus, "groupthink," or a tendency to rush work unnecessarily, and if there seems to be corroborating evidence to this effect in other statements made by group members, then the disruptive individual may have been trying to help the group rather than hinder it.

2. *Check for references to the disruptive individual's personality in assessments made by other group members.* Alderton (1980) found that personality becomes a critical factor in attributing blame for disruption when more tangible forms of evidence are unavailable. The disruptor may be characterized as having "a poor attitude" or "a negative attitude" or "a miserable personality," instead of stating the nature of the disruptive behavior (e.g., "criticizing other's work," or "escalating conflict unnecessarily," or perhaps "not completing assigned work on time"). If personality assessments are being made, try to look for more and better evidence about specific disruptive behaviors. If none is cited, then you may become more suspicious of the negative assessment given to the disruptive individual.

3. *Try to find out how the group has attempted to "punish" the disruptive person.* From your study of Equity Theory you know that group members strive to retaliate or seek restitution for injuries received during group work. If possible, find out how the disruptive individual was dealt with (or not dealt with) by group members. If no punishment was meted out by the group for disruptive acts, retaliation will probably be sought at evaluation time. Alderton (1980) also found that group members tend to increase their attribution of personal responsibility for disruption. You might infer that if personal responsibility is being attributed for wrongdoing at appraisal time, the group may have refrained from exercising its collective responsibility for meting out appropriate punishment within the group.

Guidelines for Dealing with Disruptive Individuals

You will observe that isolated incidents often distort group members' perceptions at appraisal time. A single disruption caused by a person can be blown out of proportion; a person who performed well until the last few days may nevertheless receive a negative group evaluation because the recent past is clearer than previous time spent together. There are many sources of disruption within groups. It is wise to look for information about how the disruption evolved before concluding that you have a problem person within a group. However, if your investigation confirms the group evaluations, then some authority in the organization should be asked to intervene for the protection of the group. Personal revenge may be sweet, but it is usually ineffective unless it is carried out by someone with the authority to make productive changes.

Summary

This chapter addressed the issues involved in observing and evaluating group interactions. It began with the assumption that nobody likes to be evaluated by others, especially when those evaluations become the justification for raises and promotions. My second assumption was that observing and evaluating human behavior is a complex task. Both of these assumptions lead me to conclude that one reason why organizations typically rely on quantifiable measurements of group behavior and performance is because they are simpler to use than other forms of evaluation.

I define evaluation of group performance and behavior as a *critical* act. We perform criticism when we establish standards and apply them to a group to make judgments of good and bad, right and wrong, appropriateness and inappropriateness, in appraising their methods, tasks, responsibilities, and communication. The goal of all effective criticism is to be productive, that is, to provide sound advice about how to improve future behavior and performance. To accomplish this goal, a critical evaluation should (1) state the standards used to make the evaluation; (2) make evaluations of both positive and negative aspects of the group; and (3) explain how the group can merit improvement of their collective and individual evaluations next time.

You then investigated the various standards used to evaluate groups. I defined six basic areas for group critiques: (1) the purpose of the group, (2) the level of participation by each member, (3) the effectiveness of the leader, (4) the characteristics associated with adequate or satisfactory performance by the group, (5) a description of exactly how well the group is meeting the objectives, and (6) a statement of how performance can be improved by the group. You examined some of the standards used to evaluate communication by group members. You learned that the appropriateness of speech and the ability of the individuals to adapt their language to the needs and expectations of the situation and group members are important general qualities in any assessment of a group's communication skills. However, most organizations use more precise tools for assessing the worth of verbal intercourse. You reviewed three standards used to evaluate communication by groups: (1) categorical questionnaires emphasizing evaluation (e.g., Bales); (2) general questionnaires stressing specific communication behaviors (e.g., LaForge, Hemphill, and Speroff); and (3) informal interviews and self-reports of communication.

Next you reviewed the tools of observing small groups. I discussed the comparative strengths and weaknesses of rating and ranking scales, providing an extensive list of types and examples. I believe these instruments for observing small groups have only limited value unless they are used by the group members. It is unreasonable to expect a manager to be able to observe a group session if he is limited to using any one of these tools.

Our next task was to review the tools of evaluation available to members and leaders of small groups. You examined three types of evaluative methods: (1) interviews, (2) self-reports, and (3) collective appraisals. I discussed the strengths and weaknesses of each method, and recommended consideration of collective appraisals for organizations and groups concerned about improving their behavior and performance.

Finally, I discussed some of the major problems associated with observing and evaluating groups. I reviewed the problems of (1) reluctance to evaluate behavior and performance, (2) lack of training in evaluative techniques, and (3) lack of understanding of what to evaluate when examining group behavior and performance. I then discussed solutions to these problems, including specific suggestions about (1) how to balance what is emphasized in evaluations; (2) how to avoid evaluations of personalities as such, by focusing on specific behaviors; (3) how to account for differences in communication style; (4) how to deal with the special language, history, culture, and disruptions of a group by asking them to participate directly in the evaluations.

There is no one "best" solution to the issues surrounding effective and equitable performance evaluations. Every organization will devise its own system for conducting reviews of behavior and performance. If predictions about the future of American business practices are accurate, you may expect group members and managers to move toward more collective appraisals. Only by gaining different perspectives on the behavior and performance of the group can you expect to provide reasonable advice and programs for improving productivity and quality. For this reason I recommend obtaining information about groups from at least three sources: members of the group, the leader of the group, and the person to whom the group is ultimately responsible.

References

Alderton, S. "Attributions of Responsibility for Socially Deviant Behavior in Decision-Making Discussions as a Function of Situation and Locus of Control of Attributor." *Central States Speech Journal* 31 (1980):117–27.

Asherman, I. G., and S. L. Vance. "Documentation: A Tool for Effective Management." *Personnel Journal* (1981):641–43.

Baird, J. E., and S. B. Weinberg. *Group Communication: The Essence of Synergy,* 2d ed. Dubuque, Ia.: Wm. C. Brown Company Publishers, 1981.

Baird, J. E., Jr. "Sex Differences in Group Communication: A Review of Relevant Research." *Quarterly Journal of Speech* 62 (1976):179–92.

Bales, R. F. *Interaction Process Analysis: A Method for the Study of Small Groups.* Reading, Mass.: Addison-Wesley, 1950.

Bales, R. F. *Personality and Interpersonal Behavior.* New York: Holt, Rinehart, and Winston, 1970.

Bales, R. F., and S. Cohen. *SYMLOG.* New York: Free Press, 1979.

Bass, B., J. Krussel, and R. Alexander. "Male Managers' Attitudes Toward Working Women." *American Behavioral Scientist* 15 (1971):231–36.

Bennett, E., and L. Cohen. "Men and Women: Personality Patterns and Contrasts." *Genetic Psychology Monographs* 59 (1959):101–55.

Bond, J., and E. Vinacke. "Coalitions in Mixed Sex Triads." *Sociometry* 24 (1961):61–75.

Bormann, E. G., J. Pratt, and L. Putnam. "Power, Authority, and Sex: Male Responses to Female Leadership." *Communication Monographs* 45 (1978):119–55.

Bormann, E. G. "The Paradox and Promise of Small Group Research Revisited." *Central States Speech Journal* 31 (1980):214–20.

Burgoon, J. K., and M. Burgoon. "Unwillingness to Communicate, Anomia-Alienation, and Communication Apprehension as Predictors of Small Group Communication." *Journal of Psychology* 88 (1974):31–38.

Burgoon, J. K. "Unwillingness to Communicate as a Predictor of Small Group Discussion Behaviors and Evaluations." *Central States Speech Journal* 28 (1977):122–34.

Cragan, J. F., and D. W. Wright. "Small Group Communication Research in the 1970s: A Synthesis and Critique." *Central States Speech Journal* 31 (1980):199–212.

Delia, J. G. "A Constructivist Analysis of the Concept of Credibility." *Quarterly Journal of Speech* 62 (1976):361–75.

Dertien, M. G. "The Accuracy of Job Evaluation Plans." *Personnel Journal* (1981):566–70.

Ehninger, D. *Influence, Belief, and Argument: An Introduction to Responsible Persuasion.* Glenview, Ill.: Scott, Foresman, and Co., 1974.

Faules, D. "The Use of Multi-Methods in the Organizational Setting." *Western Journal of Speech Communication* 46 (1982):150–61.

Fowler, G. D., and L. B. Rosenfeld. "Sex Differences and Democratic Leadership Behavior." *Southern Speech Communication Journal* 45 (1979):69–78.

Friedman, P. G. *Interpersonal Communication: Innovations in Instruction.* Washington, D.C.: National Education Association, 1978.

Gaylin, W. *Feelings: Our Vital Signs.* New York: Harper & Row, 1979.

Goldman, B. *Group Cohesiveness: A Study of Group Morale: Manual of Instructions.* Chicago: Psychometric Affiliates, 1958.

Goldhaber, G. *Organizational Communication,* 4th ed. Dubuque, Ia.: Wm. C. Brown Company Publishers, 1985.

Goodall, H. L., Jr., and Gerald M. Phillips. "Assumption of the Burden: Science or Criticism?" *Communication Quarterly* 29 (1981):282–96.

Goodall, H. L., Jr., G. L. Wilson, and C. L. Waagen. "The Performance Appraisal Interview: An Interpretive Reassessment." *Quarterly Journal of Speech* 72 (1986):74–87.

Hawes, L. C. "Toward a Hermeneutic Philosophy of Communication." *Communication Quarterly* 25 (1977):30–41.

Hemphill, J. *Group Dimensions: A Manual for Their Measurement.* Columbus, Oh.: Bureau of Business Research, Ohio State University, 1956.

Heiss, J. "Degree of Intimacy and Male-Female Interaction." *Sociometry* 25 (1962):197–208.

Hirokawa, R. Y. "Group Communication and Problem-Solving Effectiveness 1: A Critical Review of Inconsistent Findings. *Communication Quarterly* 30 (1982):134–41.

Jablin, F. M., D. R. Seibold, and R. L. Sorenson. "Potential Inhibitory Effects of Group Participation on Brainstorming Performance." *Central States Speech Journal* 28 (1977):113–21.

Jick, T. O. "Mixing Qualitative and Quantitative Methods: Triangulation in Action." *Administrative Science Quarterly* 24 (1979):602–9.

Kwant, R. *Critique: Its Nature and Function.* Pittsburgh: Duquesne University Press, 1967.

LaForge, R. *Research Use of the ICL.* Eugene, Or.: Oregon Research Institute, 1963.

Leathers, D. G. "Process Disruption and Measurement in Small Group Communication." *Quarterly Journal of Speech* 54 (1969):287–300.

Leathers, D. G. "Quality of Group Communication as a Determinant of Group Product." *Speech Monographs* 39 (1972):166–73.

Maier, N. "Male versus Female Discussion Leaders." *Personnel Psychology* 23 (1970):455–61.

McBurney, J. H., and K. G. Hance, *The Principles and Methods of Discussion.* New York: Harper Brothers, 1936.

McKinney, B. C. "The Effects of Reticence on Group Interaction." *Communication Quarterly* 30 (1982):124–28.

Megargee, E. "Influence of Sex Roles on the Manifestation of Leadership." *Journal of Applied Psychology* 53 (1969):377–82.

Milton, G. A. "Sex Differences in Problem Solving as a Function of Role Appropriateness of the Problem Content." *Psychological Reports* 5 (1954):705–8.

Moravec, M. "How Performance Appraisal Can Tie Communication to Productivity." *Personnel Administrator* (1981):51–54.

O'Connell, S. E. *The Manager as Communicator.* New York: Harper & Row, 1979.

Ogilview, J. *Many Dimensional Man.* New York: Oxford University Press, 1977.

Ouchi, W. *Theory Z: How American Business Can Meet the Japanese Challenge.* Reading, Mass.: Addison-Wesley, 1981.

Pepinsky, P. N., J. K. Hemphill, and R. N. Shevitz. "Attempts to Lead, Group Productivity, and Morale Under Conditions of Acceptance and Rejection." *Journal of Abnormal and Social Psychology* 57 (1958):47–54.

Phillips, G. M., D. J. Pedersen, and J. J. Wood. *Group Discussion.* Boston: Houghton Mifflin, 1979.

Phillips, G. M. *Help for Shy People and Anyone Else Who Ever Felt Ill at Ease Upon Entering a Room Full of Strangers.* Englewood Cliffs, N.J.: Spectrum Books, 1981.

Pierce, W. B. "Naturalistic Study of Communication: Its Form and Function." *Communication Quarterly* 25 (1977):51–56.

Putnam, L. L. "Paradigms for Organizational Communication Research: An Overview and Synthesis." *Western Journal of Speech Communication* 46 (1982):192–206.

Rosenfeld, L. B., and G. D. Fowler. "Personality, Sex, and Leadership Style, *Communication Monographs* 43 (1976):320–24.

Schein, V. "The Relationship Between Sex Role Stereotypes and Requisite Manager Characteristics." *Journal of Applied Psychology* 57 (1973):95–100.

Seashore, S. *Group Cohesiveness in the Industrial Work Group.* Ann Arbor, Mi: University of Michigan Institute for Social Research, 1954.

Smith, E. E. "The Effects of Clear and Unclear Role Expectations on Group Productivity and Defensiveness." *Journal of Abnormal and Social Psychology* 55 (1957):213–17.

Spence, J., and R. Helmreich. "Who Likes Competent Women? Competence, Sex-Role Congruence of Interests, and Subjects Attitudes Toward Women as Determinants of Interpersonal Attraction." *Journal of Applied Psychology* 2 (1972):197–212.

Speroff, B. *Conference Meeting Rating Scale: Manual of Instructions.* Chicago: Psychometric Affiliates, 1959.

Stogdill, R. *Handbook of Leadership: A Survey of Theory and Research.* New York: Free Press, 1974.

Yager, E. "A Critique of Performance Appraisal Systems." *Personnel Journal* (1981):129–33.

To understand how complicated the evaluation of human groups can be usually requires some direct experience with the construction of a group communication evaluation procedure. The following two exercises ask you to accomplish this task making use of the material covered in this chapter. Remember, the point of the exercises is *not* simply to choose one of the evaluation forms found in the text, but rather to construct your own, original evaluation procedure, including any questionnaires necessary.

1. Assemble your small group. The leader should announce that the purpose of this meeting is to determine the most appropriate procedure for evaluating the communication of *your* small group. Your discussion should accomplish two primary objectives: (a) determine what criteria you should use to develop an assessment procedure, and (b) state the actual contents of the assessment instrument(s).
2. When all in-class groups complete their assessment instruments, hold a general discussion session about them. Focus your comments on: (a) the goals of the assessment procedure, (b) the relative merits of the instruments, (c) the rationale behind selection of the items/contents of the instruments, and (d) ways and means to improve the instruments.

Optional Exercise: At the instructor's discretion, you may decide to use the best evaluation procedure (determined by class consensus) to assess the performance of the in-class small groups and the individuals within them.

How to Use the Skills You've Learned 11

Introduction

The use of small groups in modern organizations is widespread and varied. What you have learned about small group decision-making and problem-solving should be of special value in your search for suitable employment. Most recruiters are interested in candidates with strong communication skills and a background in organizational theory and behavior. If these skills are combined with academic preparation in accounting or finance, you will find that many private and public firms will be interested in employing you. If these skills are associated with preparation in marketing or management, you may possess valuable qualifications for an entry-level position. If these skills are combined with academic credentials in business administration or public relations, you may have more and better options for promising employment than have your peers who do not have training in small group communication.

Unfortunately, most individuals who do possess these special skills do not know how to talk about them in the selection interview, nor are they sufficiently confident about them to know how to discuss their uses with superiors on the job. This chapter addresses the question: "How can I make productive uses of these small group communication skills in the real world?" First, I will discuss how and when to talk about these skills during the interview. Second, I will explore opportunities for using communication skills on the job and how recommendations about the uses of small groups may be productively made by employees. Third, I will discuss the future of organizational small group activities. Following the chapter summary and references I will recommend some ways to practice talking about your small group communication skills to improve your skill in using them.

How to Talk about Small Group Skills When Job-Hunting

The selection interview is a unique *rhetorical* situation (Goodall and Goodall, 1982). For the interviewer the employment interview setting provides initial contact with the candidate. During the time spent together, the interviewer must ascertain which of the candidates best fits the criteria established for the position by carefully receiving, classifying, and responding to statements and questions; the interviewer must then attribute significance to the candidates' verbal and nonverbal behavior, i.e., interpret his/her conduct. The interviewer must also present a positive self-image and image of the organization, and respond to numerous questions and doubts concerning the position, salary, benefits, chances for promotion, and working conditions. The employment interviewer, and especially the campus recruiter, does not have an easy assignment. However, research consistently indicates that recruiters tend to look for the same types of characteristics in successful applicants, regardless of the position applied for. For example, Posner (1981) found that communication ability, future potential to do well in the position, and maturity (usually defined as previous work experience and a confident, but not aggressive or egotistical, attitude toward the interview) were the three most important characteristics of employability as defined by recruiters/interviewers.

For the candidate, the selection interview provides an opportunity to *persuade* the company representative of his or her ability and fitness for the advertised position. In the space of perhaps only fifteen minutes (Downs, 1969), the person being interviewed will be asked to discuss his or her past educational and vocational training, personal history, skills and abilities, goals and career aspirations, strengths and weaknesses of character, memorable classroom activities or experiences, potential to develop good interpersonal relations with co-workers, as well as preferred salary and benefits. For most people with little training or background in being interviewed for a position, the first few interviews may best be described as confusing and unsettling. There seems to be so much going on in so short a period of time! How do you answer questions about your past? About your goals and career aspirations? About your skills and abilities? How do you know what the recruiter is looking for? What "flags" might be revealed in your speech to turn off the recruiter? How can you prepare for the questions?

I believe there are approaches to the selection interview which can enhance your opportunities for obtaining the position. Although specific instructions such as how to write a resumé, how to compose a cover letter, how to interact with a recruiter are difficult to provide because of the diversity of individual responses to employment opportunities and criteria for selection, there are some general statements which can be made about effective employment interviewing (see Einhorn, Bradley, and Baird, 1982). Since my concern is primarily with how to talk about your small group skills in the interview, I will use this skill area as a focal point in the discussion. However, the information I provide about preparing for and interacting in selection interviews can be construed more broadly as a set of advisory statements that can guide your applying for virtually any post-graduate position associated with organizational life.

The resumé is a very important professional document. What it reveals about an applicant (and what it does *not* reveal) largely determines what the recruiter or interviewer will look for during the interview. Poorly constructed resumés, resumés with spelling and/or grammatical mistakes, with inadequate information, those that present a substandard appearance, all contribute to negative impressions about the *candidate*. Recruiters seldom say "this is a poorly written resumé," instead, they use the resumé as a source of empirical information about you as a person: "How could we possibly hire someone with a resumé like this?" Inferences they make about you, as a person, are based on what the resumé looks like and expresses about you.

Consequently, it is important to compose an abstract of your education and experience that can arouse enough interest in the reader so that he or she will seek further contact with you. How may this goal be attained? There is no one "good and true" resumé format. Although most colleges and universities encourage graduating seniors to limit their resumés to one page, this rule may be productively altered by individuals who have extensive work experience related to the position. While most organizations claim to use the resumé only as an index of the candidate's educational and vocational background, experience reveals that organizations are also impressed by the layout or format of the resumé, the way words are used to describe work and educational experiences, and other supplementary information.

Begin thinking about your resumé by using the following questions to guide your choice of format:

1. Are you a person possessing good educational qualifications but limited work experiences related to the position applied for? If so, the resumé format in Table 11.1 may be appropriate for you.
2. Are you a person possessing a strong vocational or experiential background in areas related to the desired position? If you have worked for five or more years and are currently in college or about to graduate, you may be interested in the resumé format presented in Table 11.2.
3. Are you a person with a mediocre college/university academic record, possessing equally limited work experiences related to the position applied for, but want the reader to know your skills and abilities? If so, the resumé format in Table 11.3 may be appropriate for you.
4. Are you a person who combines a strong educational background with an extensive background of work experiences interested in revealing these characteristics as well as a creative ability? If this description fits you, then examine carefully the resumé format in Table 11.4.

Table 11.1

Resumé

TERESA LEE D'URBERVILLE

Home Address:

2460 Technology Drive
Huntsville, AL 35805
(205)–555–7777
Birthdate: 4/22/65

Business Address:

14 Main Street
Huntsville, AL 35898
(205)–555–3333
Health: Excellent

EDUCATION

1985—Present

The University of Alabama in Huntsville School
of Administrative Science
Major: Management   Minor: Communication
Degree Sought: B.S.B.A. (May, 1989)
GPA: 2.5 (3.0 scale)

Successfully completed all major coursework in management with special work in communication skills (interviewing, interpersonal, and small group communication). President, Administrative Science Honor Society, 1989. Elected representative in Student Government Association, 1988–89. Staff writer, *The Exponent* (student newspaper).

1983–85

Von Braun Community College
Huntsville, AL 35801
General Studies/Non-Degree

Completed coursework in freshman level composition, history, and art appreciation. Dean's List both terms.

EXPERIENCE

1987—Present

Redstone Arsenal (U.S. Army Missile Command)
Huntsville, AL 35877
Job title: Student Co-op worker

Responsibilities include assisting the directorate in procurement of supplies relating to the MX missile project. Use training in BASIC and FORTRAN computer languages to assist with programming and indexing supplies; assisted in the development of monthly reports; used PERT to analyze problems and recommend solutions.

1984–85

The Best Little Burger in 'Bama
1212 S. Parkway
Huntsville, AL 35600
Job title: Counter clerk

Responsibilities included operating and maintaining counter, processing customer orders quickly and efficiently, and making change. Resigned to attend college full-time.

REFERENCES

Dr. Daniel Sherman
Prof. of Management
Univ. of Alabama in
Huntsville
Huntsville, AL 35899

Ms. Lois Hunnicutt
Procurement Director
Redstone Arsenal
Huntsville, AL 35877

Dr. C. L. Waggen
Asst. Prof. in
Communication Arts
Univ. of Alabama in
Huntsville
Huntsville, Al 35899

Table 11.2

RESUMÉ

Joseph Jeffrey Jacobs
1144 Cottonwood Drive
Huntsville, AL 35808
Phone: (205) 555–8998

I am seeking a position as a research assistant or laboratory technician in a university or hospital facility. I am prepared to take an entry-level position if advancement is possible.

Education

Pennsylvania State University University Park, PA 16802 B.S. conferred 5/88 (cum laude)	Major: Chemistry Minor: Mathematics Activities: President, Chemistry Club; Member, Johnson Research Center Internship Program (1987–88)
Edgar K. See High School 2001 Vision Road Martinsburg, WVA 25401 Graduation: 6/84	Major subjects: Chemistry, biology, math Activities: Varsity track, senior class vice-president

Work Experience

Pressure Medical Laboratories 900 Red Run Road Huntsville, AL 35802 Supervisor: Sara Brooks Employed: 7/85–9/87	I performed blood series analyses, steroid tests, and liver functions. I supervised three technicians. Resigned to devote more time to my studies.
Huntsville Hospital 101 Sivley Road, S.W. Huntsville, AL 35801 Supervisor: Art Edison Employed: 10/83–6/85	I worked as a student volunteer in the medical laboratory. Major duties included filing blood and urine samples. Resigned to seek a salaried position.

Skills: I can perform virtually all laboratory analysis tests. I have supervisory experience and can evaluate technician performance using quality control techniques. I can type 55 w.p.m. and have minimal bookkeeping background.

Personal Reference:	Winston Salem, M.D. 101 Richland Heights Huntsville, AL 35809	Work Reference:	Evita Perone, M.D. Pressure Medical Laboratories 900 Red Run Road Huntsville, Al 35802
School References:	Professor Gardenia Valentine Chemistry Department Univ. of Alabama in Huntsville Huntsville, AL 35899		Professor Lewis Lanelle Mathematics Department Univ. of Alabama in Huntsville Huntsville, AL 35899

Additional references available on request.

Table 11.3

L. Dianne Choosy
734 Regulation Drive
Huntsville, AL 35802
(205) 555-5114

EDUCATION	The University of Alabama in Huntsville
	Expected date of graduation—1990
	Major: Business-Marketing
	GPA: 2.18 (3.0)
JOB TARGET:	In areas related to quality control.
CAPABILITIES:	*Twelve years experience working for professionals.
	*Ability to work without supervision.
	*Composure under deadline stress.
	*Maintain accurate and detailed records.
	*Carry out complicated instruction and tests.
	*Ability to work long hours.
	*Write detailed reports.
	*Type and file accurately.
ACHIEVEMENTS:	*Attend college full-time while working 24–30 hours per week.
	*Maintain B-average in major.
	*Successfully handle parenting and household responsibilities while working and/or attending college.
WORK HISTORY: 1987 (Jan.)–1990 (May)	The Veterinary Dispensary
	Huntsville, Alabama
	Retail sales work.
	Maintain inventory.
	Educate customers about products and surgery.
1976–1986	Highland Veterinary Hospital
	Johnstown, Pennsylvania
	Surgical technician.
	Maintained surgical records.
	Prepared samples of laboratory tests.
	Ordered all drugs and supplies.
	Maintained inventory.
	Was responsible for operating room sterility.
	Gave surgical quotes and information by telephone.
1974–1976	Gulf Research and Development Co.
	Harrisburg, Pennsylvania
	Geology technician.
	Prepared laboratory samples.
	Read microscopic samples.
	Worked mathematical formulas on Wang Calculator.
	Kept accurate records.
	Keypunched.

References available on request.

Table 11.4

RESUMÉ
of
MARY CONTRARY
1066 Norman Drive
Salt Lake City, UT 84100
(801) 555-8818

Job Objective	Position as COBOL applications programmer in Huntsville area that would expand on current experience and education.
Experience 1984 to present	THE UNIVERSITY OF UTAH Computer Services—Data Processing. Responsible for maintaining daily, monthly and annual accounting records; coordinating with users; maintaining existing programs and producing new ones as required. Originally hired as Data Processing Assistant, promoted to Programmer/Analyst January 1981.
1973 to 1982	Bookkeeping, accounting and budgeting positions in both civilian and government service, stateside and in Europe. Adapted to various job environments, earning progressively responsible, mid-level positions.
Education	THE UNIVERSITY OF UTAH Continuing classes in Computer Science. To date have earned 15 hours (9 hours COBOL) with a QPA of 3.0.
Other	Secret clearance granted while employed by Headquarters of U.S. Army Military Intelligence in Europe.
Personal	Excellent health.
References	Furnished upon request.

These formats represent four possible alternative ways of constructing a resumé. You may want to combine desirable features of two or more formats to construct a document capable of providing the best information about you. Remember, the four formats presented in this section represent *possible* ways of writing a resumé; you may find other methods of representing your background equally capable of inducing a favorable hiring decision.

Regardless of the format chosen, a resumé should contain the following information:

1. Your full name, address, and phone number(s).
2. Your educational background, beginning with the most recent and proceeding in reverse chronological order. If degrees were granted, give dates. It is also helpful to list your major/minor fields and grade point average (if "B" or above).
3. Your work experiences, beginning with the most recent and proceeding in reverse chronological order. Give job titles and descriptions of responsibilities if relevant to position applied for.
4. Your skills, special training, or abilities relevant to the position applied for. Here are some examples:
   —typing, filing, maintaining an office
   —bookkeeping or any specialized form of record keeping
   —writing and speaking well
   —leadership (as demonstrated by offices held, responsibilities carried out, honors and awards)
   —operation of any office machines (such as keypunch, memory typewriter, any computer competencies and languages, adding machines, calculators, etc.)
   —*Small Group Communication Skills* including ability to develop and carry out agendas for meetings, use of Standard Agenda, PERT, etc., for decision-making or problem-solving groups, conflict resolution skills, negotiation abilities, presentational speaking and writing skills, especially proposals and reports.
5. Names of people who can attest to your competencies and personal character. (*References upon request* is adequate if the individuals chosen are not well-known in the community or by the organization, or if you maintain several different lists of references for different kinds of positions). These names must include *professional* titles and addresses, and should be drawn from the following categories:
   —someone who is familiar with your educational background (your advisor in your major field, the chairman of your department, etc.)
   —someone who is well acquainted with your work experiences (your most recent employer or supervisor)
   —someone who knows your character, personal strengths and weaknesses, potential to succeed (your rabbi, minister, or priest, a community leader, a civic organization leader, a friend or neighbor who may be well-known in the applicant's profession).
   Note: *Never* list the names of people until you have spoken to them about their interest in recommending you for a job.

I recommend writing a resumé for each position applied for because you will be able to adapt the *format, word choices,* and *references* to the unique demands of each job. After you have composed the final draft of your resumé format, have someone else read it for clarity, appeal, and grammatical and spelling accuracy.

After the resumé satisfies you and your reviewer, have it professionally printed or copied on 25% cotton bond paper. Consider having the printer use buff or beige colored paper and black ink. Most printers are familiar with this procedure for resumés and will be glad to help you. Their fees are nominal (slightly more expensive than traditional Xeroxing) and well worth the price. However, avoid the temptation to use any other color of paper than white, buff, or beige. Use only black or blue ink. There are other options available, but they draw attention to themselves for what seem to be the wrong reasons. The final step in composing your resumé is to staple the upper left-hand corner of the document (if two or more pages are used) and to begin writing the cover letter.

The cover letter must be adapted to the particular job for which you are applying. For this reason you may need a different cover letter for each resumé you submit, although most people find that one or two standard forms for cover letters can be modified slightly to meet this requirement.

Writing the Cover Letter

Remember: the cover letter is a source of information about you, and equally important, about *why* you are applying for this particular position. Hence, the cover letter should be written in such a way as to direct attention to (1) the resumé, where details about you are provided, and to (2) yourself as a person worth further consideration for the position. Cover letters should not be flashy nor boring, but should strive to convey precise information to reader, information which is capable of inducing favorable judgments about you.

Consider the following example (see Table 11.5).

The letter is divided into three sections. The first section states the purpose of the letter and directs attention to the enclosed resumé. The second section provides a brief summary of why the person is applying for the job, and what qualifications she or he brings to the position. In most cases the best advice about writing this section of the cover letter is to *conform to the job description* as it appeared in the announcement, newspaper, or on the bulletin board. Be sure to use the words in the job announcement when stating your qualifications. Refrain from telling the reader what a wonderful, warm, sensitive, intelligent individual you are. Avoid explaining the details of your resumé (you want the reader to peruse it after reading the letter). Avoid the pitfalls of ego, either concerning you, your college or university, or your unique skills (for example, do not write "As you know, Jagger College is considered the Harvard of Mid-America, and its program in organizational behavior is perhaps the best in the land . . ."). Everyone should have some reason to be proud of his or her education, but the interviewer is not hiring the institution's reputation; the interviewer is interested in hiring *you*. The third section of the cover letter should be a statement about your availability for an interview, when and where you can be contacted, and a brief final appeal to your interest in the position. *That's all.* Do not beg, plead, threaten, or cajole the reader. Do not belabor why you are a suitable person for the position. Finally, you must *sign* the cover letter.

Table 11.5   Cover Letter

May 1, 1989

John Eichelburger
Personnel Manager
Huntsville Hospital
101 Sivley Road, S.W.
Huntsville, AL 35801

Dear Mr. Eichelburger,

Please consider this letter formal application for your advertised position as a medical technologist. I have enclosed my resumé for your inspection.

I have had experience in all areas of laboratory analysis relevant to your job description as listed in *The Huntsville Times*. I will graduate from The University of Alabama in Huntsville at the end of this month, and will be available to begin work immediately. I have contacted my references and they will be happy to provide you with any information regarding my qualifications and potential to perform on the job. Because of my familiarity with the work done at Huntsville Hospital, and my training to perform blood analysis, I feel that I am especially qualified for your position.

I will be available for a personal interview at your convenience. Should you require any additional information, please call me and I will be happy to provide you with it.

Thank you for your time and cooperation. I look forward to hearing from you in the near future.

Cordially,

Joseph J. Jacobs

Joseph J. Jacobs
1144 Cottonwood Drive
Huntsville, AL 35808
Phone: 555–8998

JJ:hs
enclosed resumé

The cover letter is less flexible than a resumé format. Although there may be some acceptable, even preferable alternatives to the way information is presented, most cover letters are considered introductions to the resumé and to the individual applying for the job. They are not exercises in creative writing, self-promotion, or biography. Keep the covering letter simple and to the point; most readers will appreciate this. After writing the final draft of your cover letter, it is a good idea to have someone else read it for any errors. When both of you are satisfied, clip the cover letter to the resumé, and place both in an envelope. Use a $11\frac{1}{2} \times 14''$ manila envelope to avoid folding the letter and resumé, thus preserving its appearance.

Research concerning methods of preparation for selection interviews consistently indicates the need (1) to rehearse answers to standard questions, (2) to consider the effect of your physical appearance and style of dress, and (3) to be confident enough to present a calm, courteous demeanor (see Einhorn, Bradley, and Baird, 1982; Stewart and Cash, 1982; Downs, Smeyak, and Martin, 1981; Moffat, 1979; and Hollandsworth, Dressel, and Stevens, 1977). Let's explore each one of these important areas.

Preparing for the Selection Interview

Everyone agrees that *what an applicant chooses to say and do in the interview* constitutes the most important element contributing to a favorable selection decision (Posner, 1981; Hollandsworth, et al., 1979; and many others). Therefore, authorities on selection interviewing recommend thinking through the questions you may be asked by an interviewer, and preparing answers for them. Although this may seem like a rigid way to prepare for a flexible situation, it may be the best advice I can provide about successful preparation for selection interviews. There are five questions that typically are asked in selection interviews; to these you should prepare careful and precise answers:

Verbal Aspects of the Interview

1. *Tell me about yourself.* This may be the most dangerous question asked during the interview. Your response to this reveals a great deal about where you have come from, who you are, what you are interested in, and the degree of verbal fluency you possess. Answers to this question usually leads to further probes and follow-up questions, so be careful about what you decide to say. Avoid personalizing your biography. Avoid unnecessary self-disclosures. Avoid recommending yourself too highly. Try to confine your answers to a 30–45 second brief recitation of the main *themes* of your educational and personal history. For example:

Ann A., 21 That's an interesting question. I have always considered myself to be a flexible person. As you know from my resumé, I now live in Huntsville. However, I grew up in a career-military family, and spent about two years each in Japan, Germany, France, Great Britain, California, and Texas before we settled in Huntsville. Living in those diverse places has given me an appreciation of people's differences and the need to adapt communication to their needs, backgrounds, and expectations. In my studies of management I have consistently stressed the importance of communication skills, so that's why you see a minor in organizational communication and courses in small group communication, public speaking, interpersonal communication, and technical writing on my resumé. I think my emphasis on effective communication has increased my management potential because I approach decision-making from a contingency perspective, and like to receive input to the process from people with expertise and experience in the area. So, my emphasis on communication should make me a better manager because I am less rigid, more open to suggestions, and more able to see the relationships between people and goals.

2. *How has your education contributed to your ability to perform this job?* This is a tricky question to answer for a number of reasons. First, most college students tend to assume too much knowledge of their particular curriculums on the part of the interviewer. For example, they may say, "Well, I have completed CM 113, BS 412, CS 222, and AS 450" in response to a question about their educational training in management. Chances are the recruiter/interviewer will have no idea what the course numbers mean. Whenever possible, use straight-forward language to respond to questions. Second, most college students value their college education and the training it has given them. Recruiters are much less impressed by the fact that you have completed a major in Business Administration than you are. Probably every person they talk to will have completed the same major, so what makes you any different from them? Whenever possible, *talk about specific experiences* that have contributed to your understanding of organizational life and responsibilities. For example:

James W., 22 In my marketing class we were responsible for completing a demographic study of a region to promote a new product and design appropriate advertising strategies. I learned how to design questionnaires, interview people, use quantitative methods of assessing the market, and make recommendations about advertising and marketing procedures.

In most cases interviewers will be impressed by the *skills* you have mentioned. They do not care that you have completed a marketing course; they do care *what you are able to do* as a result of completing the marketing course. The same logic applies when discussing your communication skills. It is not productive simply to say you have completed a small groups course; it is much more productive to cite the specific skills you developed, such as the ability to use an agenda to run a group meeting, proficiency in the use of Standard Agenda and PERT to organize problem-solving and decision-making groups, skill in selecting group members according to their expertise and experience, ability to resolve interpersonal disputes among group members, how to gain input from shy or reticent speakers.

3. *How have your work experiences contributed to your education?* This question is designed to induce the candidate to talk about past responsibilities and accomplishments as a worker. An inadequate response to this question would be simply reciting where you worked and when. A much more productive response is something like this:

Rebecca E., 23 When I was employed at Williams' Department Store I was responsible for selling ready-to-wear to store patrons. I learned the importance of assessing a potential customer and asking the right questions to better help them make a selection. I also learned how to set goals for myself in relation to sales. Usually I tried to beat my sales record for the previous week. I learned to keep files on customers, to call them when clothes arrived which they might be interested in, and to become involved in window displays and advertising. Although selling computer parts is different from selling clothes, I believe the skills I developed at Williams will help me in this job.

4. *What are your personal strengths and weaknesses?* This is a tough question to answer. Problems occur when candidates talk only about their strengths and fail to provide some estimate of their personal weaknesses. A more mature response to this question includes consideration of *both* strengths and weaknesses. However, care must be exercised in describing them. Remember, what *you* say may not be interpreted in the same way by the interviewer. Again, the best answer to this question includes (a) inclusion of both strengths and weaknesses, (b) examples to provide evidence of what you mean, and (c) considerations of how those strengths and weaknesses contribute to your ability to perform this particular job.

David D., 23 Let me begin with my weaknesses. I tend to be a very goal-oriented person. Consequently, I am conscious of what I want to accomplish and my progress toward reaching goals. This may contribute to my ability to be a steady and hard worker, but I know it also makes me appear calculating. Which brings me to my strengths. Because I am aware of this particular weakness I strive to remember the principle of relativity in everything. I am making *some* progress, but there are improvements in my own behavior and performance I can make. I also consider communication skills to be important, regardless of one's professional field. So I have taken courses to help me better communicate with others. For example, I recently completed a small group communication course which taught me how to run meetings and be productive when other people are running meetings. It also taught me how to approach decision-making when many different people and perspectives are involved. . . . I feel these strengths help overcome my weaknesses.

5. *What are your career goals and aspirations?* This question is probably answered incorrectly more often than any other question in the selection interview. Candidates very often make the crucial mistake of either (a) aiming too high, thus appearing selfish and conceited, or (b) citing goals and aspirations that have little or nothing to do with the position for which they are applying. And perhaps even worse are the candidates who have no specific goals or aspirations, or who fail to state what they are when asked during the interview. There are some productive guidelines:
   —Avoid talking about positions within the company, and focus on the development of abilities, knowledge, and expertise in your field. For example, do not say, "I intend to be Vice-President for Finance within the next ten years." Very few individuals attain that position, even fewer within that time frame; this makes you sound more interested in status than in performance of your job.

—Avoid the appearance of using this job as a stepping-stone to other jobs. Remember, you are being hired for this position. You may prove worthy of advancement, but your primary concern now should be that of being offered the opportunity to prove yourself in this positon.

—Avoid having vaguely defined goals, such as "I want to be happy," or "I want to be successful." This usually indicates a lack of maturity and self-knowledge. Again, emphasize the specific abilities, understandings, and goals that you want to achieve within the range of the job for which you are being interviewed.

These five questions are frequently asked during the selection interview. You should prepare answers for them.

Nonverbal Aspects of the Interview

Now let us consider your appearance and its potential affect on the interviewer. In virtually every imaginable job category related to organizational life, the best advice is to dress *conservatively*. Men should wear neat, well-pressed, conservative suits, complete with tie and polished shoes. Women should wear dresses or suits that attract attention only to their taste in clothing, not to their physical assets or to their trendiness. In both sexes jewelry and other accessories should be kept to a minimum. Perfumes and colognes should be light and barely noticeable, if present at all. There are a variety of guides to dressing for success now available to people entering the job market, and you may want to consult some of them for additional information and opinion (see Roach, 1981).

Beyond your appearance, there are several important nonverbal communication components of the successful interviewee. Most researchers have established a strong correlation between nonverbal communication and judgments of confidence, assertiveness, motivation to succeed, and enthusiasm (Tschirgi, 1973; Pennsylvania State University Career Development and Placement Center, 1981). Fluency and composure go hand-in-hand in forming impressions of competency; several studies have isolated key nonverbal elements in hiring decisions:

1. *Maintaining eye contact with the interviewer:* Trust and empathy are characteristics associated with eye contact in the employment interview. Also, we tend to believe answers given by people who look at us while they speak.

2. *Leaning forward in the chair:* Interest in the position and motivation to succeed are characteristics associated with leaning forward while answering questions.

3. *Using gestures while answering questions:* Confidence, nonverbal skill, and emphasis are characteristics associated with using gestures while answering questions. The person capable of appearing natural when using gestures is preferred over the individual who seems to dramatize or who repeats the same gestures.

4. *Smiling:* It is easier to like someone who is smiling at you, and to respond favorably to the information that person is providing. This does not mean you should continuously grin at the interviewer, nor does it mean if you smile you will be liked. However, smiling connotes likeability and enthusiasm, both of which contribute to judgments of acceptance.

Nonverbal skills contribute to the impression that you are a calm, confident communicator. Though it is difficult to rehearse nonverbal skills, your awareness of their impact and your understanding of these competencies should help you improve performances in job interviews.

When you prepare for the interview, consider how and when you might make statements about small group communication skills. First, read over the job announcement. If the position you are applying for is in any of the administrative areas (management, marketing, business administration, accounting, finance, organizational behavior, etc.), or technical fields (computer science, engineering, chemistry, etc.), you can assume that communication skill training will be a significant part of the recruiter/interviewer's decision-making process. However, chances are 50–50 that you will be asked any questions directly related to communication skills training by the interviewer. Most interviewers *assess* the ability to communicate by the answers given to their questions and the general demeanor of the candidate. Consequently, you will have to prepare statements that draw upon your communication background as proof of other claims you will be making about your competencies.

How to Discuss Small Group Communication Skills

Second, consider Sandra O'Connell's idea that communication is the management *process* that creates the ability to carry out management *functions:* "A process refers to *how* something is done, not what is done. For example, when planning, you gather information, write memos, and then meet with others to explain the plan. Planning is the function; communication is the process used to achieve the function" (1979; pp. 2–3). Understanding the implications O'Connell's claim can provide you with ways and means of talking about your communication training, especially in relation to small groups. Remember, small groups are the basic organizational method for carrying out tasks; hence, the candidate who has studied how small groups operate, who can lead and participate effectively in small groups, should have an advantage over other candidates without such valuable experience.

Third, it is essential to be specific when discussing skills or competencies. What can you *do* as a result of your training in small group communication? In a course such as the one you are currently enrolled in, you probably have learned how to select people for group membership, plan agendas, use Standard Agenda, PERT, and MAT to organize decision-making and problem-solving groups, control conflict, negotiate diverse perspectives, use "brainstorming" to generate alternatives, write proposals, make presentations based on group work, delegate responsibility for researching and reporting, and so forth. These are *skills* you can talk about in the interview.

Fourth, try to use examples whenever possible. If the interviewer asks: "What makes you believe you can manage?" you might respond by drawing on past experiences in your small group. How did you perform as a leader? What steps did you carry out when preparing agendas, organizing discussions, resolving conflicts, etc.? How did your small group experiences contribute to your understanding of management? The more effectively you are able to make productive uses of your own background and experiences, the more likely the interviewer will respond to you as a person who has done something more than be physically present in college or university classes. The ability to integrate text knowledge and human experiences contributes to building character and maturity, two important considerations in any recruiter/interviewer's evaluations.

Finally, keep your answers concise. Practice talking about small group experiences in 15–30 second segments. You might be surprised how much you can say about skills and understandings if you work on it. Interviewers are not interested in listening to long stories about strengths and weaknesses. Perhaps more importantly, interviewers will be impressed by your ability to *organize* responses. Answering the question, being concise, keeping it brief and clear, these are essential elements in an interviewee's responses. Here is a pattern for most responses to interviewer questions:

Method for Organizing Answers

1. Respond directly to the question asked, using a brief declarative sentence.
2. Provide support for your response by citing evidence, past experiences, or vivid examples.
3. Relate the experiences, evidence, or example to the statement you originally made.
4. Wait for the next question, probe, or follow-up question.

If you keep this pattern in your mind when preparing answers, you will omit unnecessary details and redundancies. Remember: the more answers you provide in the limited amount of time available for most initial interviews, the greater the chances of persuading her or him to see you as the most suitable candidate.

A caution is useful here. Despite the fact that small group communication understandings and skills are vital to success in organizations, you should not rely too heavily on them when giving answers. If you are interviewing for a marketing position the interviewer may be much more interested in your ability to do market research and in the techniques you have mastered for those tasks, than he or she will be by your communication background. For most organizational positions, communication training is a valuable *additional* asset. First you must demonstrate competency in the areas immediately related to your work. Then you can add to the total impression of your competencies by talking about your strengths as a communicator. Do not allow your interest in communication competencies to appear more important to you than your skills in the area described in the job announcement.

Gayland W., 23 . . . So I went on and on about my communication classes—how wonderful they were, how important they were, and what I had learned as a result of taking them. Finally, the interviewer asked me why I didn't want to pursue graduate studies in communication, given my level of interest in the field. Before I knew what I was saying, I agreed with him. He ended the interview shortly thereafter.

How to Use Small Group Communication Skills at Work

The question addressed in this section is: Once you have been hired for a position within an organization, how do you make use of small group communication competencies? This is a difficult question to answer, primarily because of the paucity of research on the subject. We *assume* that the understandings and skills acquired in university and college classes will contribute to your perception, interpretation, and response to messages in virtually every encounter. We *assume* that the skills learned in school will shape the abilities that are demonstrated on the job. And we *assume* that we can always improve our communication skills, and should be motivated to do so. These assumptions may or may not be validated by the experiences of organizational employees. They are, however, reasonable assumptions for people entering organizational life after graduating from college.

Given these assumptions, it is no wonder authorities in communication have only recently made productive use of contacts with organizational workers. At present communication professionals are involved in research that takes us into organizations, providing us with information about how communication understandings, skills, and competencies are perceived by people in the "real world." In some cases we discover former students and colleagues who display communication competencies and add to our belief in the necessity of communication training for organizational careers. Unfortunately, we also discover people who do not share our evaluations of the importance of communicating effectively on the job, but who regard those who possess the skills with envy, jealousy, or ambivalence. So, as a result, it is difficult to generalize about how you should make use of your small group training in the given case. However, there are some observations and recommendations which can be made.

Perhaps one of the best ways to demonstrate communication competencies is to *receive* other's communication accurately (Johnson, 1956). This may be an obvious assertion, but it is so often overlooked that it bears repeating. You cannot respond to the demands of a particular situation or person unless you are capable of listening to what the other person has to say. We know good listening is associated with trust, empathy, and understanding (Barker, 1971). Upon entering organizational life, you are an unknown. In addition to completing the tasks assigned to you efficiently and satisfactorily, you will shape your identity which

Being a Good Listener

others perceive, by the responses you make to your superiors, peers, and subordinates. To make the best choices about responses, you need to develop skills in listening. Consider Bonnie's experiences:

> **Bonnie McD., 25**   How did I learn to use my communication background at work? I listened for openings. One day my boss complained to me about the shoddy manner in which decisions were made by his division. He isolated three causes: a lack of coordination between and among decision-makers, problems associated with not seeking out proper input to decisions, and time wasted circulating memos and reports. I asked him if he thought using small groups for decision-making might overcome these problems. He looked a little confused, so I explained to him how a procedure (Standard Agenda) could be used to gain input from involved parties and how this might alleviate some of his trouble. He was impressed by my idea, but skeptical. He asked me if I would be willing to try out the idea on an upcoming project. I was excited by the opportunity and agreed to try it. We had some trouble at first, but as I guided the group members through Standard Agenda they began to see how useful it was. Soon after that I was promoted and put in charge of organizing small groups for decision-making purposes. Believe me, I would not have done so well unless I had listened to what he had to say.

Listening improved Bonnie's chances for making productive use of her small group skills. Had she simply tried to institute the use of groups for decision-making, she probably would have been much less successful. However, she used her skill as a listener to provide a possible solution to someone else's problem. The result was an opportunity to demonstrate her ability to manage a small group.

Being a Purposeful Speaker

Through this text I have emphasized the need to know what your *goal* is in communication situations. I have consistently advocated planning for talk as a way of finding the available means of persuasion and adapting them to the needs and expectations of situation and of others. By making use of this advice, you can improve the responses you receive from others on the job, because you know where you want to go and how to evaluate your progress in getting there.

Planning for communication situations at work can improve your overall effectiveness. Successful sales personnel often find it advantageous to organize the next day's schedule the night before. A typical way of accomplishing this is to think through the next work day, identifying the situations in which you will interact with others. Try writing down the name(s) of people in those situations, together with their probable goals, needs, and expectations. What will you talk about with them? What goals will you pursue? What have your past experiences with them revealed to you about their content (subject matter) and style of speaking? Use this plan to determine the nature of the communication. For example, are the situations interpersonal or do they involve small groups? Are you exchanging information or contributing to a decision? Will the outcome be a formal speaking situation or an opportunity to reveal your strengths as a negotiator, conflict resolver, or leader?

A second use for a communication plan is to determine how your working relationship can be improved. If you are aware of the nature and intensity of your relationships with others, you can prepare for their unique urgencies. You can determine the subjects to be pursued and the subjects to be avoided. You can plan for opportunities to reveal specialized communication skills, such as reducing ambiguity, asking productive questions in meetings, or making recommendations about courses of action. Perceiving communication as the *method* of creating, maintaining, escalating, and de-escalating relationships can help provide you with ways and means of furthering your career and improving the quality of your work life.

Communicating determines how you participate in organizations. Recognizing this fact can reveal situations in which your understanding of and training in communication can be renumerative. For example, in virtually any organizational occupation, you will be a member of a group. You will have opportunities to use the skills you have developed as a participant in groups, even when decision-making and problem-solving tasks are minimally involved. Taking into account such data as the history of the group, how it fits into the organizational chart, the influence of interpersonal relations on the group's activities, the influence of informal groups on task groups, can prepare you for a level of participation and informed leadership beyond routine expectations.

Being an Involved Participant

I have already discussed the skills of effective participation in groups. If these skills are used in everyday organizational life, they should contribute to your advancement and satisfaction with the job. Understanding how to improve your own communication abilities and the abilities of others with whom you work can contribute to your reputation as an involved, active, capable, and respected member of the organization, and particularly of the small group.

Not everyone aspires to leadership positions in organizations, nor should they. Every career position in an organization contains its own level of expertise, and people are satisfied by knowing they are doing their job as well as anyone could. However, in most organizations leadership is associated with advancement; those individuals who aspire to higher corporate positions must first prove themselves as leaders in the lower ranks.

Accepting Leadership and Performing Leadership Tasks

Small group communication skills *are* the skills of leadership. Leading does not function apart from the communication which creates cooperative responses from others. Being an active and effective participant usually prepares a person for leadership, because it is necessary to have the experiences of being led and completing assigned tasks if you wish to understand the rewards and punishments associated with the work which you will eventually delegate. Listen to Rita:

> **Rita R., 28**   There is a certain logic to advancement in organizations like this one. I know when I graduated from college with a degree in management I thought I was ready to manage. Wrong. I was ready to participate in the organization, but I needed to learn how the organization operated, the large

and small routines and hassles that managers must deal with. It took me about two or three years of that kind of learning before I received my first real "management" opportunity. By then I was ready, at least more ready than I was straight out of school. Oh sure, I had the title of a manager, but not the responsibility. Some people get turned off by that, but I persevered and finally got a chance to prove myself. But it takes time *and* skills. You have to learn how to communicate with people, how to read their behavior, how to persuade them, how to induce their cooperation with a goal or assignment.

When the opportunity to exercise leadership occurs, you should be able to make substantive use of your small group skills. But you must be able to differentiate between acting as a participant and acting as a leader. Trying to act like a leader without having the role or status very often creates more problems than you might imagine. First prove yourself as a capable participant; the time for leadership will arrive and you will be better prepared for it if you have already legitimately gained the confidence of others because of your record of participation.

Recommending the Use of Small Groups

One problem with a text such as this one and with small group courses in general is the development of a belief in the necessity of using groups. Thus it happens that particularly zealous group-advocates try to introduce the use of small groups to deal with any and every aspect of an organization, even when the organization does not acknowledge the need for them. For this reason, you need to learn how and when to recommend the use of a small group.

First, you should only recommend the use of a small group if the problem or decision is large enough to warrant the input of several persons. People may respond negatively to the recommendation because of their previous bad experiences in groups that accomplished nothing more than a waste of time. Those who have had experience with poorly managed committees or project-teams often have a negative attitude toward any suggestion requiring working in closed quarters with others. Hence, you should develop some alternative ways of responding to perceived needs to use small groups. Remember, there are procedures that involve groups in nominal ways. The Delphi Technique is one way to gain input from group members without forcing them to risk the problems associated with poorly managed interactions. If the organization has a poor record for using groups, this technique may be a better way to accustom people to working together.

Second, you should avoid creating the impression that using groups will serve only *your* best interests. Remember, you may be a capable group member or leader, but others do not have to share your enthusiasm for the human group. In some organizations, the use of groups is a last resort. Not until every other method of carrying out a task has been exhausted will others agree to "try a group again." If this is the case you may have an excellent opportunity. One or two skilled group participants, trained in the use of procedures and group communication techniques, can greatly enhance the effectiveness of a group. However, the problem immediately becomes one of educating others about how to behave in the group. And this problem may require company time to resolve.

Third, when a recommendation to use a small group is made, particularly in an organization unfamiliar with them, it may be necessary to hire a professional consultant to facilitate the transition. Experts in organizational development seldom encourage training from within an organization. Trying to teach skills to people with whom you associate on a day-to-day basis is very, very difficult. It may even be dangerous. In most cases, it is wise to bring in someone from an outside consulting group to do the work. They will be less personally involved in the interpersonal dynamics of the organization, and more able to recommend change. They can intervene successfully where employees cannot or should not.

Finally, if your recommendation to use a group is approved, be prepared to assume the responsibilities to which you are *assigned*. If you are not appointed group leader, do not try to lead the group. Content yourself with an active role as a participant. You can do much more good using participant skills to help the group than you can if you try to be what you are not. Conversely, if you are given leadership responsibility, respond to the challenge in an appropriate manner. Remember that effective leaders induce cooperation rather than inspire jealousy or ill will. Do not seek to control the group; instead strive to influence its function and performance. Recall the goals of rhetorical sensitivity and behavioral flexibility, and then strive to help the group accomplish its task with a minimum of "strong-arming" and manipulation.

The Future of Small Groups in Organizations

The future of organizations depends to a very large degree on the small group communication skills discussed in this text. With improvements in technology, particularly those related to the computer, we will have more and better information to use in decision-making and problem-solving interactions. As society grows more complex our ability to manage change while preserving democracy and freedom will depend on individuals working in small and large groups charged with the responsibility for deciding how to allocate resources, plan for the future, organize systems of prosperity and national defense, and contribute to how we understand our collective past.

Small groups *are* the future. Technologies can be envisioned as extensions of ourselves, extensions that grant us powers far beyond what would have been our "natural" limits. Similarly, small groups can be considered another form of an extension of the individual. In addition to relying on our own knowledge, experiences, and capacity to find, categorize, and evaluate information, we can pool our resources and talents with others. Together we can better deal with the future because we are better able to process information related to change.

Small groups in organizations will continue to enjoy a position of centrality and prominence. The interdependent nature of small groups, the need to coordinate work efforts and to integrate individuals into the cultural pattern of the company are some of the functions and processes that small groups now perform and will continue to perform in the future. Participation and cooperation are the goals that organizations establish for employees. The skills of participation (and leadership) and of cooperation (and competition) are *communication* skills. I have taken the position in this text that nothing exists until it is communicated. Regardless of an individual's background and training, she or he will participate and cooperate with others in organizations through choices made about words and actions. In most cases the people who build substantive reputations for themselves as being fair in their treatment of others and competent in their work are evaluated on the bases of their verbal and nonverbal communication skills. There is no reason to believe this fact of organizational life will change.

Programs in business schools across the country are recommending a new balance between *quantitative* and *qualitative* coursework. Ouchi (1981) and others believe that American business and industry have placed too much emphasis on acquiring quantitative skills at the expense of other qualities or competencies necessary for organizational life, especially effective communication and human relations. Thus it should not be surprising to find, as a recent conference of business educators ascertained, that by the year 2000 courses in rhetoric, persuasion, technical writing, small group communication, and public speaking may be found in the undergraduate and graduate school curricula for business majors. Researchers have come to recognize that the truism "there can be no management without communication," holds more promise for redesigning our training and educating of future managers than ever before.

Communication is *how* the organization functions. One prominent American philosopher, Richard McKeon (1971) put it this way: "Communication is the architectonic art capable of informing all disciplines and subjects." He was writing about communication as the way all knowledge in all disciplines and subjects is brought into being. If we consider the organization as a subject (or as many interrelated subjects), the truth of McKeon's claim is apparent. Nothing happens apart from communication. The organization depends on communication as the human body depends on oxygen: it is the source of all information needed to operate the system.

The future is the result of choices you make now. American organizations are turning to the use of small groups to solve problems and make decisions. In turn, small groups look for individuals possessing the communication competencies necessary to ensure the smooth functioning of the group. Thus, I can end this section of the chapter as all questions concerning small groups and communication in them must end: with *you* as an individual capable of making choices about how to best prepare yourself for living and working. The choices, about communication, small groups, the modern organization, and our collective future, are yours.

This chapter considered how to use the small group communication skills that you have learned. I began by examining the selection or employment interview as a situation in which small group communication skills can be used to appeal to the recruiter or interviewer. I discussed the importance of composing a resumé and cover letter that will influence the reader to want to talk to you, and how small group communication courses and training, when appropriately described in the resumé, can be used to generate interest. I also examined the need to prepare for the questions that may be asked during the selection interview, and how to talk about small group experiences and training during this time. In this section I reviewed questions most frequently asked during selection interviews, providing information about how best to prepare yourself for them. I explored the impact of nonverbal elements on hiring decisions, recommending a conservative style of dress as well as four ways to improve your nonverbal effectiveness (maintaining eye contact, leaning forward, using gestures, and smiling). Finally, I discussed how to talk about small group communication understandings and skills in the interview. I advocated the use of a process-orientation answer to questions about organizational and management functions and suggested a way of citing examples and experiences from small groups as support for your answers.

Second, I investigated the uses of small group communication skills at work, recommending ways of improving the responses you elicit from others. I suggested that inducing others to respond to your communication competencies may be the best way to obtain their support for your goal of using small groups. I discussed the importance of (1) being a good listener, (2) being a purposeful speaker, (3) being an involved participant, (4) accepting leadership and performing leadership roles, and (5) recommending the use of small groups in response to organizational urgencies and needs as primary tools involved in creating your organizational identity.

Finally, I looked toward the future of small groups in organizations. Organizations will increase the use of small groups and thus need more and better trained small group communicators to meet the demands of technology and decision-making in the future. The new balance in undergraduate and graduate school curricula is evidence of the change to educating people in the use of both quantitative and qualitative methods. I concluded this section by looking at the organization as a system controlled by the communication within it, and by the choices made about communicating by individuals in small groups. Because the future is a result of choices made now, you should be concerned about learning how to make productive choices about communication. How you learn to communicate to achieve cooperation, consensus, and participation will determine how the future unfolds and affects you.

Summary

Barker, L. L. *Listening Behavior.* Englewood Cliffs, N.J.: Prentice-Hall, 1971.
Downs, C. W. "Perceptions of the Selection Interview." *Personnel Administration.* (May–June 1969):8–23.
Downs, C., G. P. Smeyak, and E. Martin. *Professional Interviewing.* New York: Harper & Row, 1981.

References

Einhorn, L., P. H. Bradley, and J. E. Baird, Jr. *Employment Interviewing.* Glenview, Ill.: Scott, Foresman, 1982.

Goodall, D. B., and H. L. Goodall, Jr. "The Employment Interview: A Selective Review of the Literature with Implications for Communication Research." *Communication Quarterly* 30 (Fall, 1982):116–23.

Hollandsworth, J. G., M. E. Dressel, and J. Stevens. "Use of Behavioral Versus Traditional Procedures for Increasing Job Interview Skills." *Journal of Counseling Psychology* 6, 24 (1977):503–10.

Hollandsworth, J. G., R. Kazelskis, J. Stevens, and M. E. Dressel. "Relative Contributions of Verbal, Articulative, and Nonverbal Communication to Employment Decisions in the Job Interview Setting." *Personnel Psychology* 32 (1979):359–67.

Johnson, W. *Your Most Enchanted Listener.* San Francisco: International Institute for General Semantics, 1956.

McKeon, R. "The Uses of Rhetoric in a Technological Age: Architectonic Productive Arts." In *The Prospect of Rhetoric.* Edited by Lloyd F. Bitzer and Edwin Black, pp. 44–63. Englewood Cliffs, N.J.: Prentice-Hall, 1971.

Moffat, T. *Selection Interviewing for Managers.* New York: Harper & Row Continuing Management Education Series, 1979.

O'Connell, S. J. *Communication for Managers.* New York: Harper & Row Continuing Management Education Series, 1979.

Ouchi, W. *THEORY Z: How American Business Can Meet the Japanese Challenge.* Reading, Mass.: Addison-Wesley Publishing Co., 1981.

Pennsylvania State University Career Development and Placement Center. "How Recruiters Screen and Select Students." *Journal of College Placement* (Summer, 1981):45–47.

Posner, B. Z. "Comparing Recruiter, Student, and Faculty Perceptions of Important Applicant and Job Characteristics." *Personnel Psychology* 34 (1981):329–39.

Roach, C. A. "Actions and Images May Find You Wordless." *Journal of Communication Management* 11 (1981):12–14.

Roach, C. A., P. H. Webb, Jr., and H. L. Goodall, Jr. *Thought into Action.* Dubuque, Ia.: William C. Brown Company Publishers, 1981.

Stewart, J., and W. B. Cash. *Interviewing,* 3d ed. Dubuque, Ia.: William C. Brown Company Publishers, 1982.

Tschirgi, H. D. "What Do Recruiters Really Look for in Candidates? *Journal of College Placement* (December 1972–January 1973):75–79.

Exercises

The following exercises are based on a simulation of group-generated job interviews in which the skills you learned in this class can be used. As you can see, it will take time to complete these exercises because you will be expected to conduct the job interviews in class. How long it will take will depend on your class size.

The Selection Interview: A Small Group Exercise

Day One: Assemble your small group. Your charge is to arrive at consensus concerning a job description and criteria for candidate selection which will be posted in class, and for which students from other small groups will apply.

The job description should be broad enough to attract students from a variety of educational backgrounds and experiences. Try to investigate what careers students in your class are pursuing and develop a job description applicable to many of them.

After the job description has been posted, the small group responsible for generating it should develop:

1. Criteria to be used for candidate selection.
2. An agenda to use in the selection interviews for all candidates.
3. Questions for the interviewers to ask all candidates.
4. Questions for the interviewers to use for candidates with specific backgrounds.

Day Two: When the job descriptions are posted in class, all other students from all other in-class small groups should read them. Ask students to apply for at least two or three of the jobs listed, and to develop resumés and cover letters for each of them. These cover letters and resumés should be submitted to the group responsible for interviewing candidates.

After the students have submitted their resumés and cover letters to the groups posting the job descriptions and responsible for interviewing people for them, the individuals in all groups should:

1. Prepare for questions that may be asked by the interviewers relevant to the job description and material covered in this chapter.
2. Determine ways and means of influencing positive evaluations of the applicant, using material described in this chapter.

Day Three: Small group members will choose the top three applicants for their jobs. These candidates should be announced in class, and an interviewing schedule developed by the groups in conjunction with the instructor.

If possible, arrange for video-taping equipment to be used during the selection interviews.

Days Four Through ???: Conduct the in-class interviews. Each group member should serve as *both* an interviewer (for the group) and an applicant (as an applicant for a job posted by some other group).

Critique the communication behaviors displayed by applicants during the in-class interviews. How did they present themselves? How did they make productive or unproductive uses of examples, experiences, and their knowledge of subject matter related to the job? How did they talk about their small group communication backgrounds and experiences? What recommendations would you make about performances in selection interviews next time?

Author's Index

Subject Index